AN INTRODUCTION TO PSYCHOLOGY

BY

MARY WHITON CALKINS

PROFESSOR OF PHILOSOPHY AND PSYCHOLOGY
IN WELLESLEY COLLEGE

New York
THE MACMILLAN COMPANY
LONDON: MACMILLAN AND CO., LTD.
1904

COPYRIGHT, 1901,

By THE MACMILLAN COMPANY.

———

Set up and electrotyped September, 1901.   Reprinted April,
1902 ; July, 1904.

Norwood Press
J. S. Cushing & Co. — Berwick & Smith
Norwood Mass. U.S.A.

Publishing Statement:

This important reprint was made from an old and scarce book.

Therefore, it may have defects such as missing pages, erroneous pagination, blurred pages, missing text, poor pictures, markings, marginalia and other issues beyond our control.

Because this is such an important and rare work, we believe it is best to reproduce this book regardless of its original condition.

Thank you for your understanding and enjoy this unique book!

PREFACE

FOR pressing into the crowded ranks of psychological text-books, this volume has one practical excuse to offer, — the convenience of the students to whom its author lectures. The book is written in the conviction that psychology should study consciousness, both as a series of complex mental processes, or ideas, and as a relation of conscious selves to each other. It is hoped, however, that the two points of view have been so carefully distinguished that the book may be useful to readers who reject one or other of these underlying conceptions.

As its name implies, the book is intended for students beginning the study of psychology; and, — except for the last chapter and parts of the Appendix, — it substantially reproduces a first course, as actually given. References to psychological literature and formulations of conflicting theories are included, in the belief that, in the use of text-books, "a man's reach should exceed his grasp," and with the conviction that excessively simplified statements, unsupported by reference to different writers, tend to breed in the student a dogmatic or an unduly docile habit of thought. The references, like the supplementary discussions of the Appendix, are meant also for the use of the more advanced student. The section on the structure and functions of the nervous system has been added, for the practical advantage of including, within the covers of one book, all that is absolutely essential to the first-year student.

The text-book, however, is a necessary yet a subsidiary adjunct to the study of any science. It is useful only as it stimulates, directs, verifies and supplements the individual observation of the reader. This book has been written, accordingly, with the constant purpose of leading students to the independent and careful study of their own consciousness. It is highly desirable that such introspective study should be supplemented by experiments, performed by the student under direction, and that this experimental introspection should precede, instead of following, the study of every division of the text. Detailed references are given, at appropriate points, to the two English manuals of experimental psychology.

The general reader who may open this volume should be warned against certain technical chapters. He will do well to skim Part I., omitting entirely Chapters VII. and VIII.; and he should especially devote himself to Part II., from which, however, he may drop out Chapters XIII., XVIII., and XIX.

The final paragraph in this Preface is the pleasantest, in all the book, to write, for it contains my acknowledgments to the people who have helped me. My greatest indebtedness is to Professors William James and Hugo Münsterberg. One of the distinctive theories of the book — the existence of elements of consciousness which are neither sensational nor affective — is simply a developed and systematized statement of the teaching of James, and the frequent quotations from the "Principles of Psychology" are better reading than any original paragraph in the book. The second fundamental theory of this book, the conception of psychology as a science of related selves, is closely affiliated with Münsterberg's conception of history as science of the relations of willing subjects; and few chapters of the book are uninfluenced by his vigorous teaching. A list of the text-books and monographs, by which I have especially profited, would be very long, but would certainly include the names of Külpe, Titchener, Ward, Stout, Brentano, and Flechsig. I owe, also, more than I can well express to the *viva voce* suggestions and criticisms of my colleague, Professor Mary S. Case, and of my former teacher, Professor Edmund C. Sanford. And, finally, my warm thanks are due to my father, who has indefatigably read manuscript and proof, to Mrs. C. L. Franklin, who has read the discussion of color-theories, and to my colleague, Dr. E. A. McC. Gamble, who has added a section to the Appendix and has critically read most of the manuscript. To Dr. Gamble's criticism of the chapters on sensation and on affection, I am especially indebted. Figures 3, 5, 6, 7, 9, 10, 11, 12, 13, 14 and 18, which illustrate portions of the text, are reproduced or adapted, by the kind permission of Henry Holt and Co., from James's "Principles of Psychology" and "Briefer Psychology" and from Martin's "Human Body."

SEPTEMBER, 1901.

TABLE OF CONTENTS

INTRODUCTION

CHAPTER I

NATURE AND METHODS OF PSYCHOLOGY

PAGE

I. Nature of Psychology 3
II. Methods of Psychology 7

BOOK I

INTROSPECTIVE PSYCHOLOGY OF THE NORMAL CONSCIOUSNESS

PART I

Structural Elements of Consciousness

CHAPTER II

VISUAL SENSATIONS 17
I. Sensational Elements of Color 18
II. Sensational Elements of Colorless Light 28
III. Sensational Elements of Brightness 42

CHAPTER III

AUDITORY SENSATIONS

I. Sensational Elements of Pitch and Noise 46
II. Sensational Elements of Loudness 53

ix

Table of Contents

CHAPTER IV

SENSATIONS OF TASTE AND OF SMELL

PAGE

I. Sensations of Taste 55
II. Sensations of Smell 59

CHAPTER V

SENSATIONS OF PRESSURE, OF PAIN AND OF TEMPERATURE

I.   The Sensation of Pressure. 65
II. The Sensations of Pain 71
III. Sensations of Temperature 76

CHAPTER VI

SENSATIONS FROM INTERNAL EXCITATION AND THE CONSCIOUSNESS OF MOTION

I. Sensations from Internal Excitation:
    a. Sensations of Strain 80
    b. Alleged Sensations of Position 81
    c. The Alleged Sensations of Dizziness. . . . 84
    d. Alleged Organic Sensations from Internal Stimulus . 84
II. The Consciousness of Motion 86

CHAPTER VII

THE CONSCIOUSNESS OF EXTENSITY

I. The Elemental Consciousness of Extensity:
    a. Visual Extensity 89
    b. Pressure-extensity 92
    c. Extensity of Sounds and of Other Sensation-classes . 93
II. The Developed Consciousness of Extensity:
    a. Consciousness of Surface 95
    b. Consciousness of Distance or Depth 97

CHAPTER VIII

SENSATIONAL ELEMENT AND SENSATION 103
Summaries, pp. 109, 110.

CHAPTER IX

ATTRIBUTIVE ELEMENTS OF CONSCIOUSNESS

PAGE

I   The Affections   113
II. The Feelings of Realness 124

CHAPTER X

RELATIONAL ELEMENTS OF CONSCIOUSNESS   128

CHAPTER XI

ATTENTION.   137

PART II

Concrete Conscious Experiences

CHAPTER XII

CONCRETE CONSCIOUS EXPERIENCES 149

CHAPTER XIII

FUSION AND ASSOCIATION 157

Summaries, pp. 160, 167.

CHAPTER XIV

PERCEPTION

I.   (Percept and Perceiving) 169
II. (Analysis and Classification)   173

Summary, p. 179.

CHAPTER XV

IMAGINATION

I.   (Image and Imagining)   185
II. (Analysis and Classification)   189

Summary, p. 190,

CHAPTER XVI

PAGE

IMAGINATION (*continued*): MEMORY 210

CHAPTER XVII

THOUGHT: GENERALIZATION

I. (Thought and Thinking) 218
II. (Analysis and Classification):
    a. Generalization 221

CHAPTER XVIII

THOUGHT: JUDGMENT AND REASONING

b. The Simple Judgment 234
c. Reasoning 240

CHAPTER XIX

RECOGNITION

I. (Recognition and Recognizing) 252
II. (The Feeling of Familiarity) 254

CHAPTER XX

EMOTION

I.   (Emotion as Idea and as Relation of Self) . . . 263
II. (Analysis and Classification) 265
Summary, p. 266.

a. Personal Emotion 266
b. Impersonal Emotion 276
Summary, p. 277.

III. (Physiological Conditions and Accompaniments of Emotion) 285
Summary, p. 289.

CHAPTER XXI

VOLITION AND BELIEF. WILL AND FAITH

PAGE

I. *a.* Volition 299
     b. Belief 304
II. *a.* Will 307
     b. Faith 311
III. (Classification) 313

Summary, p. 313.

CHAPTER XXII

TYPICAL PERSONAL RELATIONS. THE RELIGIOUS CONSCIOUSNESS

I. Typical Personal Relations. 321
II. The Religious Consciousness 323

CHAPTER XXIII

THE SOCIAL CONSCIOUSNESS 331
I. Forms of Social Consciousness 333
II. Imitation and Opposition 339

BOOK II

COMPARATIVE PSYCHOLOGY AND ABNORMAL PSYCHOLOGY

CHAPTER XXIV

DIVISIONS OF PSYCHOLOGY 351

Summary, p. 351.

PART I

Comparative Psychology

CHAPTER XXV

THE PSYCHOLOGY OF THE ANIMAL CONSCIOUSNESS . . . 355
I. Structural Elements of the Animal Consciousness:
    a. Sensational Consciousness 356

PAGE

b. Relational Experiences:
    1. Recognition 367
    2. Thought 367
  c. Affections and Emotions 372
II. The Personal and Social Consciousness of Animals . . 374

CHAPTER XXVI

THE PSYCHOLOGY OF THE CHILD'S CONSCIOUSNESS . . . 382
I. The Consciousness of the Baby 384
II. The Consciousness of Little Children 392

PART II

Abnormal Psychology

CHAPTER XXVII

ABNORMAL CONSCIOUS STATES OF PERSONS IN HEALTH

I. Phenomena of Abnormal Consciousness:
  a. Dreams 397
  b. Abnormal Experiences of the Waking Life:
    1. Waking Illusions and Hallucinations . . 402
    2. Automatic Writing 405
  c. Hypnosis 406
II. Analogy of Abnormal States to the Normal Experience . 413
III. Differences of Abnormal and Normal States:
  a. Changes in Personality 415
  b. Veridical Experiences. Telepathy . . . 420

CONCLUSION

CHAPTER XXVIII

THE HISTORY OF PSYCHOLOGICAL SYSTEMS 424

APPENDIX

		PAGE
SECT. I.	Structure and Functions of the Nervous System	449
SECT. II.	Aphasia	460
SECT. III.	Sensational Elements of Color and Colorless Light:	
	I. Theories	464
	II. Certain Phenomena of Color-vision:	
	a. Contrast Phenomena	473
	b. Color Blindness	475
	c. The Purkinje Phenomenon	478
SECT. IV.	The Physical and the Physiological Conditions of Sensations of Smell. By E. A. McC. Gamble	480
SECT. V.	End-organs of Pressure and of Pain:	
	I. End-organs of Pressure: Von Frey's Theory	482
	II. Theories of the Physiological Excitation of Pain	484
SECT. VI.	Bodily Movements	485
SECT. VII.	Theories of Attention	486
BIBLIOGRAPHY		492
INDEX OF SUBJECTS		504
INDEX OF AUTHORS		510

INTRODUCTION

CHAPTER I

NATURE AND METHODS OF PSYCHOLOGY

I. NATURE OF PSYCHOLOGY

ALL psychologists would agree to define their subject, at least in an introductory and provisional way, as the science of consciousness. But this definition is not enlightening unless its terms are thoroughly understood, and we must at once, therefore, proceed to discuss the nature of a science.

Science is the systematic study of facts. It must be distinguished both from philosophy and from the everyday consciousness. From the latter it differs only in method, for both science and the everyday consciousness have to do with phenomena or facts; but science studies these phenomena critically, analyzes them into their ultimate parts, and classifies them by their most essential likenesses, whereas the everyday consciousness observes facts uncritically, as conglomerates, with little or no analysis and with only a superficial recognition of the most striking likenesses. So, for example, the tourist, wandering over the ground of a recent excavation in Greece, sees a fragment of marble, and classifies it hastily as 'some part of a temple.' The trained archæologist examines the same bit of stone, finds traces of half-obliterated flutings, and unhesitatingly assigns it to a place in the triglyph of a particular temple or treasure-house. In the same way, the untrained ear hears only a multitude of mingling bird-notes, whereas the naturalist recognizes this as the note of the oriole, and that as the trill of a warbler; the careless observer sees only a scarred rock, but the geolo-

3

gist identifies the marks on its weather-beaten surface as glacial scratchings; and the ordinary reader sees nothing remarkable in a word which the philologist studies for months in his efforts to discover its exact affiliations. Now, in all these cases it is evident, as has been said, that the objects of the scientific and the everyday consciousness are the same, — architectural fragments, bird-notes, rock surfaces and words. But the two differ widely in their method; and the ordinary observer knows nothing of the close observation nor of the analytic and systematic classification of the scientist.

When we turn to the contrast between science and philosophy, we find a reversal of the situation. For metaphysics, like science, analyzes, classifies, and seeks to explain. The contrast between the two must be sought mainly in the object of the study rather than in the method. Philosophy is the attempted study of the self-dependent whole of reality, or of partial realities as related to this fundamental whole. A science is, on the contrary, a systematic study of facts or phenomena; that is, of limited or partial realities, as related to each other without reference to a more fundamental reality. We must justify this definition in some detail.

It is entirely certain, in the first place, that every science has a more or less limited sphere of study. Physics does not investigate the chemical constitution of its masses; geology does not analyze and classify mineralogical phenomena; philology, though allied to epigraphy, does not concern itself with the new forms of letters. Science never, then, "aims at the whole world generally"; its objects are always definitely limited. It is equally clear that scientific facts or phenomena are related to each other, since scientific investigation is constantly linking facts together and explaining the one by the other. The pulse-beat cannot be understood except as connected with the contraction of the heart and the dilation of the arteries; the explosion is dependent on the firing of the fuse; a national costume is related to facts of climate. Every fact, in a word, is recognized as dependent on others.

It may be shown, finally, that the scientist does not seek to relate his phenomena to ultimate or total reality. He does not ask if the rock or the bodily tissue is ultimately a spiritual or a material reality. He rests content when the physiological phenomenon has been reduced to its lowest chemical elements, when the physical fact of light or heat has been hypothetically transformed into its especial modes of vibration; and he does not ask "What is the place of chemical element and of ether wave in the system of total reality?" The problems of ultimate reality belong to philosophy, not to science; for philosophy is, as has been said, the attempt to study either the self-dependent whole of reality, or a partial reality as related to the whole. It studies, therefore, the ultimate nature of every phenomenon of science, — self and thought, bodily tissue and physical mass, — and it seeks not only to relate each phenomenon with every other, but to fit it into a complete scheme of reality.

It may now be pointed out that psychology has both characteristics of a science. From the everyday observation of consciousness, it is distinguished by its systematic method of analysis and classification. Instead of casually observing merely the more unusual psychological phenomena, pranks of the imagination, feats of logic or peculiarities of the dream-life, the psychologist carefully observes and analyzes all psychological phenomena, ordinary as well as extraordinary, and systematically classifies them. As opposed to philosophy, on the other hand, psychology sturdily refuses to study the nature of the soul, its permanence or immortality and its relation to matter, and simply analyzes the forms of self-consciousness or studies people in their social relations.

We have next to distinguish psychology from the physical sciences. All sciences deal with facts, and there are

two great classes of facts, — Selves and Facts-for-the-
Selves. But the second of these great groups, the Facts-
for-the-Selves, is again capable of an important division
into Internal and External Facts. To the first class belong
percepts, images, memories, thoughts, emotions and volitions, inner events as we may call them; to the second
class belong the things and the events of the outside world,
the physical facts, as we may name them.

There can be no doubt that we actually do make these
sharp distinctions: first, the contrast between selves and
all other facts; and second, the opposition of our percepts, feelings and thoughts, the inner phenomena, to the
outside things and events. When we examine this last
contrast we find two reasons for it. In the first place, the
inner facts, the memories, emotions and all the rest, are
realized as private, unshared experiences belonging to me
alone; whereas the things or events are public, shared
facts, common property, as it were. My fear or delight
is my own private experience, and so, for that matter, is
my perception, for I have my own particular way of looking at everything, which I share with no one else. But
the beast who frightens me, the spring day which delights
me, the sunset of which I have my own particular perception — all these are public facts shared with an unlimited
number of other selves, facts which no longer bear the
stamp of my individuality. Close upon this difference follows another. Just because the shared or public facts are
not referred to any particular self, they tend to seem independent of all selves and to become externalized; whereas
the private facts continue to be referred to a self, and in
this way, also, are contrasted with events or things which
seem to us quite cut off from selves. The physical sciences
study these common and apparently independent or externalized facts; psychology as distinguished from them is
the science of consciousness, the study of selves and of the
inner facts-for-selves. The following summary will make
this clearer : —

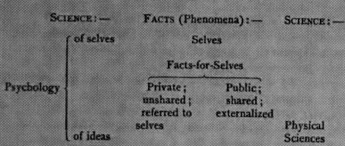

SCIENCE:—	FACTS (Phenomena):—	SCIENCE:—
of selves	Selves	
	Facts-for-Selves	
Psychology	Private; Public; unshared; shared; referred to externalized selves	
of ideas		Physical Sciences

II. METHODS OF PSYCHOLOGY

We have suggested already that science has two essential methods — analysis and classification. To the scientific treatment of any object it is necessary first, that it be reduced to relatively simple parts, and next, that these parts be grouped and arranged, according to their important likenesses and differences, in an orderly and systematic manner. Every recognized science, or division of a science, is an illustration of these statements. The chemical compound is reduced to its elements; the physical movement is shown to be a composition of interacting forces; the human body is analyzed into its tissues. Similarly, the philologist breaks up a complex verb form into stem or modified root, mood, tense, personal ending, reduplication and augment; and the historian studies a given period according to its political, its economic, its ethical and its literary aspects. The second of these methods is equally manifest in the procedure of every scientist. A chemical combination of an acid with a base is classified, for example, as a sulphate or as a chlorate, according as sulphur or chlorine is a part of it; physical phenomena are optical or acoustic, according as they consist of ether or of atmosphere vibrations; verbs are allied with each other by a common method of reduplication; and historic periods, however chronologically distinct, are grouped together by the historian as conservative or revolutionary, as creative or as imitative.

There is a third scientific method and one of great significance — explanation. In one sense, to be sure, explanation is merely a general term which covers both analysis and classification. So, for example, one may be said to explain salt when one has classified it with the chlorides and analyzed it into one part of sodium and one of chlorine. In this sense it is, of course, true that every science is explanatory simply because it is analytic and systematic. Explanation, however, has a more distinctive meaning: to explain means not merely to describe and to classify, but to assign the cause, to account for a phenomenon. The sulphuric acid, for example, is not merely analyzed into its elements and allied with the other sulphur compounds, but is explained as due to certain mechanical or thermal processes and to certain chemical affinities; the movement which has been described as an interplay of opposing forces is traced to a falling weight; the verbal form which has been analyzed into its elements is explained as the result of a peculiar conformation of lips and palate; the civic revolution is discussed as the termination of a long series of preparatory events. Explanation, however, though immensely important, is not an essential method of science. When one has reduced a phenomenon to its simplest parts, and classified it by its similarities and differences, one has treated it scientifically even if one has not gone on to explain it by reference to some other phenomenon.

The methods of psychology are, in general, these three methods of every science: analysis, classification and explanation. But besides these fundamental forms of procedure, every science has certain methods peculiar to itself; and the method which distinguishes psychology is that of introspection. This follows directly from what has been said of the subject-matter of psychology. Its facts are not the common, independent, externalized facts of the physical sciences, but the inner facts, selves and ideas. To observe the psychic fact one has not, there-

fore, to sweep the heavens with a telescope, nor to travel
about in search of rare geological formations; but one has
merely to ask oneself such questions as: "How do I
actually feel?" "What do I mean when I say that I
perceive, remember, believe?"

The method has obvious advantages. It makes no
especial conditions of time and place; it requires no
mechanical adjunct; it demands no difficult search for
suitable material; at any moment, in all surroundings,
with no external outfit, one may study the rich material
provided by every imaginable experience. In an extreme
sense, all is grist that comes to the psychologist's mill.
The apparent facility of introspection is, however, one
of its greatest dangers. Nothing seems easier than to
render to ourselves a true account of what goes on in our
consciousness. We are tempted, therefore, to overlook the
need of training in introspection and to minimize its characteristic difficulties. Chief among these is the change which
it makes in its own object. To attend to a particular experience actually alters it. If I ask myself in the midst of a
hearty laugh "Just what is this feeling of amusement?"
forthwith the feeling has vanished, and a strenuous, serious
mood has taken its place. Much the same is true of every
form of consciousness. To observe myself perceiving,
remembering or judging is no longer simply to perceive,
to remember and to judge, but to reflect upon perception,
memory and judgment. It is true, therefore, as many
psychologists have shown, that introspection is never of
the immediate present, but is rather a case of memory, and
subject, therefore, to all the uncertainties of memory.
When I introspect, I recall the experience of the immediate past; and I must safeguard my introspection by seeing
to it that the interval is short, between conscious experience and analytic observation of it. Otherwise, I shall fall
into a mistake so common that Professor James has called it [1]

[1] "Principles of Psychology," I., p. 196.

'the psychologist's fallacy' — the error of supposing that my present consciousness of a certain situation must exactly resemble my past experience of the same situation. The confusion becomes greater if I conclude that another man's experience is exactly what mine would be under similar circumstances. For the truth is, that only the attentive recollection of an experience immediately past can furnish us with the primary material for psychological analysis, classification and explanation.

This verification of our own introspection is best secured by an important subsidiary method shared by psychology with many of the physical sciences — the method of experiment. To experiment is to regulate artificially the conditions of phenomena in such wise as to repeat, to isolate, and to vary them at will. In a multitude of ways, therefore, experiment aids scientific observation. Repetition of phenomena insures accuracy of analysis, and makes it possible to verify the results of a single observation; isolation of conditions narrows the object of study, and avoids the distraction of the observer's attention; and, finally, variation of conditions makes it possible to explain a phenomenon exactly, by connecting it with those conditions only which it always accompanies.

There is an important distinction between psychological and physical experimenting. In the latter, experiment deals with conditions of the same nature as the facts which are studied. Gas, or magnet, or nerve is directly modified by some change in the physical environment, such as heat, friction or electric stimulation. But in the psychical experiment the artificial condition is physical, not psychical; that is, it is distinguished in its nature from the fact to be studied. This is because the psychic fact can be neither repeated nor varied. The stream of consciousness is a swift-flowing current whose waves and ripples never recur; and no experience is the duplicate of another. It belongs, moreover, to the very nature of the fact of consciousness that it cannot be directly compared with another. I can count the francs that I have paid for my Elzevir edition of Hobbes's " De Cive," but I can never tell how much I enjoy it; I can enumerate the details of memory image, but I can never tell how vividly I remember. Since, however, experiment requires that the conditions of a given phenomenon be repeated and varied at will, it is evident that experiment must concern itself with the physical stimulation of psychic facts, and with the physical reactions to these stimuli. For example, though I cannot measure the vividness of a memory image, I can count the number of repetitions of a series of words which I read aloud to the person on whom I experiment; and I can compare the number of errors he makes in repeating the word-series when he has heard it once only, three times or five times; or I may compare his errors after an interval of ten minutes, of an hour, of a day, or of a week. In this way I can gain, experimentally, a conclusion about the relation of memory to frequency of experience and to extent of intervening time; and by repeating the experiment many times with the same individual and with others, I may arrive at some trustworthy general conclusion.

Psychological experimenting, as is shown by the example just given, may be of a very simple sort, and may well be carried on without formal mechanism. On the other hand, it may employ very delicate and complicated apparatus for stimulating the different sense-organs in different degrees and precisely measured times, for providing exact and variable rhythms, and for recording various physical reactions, such as pulse-beats and breathing.

Experiment, it should be added, never supplants, but only supplements and strengthens introspection. Experimental psychology is not, therefore, as some enthusiasts have claimed, a 'new psychology'; and experimental methods are of value chiefly as they secure the stricter accuracy of introspection, though secondarily as they aid us to infer the consciousness of children and of animals from their reactions to artificial stimuli.

A preliminary statement must be added concerning the recognized divisions of psychology.[1] The modern tendency is toward a multiplication and a corresponding subdivision of the sciences. The reasons for this progressive subdividing are not far to seek. The more carefully one studies scientific phenomena of any sort, the more inevitable the discovery of features, unnoticed in the general survey, which mark off one group of facts from others nearly like it. So, for instance, branches of study which used to be massed together under the heading ' natural history ' were later sharply differentiated as botany, zoölogy and physiology, and within each of these general branches there are now numberless minor groups such as histology, embryology, cryptogamic botany.

Psychology is no exception to this rule of progressive subdivision. Normal and abnormal psychology, individual and social psychology, adult and child psychology, are relatively distinct branches of it. Still another distinction, not always explicitly recognized, on which this book will lay great stress, is that of the psychology of ideas, the study of succeeding facts of consciousness without reference to conscious selves, and the psychology of selves, that is, the study of consciousness as the experience of related selves. Fundamental to all these divisions, from the standpoint of methods, is still another — the division into introspective and comparative psychology. Introspective psychology is the study of one's own consciousness; and its immediate and dominant method is introspection. Comparative psychology is the study of other consciousness than one's own. The most important objects of its study are the conscious experiences of animals, of children, and of primitive men. Its methods are the careful observation of the words or actions of the animals and people whom it studies, and the inference of the conscious experience which underlies these outer manifestations. Such infer-

[1] Cf. Chapter XXIV.

ence involves introspection, because it consists in attributing one's own experience, under given circumstances, to other people; but this introspection, because imputed to others, must be distinguished from the study of one's own consciousness.

The greater part of this book will be devoted to normal introspective psychology; that is, to the study of the normal civilized and adult consciousness; for a thorough study of facts of one's own normal experience is the necessary introduction both to the introspective study of one's own abnormal experience and to the comparative study of the consciousness of other human beings.

BOOK I

INTROSPECTIVE PSYCHOLOGY OF THE NORMAL
CONSCIOUSNESS

PART I

STRUCTURAL ELEMENTS OF CONSCIOUSNESS

CHAPTER II

VISUAL SENSATIONS

My first concern as psychologist is the accurate analysis of my consciousness. For the purposes of this introspective analysis, I may seize upon any experience. I am looking out from my window, let us say, upon Gloucester harbor and the open sea beyond, happily conscious of wooded shores, rippling blue waves, cloudy horizon, white sails and salty breeze; and the dory moored to the lichen-grown rock in the foreground has dimly suggested last evening's sail and the sunset light over the harbor. In this conscious experience, I at once recognize blueness, greenness, grayness, brownness, saltiness and rippling sound as parts of the experience. Closer scrutiny will add to the list distance and form, motion (of the breeze), and further, the red, the gold and the motor sensations which belong to the image of the sunset sail. Even now the analysis is far from complete; it has left out of account the pleasantness of the whole experience and the feeling of familiarity which accompanies the memory of the sail. This superficial treatment is, however, merely preliminary to the accurate analysis of the psychologist: the experience is to be scrutinized carefully, in the hope of discovering other elements which have so far eluded introspective recollection; each one of the apparent 'elements' is then to be studied experimentally, and to be further analyzed if that is possible; the results of the analysis are finally to be classified and so far as possible explained. Following out this scheme, we shall study the elements of consciousness in the order already suggested, beginning with the consideration of colors:—

I. Sensational Elements of Color

Every seeing person knows what blue or green or red or yellow *is*, yet nobody can describe any one of these experiences. If I ask you, for example, "What is blue?" you find yourself utterly incapable of defining it, that is, of giving its meaning in other terms, and you are reduced to saying helplessly, "Why blue — is blue; it is itself and nothing besides itself." Our inability to define these color experiences is a proof that they are elements of consciousness. A definition is an enumeration of the attributes of that which is defined; and to define anything, it is therefore necessary to analyze it into its attributes. But an element is precisely that part of any fact which is irreducible and unanalyzable. So the discovery that an experience cannot be defined is equivalent to the assertion that it is an element of consciousness. If blue were made up of any simpler experiences it would not be an element, and on the other hand, just because it is an element, we cannot analyze and define it. We shall later show[1] that the color-elements belong to the class of 'sensational qualities'; but for the present we shall merely appropriate, without explanation, the terms 'sensational' and 'quality.'

Very naturally we now inquire, How many of these indescribable and irreducible color-elements can we find in our experience? And here, at the very outset of our psychological quest, we are met by a concrete illustration of the difficulty of introspection. For very different opin-

[1] Cf. Chapter VIII., p. 103.

ions are held, by close and good observers, on a question apparently so simple as this of the number of color-elements. The two most important of these theories will be outlined.

The first is the view that there are four, and only four, sensational color-elements — red, yellow, green and blue. According to this theory, neither red, yellow, green nor blue can be analyzed into any other colors; red is not a mixture of yellow with green or blue, nor a compound of any color with gray; and yellow, blue and green are equally unanalyzable. And on the other hand all other colors, except these four, are analyzable into two or more of the principal or primary colors together with colorless light sensations. The second theory holds that there are just as many elemental colors as distinguishable color experiences. It thus enormously enlarges our stock of conscious elements, for there is little doubt that we distinguish more than thirty thousand colors: one hundred and fifty spectral colors including the red, green, blue and yellow already named and many such 'hues' as orange and green-blue; and thousands of 'tints,' such as pink, lavender and sky-blue, and shades, such as wine-color and navy-blue. Upholders of the many-color-element theory admit that any sensational element of color may be occasioned by a mixture of colored lights: for example, orange by a mixture of red and yellow lights; and that a tint is occasioned by a mixture of colored with colorless light, for example, pink by a mixture of red and white light: but they insist that the color as experienced, the feeling excited by the mixture of lights, is simple and irreducible: for example, that pink is just pink, and is not rightly describable as 'red and white.'

Each of these theories has the merit of clearness and simplicity. The first regards every color experience as complex, except the four primary color-qualities of red, green, yellow and blue. The second considers every color without exception as elemental experience. In the nerve, in turn, transmits this excitation to the visual area, that is, the occipital lobes of the brain.

There is every reason to adopt this conclusion, that retinal excitation conditions the consciousness of colors. It is furthermore probable that the retinal processes which occasion sensations of color, have to do with the cones of the retina, not with the rods. The reasons for this hypothesis, which has been recently urged by Mrs. Christine Ladd Franklin and by Professor J. von Kries,[1] are the following: in the first place, the stimulation of the outer circumference, or periphery, of the retina, where no retinal cones are found, excites a sensation not of color, but of gray. For example, if I steadily look straight before me and somebody else moves a scarlet pencil from the right, so that the image of it at first falls on the outer edges of my retina, the pencil will seem gray or black until it is almost directly in front of my eye. In the second place, the purest color-sensations follow upon the stimulation of the fovea of the retina, the depression which contains only cones or, at most, few rods.

Up to this point, however, we have merely assigned the physiological conditions of the color-consciousness in general. But we are in search of a physiological explanation of each of the color-elements or, at least, of the most important color-elements. And at this point, it must frankly be confessed, physiology has only a series of guesses or hypotheses to offer. Nothing whatever is positively known of the nature of retinal activity; whether, for example, it is chemical or electrical; and nothing is certainly known of the special retinal processes which occasion the different colors. We shall, however, briefly mention two theories of the retinal conditions of sensations of color.

The first of these is that of Professor Ewald Hering. He supposes that there are in the retina three chemical substances, each of which is capable of two opposed processes,

---

[1] Cf. Appendix, Section III., I.

orange differs from a yellow by being more red, whereas a yellowish olive differs from a yellow by being more green. We rightly, therefore, distinguish between the elemental colors, red, yellow, green and blue, and the complex colors, each of which is like two of the elements or 'turning-points' of the color-square.

We must now very carefully notice that these color-elements are never actually separate in their occurrence from other sorts of experience. One can distinguish the color from a whole complex mass of conscious elements, but one can never separate it, or seclude it, so as to be conscious, at a given moment, of nothing save a color. A color, for instance, has always some sort of shape, however vague or irregular, and it is impossible to imagine a color which is not, to some degree, spread out or extended. Furthermore, a color is always experienced as more or less mixed with colorless light; and we therefore never see an absolutely pure or, as it has been called, a 'saturated' blue or red. Most of our colors, indeed, seem to us decidedly 'unsaturated,' that is to say, they are mixed with a considerable quantity of colorless light.

This account of the color elements, brief as it is, summarizes the important facts of color-experience, from the purely introspective point of view. The brevity is not an accidental feature of this treatment of the subject, for just because an element is simple and unanalyzable it cannot, as we have seen, be talked about and described. A complex phenomenon may be described by analyzing it: for example, I may tell you that the killing-stone of a Tannese warrior is blue, oblong and pointed, smooth and sharp. But I can never describe to you the nature of blue or sharp; I can only, as it were, challenge you to experience what my words suggest. If you are blind or deaf or otherwise defective, then no amount of description will make you know all these elements of consciousness.

Our purposes as scientific psychologists are, however, unfulfilled. We have still before us the tasks of classification and explanation. From the purely psychological or introspective standpoint, that is, without reference either to physiological or to physical facts, we can classify the color-elements, as a group, by the observation that they seem to us like each other, in a sense in which no one of them is like any other experience. Green, for instance, appears to us like red and blue and yellow, but unlike sour and hot. But introspection fails to distinguish one color from another according to any principle; and it does not in any way explain a color-element. Explanation, therefore, and further classification must be sought among the physiological and the physical phenomena, which condition the color-consciousness.

It will be convenient to begin with a statement of the physical stimuli of color-sensations, for there is general agreement about them. Sensational elements of color are due to vibrations of the ether, an 'incompressible medium of extreme tenuity and elasticity' which is supposed to pervade all space and to penetrate within the molecules of material substances. So impalpable a material has never been actually observed, but its existence is hypothetically assumed, because it offers the only plausible explanation of many physical phenomena. Because the ether pervades all bodies, it must be thrown into motion by their vibrating molecules, and its periodic, transverse vibrations are assumed to be the physical stimuli which condition the sensational qualities of color. Thus the colors vary according to the number of ether vibrations in a given time. The slowest vibrations, about 450 billion each second, condition the retinal process which accompanies the sensational quality 'red'; and the swiftest vibrations, about 780 billion each second, form the physical stimulus to 'violet.' The following table includes these figures for five colors, naming also the length of the ether-waves, that is, the distance from wave to wave. It is evident that the longer the waves, the smaller the number which can be propagated in a given time : —

		NO. VIBRATIONS PER SECOND	WAVE-LENGTHS
Red	(*B*)	450 billions	687 + millionths of a millimeter
Yellow	(*D*)	526 "	588 + " " "
Green	(*E*)	589 "	526 " " "
Blue	(*F*)	640 "	484 " " "
Violet	(*H*)	790 "	392 + " " "

It should be borne in mind, that each sensation-quality may be occasioned by ether vibrations varying, in rapidity and in length of wave, within a relatively wide range. For example 'red' accompanies an ether vibration varying between 450 and 475 billion vibrations; and 780 billion vibrations, as well as 790, might be the physical stimulus to a sensation of violet. When this difference of vibration numbers becomes considerable, there results a complex, retinal process and the sensational consciousness of what is sometimes known as a 'hue.' The vibration number, for example, of the hue called peacock lies between the 589 billion of the green light and the 640 billion of the blue.

We must now consider the physiological conditions of the color consciousness, and we shall set out from a study of the structure of the eye. Roughly speaking, it is a sort of spherical *camera obscura*; but instead of a plate which moves backward and forward according as objects are nearer to the lens or farther from it, the eye has an immovable plate, the retina, but a compound lens whose refractiveness (or ability to focus light-rays) changes, so that a clear image of nearer or of farther objects may be thrown upon its plate, the retina. But we must proceed to amplify this preliminary description. The eyeball is a sphere moved by six strong muscles. It consists of three membranous layers, enclosing a series of transparent substances — the aqueous humor, the crystalline lens and the vitreous humor. Each of these is a lens for the refraction of rays of light, and together they form a double convex lens. The outside layer of the eyeball is formed in part of an opaque, whitish membrane, the sclerotic (*Scl.*), and in part of a transparent membrane, the cornea (*C.*), in shape somewhat like a watch-glass. The second or middle membrane is the choroid (*Ch.*) whose inner layer is colored and whose forward portion is the iris (*I*), that is, what we know as the 'blue' or 'brown' of the eye. Connected with this membrane is the ciliary muscle (*C. P.*), a circular muscle whose contraction draws back the choroid membrane, and so enlarges the pupil of the eye, a round opening in the

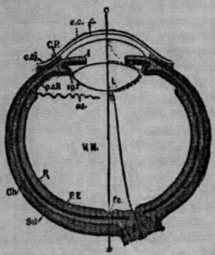

FIG. 2.— Diagrammatic outline of a horizontal section of the eye, to illustrate the relations of the various parts.

iris. The third or inner membrane, the retina (*R.*), encloses only about three-fourths of the eyeball, terminating in the ciliary muscle. The retina is the part of the eye most significant in vision, lying back of the lenses and corresponding, as we have seen, to the sensitive plate of a camera. It is composed, throughout most of its extent, of ten layers, membranous, cellular and fibrous. Of these, the most important are the layer (9) of the rods and cones, the only part of the eye on which the light can act directly, and the layer (2) formed by nerve fibres ramifying in all directions from the optic nerve (*O. N.* in Figure 2). This nerve, which pierces the sclerotic and choroid membranes from the rear, enters the retina at a spot devoid of other retinal elements, and this spot, as experiments show,[1] is unaffected by the light. Outward from this 'blind spot,' in the centre of a colored yellow spot (the *macula lutea*), there is a little pit or depression (the *fovea, f. c.*) in which the retina has thinned so that light more directly affects the cones, which here appear in unusual numbers with few or no rods among them. The eye is, in fact, a complicated mechanism constructed, apparently, for the sole purpose of focussing light-waves on its retina. The rays of light from an object are refracted by the lenses of the eye, pierce through the inner layers of the retina, and excite the rod and cone layer. The activity of

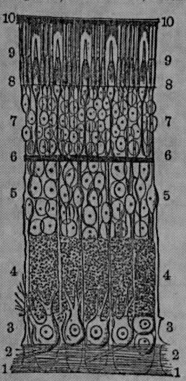

FIG. 3.— A section through the retina from its anterior or inner surface. 1, in contact with the hyaloid membrane, to its outer. 10, in contact with the choroid. 1, internal limiting membrane; 2, nerve-fibre layer; 3, nerve-cell layer; 4, inner molecular layer; 5, inner granular layer; 6, outer molecular layer; 7, outer granular layer; 8, external limiting membrane; 9, rod and cone layer; 10, pigment-cell layer.

rods and cones stimulates the optic nerve, and the optic

[1] For experiments, cf. Sanford, " Experimental Psychology," 113 and 114.

decomposition and recomposition, as they may be called. The decomposition, or katabolic process, of one of the substances occasions, Hering supposes, the sensational consciousness of red; and the recomposition of the same substance excites the sensational quality green. In the same way, the two processes of a second retinal substance excite sensations of yellow and of blue. The opposed processes of the third substance occasion sensations of white and of black.

The second theory is that of Mrs. Franklin, who supposes that different sensational elements of color are excited by the different ways in which the molecules, of a photo-chemical substance in the retinal cones, are decomposed. In more detail, the theory supposes that each completely developed color-molecule consists of four parts, of which each is fitted to vibrate to one only of the color stimuli, blue, yellow, red and green light.

Neither of these theories can profitably be considered until we have studied sensations of colorless light and their retinal condition, for both theories relate the retinal stimulus of color-elements to the retinal stimulus of colorless light elements.[1] Both theories are purely hypothetical, but, for reasons which will later appear, the Franklin theory is to be preferred.[2] We return therefore to the general conclusion already reached: The different sensational elements of color are physiologically conditioned by retinal processes, probably connected with the cones of the retina.

The retinal processes are not, of course, the immediate physiological conditions of sensational elements of color. But the retinal processes excite the optic nerve, and the optic nerve conveys these excitations to the so-called visual area, namely, the occipital lobes of the brain.[3] The immediate physiological condition of color-sensations is the excitation of cells in this part of the brain. There

[1] Cf. page 36.
[2] Cf. page 41, and Appendix, Section III., I.
[3] Cf. Appendix, Section I., I.

are several proofs of this : in the first place, a person may be conscious, while imprisoned in a darkened room, of most vividly colored sunsets or flowers or costumes. In this case, it is evident that the retina is unaffected by the ether-waves, so that retinal processes cannot be essential to sensations of color. This conclusion has been verified also by experiment. When the optic nerve is severed, however perfect the eyeball and the retina, no stimulus can bring about visual sensations. Experiment has also made it highly probable that excitation of the optic nerve is not an essential condition of visual sensations, for physiologists have established the fact that the different nerve-fibres, optic, auditory and so on, are exactly alike ; evidently, therefore, the different sensations of color, sound and the like cannot be conditioned by excitation of these undistinguished fibres.

We return, therefore, to the conclusion that excitation of brain-cells, in the occipital lobes, is the immediate physiological condition of sensations of color. But we must remark that the brain-cells are excited originally, by stimulations conveyed by the optic nerve from the retina. We should never have color-sensations, however perfect our occipital brain-lobes, if our retinæ had never been stimulated by ether-waves. But when the occipital lobes have been thus excited from without, they may later be excited, without external stimulus, by a radiation of energy from other brain-centres.[1]

II. Sensational Elements of Colorless Light

From the study of the elemental qualities of color, we must turn to the consideration of the sensational elements of colorless light. It is at once evident that these are unanalyzable experiences, distinct from any one of the sensational color-qualities. But again it is very difficult

[1] Cf. Appendix, Section I., I.

to assure ourselves, by introspection, how many kinds
there are of elemental colorless light experiences. The
writer of this book inclines to the opinion that there are
three such elemental qualities, white, black and gray, and
that only one intensity belongs with white, as with black,
whereas numberless intensities are combined with the
gray.[1] On this view, there is no such thing as an intenser
or a less intense white, or an intenser or a less intense
black, whereas there may be any number of brighter or
duller grays than any given gray; and a very light gray
resembles a dark gray but does not resemble a white in
quality, whereas it is more like the white than like the
dark gray in intensity.

This conclusion must be distinguished from four other
theories of colorless light consciousness. One of these
teaches that there are as many elemental qualities of colorless light as there are distinguishable kinds of colorless
light, and that, just as red is a different sensational element
from yellow, so one gray is distinct, as a sensation-quality,
not only from white and black, but from every other distinguishable gray. Another theory supposes that there
are two colorless light sensations, white and black, and
that gray is a complex color-experience, analyzable into
white and black. According to a third theory, black is a
sensational element which is no more closely related to
white and gray than to red or yellow or green. The last
of these theories teaches that there is but one quality of
colorless light, namely gray, and that this is combined
with numberless intensities or degrees of brightness. Such
a hypothesis means nothing less than this, that the term,
'gray' covers the whole series of visual experiences from
white through gray to black; so that white is simply 'very
light gray' and black 'very dark gray.'

It must be admitted that it is hard to choose between
these five views. Yet on the whole, introspection seems

---

[1] Cf. p. 67.

to decide against the four last outlined. The theory of an indefinite number of colorless light elements is contradicted by the fact that the different grays really seem like each other, instead of being distinct as green is from blue or yellow from red. The theory of two colorless light sensations, white and black, is opposed by the fact that gray does not really look like either white or black. Of course, this is exactly the point at issue, and one may easily be mistaken in introspection. Nevertheless, the writer of this book inclines to the view, (1) that one calls gray like black and white, merely because one knows by experience that the mixture of white and black lights gives gray, and (2) that the consciousness of gray is really distinct from the sensational elements, — white and black, and not reducible to them. The third theory, that black is as different from white and gray as from red, yellow, green and blue, also seems to the writer to contradict plain introspection.

For the same general reason, one may reject the last of these theories — that of a single colorless light impression, gray — for white and black do seem distinct from gray. Against this result of introspection, the upholders of the one-element theory urge the following fact, that it is possible, at any time, to make either a supposed 'white' or a supposed 'black' look gray by contrasting it with a whiter white or a blacker black: for example, one names the sheet on which one is writing 'white' until the sun falls upon it, when immediately it appears no longer white but very light gray; and a surface of ebonized wood which seemed black at first, grows obviously gray if placed against a black velvet background.[1] Now there is no question that this is an accurate description of the facts; but these facts certainly do not prove that the black or white surface, which grows to look gray by contrast with another hue, looked gray — not white or black — in the first place. On the contrary, we must suppose that the very

[1] For experiments, cf. Sanford, 140 a.

same object, the white paper or the ebonized wood, excites different physiological processes, and thus different conscious states, under different circumstances.[1] We come back, therefore, after study of the four theories,—the theory of innumerable colorless light qualities, the theory of two colorless light qualities, white and black, the hypothesis that black does not belong at all to the white-gray series, and finally, the theory of a single colorless light quality, —to our original conclusion that there are three qualities, white, gray and black, and that many intensities may be combined with the gray.

It will be well, before going on to study the conditions of the colorless light consciousness, to summarize the different sorts of visual sensation and visual fusion:[2] not merely the elemental colors and the colorless light sensations, but the simplest fusions, as we may call them, of elemental colors with each other, and with white, gray and black. Visual sensations and fusions are most simply represented by a color pyramid, which, as Titchener reminds us,[3] is a purely psychological (not physical or physiological) construction. The base represents the most saturated colors — those least mixed with white, gray or black. Its rectangu-

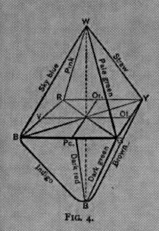

FIG. 4.

lar form suggests the fact that the red, yellow, green and blue are, as has been shown, turning-points in the color series. The dotted vertical, *WB*, represents the white — gray — black. Toward white, the surface of the pyramid represents the pale greens, straw-yellows, sky-

---

[1] Cf. Appendix, Section III, p. 475.

[2] Cf. Ch. XIII, p. 158.

[3] Experimental Psychology, Qualitative, Instructor's Manual, p. 5.

blues and pinks; toward black, the indigo-blues, the browns, the reds and the greens are represented. "All these tones," to quote Titchener again, "are the most saturated possible, the most coloured colours of their kind, but if we peel the figure (like an onion), leaving the black and white poles untouched, we get precisely what we had before, save that all the colour tones are less saturated, lie so much nearer to the neutral tones." All told — color-elements, colorless light elements, color-fusions, such as olive and peacock, tints, such as pink and sky-blue, and shades, such as indigo — the color-pyramid represents more than 30,000 color-elements and fusions.

From this introspective study, we shall go on as before to consider the physical and the physiological conditions of the consciousness of colorless light. Each sensation-quality of color, as has been stated, is physically conditioned by ether-waves of a single rate of vibration. There is no one physical stimulus to the consciousness of colorless light, but, on the other hand, three methods of bringing it about. In the first place, it is occasioned by an equal mixture of ether-waves of all lengths, and thus of all vibration rates. This is shown, experimentally, in many ways. The spectral colors, if united upon one spot, give a gray surface; and a disk containing nearly equal sectors of each of the colors, blue, green, red and yellow will appear gray if so swiftly rotated that all four stimulate the same part of the retina at one time.[1] The sensation of colorless light may also be excited by a mixture of two colored lights, which are then called complementary color-stimuli. Thus, blue and yellow light, or purple and green, or red and bluish green, combined in equal quantities, excite the sensation of colorless light.[1] And finally, there are certain cases in which sensations of colorless light are obtained, without any combination of color lights, through one color-stimulus only. There are four important cases

[1] For experiments, cf. Sanford, 148 c. and 149 ; Titchener, " Experimental Psychology," Students' Manual, Qualitative, § 8.

in which colored objects seem colorless, and we must carefully consider them.

In the first place, the excitation by any color-stimulus of very small extents of the retina, excites a colorless light sensation. This is shown by the every-day observation that distant objects lose their color. The second case is that of color-stimulation in faint light. As the proverb has it, "in the night all cats are gray." All objects lose their color when seen in faint light. The third case is that in which the peripheral parts of the retina, that is, the parts farthest from its centre, are stimulated. If a small colored object (like a half-inch square of paper glued to the end of a long strip of gray card) be brought toward the field of vision from either side, while one eye is closed and the other firmly fixated on something directly in front of the face, it will be found that the colored square at first seems gray, and that it is seen in its true color, only as it approaches the centre of the eye. Only careful experiment, with the use of a perimeter, may 'map out' the exact retinal fields for different colors, but every one may prove to himself the color-blindness of the outer rims of the retina; and this means that here any color-stimulus is accompanied by a sensation, not of color, but of gray.[1]

Fourth, and finally, we have the cases of actual color-blindness. These we shall consider in more detail, since the experience is not so common as the other three. There are probably, roughly speaking, five types of color-blind people: four classes of the partially color-blind, to whom red, green, blue or yellow seems gray, and the totally color-blind, to whom all colors seem gray. Dalton, for example, one of the first to describe the phenomena of color-blindness, could hardly distinguish his red academic gown from the grass on which he had thrown it. The first two forms of color-blindness are much the most common, and only rare cases of the other types have

[1] For experiments, cf. Sanford, 137, a ; Titchener, § 9.

D

been found.[1] Color-blindness is tested, not, of course, by
trying to discover whether names of colors are correctly
used, but by finding out whether, from a mass of differently
colored objects, the person who is being tested can distinguish all the colors. In actual tests, for instance, made
by the Holmgren method, a pile of worsted skeins in about
one hundred different shades is placed before the subject,
who is directed to put together different shades of one
color. Under these circumstances, the man who is red-
blind heaps together with the grays all reds which are not
yellowish, while he places all greens which are not bluish
with the yellows; and the green-blind person confuses
greens with grays, and reds with yellows, in a similar way.[2]

All these are cases, as has been so often repeated,
in which the physical condition of the consciousness of
colorless light, is any one color-stimulus, instead of a combination of stimuli. In other words, this, like the contrast
experience,[3] is a fact of consciousness which cannot be explained by any merely physical stimulus. For two distinct
kinds of physical phenomena, the combination of color-
stimuli and the single stimulus, are followed by one and
the same conscious phenomenon, the sensation of colorless
light; and, on the other hand, one physical phenomenon,
a single color-stimulus, conditions now a sensation of color,
and now a sensation of colorless light.

To account for the peculiarities and to find what we are
seeking, an explanation of the colorless light sensation, we
must, therefore, study no longer its physical, but its physiological conditions. Such a study must be purely hypothetical. Actual observation of the histological structure
or of the chemical constitution of the retina is, as we have
seen, almost utterly wanting. Accordingly, there has been
wide scope for theoretical constructions, and a considera-

[1] Cf. Appendix, Section III., II.   [2] For experiments, cf. Sanford, 135.
[3] Cf. p. 30, and Appendix, Section III., II.

tion of some of these will be of use to us. It will of necessity include a reference to the theories, already considered, of color-qualities : —

Chronologically first is the Young-Helmholtz theory, independently formulated by an Englishman, Thomas Young, and by the great German scientist, Hermann von Helmholtz. So far as it relates to sensational elements of color, this theory is very general, simply holding that there are three retinal elements or processes whose excitation respectively conditions three color-sensations, red, green and violet. The important part of the theory is its explanation of sensations of colorless light as due simply to the combination in equal degrees of these three color-processes. Evidently this is a reasonable explanation of the cases in which a mixture of ether-waves of all lengths conditions the consciousness of colorless light. The Young-Helmholtz theory also explains, in the following manner, the excitation of colorless light sensations through the mixture of only two color-stimuli : ether vibrations of a given rate tend to set up in the retina not only the processes specifically corresponding with them, but also those which correspond with proximate vibration numbers. So blue light excites the retinal process which conditions the sensation-quality green, as well as that which accompanies blue; and yellow light stimulates the processes for red as well as for yellow. Therefore the combination of two complementary color-stimuli produces the same effect, physiologically, as the combination of all the color-stimuli. The specific physical condition of the sensation-qualities of colorless light is thus such a mixture of ether-waves as will stimulate simultaneously and nearly equally all physiological color-processes.

It may be questioned whether the explanation just given of the excitation of colorless light, through the mixture of two complementary color-stimuli, is in full agreement with the facts. There is reason, on the other hand, to think that the third process inferred by the theory would be insufficiently excited. We need not, however, discuss this point, for however adequate its explanation of colorless light sensations through combination of stimuli, the Young-Helmholtz theory must be rejected on another ground: it fails utterly to account for the four cases in which a sensation of colorless light follows upon a single color-stimulus. It is impossible to suppose that three color-processes are aroused when a single color-stimulus falls on the outer rim, or on a small part of the retina, or when the color-stimulus is very faint. And, finally, the theory cannot possibly be reconciled with the fact of color-blindness. For in color-blindness one, at least, of the normal retinal color-processes is wanting, and there can therefore be no combination of three retinal processes.

A far more satisfactory explanation is that of Hering. He holds, as we have seen, that a sensational quality of color is physiologically due to the activity of one of two antagonistic processes of some retinal substance. Of these retinal substances, he believes that there are three, each of them capable of an anabolic, that is, assimilative or ' building up' process; and of a katabolic, that is, destructive or 'tearing down' process. To these six processes correspond the sensations of red, yellow, blue, green, white and black, whose exact relations may be seen by the following summary : —

SUBSTANCES	PROCESSES	SENSATIONS OF
Red-green	Anabolic	Green
	Katabolic	Red
Yellow-blue	Anabolic	Blue
	Katabolic	Yellow
White-black	Anabolic	Black
	Katabolic	White

In explanation of this summary, it must be stated explicitly that Hering's expressions 'red-green,' 'blue-yellow,' and 'white-black,' do not refer to the appearance of the retinal substances. Indeed, these substances have never been actually observed, for the theory is purely hypothetical. By 'white-black substance,' therefore, Hering merely means 'an inferred retinal substance whose opposite activities result in the sensations of white and black.' It follows that the katabolic process of the white-black substance excites sensations of white; the anabolic process excites sensations of black ; an equilibrium between the two processes occasions a sensation of middle gray; and an unequal combination of the two processes excites sensations of light or dark gray. Hering teaches, furthermore, that the white-black substance is excited by every light-stimulus and that it is more widely spread than the color-substances over the surface of the retina. The sensation of colorless light is, therefore, excited either through the activity of the 'white-black' retinal substance, when antagonistic color-processes have destroyed each other by simultaneous action; or through the activity of the white-black substance in parts of the retina where the red-green and blue-yellow substances are wanting.[1]

This will become clearer if we consider, one by one, all the ways in which the sensation of colorless light can be excited. Hering first explains the excitation of colorless light consciousness through combination of two color-stimuli. When, for example, blue and yellow light fall simultaneously on the retina, the blue tends to set the blue-yellow substance into anabolic activity, whereas the yellow tends equally to stimulate the katabolic activity of the blue-yellow substance. These opposite processes cancel each other; and so equilibrium is maintained and the blue-yellow substance, equally stimulated in two opposite directions, remains inactive, whereas the white-black process, as has been said, is always active. It follows that in the inactivity of the blue-yellow substance only sensa-

[1] "Zur Lehre vom Lichtsinne," E. Hering, Vienna, 1878, § 28, p. 81.

tions of colorless light result; and the combination of red and green lights must have a similar effect. It is easy to explain, after the same fashion, the excitation of colorless light sensations through the combination of ether-waves of all lengths, for this would amount to the combination of two pairs of complementary color-stimuli, red, green, blue and yellow lights, and would result in two balanced processes. Both color-substances would thus remain inactive, and the constantly active processes of the white-black substance would, as before, excite the sensational experience of colorless light.

There remain those cases, on which the Helmholtz theory was wrecked, of the consciousness of colorless light through one color-stimulus only. The superiority of the Hering theory appears most strongly at just this point. His explanations are based on the assumptions, already stated, that the white-black substance is found in all parts of the retina and that every light-stimulus, colorless or colored, excites it. In accordance then with his hypothesis, Hering supposes (1) that sensations of colorless light arise when small extents of the retina are excited by a single color-stimulus, because the stimulation of such small amounts of the red-green or blue-yellow substance is not sufficient to rouse it to activity, whereas the ever active white-black substance is excited by even a color-stimulus; (2) that the excitations in faint light are not intense enough to affect a color-substance, but do excite the sensitive white-black substance; (3) that stimulation of the retinal periphery by color-stimuli excites only sensations of colorless light because only the white-black substance is found on the periphery of the retina. Hering teaches finally (4) that a color-stimulus excites a sensation of colorless light, when the subject is color-blind, because the retina of a color-blind person is lacking in one or both color-substances, so that the color-stimulus affects only the easily excited white-black substance.

Hering has certainly, therefore, furnished a plausible

explanation for sensations of colorless light, whether conditioned by single stimulus or by a combination. But though his theory is far more satisfactory than that of Helmholtz, there are certain difficulties in the way of it. We have named the most general of these difficulties, the fact that the theory is purely hypothetical and that no histological study of the eye has discovered any trace of one of these retinal substances. In the second place, the conception of consciousness as conditioned by an assimilative bodily process directly runs athwart physiological analogy. For the assimilative bodily processes, by which nerve-cells take up into themselves materials, chiefly oxygen, from the outside world, are known to be processes which are unaccompanied by consciousness. The hours of dreamless sleep, for example, are a period of assimilation, but also of unconsciousness. The assumption of Hering that black, green and blue are conditioned by assimilative bodily processes loses sight of the probability that not assimilation, the formation of more complex compounds, but dissimilation, the decomposition of chemical compounds and consequent liberation of energy, is the physiological concomitant of consciousness.

There are other objections to the Hering theory, too technical to be considered in this chapter.[1] We shall proceed at once to outline two other theories concerning the physiological conditions of colorless light sensations. These theories, that of C. L. Franklin and of von Kries, have been referred to already in the description of color-theories. It will be remembered that they explain the sensational elements of color — red, yellow, green and the others — as due to the excitation, singly or in unequal combination, of processes connected with the retinal cones. The two theories agree, also, in the teaching that colorless light impressions result, first, when the retinal cones are excited by an equal combination of two or more color-

[1] Cf. Appendix, Section III.

stimuli, and second, when the rods of the retina are excited by a single color-stimulus. The second part of this teaching is the characteristic feature of it, and strong arguments may be urged in its favor. In the first place, it furnishes a satisfactory account of facts which the Young-Helmholtz theory failed to explain, the different cases, namely, of colorless light consciousness, through a single color-stimulus. These, as will be remembered, are four: faint light consciousness, peripheral stimulation, excitation of small extents of the retina and color-blindness. C. L. Franklin and von Kries suppose in the first case that the rod-processes are excitable by intensities fainter than those required to excite the cones; in the second case, they refer to the established fact that only rods are found in the periphery of the retina; in the third place, they suppose that the cone-process is insufficiently stimulated; and finally, they assume that the color-blind eye lacks one or two or all retinal processes connected with the cones.

So far, however, these theories have no advantage over the Hering hypothesis, for that also sufficiently explains the colorless light sensations through one color-stimulus. But the von Kries and Franklin theories have the great added advantage of corresponding accurately with the observed anatomical constitution of the retina. The first of these correspondences has already been noted, the fact that the outer edge or periphery of the retina contains rods and no cones. Thus, every color-stimulus which falls on the periphery of necessity affects the rods. But there is another argument, from actual observation, for these theories. It has long been known that the human retina and that of many invertebrate animals contains a purplish substance known as 'visual purple.' This substance is found in the retinal rods and not in the cones; and the experiments of Professor Arthur König have established, first, that it is affected by lights of different colors at different rates; and second, that these rates correspond exactly with the intensities of different colors in faint light.[1] For example, green, which has the greatest intensity in faint light, first affects the visual purple, and blue light, which has great faint light intensity, next quickly affects it. This fact, that the colors which are intensest in faint light most quickly bleach the visual purple, suggests that the functioning of this retinal substance has to do with the consciousness of faint or colorless light; and the observation that the visual purple is found only on the retinal rods confirms the view that they are, as von Kries puts it, an achromatic retinal apparatus, definitely connected with the sensational element of colorless light.

Up to this point we have treated the two theories, that of C. L. Franklin and that of von Kries, as virtually identical. But just as Mrs. Franklin developed, in the explanation of the color-consciousness, a more detailed hypothesis, so here she amplifies the theory already outlined. In brief, she supposes (1) that sensations of colorless light are due to the complete decomposition of a photo-chemical substance in either rods or cones; (2) that this substance is chemically simpler in the rods than in the cones, so that a single color-stimulus can totally decompose it; (3) that only a combination of two or more color-stimuli can completely decompose the substance in the cones and so give rise to a colorless light sensation, whereas a single color-stimulus partially decomposes this substance, thus exciting a color-sensation. A more detailed account of this theory would involve too many technicalities for the present chapter. But in the opinion of the writer the underlying hypothesis of the Franklin theory, though unsupported by experimental evidence, is the most satisfactory which has so far been formulated.[2]

We conclude, therefore, with a brief summary of our results. There are probably three elemental colorless light qualities, white, black and gray. Their physical

[1] Cf. Appendix, Section III., I.   [2] *Ibid.*

stimuli are of two kinds, an equal combination of color-stimuli, or a single color-stimulus. The retinal conditions of the colorless light experiences are not definitely known, but it is reasonable to conjecture that, in the first case, the retinal cones are excited, very probably with complete decomposition of their molecules, and that, in the second case, the retinal rods are stimulated. The immediate physiological occasion of the colorless light consciousness is the excitation, primarily through the optic nerve, of the 'visual area' in the occipital lobes of the brain.

III. Sensational Elements of Brightness

One cannot be conscious of a color, a red or a blue for example, or of a colorless light, a white or black or gray, without being at the same time conscious of its brightness and of its bigness or extensity. The combination of these sensational elements, which invariably accompany each other, is called a sensation. The problem of extensity is so complicated and so difficult that we must postpone it for a later discussion.[1] We shall, however, at once consider the nature of visual intensity or brightness. There is no doubt, in the first place, that a brightness, as well as a color or a gray, is a distinct and unanalyzable element of consciousness. It cannot, of course, be separated from the color or the colorless light with which it is combined, but it may be perfectly distinguished from it. Some psychologists, it is true, have denied the distinctness of visual intensity elements, and have instead identified the series of brightnesses with the sensational colorless light series from black through gray to white.[2] According to this view, an intense color is simply a color combined with white. But observation shows a striking difference between a highly illuminated color — for example, a red intensely lighted from behind — and the same color mixed

[1] Cf. Chapter VII., p. 89.   [2] Cf. Appendix, Section III., II.

with gray or white light — for example, a lighter red or pink. We may, therefore, reaffirm that the visual intensities are distinct elements of consciousness.

The visual intensities are, as every one admits, indefinite in number. They are furthermore distinguished from sensational qualities of color and of colorless light, by their capacity for direct and simple serial arrangement. We are not yet prepared to discuss in detail the nature of what we know as series, but for our present purpose it suffices to describe a psychological series as composed of successive facts of consciousness, of which each includes within itself a feeling of 'more,' that is, of increase. Now, in the series of brightnesses each successive feeling of 'more' is directly connected with the sensational element brightness so that the series may be thus expressed: 'bright — more bright — still more bright.' In the series of color-elements, on the other hand, the feeling of 'more' attaches itself to a feeling of difference, not directly to a sensational element of color. The series 'red, yellow, green, blue,' cannot therefore be described as 'red — more red — still more red,' but is rather to be described as —

Red [1]	
Yellow	different from red
Green	{ different from yellow
	more different from red
Blue	{ different from green
	more different from yellow
	still more different from red

Partly because of their direct serial arrangement, and partly because our practical and æsthetic interests are concerned only with extremes of intensity, we are not interested in naming the brightnesses as we are in nam-

[1] Such a series as 'red, reddish yellow, yellowish green,' etc., is a direct series, but not a simple series. Cf. p. 105.

ing the colors. For these reasons, the visual intensities are estimated by comparison with each other, and not with reference to absolute standards.

Some psychologists have argued that we have no data for the physical and the physiological explanation of brightnesses, basing their view on the assumption that ether-vibrations, retinal processes and cerebral excitation are sufficient only to the explanation of sensational qualities, the colors and the colorless light elements. This assumption, however, overlooks the fact that, in the case of a physiological process, we may distinguish the locality of the functioning bodily organ and the degree of its activity. Now the colors and the colorless light elements correspond with the activity of a substance in the cones or rods of the retina, and with the activity of cells in the occipital lobe. The brightnesses, therefore, may well correspond with the different degrees of the activity of these different organs. In a physical process, also, we distinguish the mode and the degree of the activity; and we know experimentally that variations of degree in atmospheric vibrations, that is to say, differences of amplitude in an atmospheric wave, occasion differences in sound-intensity. It is reasonable to infer that the visual brightnesses are due to the degree of ether-vibrations, or the amplitude of the ether-waves.

We must now sum up the conclusions of this chapter. Within our conscious experience we have found, by introspection, these three sorts of elemental consciousness: (1) the colors: red, yellow, green, blue; (2) the colorless light elements: white, gray and black; and (3) the brightnesses, always combined with colors or with colorless lights. We have found, also, that white is combined with but one intensity and that the same is true of black; whereas numberless intensities may be combined with gray.

The probable physiological conditions of the color-elements are, first, the mode of activity of a substance in the retinal cones, and second, the mode of activity of cells in the occipital lobes of the brain. The physiological condition of the white, gray and black is the mode of activity of rod-substance and of brain-cells. The physiological condition of brightnesses is, however, not the mode, but the degree, of retinal and of brain activity.

The physical condition of sensational elements of color is the mode of ether-vibration, that is, the length of the ether-waves which fall on the retina. The physical condition of the colorless light consciousness is a combination of the ether-waves of all possible wave-lengths. The physical condition of visual intensities or brightnesses is, in all probability, the degree of the ether-vibration, that is, the amplitude of the ether-waves which excite the retina.

lower, C, is a difference between two unanalyzable elements of pitch, whereas reddish purple (at least in the opinion of many observers) differs from red, as a complex from an element. It should be added that individuals and species vary greatly in their ability to distinguish very high and very low tones. Some people, accordingly, are spoken of as deaf to low or to high tones, and some animals hear notes inaudible to human beings. Cats, for example, give every indication of hearing the high tones of a Galton whistle, sounds so high pitched that they are inaudible to us.

The most characteristic feature of the series of tones, as compared with that of colors, is the recurrence of parallel series of elements of pitch. These are the octaves, which resemble each other as wholes. The series of differently pitched tones may, therefore, as has been suggested, be symbolized by a spiral, ascending from base to apex, of which each curve represents an octave. The study of the octave involves, however, a consideration of the interval, and the interval is a complex and not an elemental experience, so that it is not appropriately discussed in this connection.

Unlike tone, noise is devoid of pitch. Certain observers, it is true, speak of the pitch of a simple noise, but, closely observed, anything which has pitch appears to be what we mean by tone.[1] Others believe that a noise is merely a very complex, and thus an utterly discordant, mixture of tones, and that, so far from lacking pitch, it is a confused mass of innumerable pitches. Now it is true that what we ordinarily know as a noise includes an irregular combination of tones of different pitch.[2] If one listen to the common-place noises of falling footsteps, rolling wheels and clanging bells, holding to one's ear successively a set of resonators, each fitted to transmit to the ear only air-waves exciting a single pitch, one may assure oneself experimen-

[1] Cf. W. Wundt, "Physiologische Psychologie," 4te Aufl., I., p. 448.
[2] For experiments, cf. Titchener, § 12 (2) and (3).

tally that the so-called noise contains differently pitched tones. But though containing these discordant tones, this mass of sounds probably includes, and is characterized by, a certain elemental noise-quality. For if the stimulus to a simple tone is continuously varied, so that its pitch becomes gradually lower or higher, there will come in each case a point of transition to some sensational element, distinguishable from a pitch, which may be named (in lieu of a more characteristic designation) a 'noise-quality,' that is, the element characteristic of the complex experience, noise. It, however, so seldom occurs, in even relative isolation, that it often is not even identified by the ordinary observer. There is, for this reason, no enumeration of 'primary' or absolutely unanalyzable noise-qualities, like the list, red, green, blue, yellow, of primary color-elements. Such words as 'snap,' 'puff,' 'thud,' do, however, point to certain distinct noise-elements. From the sensibility to differences of noise, 553 (alleged) noise-qualities have been calculated, but most of these probably are capable of analysis, and therefore are not strictly elemental.

Once more, we shall find it convenient to consider the physical, and therefore secondary and remote, conditions of pitch and noise-quality, before regarding the more immediate physiological antecedents. The physical condition of sound in general may be described as oscillation of air-particles, producing rarefactions and condensations of the air. A rarefaction followed by a condensation is called an atmospheric wave. Pitch is, in all probability, occasioned by a succession of simple and regular atmospheric waves, or even by a small portion of a simple atmospheric wave.[1]

[1] It is usually held that at least two complete air-waves are necessary to excite sensations of tone. Experiments, however, indicate that even a portion of a single, simple air-wave excites a sensation of tone, whose pitch corresponds to the length of the complete air-wave of which a part only has stimulated the ear. Cf. C. R. Cross and M. E. Maltby, "On the Least Number of Vibrations Necessary to Determine Pitch," Proc. of the Amer. Acad., 1892, p. 222.

Noise, on the other hand, is probably due to a complex and irregular combination of air-waves, that is, to an irregular and unperiodic vibration of air-particles. Different qualities of pitch are found by experiment to correspond to the varying length of the atmospheric waves. The swifter the atmospheric vibrations, that is, the greater the number and the shorter the length of the air-waves in any second of time, the higher is the pitch; and, on the other hand, the slower the vibrations, that is, the fewer and longer the air-waves of a second, the lower or deeper is the pitch. This is the principle on which all stringed instruments are constructed. The shorter strings of the piano are struck to produce its higher notes; and the violinist's finger divides his string to obtain from the swifter air-vibrations, propagated by the motion of each half, a tone an octave higher than that produced by the slower vibration of the entire length. As, therefore, a definite number of ether-vibrations corresponds with each experience of color, so each pitch has its vibration number: low c, for example (in what is called the small octave) is produced, through the excitation of nerve-endings and brain-cells, by 128 vibrations; and its octave, c', is excited by exactly twice as many, or 256 vibrations.

But these physical phenomena are conditions of sound only indirectly, as they bring about neural changes. They stimulate nervous end-organs enclosed within the ear, whose structure, therefore, we have next to consider. The external ear, or *concha* (*M*), reflects the air-waves and air-shocks into the hollow tube, or external *meatus* (*G*), which is closed by a surface, the tympanic membrane (*T*). This is thrown into vibration by the motion of the air-particles, and its motion is transmitted to a series of three bones called, from their shape, *malleus, incus* and *stapes* (that is, hammer, anvil and stirrup). These bones lie within the drum or middle ear (*P*), a hollow in the temporal bone from which the Eustachian tube leads to the pharynx. The middle ear communicates by two openings with the

4

inner ear. Into one of these openings, the *foramen ovale* or oval window (*O*), the stapes or stirrup-bone fits closely; the other opening, the *foramen rotundum* (*r*), is closed merely by a membrane.

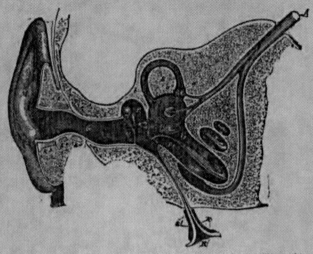

FIG. 5.— Semidiagrammatic section through the right ear (Czermak).

The inner ear is composed of hollows in the temporal bone, with membranous lining throughout. These consist of a middle chamber, the vestibule (*V*), which divides the three semicircular canals from the *cochlea* (*S*). The canals, however, are almost certainly unconnected with phenomena of hearing, and it is doubtful whether the vestibule has to do with sound-sensations. We are, therefore, chiefly concerned with the structure of the cochlea. It is in form a spiral, consisting of two and one-half coils around a bony axis. From this axis projects a bony shelf, the *lamina spiralis* (*lso* in Figure 6) ending in the basilar membrane (*b*). Together, bone and membrane divide each spiral into two winding half-coils, the *scala tympani* (*ST*) and the *scala vestibuli* (*SV*). The former opens by the round foramen into the middle ear; the latter is con-

nected with the vestibule. (A third division, the *scala
media (CC)* is partitioned off, by a membrane, within the
scala vestibuli.)

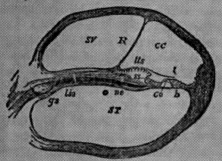

FIG. 6. — Section of one coil of the cochlea, magnified.

The structure of the basilar membrane is of great importance for our present study. It consists of cross-
fibres, varying in length from beginning to apex of the
cochlea, and carrying nerve-cells. From some of these
cells, hairs project, and in these same cells ramifications of
the acoustic nerve have their termination. Other cells support the inner and outer 'organs of Corti,' which number
respectively six thousand and forty-five hundred. They
are tiny, membranous rods, leaned against each other at
their upper ends so as to form a sort of arch, and decreas-
ing in length from base to apex of the spiral. It used
to be thought that the organs of Corti play the part in our
ears of strings in a piano, vibrating because of their differing length and span with air-waves of different rates.
Several arguments, however, tell strongly against this view.
The rods are neither sufficient in number, nor sufficiently
varied in size, to serve this purpose; they are not found in
the auditory end-organs of birds whose ability to discriminate pitches can hardly be doubted; and finally, they are
not directly connected with the fibres of the auditory nerve,
which terminate, as has been said, in the hair-cells of the
basilar membrane. It is possible, therefore, though it is

not certain, that, not the organs of Corti, but the cross-fibres of the basilar membrane, which increase in length from the bottom of the spiral nearly to the apex, are fitted, or tuned as it were, to vibrate with air-waves of all different periods. This independent vibration of basilar membrane fibres is certainly possible, for though the basilar membrane is 'tense radially,' it is loose in one direction, namely 'longitudinally along the spiral of the cochlea.'[1] If this view is correct, the vibration of these fibres excites some of the sixteen to twenty thousand overlying hair-cells, and the hair-cells in turn affect the fibres of the auditory nerve. In this case, the organs of Corti and the hairs projecting from the hair-cells probably serve, like the dampers of a piano, merely to stop the movements of the vibrating fibres.

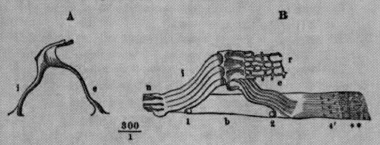

$$\frac{300}{1}$$

FIG. 7.—The rods of Corti. *A*, a pair of rods separated from the rest; *B*, a bit of the basilar membrane with several rods on it, showing how they cover in the *tunnel of Corti; i*, inner, and *e*, outer, rods; *b*, basilar membrane; *r*, reticular membrane.

The outline, which follows, of the process in the ear is, in great part, merely tentative. We consider, first, the case in which all or part of a simple air-wave, of perhaps 128 vibrations per second, sets the tympanic membrane in motion. This motion is communicated by the bones of the middle ear to the membranous covering of the oval foramen, that is, the window opening into the inner ear. The

[1] Cf. Foster, "Text-book of Physiology," Bk. III., Chapter IV., p. 1015.

vibrations of this membrane indirectly set in motion the endolymph, a liquid with which the membranous cochlea is filled, and the movement of this liquid excites those only of the cross-fibres of the basilar membrane whose vibration number is either exactly or approximately 128. But, in the second place, the tympanic membrane, the ear-bones, and the endolymph may be stimulated by a compound and yet regular air-wave; in this case several basilar membrane fibres of varying length will be excited, and the consciousness of a clang or chord will result, instead of the simple sensation. A complex and irregular, or unperiodic, vibration may, finally, affect the organs of the ear. To this, the fibres of the basilar membrane must respond with an irregular movement—what has been called a 'twitch,' and the sensation which follows is that of noise.

The cerebral condition both of tone and of noise is, as we have seen, the excitation of a temporal lobe of the brain. Originally and primarily, this cerebral centre is excited by impulses conveyed along the auditory nerve from the basilar membrane; but later, the brain-centre may be excited from within, so that the music of our reveries and the voices of our dreams probably occur without the functioning of end-organs in the ear.

II. SENSATIONAL ELEMENTS OF LOUDNESS

Another sensational element, loudness or sound-intensity, is invariably connected both with pitch and with noise-quality. It is, of course, impossible to describe sound-intensity, but everybody who can recognize either a tone or a noise knows that it may be soft or loud, and that what is called its intensity may vary indefinitely, while its pitch or noise quality remains the same. For the rest, sound-intensities, or loudnesses, are parallel with the color-intensities or brightnesses. For they are not well provided with designations, they shade gradually into each other, and they are capable of direct serial arrangement: 'loud — louder — still louder.' In these series, the feeling of 'more' is always directly combined with the intensity, whereas in pitch-series, which resemble color-series, the tones are successively 'more different' or 'less different' from each other, forming such series as —

C	.	.	.	
D	.	.	.	different from C
E	.	.	.	different from D *more* different from C
F	.	.	.	different from E *more* different from D *still more* different from C

The physiological and physical conditions of sound-intensities are like those of the color-intensities. The amplitude of the air-wave, that is, the extent of vibrations of each air-particle, is known to condition the intensity of sound, and the greater the movement of each particle, the louder is the sound. This is, of course, the principle of the speaking-tube: the confinement of the air within narrow limits prevents radiation of the voice-impetus in many directions, and gives greater force to the movement of the fewer particles of air. We have also every reason to suppose that the degree of nervous excitation both in the end-organs and in the brain-centre, or in the cerebral centre alone, is the physiological condition of sound-intensities.

The writer, in common with many psychologists, recognizes a third factor of sound-sensations, voluminousness, or sound-extensity, the element of sounds which distinguishes tones of the same pitch and intensity, as played on different instruments. The existence of this element is, however, denied by many authorities; and the discussion of it will, therefore, be postponed to the general chapter on the consciousness of extensity.

CHAPTER IV

SENSATIONS OF TASTE AND OF SMELL

I. SENSATIONS OF TASTE

WE are familiar already with the psychologist's method of approaching every experience, — the analysis of it into its ultimate elements. The method has now to be applied to the experiences which we know as tastes.

The ordinary individual, asked to name what he had 'tasted' at dinner, might respond with some such list as the following: beef-boullion, roast duck, potato, onion, dressed celery, peach ice and coffee. But the psychologist would conclude at once that some of the tastes enumerated were complex experiences, made up of simpler elements. And the experimentalist would go further: he would take means to isolate, so far as he could, the conditions of taste, so that other sense-elements should be shut out from consciousness. To this end he would select, if possible, as subject of the experiments, an anosmic person, that is, one without smell-sensations, or else he would close the subject's nostrils, so as to eliminate most of these smell-sensations; and he would certainly blindfold the subject, to prevent his seeing the articles which he tasted. These substances would be presented to him at an even temperature, and the solids would be finely minced so as to be indistinguishable in form. Judging by the results of actual experiments, in particular those of Professor G. T. W. Patrick,[1] the results of such a test as applied to our

[1] "University of Iowa Studies in Psychology," Vol. II., p. 85, or *Psychological Review*, 1899, p. 160.

suggested *ménu,* would be the following : the blindfolded
and anosmic subject would as likely as not suppose that
he had tasted chicken broth, beef, potato, an unknown
sweetish substance, another unknown material mixed with
a thick tasteless oil, a sweet unflavored substance and a
slightly bitter liquid — perhaps a dilute solution of quinine.
A normal person, also blindfolded, but without closed nostrils, would recognize the onion, the peach, the coffee and
often the olive oil ; but would be as likely to confuse the
beef and the duck ; whereas, if these were unsalted, the
anosmic subject would fail to recognize them even as meats.
Certain substances, on the other hand, for instance, the
different sorts of bread, of white, graham and rye flours,
would be better discriminated by the anosmic subject.

These results are easy of interpretation. What we know
as the different tastes are complex experiences, made up
of odors, motor experiences, pressure and pain sensations,
visual elements and a far more limited number of taste-
elements than we ordinarily suppose. The odor is the
significant element in such ' tastes ' as egg, milk, fruit,
wine, onion, chocolate, coffee and tea. Tea and coffee
are, indeed, undistinguished from quinine, when the odor-
elements are excluded, and are differentiated from each
other only by the slight astringency of the tea, that is, by
the peculiar pressure-experience, the ' puckering,' which
it incites. The so-called tastes of nuts, vegetables and
grains form a second class, for they consist, in large part,
of pressure-sensations excited by stimulation of the tongue.
It follows that because of his trained attention to degrees
of roughness, smoothness, hardness and softness, the
anosmic person can distinguish better than the normal
person, if both are blindfolded, breads made of different
grains. The pungent tastes, in the third place, like the
spices, are largely distinguished by sensational elements
of pain and perhaps of heat. And, finally, in another
class of tastes the important feature is visual, as is
proved by the fact that the varieties of meats and of

breads are so frequently undistinguished by the blind-folded observer.

But the proof that most of the so-called tastes are complexes of smell, touch and color, with or without taste, leaves us still with the question, How many of these taste-elements are there, and how are they named? The most probable theory recognizes precisely four tastes: sweet, salt, sour and bitter. For this conclusion, there are two main arguments. The first is introspective: these four experiences are actually distinct and unanalyzable. The effort to analyze them further, and to reduce all tastes to two elements, for example, sweet and bitter,[1] is admitted by almost every observer to be unavailing. Neither salt nor sour is any fusion of other elements; each is itself and is further irreducible. The attempt to discover, embedded in our experience, a new taste-element, has been equally fruitless. Such a fifth element is the alleged alkaline or insipid taste,[2] but close introspection pronounces it a faint degree of saltness.

It should be noted, finally, that tastes have a strong affective value, that is, that they are emphatically pleasant or unpleasant and seldom indifferent. The common confusion of the words 'sweet' and 'good' is, therefore, no accident; and such expressions as 'bitter grief,' 'sour face,' 'sweet dreams,' are metaphors founded on this essentially affective nature of the tastes. The pleasantness or unpleasantness of the tastes, it will be observed, has a significance in the evolution of animal life, for harmful foods, which are also unpleasant, are more readily rejected, and healthful foods are more likely to be eaten if they are also pleasant.

We shall next consider the physiological conditions of taste. In spite of great individual differences, it may be said, in a general way, that the surface of the tongue,

---

[1] Ladd (quoting Valentine) "Elements," p. 166.

[2] Cf. Kiesow in Wundt's "Philosophische Studien," X. and XII.; Wundt's "Physiologische Psychologie," 4te Aufl., I., 439; and Patrick, op. cit., p. 92.

especially the back and tip of it, the forward surface of the palate and sometimes other parts of the mucous membrane lining the mouth cavity, are known to be sensitive to taste-stimuli, and to be connected with nerves leading to the 'taste-centres' in the temporal lobes of the brain.[1] Examination discloses on these surfaces slight elevations, consisting of membranous folds, called papillæ. These differ in structure, and two forms of them are probably of especial importance.[2] These are, first, the small, reddish papillæ, readily recognized on the forward and middle surface of the tongue, and second, the large circumvallate papillæ, shaped like castles with moats about them, which are found near the root of the tongue. On the circumvallate papillæ are certain minuter structures known as taste-buds, but these cannot be essential to taste, since they are not found on the papillæ of the tip and sides of the tongue. No certain connection of a distinct end-organ with each of the different tastes has been made out. But whatever their structure and their mode of functioning, the end-organs of taste occasion contrast effects.[3] The contrast between sweet and sour is especially noticeable; candy is oversweet when one has been drinking lemonade, oranges very sour after ice-cream.

Of the physical stimuli of taste-sensations, we know even less than of the indefinitely localized physiological organs. Chemically distinct substances may even arouse the same sensational quality, for example, both sugar and acetate of lead give a 'sweet' taste. Only one general statement may be hazarded: the taste-stimulus is always in liquid form. If the tip of the tongue be carefully dried, a crystal of sugar placed upon it will seem tasteless, until the tongue again becomes moist enough to dissolve it. The sum of our knowledge of the physiological and physical

[1] Cf. Appendix, Section I, I.

[2] For experiments, cf. Sanford, 53; Titchener § 24, 25.

[3] Külpe, "Outline of Psychology," § 12. For experiments, cf. Titchener, § 26.

conditions of taste amounts simply, therefore, to this: stimuli in liquid form affect end-organs situated in the papillæ of the mucous lining of the mouth cavity, and these are connected by afferent fibres with the temporal lobes of the hemispheres.

Besides the taste-quality, a total sensation of taste (that is, the compound of the feeling of either sweet, salt, sour or bitter, with its invariable accompaniments) includes a sensational element of taste intensity. This is unnamed, but it is as clearly distinguished and as unanalyzable a sensational element as a brightness or a loudness. For example, the taste of highly salted food differs in its feeling of salt-intensity from the taste of slightly salted food; and the taste of a one per cent solution of quinine differs from that of a thirty per cent solution in its feeling of quinine-intensity. These intensities, moreover, like the brightnesses and loudnesses, are capable of simple serial arrangement. We may assume that they are conditioned by the degree of physical stimulus and physiological excitation.

Some psychologists also teach that tastes, like tones and noises, have a certain volume or extensity. It will be convenient, however, to discuss all forms of extensity together, in a later chapter.

II. Sensations of Smell

We have little scientific knowledge of odors. Even our names for them are borrowed, usually from the objects to which we chance to refer them, and occasionally even from their affective accompaniments. Thus we know some odors only vaguely as good or bad, that is, pleasant or unpleasant, and at the best we can say nothing more definite than 'heliotrope fragrance' or 'kerosene odor.' This chaotic state of affairs is largely due to the limited significance of odors in our intellectual and our artistic life. Language, the great medium of intellectual achievement,

is invariably, because most readily, made up of visual and
of auditory symbols; and art employs visual and auditory
materials, both because they admit such numberless combinations, and because, also, forms and colors are relatively permanent and sounds are readily reproducible. Odors, on the
other hand, are far less capable of fusions, and are neither
permanent nor easily revivable, hence they are of little importance in art; and so it comes about that the perfumer is
even less likely than the cook to be reckoned among artists.

The closer knowledge, so greatly needed, of odors and
their conditions can be gained only by experimental introspection.   This, however, is unfortunately of extraordinary
difficulty, because we are so ignorant of the physiological
processes and the physical conditions involved.   Many
smells are, of course, like tastes, obviously complex experiences containing elements of taste, touch and vision,
as well as of smell.   The pungency of such smells as that
of ammonia is thus a touch-quality; and such experiences
as smelling sour milk are perhaps due to the entrance of
particles through the nose into the throat.   But this does
not alter the need for the discovery and classification of
the real smell-qualities.

The most satisfactory classification of smells, as we
meet them in nature, is that adapted by the Dutch physiologist, Zwaardemaker, from the classification of Linnæus.
It recognizes the following classes : —

1. Ethereal smells, including all fruit odors.
2. Aromatic smells, for example, those of camphor, spices, lemon, rose.
3. Fragrant smells, for example, those of most flowers.
4. Ambrosiac smells, for example, all musk odors.
   Alliaceous smells, for example, those of garlic, asafœtida, fish, chlorine.
   Empyreumatic smells, for example, those of tobacco and toast.
   Hircine smells, for example, those of cheese and rancid fat.
   Virulent smells, for example, that of opium.
   Nauseating smells, for example, that of decaying animal matter.[1]

E. A. McC. Gamble, "The Applicability of Weber's Law to Smell," p. 10;
~ardemaker, "Physiologie des Geruchs," 233–235.

This classification, however, aims simply to group natural objects according to obvious similarities, not to classify odors by the unanalyzable smell-elements which distinguish them. It is not surprising, therefore, to discover that many of the smells which it enumerates are capable of further analysis. Thus, in the odors of the strawberry, the rose and the violet, — as compared, for instance, with the odors of benzine and of laudanum, — there certainly seems to be an unnamed common element to which this list makes no reference. This introspective conclusion, that so-called smell-qualities are reducible to simpler ones, is supported by a study of the end-organs of smell, which are fitted, as we shall see, for functioning in only a limited number of ways. In the present state of experiment and discussion, the question of the number of odor-elements must, however, be turned over to the expert.

Our conclusions are, therefore, very indefinite: we have sensational experiences, known as smells or odors, distinguished from each other, but not designated by special names; they are probably analyzable into a few distinct elements, but this analysis has never been satisfactorily made; and they are often compounded, and sometimes confused, with tastes and touches. The arguments for the existence of smell-intensities are so closely parallel to those concerning taste-intensities that they need not be enumerated. The discussion of smell-extensity or volume is postponed to another chapter.

The structure of the physiological end-organs of smell is not very clearly made out. Two phenomena indicate, however, that these organs are so distinct that they correspond both with different physical stimuli and with different smell-experiences. One of these phenomena is that of exhaustion. Experimental investigations show, for example, that "a subject whose organ is fatigued by the continuous smelling of tincture of iodine can sense ethereal oils almost or quite as well as ever, oils of lemon, turpen-

tine and cloves but faintly, and common alcohol not at
all." [1]   Evidently, therefore, different parts of the end-
organs are affected by these distinct smell-stimuli, else the
nostrils would be exhausted for all smells at the same
time. [2]   The infrequent experience of partial anosmia, or
insensibility to smell-stimuli, also suggests that the end-
organs of smell are differentiated, for the partially anosmic
subject is sensitive to certain smell-stimuli and insensitive
to others.   This is supposed to indicate that the physiological mechanism of smell has distinct parts, of which
one may be impaired without injury to the others; just
as the phenomena of partial color-blindness indicate the
existence of distinct retinal structures or substances, corresponding with the different color-stimuli.

The nasal cavities are divided, one from another, by
a wall, or septum, of bone and of cartilage, and the bony
portion of each is partially divided within itself by the
three turbinate bones.   Each nasal cavity opens at its
further end into the pharynx, and this explains, of course,
the confusion between tastes and smells, since gaseous
particles from the mouth cavity may enter the nostrils in
expiration, and sapid particles, on the other hand, may
reach the mouth through the nostrils.   The nasal cham-
bers are lined in their upper part with mucous membrane
of yellowish color consisting of several layers of cells;
with the outermost, or epithelial, layer of these cells the
branches of the olfactory nerve are connected.

Zwaardemaker has a very ingenious theory which sets
forth that the stimulation of different localities of the
olfactory region corresponds with smells of his nine different classes.   For example, the excitation of the part
nearest to the pharynx and the reflex centre of coughing
brings about, according to his scheme, the nauseating and
virulent smells; and, on the other hand, the fragrant, aro-

---

[1] E. A. McC. Gamble, *op. cit.*, p. 7.
[2] For experiments, cf. Sanford, 59; Titchener, § 29.

matic and ethereal smells are due to the excitation of the region nearest the front of the nose and the sneezing centre. There is as yet, however, no direct proof of such a hypothesis.[1]

The immediate physiological condition of the consciousness of smell is, of course, the excitation of cells in its ‘cerebral centre,’ which is part of the temporal lobe. The human brain, as is well known, is far less developed, in its olfactory centres, than the animal brain. The other vertebrates have distinct olfactory lobes projecting forward from the hemispheres, but these have shrunk, in the human brain, to mere excrescences on the frontal lobes. Corresponding with this degeneration of physiological structure is the fact that smell plays a far less leading rôle in the life of men than in that of animals.[2]

We know little of the physical conditions of smell. Two statements only can be made with any degree of assurance. It is highly probable, in the first place, that the smell-stimulus is always gaseous, not liquid; and it is almost certain that the property of stimulating the end-organs of smell is a function of the physical molecule, not of the atom, since most of the chemical elements are odorless. Summing up both physiological and physical conditions, we may say, therefore, that certain gaseous particles are carried by inspiration into the nostrils, where they stimulate cells composing the mucous membrane, and that these nerve-impulses are conveyed by the olfactory nerves to the temporal lobe of the brain.

In conclusion, we may briefly compare smell-sensations with taste-sensations, and the stimuli and organs of smell with those of taste. We shall find important likenesses, but marked differences also. Both smell and taste sensations have a strong affective quality, that is to say, they

---

[1] For experiment, cf. Titchener, § 28 ; cf. Appendix, Section IV.
[2] Cf. Chapter XXV., p. 359.

are likely to be distinctly pleasant or unpleasant. They resemble each other, also, in function, for both serve to test the wholesomeness of food. On the other hand, the delicacy of smell-sensations is remarkable, and there may be a great number of smell-qualities, whereas only four qualities of taste are established. A very small quantity of odoriferous material is required to occasion a smell-sensation, but the taste-stimulus is required in comparative bulk. The organ of smell is extensive, is situated at the entrance of the respiratory passages, and is excited by a stimulus at a distance; the organ of taste cannot be surely identified, is situated at the entrance of the alimentary canal, and is affected only by objects which come into contact with it. And, finally, the brain-centre of smell is very distinct, but the taste-area is so small or so ill demarcated that anatomists are so far not even sure where it is.

CHAPTER V

SENSATIONS OF PRESSURE, OF PAIN AND OF TEMPERATURE

I. THE SENSATION OF PRESSURE

"THE famous town of Mansoul," said John Bunyan, "had five gates, in at which to come, out at which to go. . . . The names of the gates were these, Ear-gate, Eye-gate, Mouth-gate, Nose-gate, and Feel-gate." Everyday opinion agrees well with Bunyan and credits us with a fifth sense, touch, besides sight, hearing, taste, and smell. But long ago a better observer than Bunyan — Aristotle, first of psychologists — said truly, " It is a question whether the sense of touch includes several senses or whether it is one sense only, . . . for . . . the object of touch presents us with many pair of opposites — such as hot and cold, dry and moist, hard and soft, and others.[1]" On reflection, we are tolerably certain to take sides with Aristotle. The different experiences, warmth and cold, pressure and pain, which result from stimulation of the skin, are as radically different from each other as colors from sounds or tastes from smells. Evidently, therefore, the word ' touch ' does not designate an elemental consciousness, but rather loosely covers a multitude of experiences which arise through stimulation of the skin.

Of all the elemental experiences which the word 'touch' implies, the fundamental one is that of pressure. A proof of its significance is the curious fact that the reality of our experience is always put to a pressure-test, as we may call

---

[1] " Psychology," Book I., Chapter II., § 11.

it. Macbeth clutches at the dagger to assure himself, by
touching it, whether or not it is an apparition; and one
feels of an object to know what its shape 'really' is.
Our first impression is, that just as there are several
distinct colors and several tastes, so also there are many
varieties of pressure. There are, for example, the distinctions which Aristotle has noted, of hard and soft, wet
and dry; there are other opposites of the same sort, such
as rough and smooth, blunt and sharp; and sensational
elements of 'contact' and of 'tickling' are sometimes
added to the list. But instead of being pressure-qualities
and, therefore, elements of consciousness, these experiences
are complex ideas in which the feeling of pressure is
prominent. The simplest of them is 'contact,' which is
merely faint pressure, that is, pressure-quality accompanied
by a low degree of pressure-intensity. 'Sharp' and 'blunt,'
are terms applied to the extents, great or small, of the pressure. The feelings of 'smoothness' and 'roughness' are
experiences of continued and of interrupted pressure. What
we call the sensation of 'resistance' may be analyzed into an
experience of pressure and of strain, and ordinarily includes
also visual images of one's own body and of the resisting
object. The consciousness of 'hardness' and of 'softness'
is really the experience of the varying intensities accompanying the resistance. The experience of being tickled
involves the consciousness of contact and of motion, usually
also a temperature feeling and an affection of pleasantness
or of unpleasantness.

Only one alleged pressure-quality remains to be analyzed. This is the feeling of 'wetness,' which is seemingly the most elemental of them all. At first thought, it
appears to be immediately experienced and incapable of
resolution into any other factors. Yet everybody knows
that it is impossible always to be sure by the mere 'feeling'
whether one's feet are wet or merely cold; and whether a
hot application has been wrung out in water or heated
over a fire. The idea of humidity is indeed very complex,

made up of the sensational experience of temperature, either warm or cold, and of the more complex experience of smoothness — combined usually with the visual image of a liquid, and with the consciousness of resistance.[1]

In spite, therefore, of their brave showing, no one of the alleged pressure-qualities has survived the test of attempted analysis. Each of them turns out to be a more or less complex experience, whose centre and core is the conscious element 'pressure,' capable, like the element 'gray,' of ultimate combination with an indefinite number of intensities, but itself a single quality.

These pressure-intensities, like taste and smell intensities, have no special names, but are, nevertheless, distinguishable from the qualities which they accompany, and are, therefore, sensational elements.

The sensation of pressure, which is a complex of invariably coalescing elements, certainly includes, besides the one pressure-quality and any one of the innumerable pressure-intensities, still another factor, the 'pressure-extensity,' parallel with the color or light extensity to which we have already alluded. The consideration of 'extensities' is, however, postponed to another chapter.

The erroneous assumption that we have one sense of touch has arisen, doubtless, from the supposition that the skin as a whole is the end-organ of touch, in the sense in which, for example, the retina is the end-organ of vision. The truth is, however, that the skin has many functions. It protects the organs which lie beneath it; it is of extreme significance as an excretory organ; and it also contains specific sensational end-organs of distinct sorts. An experiment which may be very simply carried out shows conclusively that the skin, though apparently sensitive, as a whole,

---

[1] Cf. throughout Titchener, "Outline of Psychology," § 16, and Külpe, *op. cit.*, § 10.

to pressure-stimulations, is really merely the protector of distinct and scattered end-organs of pressure. If a blunted bit of cork be passed slowly along any portion of the skin, the wrist, for example, the subject of the experiment, if his eyes be closed, may be for several moments at a time unconscious of any pressure. But suddenly, now and again, as the cork touches certain definite points, there ' flashes out' a distinct sensation of pressure, evidently brought about by the stimulation of a separate organ.[1] These pressure-spots, so called by Goldscheider, their discoverer, are scattered all over the surface of the body, but are more or less closely grouped together in different surfaces. Minute experiments in which carefully graded hairs replace the cork points of our proposed test, have ascertained that at some specially sensitive points, as the palm of the hand, one hundred such pressure-spots may be found within one square centimeter.[2] Almost without exception, a pressure-spot is found at the base of every one of the tiny hairs with which the skin is overgrown ; but there are also hairless regions of the body, the palm of the hand, for instance, which are yet very sensitive to pressure-stimuli.

The exact structure of the end-organs of pressure, which lie beneath the pressure-spots of the skin, is not known. No less than four sorts of differentiated nerve-endings, besides the hair-bulbs, have been discovered. All are relatively simple, ' little bunches of fibrils,' as Titchener calls them. There is much probability in von Frey's theory of two types of pressure end-organs, first, hair bulbs, and second, the so-called 'tactile corpuscles,' found under little elevations of the skin and penetrated by several nerve-fibres.

One very curious phenomenon[3] connected with the

[1] For experiments, cf. Sanford, 21 ; Titchener, § 21.

[2] Cf. Appendix, Section V., and von Frey, "Über die Sinnesfunctionen der Menschlichen Haut," Abhandlung der Königl. Sächs. Ges. der Wiss., Math-phys. Kl., XXIII., 1896, p. 254.

[3] For experiment, cf. Sanford, 7 ; Titchener, § 49.

situation of the pressure end-organs is the following: if two points be placed upon any surface of the skin, some distance may be found at which they will excite the consciousness, not of two pressures, but of a single one. This distance varies in different localities, and is smaller on the mobile organs: about one millimeter, for example, on the tongue, two millimeters on the finger-tips, and sixty-five millimeters on the middle of the back. These areas within which two points are felt as one are called 'sensory circles,' and it is important to notice that they are relatively, not absolutely, defined. That is to say, the skin is not mapped off into definite portions, such that a point near the edge of one portion is felt as distinct from a very near point which, however, is over the border of the given 'sensory circle.' On the contrary, the distance between any two points felt as one must be virtually the same in neighboring regions of the skin. The physiological explanation is not yet definitely established. E. H. Weber suggested, years ago, that the distinction of pressure-stimuli as two must be supposed to occur only when unstimulated nerve-fibres intervene between the two which are excited; and though this state of affairs has no known physiological analogy, yet no more probable or adequate hypothesis has been proposed.

It should next be observed that end-organs of pressure, whatever their structure, are found, not only in the skin but inside the body. Pressure is thus a sensational element, excitable through internal as well as through external stimulation. The most important inner locality of the pressure end-organs is on the joint-surfaces. Anybody can convince oneself, by a simple experiment,[1] of the sensitiveness of these surfaces. Let one lower a weight, by a string attached to one's forefinger, till it strikes floor or table. At the moment when it strikes, one experiences a sensation, evidently of pressure, which can only be due

---

[1] For experiments, cf. Sanford, 39, 40.

to the backward movement of the lower upon the upper joint-surfaces of the arm.

Pressure end-organs are not only situated on the joint-surfaces, but are probably, also, to be found embedded in the muscles.[1] In fact, if the skin be made anæsthetic by spraying with ether, for example, and if then the muscle be flattened by hard pressure or contracted by electrical stimulation, a dull sensation, whose quality is that of pressure, is obtained. There is a difference, however, in the intensity of the pressure-sensations occasioned by these two methods. Many experiences tend to prove that pressure-sensations through bending of the joints are stronger and more readily discriminated than pressure-sensations through muscle-contraction.[2] When the arm is mechanically lifted, without any muscular contraction at all, very small differences of pressure can be detected, and the larger the joint, the smaller may be the motion which is noticed. For example, if one lift the forearm of a blindfolded person through less than an angular degree, he will feel the pressure, which must therefore be due to the movement of the lower on the upper surface of the elbow-joint. And the accurate consciousness which we have of our finger-movements — a pressure-experience, as we shall later discover[3] — is far more likely due to the movements of the finger joint-surfaces on each other than to the contraction of the muscles which move the fingers, for the muscles which do the chief part of this work are not in the fingers at all.

The cerebral condition of pressure-sensations is the excitation of the area about the fissure of Rolando, and of part of the median surface of the brain. This accords well with the fact that the fissure of Rolando is that which first appears in the embryonic brain, for the ' sense of touch ' is certainly earliest developed and must be of special significance in the pre-natal life. An incidental proof from

[1] Foster, "Textbook on Psychology," Book III., p. 1063.
[2] Foster, *op. cit.;* James, *op. cit.,* II., p. 197.
[3] Cf. p. 87.

biology, that pressure-sensations are primitive experiences, is the fact that all the end-organs are developed from structures embedded in the skin, such as the 'pigment spots' which are the predecessors of eyes, and the 'auditory pits' from which ears have been developed.[1]

The physical stimulus of pressure-sensations, like that of sounds is mechanical, and is thus contrasted with the chemical stimulus of taste, of smell and, probably also, of visual sensations. To excite the end-organs of the pressure-consciousness, these mechanical stimuli must, however, produce an actual deformation. This is the reason why one does not feel even pressures over large surfaces except at their terminal lines, so that if the hand be plunged into a liquid, the pressure will be felt only where the wrist emerges. It should be added that the mechanical stimulus serves merely to initiate a change which is probably chemical, in the nerve itself.

II. The Sensations of Pain

The knife-blade which, gently applied, excites a sensational experience of pressure, may bring about also a very different sort of consciousness, that of pain. This is evidently distinct from all other sensation-elements through stimulation of the skin, and no good observer confuses the mere pressure with the painfulness of a heavy weight, or the heat with the painfulness of a poultice. But it is, perhaps, less easy to realize that painfulness is quite distinct also from disagreeableness or unpleasantness. Half the experiences which we ordinarily call 'painful' are probably merely unpleasant. It is unpleasant, for example, but not painful, to mistake an ice-cream fork for an oyster fork at a dinner-party; the magenta of the hat which obscures my view in the concert room is a disagreeable, not a painful,

[1] The eye is a partial exception, — for the retina, the part most significant for vision, is in reality an outgrowth from the brain, not the development of a pigment spot in the skin. Cf. Chapter XXV., and Appendix, Section I., I.

color; nausea and suffocation are unpleasant, not painful, experiences. The confusion is mainly due to the fact that sensational elements of pain are always accompanied by unpleasantness, in other words, that painful things are also unpleasant. In the case of apparent exceptions, as of slight pains which we intentionally inflict upon ourselves to see how they will feel, the pleasantness is probably that of the novelty, not of the pain. But it does not follow from the fact that pains are always unpleasant, that unpleasant-nesses are always painful, still less that the two are iden-tical. Our first conclusion, therefore, is that painfulness, an experience which follows upon the burning, bruising, or cutting of the skin and upon certain internal changes, is different from unpleasantness or disagreeableness.

In the next place, we must observe that there is prob-ably only a single quality of pain-sensation, just as there is only one pressure-quality. That is, however distinct the methods by which it is induced, whether by heat or pressure or laceration, pain is just pain, the same inde-scribable sensation. At first thought, this statement may seem to contradict our ordinary experience. For we do actually distinguish acute, dull, stinging, gnawing, whirl-ing pains, and many others besides. The truth is, how-ever, that, carefully examined, these different sorts of pain are distinct from each other, not by any difference in their painfulness or pain-quality, but in one of three ways: they may differ of course in intensity; they may, perhaps, differ also in bigness or voluminousness, for some pains seem vaster and more enveloping than others; "they may differ also in steadiness, and if unsteady, they may vary in regularity, and regular pains may even vary in their rhythm. A throbbing headache, for example, follows the pulse-beat, and is very distinct, not only from a steady headache but from an irregular, stabbing, neuralgiac pain."[1] Pains, finally, may have widely differ-

---

[1] Quoted from manuscript notes of E. A. McC. Gamble.

ent accompaniments. They are normally combined with sensations of pressure and of warmth or of cold; and the alleged differences in pains are most often variations in these other sensations, which accompany them. A stinging pain, for example, is a complex experience of painfulness, of warmth and of a small extent of pressure.

The close connection of painfulness with pressure-sensations is readily explained from the evolutionary standpoint. Objects which come into actual contact with an organism are more likely to be dangerous than those which it merely sees or hears from a distance. Animals to whom, from spontaneous variation of their nervous organs, pressures were usually painful, would survive the dangers which overwhelmed their less highly organized comrades. The peculiar differentiation of their nervous apparatus, by which mechanical and thermal stimuli brought about pain as well as pressure and temperature sensations, would, therefore, tend to be perpetuated.

It will be convenient to consider, briefly, the physical condition of pain, before discussing its physiological excitation. We are met at the outset by a deviation from the ordinary relation. For every other form of sense-quality, we have found a definite, even if vaguely characterized, physical stimulation. In the case of pain, however, it is obvious at once that no specific form of energy occasions it, but that the same stimuli which excite sensations of pressure, warmth and cold, and possibly even those which excite visual and auditory sensations, may bring about painfulness also, if only they are very intense, long continued or often repeated. Hard or long-continued pressure, intense heat and cold, and, possibly, blinding lights and crashing sounds may be called painful; whereas excessive sweetness and heavy fragrance are merely unpleasant.

We have next to ask for the physiological conditions, and first, therefore, for the peripheral or surface organs of the pain-sensations. The oldest theory is based on the undoubted fact that pain follows on high degrees of mechanical stimulus. It teaches that there are no specific pain-organs, but that the excessive functioning of other end-organs, especially those of pressure, condition pain-sensation. This teaching, that excitation of pressure end-organs may occasion pain, is disproved by the discovery that certain anæsthetics destroy pain and pressure-sensation independently of each other, however high the degree of physical pressure. If the oculist treats one's eye with cocaine, one is distinctly conscious of the contact of his instruments but feels no pain; a similar use of saponin annihilates pressure-sensations and leaves pain. Certain injuries to the spinal cord result in a similar separation of pain and pressure-sensations. Evidently then, pain is not always produced by the hypernormal excitation of pressure end-organs.

A second theory holds that pain is occasioned only by the excitation of distinct end-organs of pain. This view is based on the important discovery of pain-spots on the skin, like the pressure-spots already described.[1] These pain-spots, have not, however, up to this time been found on all parts of the body. In fact, careful experiments have discovered these spots, which are sensitive to pain and not to pressure, on no other parts of the body than the elbow-joints and the membranous coverings of the eye. Von Frey explains this infrequency of the pain-spots actually discovered, by supposing that the pain end-organs are far less easily excited than the pressure-organs.

A third theory of the physiological condition of pain is especially worthy of attention, because it is that of Gold-scheider, the discoverer of the pain-spots on the skin. He holds that these 'pain-spots,' are not, as has been supposed, pain end-organs, distinct from pressure-organs, but that they are merely exposed pressure-organs, located

---

[1] For experiments, cf. Sanford, 32; Titchener, § 22.

under an unusually thin part of the epidermis or upper skin; and that pain is physiologically due, not to the activity of any nerve end-organs in the skin, but to a transformation, in the gray substance of the spinal cord, of nerve-excitations conveyed from these exposed pressure end-organs.[1]

It should be added that pain is usually due to conditions on the surface of the body, not inside it. "A muscle or a tendon, the intestine, the liver, or the heart may be handled, pinched or cauterized," Foster says,[2] " without any pain or indeed any sensation being felt." This suggests the view that so-called 'internally excited' sensations of pain, as of warmth and of cold, are usually due to the spread of nerve-excitations to end-organs in the skin; and from the standpoint of evolution, this infrequency of internally stimulated pains is readily understood. All pain is an exhausting experience and positively injurious to the organism; but external pains serve as signals of danger, warning animals from harmful food and environment. The race of animals with external pains would tend, therefore, to be perpetuated, in spite of the harmfulness of the pain in itself; but animals who are internally sensitive to pain would tend to die out, since internal pains serve no useful purpose to offset their harmfulness.

No definite brain-centre has ever been localized whose functioning is found to condition pain-sensations only. The Rolandic region has been, up to this time, considered as centre for dermal sensations of pressure, warmth, cold, pain. What particular area or special cortical layer within this region has to do with pain-sensations is not known.

A distinct treatment of 'intensities' and 'extensities' of pain would merely repeat, *mutatis mutandis*, what has been said of smells and tastes.

---

[1] Cf. Goldscheider, " Über den Schmerz," p. 18.
[2] "Textbook of Physiology," Book III., p. 1045.

The most important of these results are included in the following summary: we have unanalyzable experiences of pain and pain-intensity, usually accompanying other sensations, especially those of pressure, and invariably accompanied by unpleasantness, yet perfectly distinct from both. These have no definite physical stimulus but are usually or always conditioned by the extreme intensities of mechanical and thermal stimuli. They are physiologically caused by the activity of cerebral centres (probably of the Rolandic region) originally set up either by the functioning of special nerves and end-organs, or by some more central process, very likely in the gray substance of the spinal cord.

III. SENSATIONS OF TEMPERATURE

We all know what it is to be warm and to be cold, and reflection will convince us that warmth and cold are distinct, unanalyzable experiences, and, therefore, elements of consciousness. They are distinct, in the first place, from pressure and from pain, though often combined with each. For instance, I am conscious at the same time of the pressure and of the warmth of a warm poultice, but the warmth is an experience quite distinct from that of pressure. The sensational qualities, warmth and cold, are also quite distinct from each other, so that it is really misleading, though convenient, to group them together as sensational elements of temperature.

The nature of the experience which we know as hotness is far harder to determine. Three opinions have been held. It has been taught by most psychologists that hotness is simply warmth, combined with a high degree of warmth-intensity. But introspection opposes this conclusion; there is a qualitative difference, for example, in the feeling of a red-hot stove and the feeling of a rock warmed by the sun. It is sometimes, therefore, held that hotness is a complex experience including feelings of warmth and of pain. But though it is certain that hot objects are often also painful, it is probable that the feeling of hotness is distinct from that of pain. On the whole, therefore, we conclude that hotness is a distinct and simple sensational element, although, as we shall see, its physiological condition is complex.[1]

Warmth, cold and heat intensities demand no special treatment. There is no reason to deny their elemental quality and their capacity for direct serial arrangement. There is perhaps, also, voluminousness, or bigness, of temperature experiences.

No direct relation can be discovered between the degree of the thermometer and the cold or warmth or heat sensation. In other words, we are not always warm when the thermometer registers a high degree and cold when it stands at a low figure. On the contrary, the room which seems warm to me as I enter it after a brisk walk seems chilly an hour later, though the height of the mercury is unchanged; and if I warm one hand and cool another the same lukewarm water will seem cool to the first and warm to the second.[2] These experiences, and others like them, clearly show that the sensation of warmth or of cold or of heat is not determined by the actual temperature of the body, but by the relation between the temperature of the body and that of its environment. When these two are identical, however high or low, the bodily temperature is described as that of the physiological zero, and there is no sensation either of warmth or of cold. When the physical temperature of the body exceeds that of its environment, the sensation is of cold, and, on the other hand, when the temperature falls below that of the environment, one has the experience of warmth, changing — as we have seen — at a certain point to that of heat. The physiological conditions of this sensational element, hotness, are complex, as will be shown later.

[1] Cf. p. 78.
[2] For experiments, cf. Sanford, 18 ; Titchener, p. 53, last paragraph.

The thermal stimulation of the skin is occasioned in two ways: by radiation of heat from outer objects and by muscular activity, which means loss of energy in the form of heat. I may grow warm, for example, by basking in the sun, or by swinging dumb-bells. Not the skin as a whole, however, but certain definite end-organs are affected. This is shown by applying warm and cold surfaces of very small extent to different parts of the body. A bit of metal may be moved along for some little distance on the surface of the body, without rousing the experience of cold, which, however, will suddenly occur as the stimulus reaches one of the 'cold spots' over an end-organ of cold.[1] There are fewer of these than of the pressure or pain end-organs, and the organs of warmth are least frequent of all, and most scattered. The cornea of the eye is sensitive to cold, but not to pressure, and both warmth and cold end-organs are found within the mouth-cavity where no 'pain spots' have been discovered. Most of the inner surfaces of the body, however, are without these warmth and cold organs, so that internal sensations of 'cold,' 'warm' and 'hot,' though localized within the body, are usually due to outward radiation of cold or heat and to stimulation of the end-organs in the outer skin. Even the mucous lining of the mouth-cavity is less sensitive than the outer skin, so that one may drink, with perfect comfort, coffee which seems unbearably hot if it touches the lip.

It has been indicated by experiment[2] that sensations of hotness are conditioned by the simultaneous functioning of end-organs both of warmth and of cold. The most important reasons for this conclusion are the following: (1) If an area of the skin be stimulated containing warm spots, but no cold spots, no feelings of hotness, but only feelings of warmth and of pain result, however hot the stimulating object. If (2) a region of the skin, that of the upper forehead for instance, which contains cold spots and

1 For experiment, cf. Sanford, 13; Titchener, § 19.
2 Cf. S. Alrutz, *Mind*, N. S. VI., 445 *seq.*; VII., 141 *seq.*

a very few warm spots, be tested with a series of points graduated from cold to hot, sensations of cold, of slight warmth, and then at once of hotness are obtained, with no intermediate sensations of extreme warmth.

The structure of these end-organs is not definitely determined, but von Frey may be correct in his theory that the so-called end-bulbs of Krause, found in most parts of the outer skin, on the cornea and in the mouth, are end-organs of 'cold,' and that certain deep-lying cells, recently discovered by Ruffini are warmth end-organs.[1] The cerebral locality whose excitation is the immediate physiological cause of warmth and cold sensations is, so far as discovered, the Rolandic region.

To recapitulate therefore: we have distinct sensational elements of cold, warmth and hotness; of cold-intensity, warmth-intensity and heat-intensity; and perhaps a parallel series of sensational elements of voluminousness. The physical conditions of these sense-elements are modifications of a thermal stimulus. The physiological conditions are primarily the excitations of end-organs (1) of cold, (2) of warmth or (3) both of cold and of warmth. These end-organs are situated mainly in the skin; their excitation depends on the temperature of the body relative to that of its environment; their excitation, by way of ingoing nerves, occasions the activity of cerebral cells, probably in the Rolandic area; and this cerebral activity is the immediate condition of the feelings of cold, warmth and hotness.

[1] Cf. throughout, Max von Frey, "Beiträge zur Sinnesphysiologie der Haut," Berichte der Gesellsch., d. Wissenschaft, zu Leipsic, Math-Phys. KL, 1894–95, pp. 165 *seq.*

CHAPTER VI

SENSATIONS FROM INTERNAL EXCITATION AND THE CONSCIOUSNESS OF MOTION

I. SENSATIONS FROM INTERNAL EXCITATION

WE have found that pressure and pain sensations, and, on a more limited area, sensations of warmth and cold, are excitable not merely by the stimulation of organs on the outer surface, but by the excitation also of end-organs within the body. There are still to be considered certain alleged sensations whose excitation is invariably internal.

a. SENSATIONS OF STRAIN

The first of these is the sensation of strain. It is occasioned by lifting weights and by assuming rigid bodily attitudes. A simple way to excite it, for example, is to clench the hand firmly but in such wise that its surfaces do not touch each other. No external pressure can then be felt, but the resulting experience is said to include, not only a weak sensation of pressure from the moving of the surfaces of the finger-joints on each other, but also a new and elemental experience, that of strain. There is no doubt, of course, about the existence of this consciousness of strain; but it is not so certain that it is really a sensational experience and not rather a combination of pressure and of pain. The writer of this book is unable, in fact, to decide between these two hypotheses, vibrating between the view that strain is an elemental experience and the theory that it is a complex experience, analyzable into pressure and pain sensations; in either case it may be accompanied by any one of an indefinite number of intensities.

A simple experiment[1] will show that this strain-experience, whether elemental or complex, is due to stimulation of the tendons, that is, the fibrous cords which connect muscles with bones. If one's arm be drawn down by a heavy weight attached to one of the fingers, strain-sensations are felt. But the weighting of the arm prevents either muscular contraction or pressure of the joint-surfaces. The only change, therefore, which the weight can effect in the arm is the excitation of its tendons. The cerebral centre of the strain-sensations is the Rolandic area.

b. ALLEGED SENSATIONS OF POSITION

The experiences next to be discussed are more obviously, in the writer's opinion, complex, not elemental. Both are due to excitations of the semicircular canals. The first of them is the alleged static sense of consciousness of the body's position.

I unquestionably possess in my normal waking life a consciousness of my position. I know whether I am standing or lying down, whether my head is straight or tilted, whether my body is inclined to right or to left. More than this, I am constantly making little compensatory movements forward or back, right or left, to preserve the balance of my body when its position changes. I ordinarily reflect little on the consciousness of bodily position, and I may be perfectly unconscious of the movements which I make to keep my balance, but whenever these are checked — for example, on first trying to walk after a long illness — I discover myself staggering and falling for want of these quick, recovering movements. Before discussing the consciousness of position, we shall, therefore, consider

[1] Cf. Titchener, § 31, p. 87, Exercise (1).

G

82 *Sensations from Internal Excitation*

the origin of these compensatory movements. We shall later show that the two phenomena, psychical and physiological, are often confused, that is, that the consciousness of bodily position is often argued from the mere observation of the bodily movements. These compensatory movements are probably excited in the following way: end-organs in the semicircular canals of the ear are stimulated, and these nervous impulses are conveyed to the cerebellum, which is a brain-centre for the motor nerves whose excitation causes the balancing movements of the body. This summary statement must now be expanded. The semicircular canals are organs within the ear, separated from the cochlea by the vestibule, a rounded, bony envelope, containing two small, membranous bags. The canals themselves consist of membranous tubes each completing nearly a circle. Each canal is enclosed in a bony sheath, is surrounded by a liquid (the perilymph) and is filled with a liquid (the endolymph). The bony canals, vestibules and

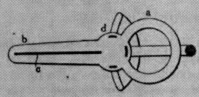

FIG. 8. — Diagram (schematic) of the internal ear, in longitudinal section. *a*, semicircular canals; *b*, cochlea; *c*, basilar membrane; *d*, vestibule.

cochlea together form a continuous body, lying in a spongy portion of the temporal bone. The canals are at right angles to each other, one of them lies horizontally, a second curves from front to back and the third runs from right to left. Each opens into the vestibule and terminates at one end in a sort of swelling or dilation called an *ampulla*. A branch of the auditory nerve penetrates each of these ampullæ and the vestibule as well, ending in cells from which hairs project; and in the vestibule, at least, there are small hard substances, the ear stones or otoliths. The essential feature of the apparatus is its extreme sensitiveness to changes of bodily position. The slightest movement which tends to unbalance the body must alter the position of the semicircular canals, and thus put in motion the endolymph. This movement, with or without the additional pressure of an otolith, bends the hairs of the ampullæ and stimulates the vestibular section of the acoustic nerve, and this excitation reaches the cerebellum, which is, as has been said, the nerve-centre for the movements affecting bodily equilibrium. Actual experiments show the connection of these organs with the preservation of balance. Animals deprived either of cerebellum or of semicircular canals stagger and fall about in an unbalanced and helpless way ; and deaf people whose semicircular canals are injured cannot preserve their equilibrium, if they are blindfolded and therefore unable to regulate their movements by the visual perceptions of bodily position.

If we now carefully consider what has so far been established, we find this result : the movements which keep the body balanced are due (1) to the disturbance of the position of semicircular canals and the consequent pressure of endolymph on nerve-endings, (2) to the excitation of motor-centres in the cerebellum, (3) and finally, to the excitation of outgoing, or motor, nerves and the muscular contractions which preserve the balance. We have thus discovered the origin of the balancing movements of the body. Undoubtedly they are initially due to excitation of the semicircular canals. But this is no foundation for the statement of certain psychologists, that there are 'sensations of bodily position' whose organs are within the semicircular canals. On the other hand, when we examine introspectively the nature of our consciousness of bodily position, we shall almost certainly find it made up of pressure and of strain experiences. The latter are mainly due to bodily rigidities and to cramped attitudes. The pressure-sensations are from two distinct sources : first, from external stimulus, as when one is conscious of the pressure of the foot to the floor, of the body to the chair and of the skin more tightly drawn over a moving hand ; and second, from internal movements, of the joint-surfaces, for example, of shoulder and elbow joints upon each other. The most careful analysis fails to find more than this in our consciousness of position, and we are forced, therefore, to deny that there is any static sense, any elemental sensation of position.

c. ALLEGED SENSATIONS OF DIZZINESS

To the excitation of semicircular canals still another sensation is referred, that of dizziness. What is known as dizziness is probably either a complex experience or a mere pressure-sensation. It includes, or is closely accompanied by, moving visual images of objects and figures rotating slowly, or slipping and swimming about in one's field of vision. It is furthermore, sometimes, though by no means invariably, accompanied by the feeling of nausea. For the rest, it seems to consist of a pressure-sensation 'located' within the head.

No definite physiological cause of dizziness can be assigned. It is often, as has been said, explained by semicircular canal-excitation, and certainly the loss of balance is its most frequent cause. Deaf-mutes, whose semicircular canals are affected, may therefore lose their equilibrium without being giddy. But the loss of balance and the consequent pressure of the liquid in the canals is not sufficient explanation of dizziness, which occurs sometimes when the head and the whole body are unmoved. On the whole, therefore, we are not able to assign to it a definite bodily cause, though it probably is a pressure-sensation due to some stimulation within the head.

d. ALLEGED 'ORGANIC' SENSATIONS FROM INTERNAL STIMULUS

Certain alleged sensational qualities, due to internal and not to external stimulation, still remain open to discussion. Among them are (1) the so-called sensations from the alimentary canal, hunger, thirst, nausea, and (2) the so-called circulatory and respiratory sensations. Carefully analyzed, however, each of these, in the writer's opinion, will disclose itself as a complex experience, and not, in any sense, a simple feeling. Thirst, for example, is a complex of pressure and warmth sensations; it is due to a drying of the mucous membrane of the mouth-cavity, which becomes a poorer conductor of warmth. The chief element in hunger, also, is probably that of pressure, brought about by some chemical action on the lining of the stomach. What is called nausea is a still more complex experience, but its essential ingredient is pressure, due to the antiperistaltic reflexes of the œsophagus.

The alleged respiratory sensations, such as breathlessness, suffocation and stuffiness, are evidently experiences including several elements: first, and most important, pressure-sensations; often also, sensations of strain, as when one holds one's breath; and, finally, for most people, a visual image of the part of the body — chest or throat — which is affected. The 'circulatory' sensations are either, like itching and feverishness, compounds of warmth and pressure-sensations, or else they are the massive pressure-sensations from difficult breathing or from abnormally strong heart-beat.

These 'organic' experiences, though seldom attended to, are nevertheless of great significance, for they may form part of our most complex ideas and moods. Emotions are, as we shall see, especially rich in 'organic sensations.' When, for example, I am afraid, my heart flutters; when I am grieved, my throat is choked; when I am perplexed, there is a weight on my chest. And though I concern myself little with these seemingly unimportant experiences, they none the less effectively color my moods.[1]

We have thus examined four sorts of alleged sensation from internal stimulus. But with one possible exception,

---

[1] Cf. Chapter XX., p. 286 *seq.*

the sensation of strain, these have resolved themselves into complex experiences, mainly of pressure. Our important results are, therefore, two: we have found a probability that pressure end-organs of some sort are situated in certain unexpected bodily localities. Not merely the mechanical stimulation of skin, joint-surfaces, and voluntary muscles, but that of the alimentary canal and perhaps, also, that of the tendons, results in pressure-sensations. We have found, also, that these pressure-sensations from internal excitation form, not only an important part of the consciousness of our bodies, but a constant though unnoticed feature of all types of experience.

II. The Consciousness of Motion

So much is made, in these days, of what has been called the 'motor' consciousness, that it is well to devote a brief section to the study of it.[1] We must begin by distinguishing two experiences: the consciousness of bodily movements, of head or limbs or trunk; and the consciousness of motions on the surface of the body, like that, for example, of an ant crawling slowly over the forehead or the wrist. We are mainly concerned with the consciousness of movements of the body.

The mobility of the human body is its most obvious characteristic. Movements of the limbs and fingers, and of jaws, nostrils and eyeballs are constant during one's waking hours; and others, such as the movements of lungs and diaphragm and the rhythmic contractions of heart and arteries, are normally continuous throughout life. Only the effort to control these movements, to fix the eyes, to compose the hands or to hold the breath, makes clear to us the utter restlessness of our bodies. The psychologist is interested in bodily movement from several points of view. Even if the movement is unconscious, it is inevitably either

[1] For fuller treatment, cf. James, *op. cit.*, II., 493, *seq.*

the antecedent, the accompaniment or the consequent of particular facts of consciousness, and it is, therefore, useful in the explanation and classification of these psychic facts. We are here concerned, however, with the direct consciousness of bodily movements. One important school of psychologists has held that it is a sensational, that is, a distinct and unanalyzable experience. But careful analysis of any experience of the moving body, the consciousness, for example, with eyes closed, of a moving arm, will convince any one that it is a very complex idea, involving some or all of the following factors: (1) the visual images of the appearance of the arm in successive positions, (2) the sensations of pressure of the surfaces of the joints against each other, (3) the vague sensations of pressure from the contraction of voluntary muscles, (4) the sensation of pressure from contraction of the sympathetic and involuntary muscles, (5) the experience of dizziness. And of all these constituents of the idea of the body's movement, the sensations of pressure through movements of the joints are doubtless the most important. James says truly that "no more favorable conditions could be possible for the delicate calling of the sensibility into play than are realized in the minutely graduated rotations and firmly resisted variations of pressure involved in every act of extension or flexion." [1]

The consciousness, not of movements of the body, but of motions on its surface, may be even more briefly considered. It consists essentially in the consciousness of successive positions. My experience, for example, of a pencil point drawn slowly over my cheek, as I sit with eyes closed, is a consciousness of the object as first near my hair, then closer to my ear, then approaching my chin. We are not yet prepared for the thorough analysis of this consciousness of successive positions. Evidently, however, it requires that at the moment when one point of my skin is stimulated, I retain the image of a previous stimula-

[1] *Op. cit.*, II., 191.

tion. And evidently this is no simple sensational experience but a very complex one, including, as it does, the consciousness of position and of succession, besides purely tactual and often visual sensations.

Our most important result is, therefore, negative: the failure to discover any 'motor sensations.' The consciousness of bodily movements has been shown to be a complex experience mainly of pressure, and the consciousness of surface-motions is at least equally complex.

CHAPTER VII

THE CONSCIOUSNESS OF EXTENSITY

I. The Elemental Consciousness of Extensity

a. VISUAL EXTENSITY

EVERY color has a certain bigness or extensity. The discussion of the nature of this experience involves great difficulty: we have already dodged the problem at several points of our study, but it definitely confronts us now. Its most natural solution treats extensity as a sensational element of consciousness, on the ground that it is an unanalyzable experience quite distinct from every other. In the words of James, it is "an element in each sensation, just as intensity is. That, every one will admit to be a distinguishable though not separable ingredient. . . . In like manner, extensity being an entirely peculiar kind of feeling, indescribable except in terms of itself, and inseparable in actual experience from some sensational quality which it must accompany, can itself receive no other name than that of sensational element."[1]

This testimony of introspection to the elemental nature of extensity has, however, been challenged by acute and learned psychologists.[2] Their position has, therefore, to be carefully considered. They point out that no definite physical and physiological conditions of the extensity consciousness have ever been discovered. The lack of a corresponding form of physical energy is common, to be sure,

---

[1] *Op. cit.*, II., p. 136.
[2] Among these may be named the English psychologists, Mill, Bain and Spencer, and the German writers Helmholtz and Wundt. The sensational theory is supported by James, Ward, Stumpf, Hering and others. Cf. Bibliography.

to several admitted forms of sensational element, and is comparatively unimportant, since the physical is never the immediate explanation of the psychical. But there is no instance, it is argued, of sensational element without corresponding physiological end-organs; and no organs of visual extensity have ever been discovered in the retina. The natural conclusion, it is urged, is that the consciousness of visual extensity must be unsensational.

The opponents of the sensational theory endeavor, also, to undermine, at its foundation, the value of the introspective observation. The naive, unverified consciousness, they observe, is notoriously untrustworthy in its discovery of conscious elements. Experiences such as alleged sensations of wetness and of tickling, which it unhesitatingly labels as simple, turn out to be highly complex. The fact that extensity seems to introspection an unanalyzable sensational experience proves only, therefore, that the elements of which it is made up so invariably accompany each other, that they are no longer noticed separately. Positively, therefore, this 'empirical' theory of extensity, appealing to our trained and attentive introspection, teaches in opposition to the 'sensational' theory, that the consciousness of visual extensity is a complex experience, made up of a combination of the sensations resulting from the movement of the eye-muscles. According to this empirical or motor theory, my idea, for example, of the extensity of the paper on which I write, is composed of the sensations of pressure which I gain from the moving of my eyeballs as I glance, involuntarily, from top to bottom and from right to left of the sheet, and my idea of the extensity of my watch is the complex of sensations due to the sweep of my eye-muscles, actual or imagined, as I follow its curved outline. The fact that our extensity-consciousness is mainly, at least, visual or tactual, follows naturally, it is argued,[1] on this hypothesis, from the peculiar mobility of eyeball and of hand.

[1] Cf. Spencer, "Principles of Psychology," Vol. II., Pt. VI., Chapter 14, pp. 196-197.

Let us now, however, examine critically the arguments which oppose the sensational theory and which indirectly, therefore, support the empirical or motor hypothesis. In the first place, the sensationalist may reject the implication that assignable physiological end-organs are the condition *sine qua non* of sensational elements. Admitting, from analogy, the probability that sensational elements are so distinguished, he will nevertheless insist that their only essential criteria are (1) observed distinctness and (2) the fact that they are not analyzable. It is quite unnecessary, however, to concede to the empiricist that no physiological differentiation corresponds with the experience of extensity. We know very little of the membranous structure and muscular processes of the eye, and we are ignorant, above all, of the cerebral areas and modes of activity which are immediate conditions of psychical facts. There may, therefore, be physiological structures and functions, as yet unobserved, which specifically correspond with the extensity consciousness. For example, it is conceivable, as has been suggested, that visual extensity is physiologically conditioned by the *number* of retinal processes, optic nerve-fibres and cerebral cells, which are excited, that is, by the number, as distinguished from the degree and the locality, of nerve-excitations. Such an hypothesis may be supplemented by the theory that the number of ether-waves of a given length and amplitude, impinging at a given time upon the retina, is the physical correlate of the consciousness of extensity.

But far more serious is the aspersion cast by the empiricist theory on the trustworthiness of adult introspection. Nobody can deny, indeed, that the 'naive consciousness' is peculiarly prone to err in its enumeration of elements, and likely to mistake, through inattentiveness or through positive inability, the constantly combined for the elementally simple. Untrustworthy as it is, however, introspection is the only resource of the psychologist. He must guard it by experimental methods and verify it by comparison with the experience of others, but in the end he must trust it. The object of his study consists simply of the facts of his own consciousness, and for these he is the final authority. In the end, therefore, the issue is between the introspection of the sensationalist and that of the empiricist. The writer sides with the former, and maintains that our consciousness of extensity simply is not a consciousness of motion or a complex of pressure-sensations; and that, on the other hand, by bigness or extensity we do mean an experience as distinct, as unlike every other and therefore as elemental, as color or pitch or brightness.

It is, however, of the utmost importance to distinguish between the elemental consciousness of mere bigness or extensity and the developed ideas of space, surface, depth and figure, which replace it in the adult consciousness. No one of these experiences is what we mean by the sensational element of 'crude extensity,' in which, as James[1] well says "there is no question as yet of surface or of depth." These ideas of 'total space,' of surface or space of two dimensions, and of depth or distance, like the ideas of definite shapes, of triangles, circles or cubes, are without doubt highly complex. In all probability the consciousness of movement is an important factor of them. They certainly include, also, the consciousness of position and the consciousness of relation — experiences which have not been carefully discussed. Engulfed as it is in this consciousness of surface, depth and form, almost never appearing in even relative simplicity, the consciousness of mere bigness seems nevertheless to be a distinct experience unlike all others, and thus a sensational element of consciousness.

b. PRESSURE-EXTENSITY

Everybody admits that we are conscious not only of visual extensity but of the bigness or extensity of objects of touch. The feeling of extensity, occasioned by an object

---

[1] *Op. cit.*, II., 136.

which touches forehead or hand or leg, is indeed as distinct and indescribable an element of experience as the feeling of pressure from the object. The empiricist, to be sure, denies this, and describes the consciousness of pressure-extensity as a consciousness of the movements, real or imagined, with which we 'outline' the object. But the arguments which inclined us to the view that visual extensity is elemental apply equally to the tactual experience. It is, however, an open question whether the extensity is identical in the visual and tactual experience, or whether there are at least these two kinds of extensity, visual and tactual, just as there are different sorts of intensity, like brightness and loudness. The writer inclines to the latter view.[1]

c. EXTENSITY OF SOUNDS AND OF OTHER SENSATION-CLASSES

Sounds certainly differ from each other in some other way than in pitch, in noise-quality and in loudness. The roar of the waves on the beach is not merely a deeper-pitched nor always a louder sound than the voice of the child at play beside them; it is also what we may call 'bigger,' 'vaster,' more 'extensive' or more 'voluminous.' This difference, whatever it is, is best illustrated by playing the same tone with equal intensity on different instruments — on flute and on horn, on violin and on harp, or on cello and on trombone. There is an unmistakable difference between these tones, yet the one is not higher nor lower, louder nor softer, than another. Physicists have been wont to name the distinction one of 'quality,' but most people express it by saying that the trombone tone is bigger than the cello tone; and that the violin has a larger sound than the harp. This sound-bigness, or volume, it should be added, varies with the pitch, for the lower the pitch the 'bigger' is the sound; yet volume is

[1] Cf. *op. cit.*

not identical with pitch, since it may vary, as we have seen, when the pitch is unaltered.

Physicists are probably correct in attributing sound-volume, or sound-quality as they call it, to a complex atmosphere-vibration. The physical correlate of sound-extensity, as thus considered, is roughly parallel with that of visual extensity. It consists of the complexity of vibration of the air-particles, depending on the number of simple vibrations into which each complex vibration can be analyzed. The physiological correlate of the consciousness of extensity is probably the number of functioning basilar-membrane fibres and brain-cells.

The usual view, it should be added, of the experience which we have called that of sound-extensity is that sounds are called 'larger' or 'vaster' simply because we imagine them as coming from a greater distance or as pervading a greater visual space or as occasioned by objects which are big to vision or to touch. On this hypothesis, the sound of a cannon, for example, is vaster than that of the squeaky slate pencil, because the cannon is bigger than the slate pencil or because the explosion can be heard for a greater distance than the squeak. The difficulty with this theory, in the writer's opinion, is its contradiction of a fact of introspection, the distinct, unanalyzable, elemental character of sound-bigness which is quite different from the imagined visual or pressure extensity.

James teaches that the element of crude extensity or bigness or voluminousness is 'discernible in each and every sensation, though more developed in some than in others.' He instances the 'massive feeling . . . [from] . . . entrance into a warm bath,' contrasting it with the 'prick of a pin'; the 'little neuralgiac pain, fine as a cobweb,' comparing it with the 'vast discomfort of a colic or a lumbago'; and the voluminousness of the 'complex flavor . . . of roast meat or plum pudding' or of the 'heavy odors like musk or tube rose.' In all these cases introspection is difficult, because it is so easy to mistake for a new sort of extensity, what is really an image of the visual extensity, or bigness, of the bodily area which is affected. For this reason, we shall not attempt even a tentative decision of the disputed question.

II. The Developed Consciousness of Extensity

The most fruitful source of difficulty, in the study of the consciousness of extensity, is the constant confusion of the elemental extensity feeling with the developed and complex consciousness of breadth or of depth or of figure. We shall try, therefore, to distinguish with care the complex from the elemental experience. It should be noted that only ideas of visual and of pressure extensity have attained any marked complexity. For lack, indeed, of a high degree of development, the very existence of sound-bigness is often denied — most unjustly, because the crude feeling of extensity can be better observed in the relative simplicity of a sound idea than in the confused tangle of a visual or of a pressure idea.

The primitive pressure-extensity and visual bigness have given place to two main forms of consciousness of the spatial: —

a. CONSCIOUSNESS OF SURFACE OR SPACE-IN-TWO-DIMENSIONS

The consciousness of surface or 'spread-out-ness' is sometimes supposed to be an elemental experience. James suggests this view by the expression 'breadth-feeling,' but closer introspection shows that the feeling of spread-out-ness (so far as the term is not a mere synonym for 'bigness') is the consciousness of a complex of related lines or points or angles, and therefore no elemental experience.

The study of this complex experience does not belong to our present discussion of elements of consciousness; it is indeed a subject of such technical difficulty that it cannot profitably be undertaken by the elementary student. It will be convenient, however, to consider briefly in this section certain features of the developed consciousness of surface. Its centre and nucleus is the elemental feeling of extensity or bigness. With this is combined, in the second place, a consciousness of certain bodily movements, usually of eye or hand, which may be actually performed or merely imagined. The incorrect 'empirical' account of the sensation of extensity [1] turns out, therefore, to be a good account of the developed consciousness of surface. My consciousness of the outline or figure of a church spire is distinguished from my consciousness of its clock, because the one includes the sensations from long upward movements of my eye, whereas the other contains sensations from a sort of circular sweep of the eyeball. The difference between rectilinear and circular figures is the most fundamental of the distinctions based on these bodily movements.

The consciousness of surface may include, in the second place, the consciousness of the subdivision of surfaces.[2] A rectangle, for example, may be thought of as a combination of two triangles or of four rectangles, and as subdivided in innumerable other ways. This consciousness of subdivided surface is doubtless brought about by comparing with each other objects of different size and shape; and it involves what we shall later know as relational feelings: the consciousness of 'whole' and of 'part.'

We may have, finally, the spatial consciousness of the locality or position of a figure with reference to another figure. Such a consciousness of locality includes (1) the consciousness of the first figure, (2) the consciousness of the second figure, with which the first is compared, (3) a relational feeling of the connection of the one with the other, (4) the consciousness of the surface between the

[1] Cf. p. 90.   [2] Cf. James, *op. cit.*, II., p. 167 *seq.*

two, and (5) the consciousness of the direction, right or left
and up or down, of one from the other.   This consists, in
whole or in part, in imagined movements — for most of us,
eye-movements.   When, for example, I am conscious of
my collie as lying to the right of his kennel, I imagine the
sensations which would be involved in moving the eye so
as to bring the retinal images of collie and kennel successively upon the point of clearest vision.

b. CONSCIOUSNESS OF DISTANCE OR DEPTH

We unquestionably have a consciousness of the depth
of objects or of their distance.   " It is impossible," James
says,[1] " to lie on one's back on a hill, to let the empty abyss
of blue fill one's whole visual field, and to sink deeper
and deeper into the merely sensational consciousness regarding it, without feeling that an indeterminate, palpitating, circling feeling of depth is as indefeasibly one of its
attributes as its breadth."   In somewhat the same way,
as James quotes from Hering, darkness seems to us to
' fill ' a room instead of covering its walls, and a transparent cube appears more ' roomy ' than the ' mere surface '
of an opaque one.

We are therefore concerned to discover the nature of
the consciousness of depth.   And we are met at the outset
by the theory, embodied by James in the words ' depth
feeling,' that it is an element of consciousness.   At first
thought, it does indeed seem to contain an elemental, a
distinct experience, unlike any other, and like only to itself.   But closely scrutinized, this elementalness turns out
to be the mere vague consciousness of extensity, and that
which distinguishes the depth-consciousness from other
forms of extensity-consciousness is rather the dim consciousness of one's whole body in motion, the experience
of what Mill describes [2] as ' muscular motion unimpeded.'

[1] *Op. cit.,* II., p. 212.
[2] " Examination of Sir William Hamilton's Philosophy," Vol. I., Chapter 13,
p. 282.

H

The epithets 'palpitating' and 'circling,' applied by James in the passage quoted, to what he names the feeling of depth, suggest that the consciousness of the depth of the blue sky and the roominess of the dark enclosure are really a vague realization of this freedom of possible movement. Thus, my consciousness of the depth of the sky includes an indistinct image of my body as moving upward; and the roominess of the dark room implies my groping motions. My consciousness of an object as a volume and not a mere surface includes very definitely, to the introspection of the writer, an image of my body moving about in such a way as to see also the hidden side and back of the object. In other words, every experience of depth includes an elemental feeling of extensity, and beyond this — not a specific 'depth feeling' but a consciousness of the movements of the body. In favor of this interpretation, and against the theory of a definite depth-sensation, an argument from the physical side may be adduced in support of our introspection. Bishop Berkeley long ago called attention to the fact that no point, situated directly behind a fixated point, can by any possibility affect the retina. " Distance," he said,[1] "of itself and immediately cannot be seen. For distance being a line directed endwise to the eye, it projects only one point in the fund of the eye. Which point remains invariably the same, whether the distance be longer or shorter." But this situation of one point directly behind another is of course the only case of absolute depth, for the position of an object in which some points are behind others, but also at one side of them, gives the effect of surface or spread-outness. The only fair physical test, therefore, of the existence of depth-sensations seems to rule out the possibility of them.

On the physiological side, also, there is a certain difficulty for the hypothesis of a particular sensation of visual depth. The only physiological explanation which can be

---

[1] " Essay towards a New Theory of Vision."

given of these alleged sensations of visual depth is the
following: when one looks at an object with the two
eyes, the right eye undoubtedly sees slightly more on the
right and the left eye a little more on the left of the object,
so that the images which it produces on the retina differ a
little in the two eyes; and the difference increases with
the distance of the object.[1] Corresponding, it is said, with
this double retinal stimulation and with the cerebral activity which accompanies it, is the consciousness of visual
depth or voluminousness. But this explanation altogether
overlooks the fact that the two eyes ordinarily function as
one, probably because from each retina fibres of the optic
nerve go to the occipital lobe of each hemisphere; and it
accordingly is very improbable that any cerebral distinction
results from the slight difference of the retinal images.

It is fair to conclude that the existence of specific depth-
sensations is wholly unproved. Both breadth and depth
may best be defined as visual or tactual experiences, involving a consciousness of motion and including, as their
nucleus, the sensational experience of mere crude extensity.
Breadth and depth are differentiated in that the motor idea
included in consciousness of breadth is that of motion of a
limited part of the body, as eyeballs or fingers; whereas
the consciousness of depth requires also the idea of
motion of my body as a whole, from one position to another. Depth or distance, therefore, is not perceived until
one has gained the consciousness of the peculiarly constant
combination of visual, pressure and pain sensations which
one calls one's own body. Mere sensations of extensity,
on the other hand, may accompany a baby's very first
color and light sensations, and may precede by many weeks
his acquaintance with his body. The consciousness of distance thus includes (1) a feeling of crude extensity, (2) a
certain consciousness of the relation of objects, (3) a more

[1] For experiments cf. Sanford, 212-217; Titchener, § 42. Cf. Titchener,
"Outline," § 44.

or less vague consciousness of movements, of my body as a whole, toward or around an object, and (4) the sensations due to the convergence of the eyes. When, for example, I look from a boulder six feet away to a light-house a mile distant, the angle of vision becomes more acute, that is to say, the pupils of the eyes turn toward each other, and I get sensations of pressure from the muscle contractions which bring about the movement.

It should be added that the consciousness of distance is often occasioned by the observation of certain visual characteristics of an object, 'signs of distance,' as they are called. The consciousness of dimness of color and of hazy outlines, and of the reduced size of a familiar object is followed by the consciousness of the object's distance.

This discussion of the extensity-consciousness has so far left out of account a distinction which has often confused the point at issue. The sensational theory has been supposed to imply that the consciousness of extensity is innate, and has accordingly gone by the name of the nativistic theory of space. On this basis the 'nativists' have occasionally argued, from the exactness of the motor adjustments of new-born animals, that an innate consciousness of space relations is possible. Because chicks, which are hooded as soon as they leave the shell, are able when first unhooded on the second day to pick up grains of corn,[1] it is argued that they are innately conscious of the position of the grains of corn. To this argument, the opponent of the nativist theory rightly retorts that the nativist's argument from the reactions of young animals loses sight, first, of the fact that these may be merely unconscious reflexes, and second, of the impossibility of arguing from the animal to the human consciousness.

The upholders of the opposite hypothesis — the genetic theory, as from this point of view it is called — then argue

[1] Cf. D. A. Spaulding, *Macmillan's Magazine*, Vol. XXVI, esp. 283–287.

positively that there can be no innate consciousness of space because of the uncertainties of a baby's early motions, its efforts to seize the moon and its inability to grasp the object close before it, and because of the long training necessary to enable a patient recovered from blindness to calculate the size and distance of an object.[1] But these arguments prove only, what no one ever doubted, that exact measurements of depth and distance are the results of education; they certainly do not prove the utter absence of crude, elemental experiences of extensity, in the earliest hours of consciousness.

Even more serious than the insufficiency of both arguments is the false conception which underlies them. The truth is that an elemental, sensational consciousness is not necessarily innate. On the contrary, an experience, though absent in the first moments or days or months of the individual human life, may prove, when it appears, to be a distinct and unanalyzable, and therefore, an elemental form of consciousness. The sensational character of extensity would not, therefore, be disproved, though it were shown to be a later, not an innate, experience. But the truth is that, in the nature of the case, the problem of innateness is as insoluble as it is unessential.

The conclusions of this whole difficult discussion may now be summarized: (1) What is ordinarily called the consciousness of the spatial is a sensational experience of mere 'bigness' or 'crude extensity,' varying with different sense-types but most developed in vision and in touch. (2) This extensity-consciousness has a probable physiological correlate, the diffusion of excitation, that is, the number of nerve-elements which are excited. (3) Visual and pressure extensities are combined with other, and especially with motor elements, and thus merged in very complex experiences of two sorts, breadth and depth.

[1] Cf. Bibliography.

(4) The consciousness of breadth, or surface, is a complex experience including extensity, and the consciousness of motion of the eye and the limbs. (5) The consciousness of depth or distance is a complex idea including extensity, or bigness, and the consciousness of the motion both of eye and limbs and of the body as a whole.

CHAPTER VIII

SENSATIONAL ELEMENT AND SENSATION

WITH the end of our outline study of all reputed sense-elements of consciousness comes a natural opportunity to review our results and to define our terms from the vantage ground of a completed examination of the facts. The element of consciousness has already been defined as a distinct and further unanalyzable feeling, or fact of consciousness. This definition has been justified by the discovery, in our complex experience, of a multitude of such indescribable and irreducible elements. The conception of 'sensational element,' we have, however, taken for granted, and we have now, therefore, to frame a definition of it. The definition must of course take account of the elements of consciousness already enumerated as sensational, and must definitely mark them off from others in a class by themselves. A careful review of the psychic phenomena which we have called sensational elements discloses the following general characteristic: sensational elements are actually present in every concrete, conscious experience. However lofty one's thought, or however impassioned one's emotion, whether one reflect on the infinite, or thrill with the love of humanity, always, included within the experience, are sensational elements, those, for example, which make up the verbal images 'humanity' and 'infinite,' and the feelings of quickened or retarded breath which make part of one's emotional experience. It must be noted carefully, that this characteristic, invariable occurrence, is in no sense a part of the sensational element itself. On the contrary, the element, as we know, is simple and unanalyzable, mere blueness, or loudness, or bigness. The fact that sensational elements are always present in our experience is only discovered by after reflection, and is, therefore, a fact about the sensational element, not a fact within it. This reflectively observed characteristic may be named the psychological criterion of the sensational element, because it is established without reference to any physiological and physical phenomena.

But psychology does also correlate its facts, for purposes of classification, with the facts of physics and physiology. The physiological criterion of the sensational element is the fact that, corresponding with every sensational element, there is some assignable change, both in an area of the brain and in a peripheral nerve end-organ. This statement, of course, does not imply that the unsensational psychic elements are without corresponding neural excitation ; on the other hand, we have reason to suppose that every element of every emotion, belief or volition is physiologically conditioned by some change within the nervous system. What is asserted is merely, first, that the neural excitation of the sensational element is more readily assigned, and second, that this neural excitation involves peripheral organs of the body. By 'peripheral organs' are meant, in this connection, all parts of the body outside the brain and spinal cord, for example, the retina, the basilar membrane, the taste-bulbs, and the joint-surfaces. The excitation of these peripheral organs is conveyed by nerve-fibres to the brain, and the cerebral excitation is, as we have seen, the immediately antecedent condition of the sensational consciousness.

The situation of most of the important sense-organs, near the surface of the body, explains the possibility of assigning a third characteristic of the sensational element. This may be named its physical criterion, and may be ᵉmulated thus: for almost every sensational element : is a distinⅽt physical condition. Thus, the rate of ether-vibrations is the physical condition of each color; the amplitude of the vibrations is the condition of each brightness or color-intensity, and the rate of atmosphere-vibrations is the condition of each musical pitch.

Within the class of sensational elements, thus marked off from others, psychological method recognizes three sub-classes, usually distinguished as qualities, intensities, and extensities. The fundamental ground for this division is the observed distinctness of these groups of elements, the fact that hues and pitches and tastes seem, from one point of view, to belong together, and to be equally distinct from brightnesses, loudnesses, and taste-intensities, or from visual and auditory bignesses. But besides this immediately observed distinctness, the sensational qualities differ, as has been shown, from intensities and from extensities, by their incapacity for direct serial arrangement.[1] Aside from what may be called the complex series in which sensational qualities may figure (color-series like 'red, orange, yellow, yellow-green,' or tone-series like C-CE-EG, in which the likeness of the successive terms is due to the presence of identical elements), sensational qualities are also capable of simple serial arrangement. Such series as 'red, yellow, green, blue,' or C-D-E-F are illustrations. Now the serial character of this succession is due to an increase, not of the quality, but of the difference. In other words, the consciousness of 'more,' which characterizes every step of a series, attaches itself, not directly to each quality, but to the recognized likeness or difference of each quality as compared with its neighbors. Fully expressed such a tone-series is not, therefore, C-D-E-F-G, nor yet:—

$$
\begin{array}{lll}
\text{C} & \cdot \quad \cdot \quad \cdot & \\
\text{D} & \cdot \quad \cdot \quad \cdot & \text{more C} \\
\text{E} & \cdot \quad \cdot \quad \cdot & \left\{ \begin{array}{l} \text{more D} \\ \text{still more C} \end{array} \right.
\end{array}
$$

[1] The theory of the series underlying the distinctions which follow is stated by James in " Principles of Psychology," Vol. I., pp. 489 *seq.*, 530 *seq.* Cf. also

but rather, as has been shown already,

C . . .
D . . . different from C
E . . . { different from D
          more different from C }
F . . . { different from E
          more different from D
          still more different from C }

Intensities, on the other hand, and extensities, are capable of direct, simple serial arrangement. The increase is of the intensity or the extensity, that is, the 'feeling of more,' as James calls it, is directly connected with the consciousness of 'bright' or 'loud' or 'big,' and our series become 'bright—more bright—still more bright,' 'loud—more loud—still more loud,' 'big—more big—still more big,' and so on.

The attempt to indicate a similar psychological distinction of extensity from intensity has, so far as the writer is concerned, been unsuccessful. As has been shown, however, the extensity has distinct physiological and physical conditions. From the consideration of the psychic experience we shall, therefore, proceed to an enumeration of physiological correlates.

The physiological condition of the sense-quality is admitted to be the locality of the excitation. For example, the physiological explanation of the sensational element blueness is the fact that it is preceded by excitation of the retina and of the occipital lobe; the explanation of the sensational element bitterness is the excitation, first, of a taste-papilla on the back part of the tongue, and second, (in all probability) of an area of the temporal lobe. Our more detailed study of these physiological conditions has shown, to be sure, great gaps in our knowledge of neural

throughout, "Elements of Conscious Complexes," M. W. Calkins, *Psychological Review*, VII., 377, from which certain paragraphs are transferred.

localization, but everybody admits the general correspondence of sensational quality with neural locality.

At first sight there seems, however, no distinct physiological condition for the sense-intensity, but, on the other
hand, intensity as well as quality seems to vary with the
place of excitation of the nerve endings and centres. The
excitation of the basilar membrane and the temporal lobe
seems to occasion the feeling of loudness as well as that
of pitch; and the excitation of retina and occipital lobe
appears to condition the sensational intensity, the brightness, as well as the sensational quality, the color. Because
of this alleged absence of a specific physiological condition, many psychologists have indeed refused to admit the
intensity as a sensational element coördinate with the
quality. Now we must first oppose to this view the truth,
that no argument from physiology can stand against the
testimony of consciousness to the distinct and irreducible
character of the sense-intensity. We have, however, no
need to admit that there is no assignable physiological
correlate of sense-intensity, for there are innumerable variations in the degree of excitation of the given end-organ
and brain-centre; and we may well suppose that delicately
graded intensities correspond directly with the different
degrees of energy with which the nerve-cells of end-organs
and brain are decomposed.

As physiological correlate of sensational elements of
extensity, we may finally suggest the specific relation of
these feelings of extensity to the number of nerve-cells
excited at a given time. The more extensive color or
pressure is, on this view, conditioned by the greater number of retinal or Meissner cells and of cerebral cells which
are decomposed, at a given time.

The physical criteria of the different types of sensational elements are even less certainly known, and this is
natural, since there are so few sorts of physical stimulus
about which we can even make plausible guesses. It is,
however, possible to observe in physical stimuli the mode,

degree and complexity of stimulation, and these distinctions correspond in general with those of the locality, degree and number of the physiological processes. Thus, the quality normally varies with the different modes of physical stimulation. In the case of most sensations, this distinction can only be indicated roughly by the use of the terms 'mechanical,' 'thermal' and 'chemical stimulus'; but the better-known stimuli of visual and auditory sense-elements are distinguished from each other by the difference in the vibratory medium, ether or atmosphere. Moreover, each distinct element of a given quality, the red, green, blue or yellow, the C, D, E or F, is conditioned by a definite rate of ether or of air vibration. The intensities of these different sensation-classes vary with the degrees of the excitation (in the case of ether and air vibrations, with the amplitudes of the waves). And finally, the extensities vary with the complexity of stimulation, for example, with the complexity of ether-waves or atmospheric vibrations of similar length and amplitude.

This relation of the psychical element to the physical stimulus is, however, as has been said, merely a normal or usual, not a necessary relation. A given sense-element is not invariably produced by the mode, degree or amount of a definite form of physical energy. On the contrary, the sensation following upon excitation of a given nerve-fibre is the same, whatever the mode of the physical stimulus. When the optic nerve, for example, is mechanically stimulated by the internal jar from a fall, we 'see stars,' that is to say, the sensation is the characteristic one of light; and when a 'cold-spot,' the skin which covers an end-organ of cold, is mechanically stimulated, an experience not of pressure but of cold is the result. This phenomenon, known as the specific energy of nerve-substance, is a striking illustration of the truth that psychical facts are direct accompaniments, not of physical, but of physiological phenomena. There is, therefore, only a normal, not a constant, physical criterion of the sense-element.

All these criteria may be grouped together in the following summary: —

A. Criteria of All Elements of Consciousness: Distinctness and Unanalyzableness.
B. Criteria of Sensational Elements.
    I. General criteria.
        a. Always present, conceivably without elements of another order.
        b. Conditioned by definite form of peripheral and of central excitation.
        c. Originally conditioned (except pain) by definite form of physical stimulation.
    II.
        a. Criteria of sensational qualities.
            1. Capable of indirect, simple serial arrangement only.
            2. Varying with locality of physiological excitation.
            3. Varying with mode of physical stimulation.
        b. Criteria of sensational intensities.
            1. Capable of direct, simple serial arrangement.
            2. Varying with *degree* (and with locality) of physiological excitation.
            3. Varying with degree of physical stimulation.
        c. Criteria of sensational extensities.
            1. Capable of direct, simple serial arrangement.
            2. Varying with *diffusion* (and with locality) of physiological excitation.
            3. Varying with complexity of physical stimulus.

By still another table we may summarize the different elements themselves, grouping them into sensations, that is, into complexes of invariably combined sensational elements. There is no color, for example, which is not bound up with a certain brightness and a certain bigness, and no pitch which is not combined with loudness and volume. Therefore, the combined color, brightness and bigness are called a visual sensation, and the combined pitch or noise-quality, loudness and volume are called an auditory sensation. Some psychologists accordingly regard the sensation as the unit of psychology, and speak of the sensational elements, the quality, intensity and extensity, as attributes of the sensation.

SENSATIONAL ELEMENTS

A. FROM EXTERNAL STIMULUS

(*Psychic nature*)   (*Organ stimulated*)

(*Periph.*)   (*Central*)

I. VISUAL SENSATIONS

(Quality) (Intensity) (Extensity)	RETINA	OCCIP. LOBE	ETHER-WAVES
a. 1. Color —— ——	"	"	Length of waves
2. Colorless light —— ——	"	"	"
b. Brightness	" (degree of excitation)	" (degree of excitation)	Amplitude of waves
c. Bigness	" (number of cells excited)	" (number of cells excited)	Number of simultaneous waves

II. SOUND-SENSATIONS

	COCHLEA	TEMPORAL LOBE	AIR-WAVES
a. 1. Tone	"	"	Length of waves
2. Noise	"	"	"
b. Loudness	" (degree of excitation)	" (degree of excitation)	Amplitude of waves
c. Volume	" (number of fibres excited)	" (number of cells excited)	Complexity of waves

III. TASTE-SENSATIONS

	MUCOUS MEMBRANE OF MOUTH	TEMPORAL LOBE (median surface)	LIQUID CHEMICAL STIMULUS
a. Taste	"	"	Mode of stimulus
b. Taste-intensity	" (degree of excitation)	" (degree of excitation)	Degree of stimulus
c. Taste-extensity (?)	" (extent of excitation)	" (number of cells excited)	Amount of stimulus

IV. SMELL-SENSATIONS

	MUCOUS MEMBRANE OF NOSE	TEMPORAL LOBE (median)	GASEOUS CHEMICAL STIMULUS
a. Smell	"	"	Mode of stimulus
b. Smell-intensity	" (degree of excitation)	" (degree of) excitation	Degree of stimulus
c. Smell-extensity (?)	" (extent of excitation)	" (number of cells excited)	Amount of stimulus

B. FROM EXTERNAL OR FROM INTERNAL STIMULUS

V. PRESSURE-SENSATIONS

	Meissner cells (?) in { Cutis, Joints, Muscles (?) }	Rolandic region	Mechanical stimulus
a. Pressure-quality			
b. Pressure-intensity	"	"	"
c. Pressure-extensity	"	"	"

VI. PAIN-SENSATIONS

	End-organs in cutis, etc.	Rolandic region	Mechanical and Thermal

VII. TEMPERATURE(?)-SENSATIONS

a. Cold [1]

	End-organs in cutis, membranes, etc.	Rolandic region	Thermal stimulus
b. Warmth [1]	"	"	"
c. Hotness	"	"	"

C. FROM STIMULUS OF INTERNAL ORGAN ONLY

VIII. SENSATIONS OF STRAIN (?) [1]	End-organs in tendons	Rolandic region	Mechanical stimulus by external weight or internal pull

An illustration of the relative interdependence of physical and psychical phenomena will conclude this chapter. It is formulated in what is named the psycho-physic law,[2] that is, in general outline, the probability that sensations vary regularly but not directly with the quantitative variations of their physical stimuli. Many illustrations of this law are matters of everyday observation. A room grows lighter with the number of lighted gas jets, but a single jet more in a brilliantly illuminated room does not make it observably lighter; the feelings of pressure and of strain-intensity change with the addition of weights to an extended arm, but the addition of a single ounce to a four-pound weight cannot be distinguished. The early psychological experimenters confined themselves closely to the verification and extension of this law, first suggested by E. H. Weber and later minutely discussed and formulated by G. T. Fechner. The experiments, which have dealt exclusively with sensation-intensities, have resulted in the following general conclusion: to obtain a series of sensa-

[1] The specific mention of quality, intensity and (probable) extensity is here omitted, and should be supplied.
[2] Cf. Bibliography.

tion-intensities, just perceptibly different from each other, the series of physical stimuli must differ, one from the other, by a certain definite proportion. The proportion varies with the form of stimulus: the degree of sound stimulus must increase by one-third, of gaseous olfactory stimulus by about one-fourth, of mechanical surface stimulus by one-twentieth, of mechanical pull by one-fortieth, and of light stimulus by one one-hundredth. For example, if one can just tell the difference between weights of one hundred and one hundred and five grams applied to the ends of the fingers, one will not be able to distinguish weights of two hundred and two hundred and five grams, but will barely discriminate weights of two hundred and two hundred and ten.

CHAPTER IX

ATTRIBUTIVE ELEMENTS OF CONSCIOUSNESS

I. THE AFFECTIONS: FEELINGS OF PLEASANTNESS AND OF UNPLEASANTNESS

IT needs no text-book in psychology to convince us that our analysis of consciousness is incomplete when we have merely enumerated the sense-elements. For, quite as prominent as the sights and sounds and fragrances and all the other sensational parts of our experience are the pleasantnesses and unpleasantnesses. Now these are clearly elemental feelings. One can no more tell what one means by agreeableness or by disagreeableness, than one can tell what redness and warmth and acidity are: in other words, these are irreducible experiences, and they are perfectly distinct from each other as well as from the sensational elements.

From the class of sense-elements they are, however, plainly differentiated. Unlike sensational elements, the affections are not always present in consciousness, and cannot conceivably occur by themselves without belonging, as it were, to elements of another sort. The fact that we are not always conscious of either pleasantness or unpleasantness is ordinarily expressed by saying that much of our everyday experience is 'indifferent' to us. Another characteristic is clearly shown by the reflection that we are conscious, not of agreeableness or disagreeableness by itself, but always of an agreeable or disagreeable somewhat, of a pleasant familiarity, for example, or of an unpleasant taste. These distinctions, of course, are not immediate constituents of either pleasantness or unpleasantness, that is to say, when one is conscious of pleasure one does not necessarily say to oneself, " this experience might have been perfectly indifferent, and the pleasantness of it belongs to its brilliant color." On the contrary, these are only possible after-reflections about the agreeableness or disagreeableness. The fact that the affections are not always present in consciousness, and that they seem, as has been said, to ' belong to ' other elements, may be indicated by calling them ' attributive ' elements of consciousness.

Some psychologists, notably Wundt,[1] express this relation by calling the affection an ' attribute ' of sensation. There are two objections to this conception, as usually held. In the first place, it often treats the affection as if it were exactly on a par with sensational quality, intensity and extensity, forgetting that these invariably occur together, whereas the affection is, as we have seen, sometimes lacking. For example, a visual object is always colored, bright, and extended, but not always either pleasant or unpleasant. In the second place, the definition of affection as attribute of sensation leaves no room for a pleasantness which belongs, not to sensations, but to unsensational experiences. The familiarity, for example, not the color of a landscape, may be its pleasant feature. This possibility will later be discussed more fully. The term ' attributive ' is used in this book to contrast the affections with the sensations, which James calls ' substantive ' facts of consciousness.

Reflective introspection thus discloses that affections are not invariably present, and that they occur in close relation with non-affective experiences. We have now to go beyond mere introspection, and to discover, if we can, the physical stimuli and the physiological excitations of the affections. At once there appears a marked distinction between sensational and affective elements. For the affec-

1 " Physiologische Psychologie," 4te Aufl., L, p. 281.

tions have no definite physical stimulus, no distinct form of physical energy which corresponds with them, in the way in which vibrations of the ether normally condition sensations of color, and atmospheric waves condition sensations of sound.

This independence of physical stimulation is admitted by everybody, so far as the mode of physical stimulus is concerned. Ether or atmosphere vibrations, and mechanical or electrical, liquid or gaseous, stimulus may bring about now a pleasant, now an unpleasant, now a perfectly indifferent, experience. It is true that certain sense-qualities, pain and probably also certain smells and tastes, are always unpleasant, and there may be certain sense-qualities which are always pleasant; but, none the less, every class of sense-qualities (except pain) includes both agreeable and disagreeable experiences; and many sense-qualities are sometimes pleasant, at other times unpleasant and again indifferent.[1] It follows, as has been said, that the affective tone cannot vary with the mode of physical stimulus.

Some psychologists have, however, supposed that a definite relation may be found between the degree — and possibly also the duration — of physical stimulation and the affective experience. This relation is usually formulated as follows: any stimulus of great intensity, and many stimuli of prolonged duration, occasion unpleasantness, whereas stimuli of medium intensity bring about pleasantness,[2] and very faint stimuli excite indifferent experiences. But this is not an accurate statement of the facts. Both moderate stimuli and even stimuli, which at one time are strong enough to be unpleasant, may become indifferent — for example, workers in a factory may grow indifferent to the buzz of the wheels which is intolerable to visitors; and low intensities, for instance, the faint pressure

[1] Cf. Külpe, *op. cit.*, § 37, 5 and 6. For experiment, cf. Titchener, § 34.
[2] Cf. statement and illustrative diagram, Wundt, *op. cit.*, 4te Aufl., I., 558; and Külpe, *op. cit.*, § 37.

logical basis for the affections. In the writer's opinion, the most plausible account of this physiological condition is the following: pleasantness and unpleasantness are occasioned by the excitation of fresh or of fatigued cells in the frontal lobes of the brain, and this frontal lobe excitation is conveyed by fibres from the motor cells of the Rolandic area of the brain. When the cells of the frontal lobes, because of their well-nourished and unfatigued condition, react more than adequately to the excitation which is conveyed to them from the Rolandic area, an experience of pleasantness occurs; when, on the other hand, the cells of the frontal lobe, because they are ill-nourished and exhausted, react inadequately to the excitation from the Rolandic area, then the affection is of unpleasantness; when, finally, the activity of frontal lobe cells corresponds exactly to that of the excitation, the given experience is neither pleasant nor unpleasant, but indifferent.

Important considerations favor this theory. It accords, in the first place, with an established fact concerning the structure of the brain: the area about the fissure of Rolando is known to be closely connected with every sensory centre of the brain, and to be connected also with the frontal lobes; a stimulation from without, conveyed to a sense-centre of the brain, would be likely, therefore, to spread to the Rolandic centre, and might be carried even further to the frontal lobes.

There is, moreover, a certain antecedent probability that the excitation of cells of the frontal lobes should condition the affections: the fact that sensations are conditioned by the excitation, not of fibres, but of cells in the brain, suggests the probability that the affections also are occasioned by cell-activity; but it has been found to be probable that excitation of cells in the sense-centres does not condition the affections; there remain the cells of the two association-centres, as Flechsig calls them,[1] and it is likely that

[1] Cf. Appendix, Section L, I.

the forward association-centre, namely, the frontal lobes, rather than the hind association-centre should be the area of the excitations of affective experience. One reason for this conclusion is the following: the affections are, as we have seen, very inconstant elements of our consciousness, that is to say, we often have perfectly indifferent experiences, and the frontal association-centre has least connections with the rest of the brain, and is therefore most likely not to be excited at a given moment. The study of diseased brains has shown, moreover,[1] that injury to the frontal lobes has been accompanied by derangements of the emotional life.

This theory, in the third place, accords well with the observation that motor bodily changes are the constant correlates of pleasant and unpleasant states of mind. Everybody realizes that he holds his head higher, makes more vigorous movements[2] and often breathes more deeply when he is pleased than when he is sorry.

Our theory, furthermore, relates pleasantness and unpleasantness to admitted and constant bodily processes, nutrition and waste, or anabolism and catabolism. For it explains the adequate and inadequate response of cells in the frontal lobes to excitation from the Rolandic area, as due to their well or ill nourished condition, that is, to the sufficient or insufficient supply of oxidated blood.

The theory, finally, can account in a general way for those puzzling facts of the affective experience disclosed by our unavailing search for a definite physical stimulation. These facts, with the corresponding explanations, may be grouped as follows: (1) Every mode of physical stimulus may occasion either pleasantness or unpleasantness, because an excitation may be carried from any sensory centre through the Rolandic area to the frontal lobes. (2) No stimulus is invariably pleasant or unpleasant because the

---

[1] Flechsig, " Gehirn u. Seele," pp. 89 *seq.*
[2] For experiment, cf. Titchener, § 36.

frontal lobes are not so closely connected as other centres with all parts of the brain. (3) Novel stimuli, unless over strong or greatly prolonged, occasion pleasure, because the infrequency of the stimulus gives opportunity for the complete nutrition and upbuilding of cells in the frontal lobes. (4) Great degrees of physical stimulation, if they are not habitual, occasion a feeling of unpleasantness, because they invariably spread to the frontal lobes, which probably are readily fatigued. Prolonged stimulation may have a similar effect. (5) Intermittent stimuli are perhaps unpleasant for the following reason: they require constant changes of muscular adjustment, for example, changes in the muscles which focus the eye; this muscular work makes unusual draughts on the blood-supply, and the frontal lobes are not, therefore, in an adequately nourished condition. The following analogy (6) may partially explain the indifference of habitual stimuli. Repeated acts tend to become unconscious; and this means that the lower centres (through which excitations pass to the brain), not the brain-centres themselves, are excited. In a similar way, it may be that repeated stimuli excite only the sensory and motor centres, and are not carried through them to the remoter frontal lobes.

This theory of the physiological conditions of pleasantness and unpleasantness is thus supported by a general correspondence with the facts of brain anatomy, and by the facility with which it explains the known relations of intense, prolonged, novel and habitual stimuli to affective experience. Two objections to the theory must be briefly considered.[1] It is urged that unpleasantness accompanies not merely over-exertion (as this hypothesis supposes), but under exercise as well; the enforced quiet of the schoolroom, for example, is intensely unpleasant to the active child. To this it may be replied that, even in such situations, certain organs of the body are actually overstrained.

[1] Cf. Marshall, *op. cit.*, Chapter IV., §§ 12 and 13.

For instance, the flexing muscles by which the child checks the swinging of his feet may be strained in his efforts to be quiet. This would indirectly produce the overstimulation of motor brain-centres, and thus the overstimulation and consequent inadequate reaction of the frontal lobes. The opposite difficulty, that extremes of bodily exercise are sometimes pleasant, may be met by the supposition that in these cases the frontal lobes, through some internal conditions, are especially well nourished, so that they are unfatigued in spite of the high degree of bodily activity.

This theory of the physiological basis of affection will be better understood by comparison with certain theories which it closely resembles. It is, in fact, a sort of composite of important features of the teaching of Münsterberg, Wundt, Flechsig and Marshall.

Pleasantness and unpleasantness (which Marshall names ' pain ') depend, according to the Marshall theory, upon the ease or difficulty with which any bodily organ reacts to the physical stimulus of any moment; this ease or difficulty depends upon the 'stored force' of the stimulated organ; and this force finally depends upon the nutriment of the organ. Marshall's condensation of the theory is the following: "Pleasure is produced by the use of surplus stored force in the organ determining the content; and pain is determined by the reception of a stimulus to which the organ is incapable of reacting completely. Indifference occurs where the reaction is exactly equalized to the stimulus."[1] From this Marshall theory, we have borrowed the conception of unpleasantness and pleasantness as indirectly due to exhaustion and vigor, and as dependent not on the absolute degree of reaction but on the relation of reaction to stimulus. The Marshall theory, however, differs from that of this book in an important feature. It supposes that the motor reaction of any organ, of eye or hand, for example, not the excitation of frontal

[1] "Pain, Pleasure, and Æsthetics," Chapter V., § 3, p. 222.

lobes, occasions the affection. The main reason for reject-
ing this feature of the theory is the fact that the motor
reactions of bodily organs directly stimulate, so far as we
know, no other organs than the pressure end-organs of
joints, tendons, muscles and skin. Unless, therefore, we
suppose some additional cerebral condition, such as the
one outlined by our own theory, the motor reactions would
occasion only pressure-sensations.

This difficulty is met by Titchener's combination of
Wundt's and Flechsig's teaching with Marshall's. Titchener supposes [1] the affection to be occasioned not by the
well or ill nourished condition of some one organ of the
body, but by the general effect produced by every stimulus
upon the nervous system of the body as a whole, and thus,
indirectly, upon the frontal lobes. This general effect is
either "the building-up process (anabolism) or the break-
ing-down process (catabolism). . . . The conscious processes," he says, "corresponding to the general processes
thus set up by stimuli, are termed affections." The affections, moreover, he points out, are closely related to motor
excitations. The theory of this book, while resembling
Titchener's, teaches that the well or ill nourished condition
of the frontal lobes of the brain, the immediate occasion of
pleasantness and unpleasantness, does not always correspond exactly with the general process — anabolic or catabolic — of the body as a whole.

Our theory, finally, resembles Münsterberg's, in that he
teaches that the excitation of motor structures in the brain
conditions pleasantness and unpleasantness. He does not,
however, suppose any excitation of the frontal lobes as
immediate occasion of affective experience; and his motor
hypothesis is more detailed than that of this book, for he
holds that the innervation of cells and fibres connected with
the extensor muscles conditions pleasantness, and that the
excitation of cells and fibres connected with the flexor mus-

[1] "Outline," §§ 31, 32, 33(2).

cles conditions unpleasantness. The theory is based on experimental observations. A long succession of daily records of the errors in distance-estimation in certain simple movements unexpectedly disclosed the following facts: (1) In moods of pleasure these movements tended to be in excess of the normal and (2) in depressed moods, the errors tended in the opposite direction.[1]   From these results, which are supported by biological considerations, Münsterberg concludes that excitation of extensor and of flexor muscles conditions pleasant and unpleasant experiences respectively.   It is, however, more likely that the vigorous contraction of *any* muscle, flexor or extensor, is the accompaniment of pleasure,[2] and that the phenomenon observed by Münsterberg is due to the fact, that the normal position of many muscles is relative flexion, so that slight motions are more apt to be those of the flexor muscles.

The discussion of the physiological conditions of affection suggests certain considerations bearing on two disputed problems of introspection. The first is the question of the number of affective elements. If these are physiologically conditioned by the opposite processes of upbuilding and dissimilation in the frontal lobes, then there is physiological support for the introspective conclusion that there are two, and only two, affections, pleasantness and unpleasantness.

The second of these problems may be stated thus: is any experience at one and the same moment both pleasant and unpleasant? Unquestionably, we usually suppose that such a combination of affections is possible. More than one poet has repeated *Dante's* assertion that sorrow's crown of sorrow is the memory of happy days; and literature is full of such expressions as the exclamation of Constance, in "King John": —

[1] " Beiträge zur Psychologie," IV., 216.   For experiment cf. Titchener, § 35. See also Primer, § 26.
[2] Cf. Lange, " Ueber Gemüthsbewegungen," p. 19.

"Then have I reason to be fond of grief."

Many psychologists, nevertheless, insist that the mixed emotion is impossible. "The total feeling of a given moment," Titchener declares,[1] "must be either pleasant or unpleasant; it cannot be both." He proceeds to explain the apparent combination of pleasure and unpleasantness in one experience as a "quick alternation of pleasurable and unpleasurable — a see-saw of joy and sorrow — in which now the pleasurble, now the painful, factor is uppermost." The argument most emphasized by Titchener, for this incompatibility of the two affections, is physiological in its nature. He holds, as we have seen, that the condition of the body as a whole, either the upbuilding (anabolic) or the decaying (catabolic) condition must be uppermost, if indeed they do not equalize each other. On this supposition, therefore, the resulting affection must at any given moment be agreeableness or disagreeableness. On the theory, however, which we have adopted, some of the frontal-lobe cells may be in a well-nourished condition, and their action may therefore be unfatigued, whereas other cells in the frontal lobes may respond in an inadequate manner. The result in consciousness would be a mixed emotion, both pleasant and unpleasant. It must be admitted, therefore, that the testimony, on this point, of everyday observation and of literature is capable also of justification from the standpoint of physiology.

No attempt will be made to discuss the occurrence and the nature of affection-intensities. There may be such intensities, but introspection is at this point so difficult that the limits of this book preclude consideration of the question.

Our more positive, though still, in great part, hypothetical conclusions, are therefore the following: we find in our conscious experience two distinct and unanalyzable

[1] "Primer," § 65.

feelings, pleasantness and unpleasantness, the affective elements. These are (1) introspectively distinguished from the sensational elements, in that they are not always present and are reflectively observed to 'belong to' other elements. They are probably (2) physiologically conditioned, not by any modification of peripheral endorgans, of afferent fibres or of sensory brain-cells, but by the excitation of well or ill nourished cells in the frontal lobes, directly excited by fibres from motor cells in the Rolandic area. There is (3) no definite form of physical energy which conditions the affective elements.

II. THE FEELINGS OF REALNESS

Allied with the affections, the feelings of pleasantness and unpleasantness, is another elemental experience, the 'feeling of realness.' We can most readily illustrate it by a contrast. If I compare my memory-image of the ruins at Tiryns or of the Doge's palace, which I have seen or of which I have read descriptions, with my image of the towers of Kubla Khan or of Camelot, I shall find embedded in the first experience a certain elemental consciousness, a feeling of realness, as we have called it, utterly lacking in the poetry images. It is an 'ultimate and primordial' experience, as Stuart Mill says,[1] 'a state of consciousness *sui generis*,' to quote James.[2] "It cannot be explained," Baldwin rightly comments, "any more than any other feeling, it must be felt."[3]

For two reasons, the feeling of realness is classed as coördinate with the affections. Like the feelings of pleasantness and unpleasantness, it is always realized as belonging to some element or complex of elements. There is always a something which is real: a 'real' mouse or explosion or smell of onion. Like the affections, also, and

[1] Note to James Mill, "Analysis of Human Mind," Vol. I., p. 412.
[2] "Principles," Vol. II., p. 287.   [3] "Feelings and Will," p. 155.

unlike the sensations, the feeling of realness is not always present: one may look at objects or imagine scenes without at the same time feeling their reality. This last assertion is sometimes disputed, and it must therefore be illustrated in some detail.

We are often, as has been said, conscious of things which do not seem to us either 'real' or 'unreal,' but which simply seem to be what they are, for example, red, smooth, fragrant, pleasant and familiar, without our being at the moment conscious either of their reality or their unreality. It is in truth a great mistake to suppose that every fact of even the adult consciousness is invariably tagged with the epithet 'real' or 'unreal.' True, a given experience may always, in our adult life, seem real or unreal to us; but there is every reason to suppose that we have hosts of experiences, unclouded by a feeling either of their realness or their unrealness. The æsthetic consciousness is a good example. Our enjoyment of a beautiful scene or object never goes hand in hand with an estimate of its reality. For this, as we shall later see,[1] accompanies the recognition of an idea as connected or congruent, whereas the beautiful object is always a self-sufficient, isolated, unrelated thing. To be always concerning oneself about reality is, indeed, an unhealthy, narrowing and spoil-sport sort of existence. We all know the literal, conscientious type of person who breaks the spell which the "Arabian Nights" or "Alice in Wonderland" casts about us, by the stupid observation that it is none of it real. Thus challenged, we reply indignantly that it is all very real; yet the truth is, probably, that we have up to this time been utterly unconscious of either the reality or the unreality of the story which we have been living through.

By all these illustrations, we must try to drive home the truth that one is often conscious of things without,

---

[1] Cf. Chapter XXI., p. 304.

at the moment, feeling either their realness or their unrealness. The feeling of the not-real is evidently a composite
of the consciousness of opposition and the consciousness of
reality. The two experiences grow up, side by side, for
I am never conscious of unrealness without being at the
same time conscious of an opposite realness. I am conscious, for example, that Bacon did not really write "The
Tempest" because of my consciousness that Shakespeare
really did write it.

We must next observe that neither the feeling of realness
nor the feeling of unrealness can be a first experience in
any life, because both are learned through experience of
such contrasts as that between percept and image, fulfilment and hope, execution and volition. In illustration
of the fact that the feeling of unrealness is not a primitive
experience, James supposes [1] 'a new-born mind' for whom
experience has begun 'in the form of a visual impression
of a hallucinatory candle.' "What possible sense," he asks,
"for that mind would a suspicion have that the candle was
not real? . . . When we, the onlooking psychologists, say
that it is unreal, we mean something quite definite, *viz.*, that
there is a world known to us which is real, and to which
we perceive that the candle does not belong. . . . By
hypothesis, however, the mind which sees the candle can
spin no such considerations about it, for of other facts,
actual or possible, it has no inkling whatever. The candle
is its all, its absolute. Its entire faculty of attention is
absorbed by it."

From the correct doctrine that the naive mind has no
inkling of an unreality, James and Baldwin and other
psychologists draw the erroneous conclusion that the
undisputed, uncontradicted facts of the primitive consciousness are felt as real. The "new-born mind,"
James says, "cannot help believing the candle real,"
because, "the primitive impulse is to affirm the reality of

[1] *Op. cit.*, Vol. II., p. 287.

all that is conceived." But the proof that no primitive idea is thought of as unreal falls far short of a proof that it is thought of as real; and, on the contrary, our observation of ordinary experience has shown us many instances in which we are conscious neither of realness nor of unrealness.

There is no specific physical stimulus to the feeling of realness, and in the utter absence of experimental observation, it is idle to attempt to assign its psychological condition. There is, however, reason to suppose that excitation of motor cells and fibres of the brain is involved; and this supposition is in accord with the doctrine that affections and the feeling of realness are allied.

CHAPTER X

RELATIONAL ELEMENTS OF CONSCIOUSNESS

WE have thus distinguished, in our everyday experience, certain irreducible elements, sensational and affective. The question, however, remains, Are there any other elements of consciousness, that is, are there any simple and distinct experiences which are not to be classed as sensational elements, of quality, intensity or extensity, or as affective elements of pleasantness and unpleasantness? Two schools of psychologists answer this question by a decided negative, and we must carefully consider the position of each of these groups.

Most of those who are somewhat inaccurately named 'sensationalists' assert, as unequivocal result of their introspection, that all contents of consciousness, the most soaring fancies, the most subtle speculations, as well as the most ordinary percepts and the most primitive feelings, are reducible in the end to merely sensational and affective constituents: to colors, sounds and smells, to organic and joint sensations, to visual, auditory and motor word-images, and to feelings of pleasure and unpleasantness.

The intellectualists bring forward a very different theory. They teach that our consciousness includes far more than mere sensations and affections, a knowledge, namely, of relations and 'forms' of thought, but that this conscious-ness of relation is a higher order of psychic reality than the mere sensation or affection, so that it may not be named an element of consciousness.

To this second theory we have the right to interpose an immediate objection. It is certainly inconsistent to make use of the conception of conscious elements and at the same time to limit the range of its application. Either it is altogether unjustifiable to regard consciousness as a complex of analyzable elements, or else, if it is admitted to be proper to analyze conscious contents into sensational and affective elements, it is also necessary, if introspection discloses other unanalyzable contents, such as 'like' and 'more,' to admit that they also are elements. The intellectualist says in effect, "While you are treating of perceptual and even of emotional experience, you may regard consciousness as a succession of percepts, images and emotions, and you may analyze these into their elements; but when you come upon a judgment, a memory or a volition, and are conscious of other than sensational and affective experience, you must change your point of view and drop your conception of elements, and talk only of forms of thought or mental activities." But this, as we have seen, is illogical. The method is valid throughout or it is utterly invalid.[1]

The intellectualist theory in psychology is practically always due to a confusion of metaphysics with psychology. It may be traced back at least to Plato's undervaluation of sense-realities, and in modern times it is clearly discernible in Descartes's exaltation of reason, in Spinoza's treatment of sense as illusion, and in the curious opposition of truths of reason to matters of fact, by which Leibniz contradicts his own doctrine of the unity of sense and thought. The opposition of thought to sense forms the foundation of Wolffian philosophy and psychology, but its influence on modern thought is most pronounced in the Kantian doctrine of the categories, or forms of thought, opposed to the matter of sense.

Admitting that the intellectualists are clearly wrong in their theory, that psychology must recognize 'forms of thought' in addition to elements of consciousness, sensational and affective, our next question is, Are the sensa-

---

[1] Cf. "Elements of Conscious Complexes," by M. W. Calkins, *Psychological Review*, VII., 387.

tionalists right in asserting that sensational and affective elements of consciousness are the only ones? The writer of this book is convinced that the introspective analysis of sensationalists is inadequate. It fails to recognize certain undoubted experiences, which are not completely described when the sensational and affective elements entering into them have been fully enumerated. This means, of course, that there are elements of consciousness other than the sensational and affective ones. We shall call them 'relational elements,' and shall later attempt to justify the name. When, for example, I try to match one blue with another, the blueness, the colorless light, the brightness and the extensity are not the only elements of my consciousness. On the contrary, the consciousness of the likeness or difference of the given blue, as compared with the standard, is the very essence of this experience. Again, when I see a familiar picture, in the *Salon Carré*, my idea includes, not merely (1) the elements of color and form, flesh tints, dull blue, bending figures and the like, (2) the verbal image of the names of pictures and painter, " Holy Family " by Andrea del Sarto, (3) the organic sensations due to my relaxed attitude as I come upon a well-known picture, and, finally, (4) a feeling of pleasure. Besides all these, and distinct from them, there is in this experience a certain feeling of familiarity which can neither be identified with sensation and affection nor even be reduced to them.

An attempt to enumerate the relational elements discloses extraordinary obstacles. They have, as will later be explained, no special physical stimuli, and they are physiologically conditioned by brain changes only, and not by any changes of nerve end-organs. For this reason, these relational elements cannot easily be isolated and varied by experimental devices ; for experiment, as we have seen, must be applied to the stimuli of physical phenomena, and not directly to the facts of consciousness themselves.[1] In

[1] Cf. Chapter I., p. 11.

our study of these relational elements, we are, therefore, for the most part thrown back upon individual introspection, notoriously untrustworthy and at this point especially difficult. We are thus likely to mistake a relatively simple and yet analyzable experience for one which is really elemental. For all these reasons, it is unwise to attempt a complete classification of relational elements. The following enumeration is merely tentative; it is probably incomplete, and it very likely includes feelings which are not entirely simple. The experiences which it names are, however, irreducible to merely sensational and affective elements. The feelings of 'one' and of 'many' are peculiarly constant elements of this class, that is, they seem to lie at the basis of most complex relational experiences. What James calls the feelings of 'and' and of 'but,' — that is, the consciousness of connection and of opposition, — and the feelings of 'like' and of 'different,' of 'more' and of 'less,' are certainly relational experiences and are probably also elemental. Our study of complex conscious experiences will disclose certain simple combinations of these elements as constituents of perception, of recognition and of thought. Thus, we shall find recognition distinguished by a feeling of familiarity, and though this is no elemental experience, we shall find that it must contain relational elements. What is known as judgment involves a feeling of wholeness; generalization includes a feeling of generality; even perception and imagination are distinguished, we shall find, by certain feelings of combination and of limitedness. Our later discussion of these complex experiences will, therefore, include a closer study of the relational elements embedded in them.

The most vigorous upholder of this theory of relational elements is William James. "We ought to say," he insists, "a feeling of *and,* a feeling of *if,* a feeling of *but* and a feeling of *by,* quite as readily as we say a feeling of *blue* or a feeling of *cold.*" He attributes the ordinary denial of these experiences to the difficulty of introspecting them, and the consequent lack of names for many of them.   It should be added, however, that certain sensationalists, as James points out,[1] admit the existence of relational elements.   Prominent among these writers is Herbert Spencer, who, in spite of his baffling terminology, clearly teaches that there are 'relational feelings' as well as 'conspicuous feelings' (sensations and affections).

Admitting the existence of relational elements, whether or not we can exhaustively enumerate them, we have next to discover, if we can, the characteristics which mark them off from the simple sensational and attributive experiences. This is not, indeed, an easy task.   But it cannot be too often repeated that an obstinately realized difference between one set of psychic phenomena and another, even if the difference cannot be analyzed and explained, is nevertheless a sufficient reason for distinguishing the experiences.   Now there certainly is a recognized difference between the feelings of 'like,' 'more' and 'one,' and the feelings of 'red,' 'warm' and 'pleasant'; and this difference in itself suffices to mark these off as distinct groups of conscious elements.

We may, however, suggest an explanation of this realized difference.   The relational elements, like the attributive, are not necessarily present in all our experience, though unquestionably they almost invariably occur.   The utterly undiscriminated experience, the conscious content without observed oneness, likeness or difference, in a word, devoid of relational elements, is certainly possible. The animal consciousness, the baby consciousness and the sleepy consciousness probably approximate to this type. From 'attributive,' as well as from 'sensational,' elements, relational elements are furthermore distinguished by another characteristic: each seems, as we reflect upon it, to be closely connected with more than one other conscious experience.   The feelings of 'and,' of 'like' and of 'dif-

[1] *Op. cit.*, Vol. I., p. 247, note.

ferent' obviously require the presence of at least two facts which are alike, different, united or contrasted. The feelings of 'more' and 'less' imply a standard and a compared fact; and each relational feeling 'belongs,' as it were, to these other feelings.

There is one apparent exception to this statement. The feeling of 'one' or 'single' is a relational experience, which certainly does not seem to 'belong to' more than one feeling other than itself. It may be pointed out, however, that we never actually have the feeling of 'one' except as the consciousness of one in contrast with many, and that, therefore, the feeling of 'one' itself requires a complex experience.

It is furthermore true that relational feelings are, ordinarily, less prominent and less attended to than the other experiences to which they are supposed to 'belong.' James has laid stress on this characteristic, noticing especially the greater duration of the unrelational feelings, or 'substantive parts of the stream of thought,' as he calls them, as compared with the relational or — in his terms — the 'transitive' states. "As we take," he says, "a general view of the wonderful stream of our consciousness, what strikes us first is this different pace of its parts. Like a bird's life, it seems to be made of an alternation of flights and perchings. The resting-places are usually occupied by sensorial imaginations of some sort, whose peculiarity is that they can be held before the mind for an indefinite time, and contemplated without changing; the places of flight are filled with thoughts of relations, static and dynamic, that for the most part obtain between the matters contemplated in the periods of comparative rest. *Let us call the resting-places the 'substantive parts,' and the places of flight the 'transitive parts,' of the stream of thought.*" This greater stability and self-dependence of the unrelational experiences explains the difficulty of introspecting relational feelings. We are so full of interest in the colors which are

different, the sounds which are identical, or the emotions
which are alike, that feelings of difference, identity and
likeness are, as James says,[1] quite eclipsed and swallowed
up in the color, sound or emotion.   On the other hand, if
we lose consciousness of the feelings to which the relational element belongs, this must vanish with them; as there
is no such thing as likeness which is not the likeness of
something to something else.   "Let any one," James says,
"try to cut a thought across in the middle and get a look
at its section, and he will see how difficult the introspective
observation of the transitive tracts is.   The rush of the
thought is so headlong that it almost always brings us up
at the conclusion before we can arrest it.   Or, if our purpose is nimble enough and we do arrest it, it ceases forthwith to be itself.   As a snowflake crystal caught in the
warm hand is no longer a crystal but a drop, so, instead of
catching the feeling of relation moving to its term, we find
we have caught some substantive thing, usually the last
word we were pronouncing, statically taken, and with its
function, tendency and particular meaning in the sentence
quite evaporated."

Spencer's term, 'relational feeling,' has been adopted
in this book, in place of the equivalent expression,
'transitive feeling,' usually employed by James, because
the term 'transitive' is based merely on the supposedly
short duration and the temporally midway position of
the conscious state and its brain process.   This overlooks the possibility that one may be simultaneously
conscious of relational feeling and of its terms, as
when, in an indivisible moment, one is conscious of
the present recognized percept and its likeness to past
experience.   The essential feature is neither the duration nor the position of the relational element, but the
fact that the relational element is recognized as 'belonging' to others, as occurring only in connection with them.

[1] *Op. cit.*, Vol. I., p. 244.

The relational element, it should be noted, occurs not only with emotional and affective elements, but also in connection with other relational experiences. We may be conscious, for example, of the likeness of the feeling of familiarity with that of sameness.

There certainly are no specific forms of physical energy which correspond with the relational feelings of 'like,' 'whole,' 'more' and the rest. For every known kind, degree and amount of physical force conditions a sensational experience which may occur without relational feeling, or which, on the other hand, may be accompanied by any one of many relational feelings. The physical phenomenon cannot, therefore, be considered the condition of the relational feeling.

As there are no external physical stimuli, so also there are no end-organs of relational elements. The physiological changes which condition them must, therefore, lie within the brain. These conditions are not definitely known, but two hypotheses may be advanced. The relational elements may be conditioned not by nerve-cell activity, but by the excitation of so-called 'association-fibres' connecting different brain areas with each other. This is the theory suggested by James. It must be supplemented, if Flechsig's results are accepted, by the theory that the excitation, not only of the nerve-fibres, but of the nerve-cells, in the association-centres [1] is a condition of the 'relational' experience. The brain condition of the relational element differs, on this view, from that of the sensational consciousness, in that the latter involves the excitation of ingoing fibres and of cells in the 'sensory' centres of the brain in which these fibres terminate; whereas the former demands the excitation of connecting fibres and of cells in the association-centres, which are not directly connected with outside bodily organs.

[1] Cf. Appendix, Section III, p. 459.

To recapitulate : we find that we have experiences which
are not wholly reducible to sensational and affective elements.   We thus establish the existence, in our consciousness, of relational elements.   These relational elements
(1) are not invariably present, and they seem to 'belong
to' other elements or ideas with which they occur.   They
are (2) physiologically conditioned by excitation of connecting fibres and probably also of association-centre cells.
They have (3) no specific physical condition.

CHAPTER XI

ATTENTION

THIS chapter discusses a difficult problem, and we find ourselves, as we approach it, in immediate perplexity, a prey not merely to conflicting theories, but to doubts and indecisions of our own. Our problem concerns the nature of attention and of the idea attended-to. Psychologists who consider consciousness as the experience of a self use the former term; those who regard consciousness as a mere series of ideas should use the latter or one of its equivalents; we, who admit the validity of both conceptions,[1] shall shift our point of view, with the idiomatic turns of the English tongue, and shall speak now of attention and again of the idea as attended-to. The term 'attention' is a psychological synonym of the expression 'interest.' To be attended-to means precisely to be interesting. The common theory, that uninteresting things may be attended-to, is therefore, in the opinion of the writer, entirely erroneous. Things which are naturally uninteresting, such as dull books or difficult problems, may, it is true, be attended-to, but they grow interesting in the process; for being interested and attending are one and the same experience. Naturally uninteresting topics do usually, it is true, lose their temporary, acquired interest, but this happens only in so far as they become unattended-to.[2]

In a strict and limited sense, the attended-to or interesting is a relational experience, elemental or at least very simple. 'Clear' and 'vivid' are other synonyms of

[1] Cf. Chapter I., p. 6, and Chapter XII.
[2] Cf. Appendix, Section VII.

attended-to and interesting, in this narrow use of the terms.
The last paragraph of this chapter will indicate a broader
conception of interest, or attention.

An account of matters of general agreement shall intro-
duce our study. Psychologists teach that every sort of
conscious experience may be interesting or attended-to.
Pleasant and unpleasant things, beautiful and ugly objects,
varied and monotonous scenes alike may be attended-to.
The interesting experience always is, however, a narrow or limited part of the total experience of a given
moment. The darkness, the dull sounds and the faint
odors of the room are present to my consciousness but
uninteresting : only this one bit of experience, the flash of
light, is vivid or attended-to. This narrowness of the
fact attended-to is evidently a constant characteristic.
Not the entire scene spread out before me and stimulating my retina, but some one object, as the moving figure,
or the brightly colored cloud, not the complete harmony of
voices and instruments, but the liquid note of the harp or
the soaring tenor voice — are the 'attended-to' or interesting parts of my total consciousness. Experimental observation,[1] which has greatly concerned itself with this question,
has found that one can attend to a limited number only of
distinguishable impressions : to four or five visual impressions and to eight auditory impressions. In all these cases
the different impressions are realized as making up one
complex. From this limitation of the extent of an object
of attention, it follows that attention to one subject always
implies inattention to another. The 'absent-minded' person, who is blind and deaf to the sights and sounds of his
environment, is inattentive to them precisely because he is
attentive to something else, for example, to some imagined scene or some ideal project.

All psychologists are agreed, furthermore, in distinguishing two sorts of attention, passive and active, as they

[1] For experiment, cf. Titchener, § 38, Exp. 4, p. 113. Cf. also Titchener,
"Outline," 42; James, *op. cit.*, Vol. I., pp. 405 *seq.*

are usually named. These precise terms must be abandoned, for they have either a metaphysical meaning which plainly disqualifies them for psychology, or else they are applicable, not to psychical, but to purely physical, phenomena. The distinction which they indicate is, however, an actual one; it is that, namely, between (1) natural or primary, and (2) acquired or secondary attention. For example, brilliant colors, moving objects, sounds, even faint ones, in the stillness of the night and pleasant or unpleasant situations are naturally and primarily interesting or attended-to; but, on the other hand, monotonous percepts or images and relational ideas, such as ideas of difference or of causal connection, are secondarily, not naturally, interesting or vivid. We may classify these types of interest or attention as follows: —

    I. Natural or Primary Attention or Interest, in
       (*a*) The Unusual (including the Intense),
       (*b*) The Instinctively Interesting.

    II. Acquired or Secondary Attention.

Everybody will admit that a relational experience, the consciousness, for example, of likeness or of generality is secondarily and seldom, if ever, naturally interesting. Yet, not all sensational experiences are primarily interesting. Unusual things, however, including intense sense-stimuli, are always interesting, standing out in sharp contrast to their commonplace background. As we say, we cannot help attending to bright colors, loud sounds and intense odors.

Under the head of instinctively interesting experiences, we vaguely mass together all those whose vividness is unquestionably primary yet psychologically inexplicable. I know that the nest full of eggs is an 'utterly fascinating' object to the broody hen, that scarlet is hatefully interesting to bulls and entirely indifferent to sheep, that I cannot keep my eyes from the waves that are breaking on the shore, whereas my neighbors are tranquilly playing cards or making Battenberg lace. Biologically, I may assign a reason for each of these interests, but psychologically, from my own introspection or inference, they are inexplicable. The hen attends to the eggs, the bull to the scarlet parasol, I to the beating waves — because we must; we are interested — because we are interested! One is either veiling one's ignorance by a word, or else one is appealing to biology, when one names these interests instinctive.

The existence of acquired interests attests, it should be added, the capacity for intellectual development. For education is a widening as well as a deepening of one's interests; it not only lays emphasis upon the natural and instinctive interests, but creates new interests as well, supplementing the primary attention to glowing colors, loud sounds and instinctively attractive objects by acquired interests in likeness, contrasts and causes.

We are ready now to discuss the nature of attention, in its primary meaning of clearness or vividness. We have already defined it as a relational experience, elemental or very simple. Whatever the stage of attention, natural or acquired, and whatever the object of attention, flash of light or Greek word or nebular hypothesis, the attended-to experience includes a certain attribute of clearness which simply does not belong to the unattended-to or uninteresting. The presence of such a feeling of clearness becomes evident, if we compare a moment of attention with the dazed and sleepy consciousness of the barely wakened moments.[1] The attentive or interested consciousness of lights, sounds and odors differs, on this view, from the sleepy consciousness in that it contains this distinct element, 'vividness' or 'clearness,' radically different from sensational and affective elements of consciousness.

Another way of bringing out the relational nature of

---

[1] Cf. James, *op. cit.*, Vol. I., p. 404, for mere suggestion of this contrast. For experiment, cf. Titchener, *Laboratory Manual*, Exp. 1, p. 110.

clearness is the negative method of considering different accounts of this attention-feeling. Some psychologists have suggested that attention is virtually another name for affection: the interesting, or attended-to, is that which is either pleasant or unpleasant; inattention is mere indifference; the apparently indifferent object which is attended-to is really, for the moment, faintly pleasant or unpleasant; and this affective tone is its interestingness.[1] The chief objection to this theory is the introspective discovery that we do sometimes attend to experiences which are not affectively toned, in other words, that psychic facts, neither pleasant nor unpleasant, are nevertheless vivid. The most striking illustrations of this fact are found within the circle of our habitual experiences. A well-known phrase, however insignificant, will catch the attention in a context of far greater emotional value, and an æsthetically indifferent face, if familiar, may be attended-to. Most, if not all, primarily interesting experiences are pleasant or unpleasant, whereas many acquired interests are indifferent. The arithmetic lesson, the list of prepositions and the butcher's book, which were utterly uninteresting, may become the objects of attentive study and still remain indifferent.

It is fair then to conclude that clearness, or attention in the narrow sense, is not identical with pleasantness or unpleasantness, that is to say, that it is no affective experience. We have next to show that clearness is not sensational. It has sometimes been confounded with sense-intensity, but the two are utterly unlike. As Münsterberg says,[2] "The vivid impression of a weak sound and the faint impression of a strong sound are in no way interchangeable. . . . The white impression when it loses vividness does not become gray, and finally black, nor the large size small, nor the hot lukewarm." But though a faint im-

---

[1] Cf. Titchener, "Primer," § 33. Titchener, however, in other passages suggests a view of attention as clearness — resulting in motor accompaniments, permanence, etc. — which is somewhat like that of this book. Cf. "Outline," § 38; "Experimental Psychology, Qualitative, Student's Manual," § 38, p. 109.
[2] "Psychology and Life," p. 86.

pression does not gain in intensity, it may gain in interest, that is it may be better attended-to. The truth is, therefore, that both intense and dull experiences are attended-to; and this shows that intensity is not identical with clearness, that is, with elemental attention. By a parallel argument it may be shown that clearness, in this sense of interest, and visual clearness of outline are not identical, for we may attend to very vaguely outlined and indistinct objects, for example, to shadowy figures on a dark night.

Of course it is none the less true that objects of attention are very often intense and clear in outline. Indeed, the intensity and visual distinctness are, in a way, the results of the relational clearness or attention. For example, we change the accommodation of our eyes in order to obtain a distincter outline of the object which interests us, and we turn our heads that the music to which we are attending may seem louder. Even a faint experience, therefore, has, if attended-to, the greatest intensity possible. These motor results or accompaniments are often known as marks of attention.

Still another result of the clearness of an experience is its relatively long duration. We make bodily movements to prolong it, if it is a sense-experience — for example, we follow a moving light with our eyes; and, whatever its nature, it has a tendency to persist in the memory. To say that interest or attention is relatively prolonged contradicts, we must admit, the constant assertion of psychologists, that the duration of attention is limited.[1] Now it is true that a sensational impression retains its intensity for no more than five or six seconds.[2] The fixated object grows alternately bright and dull, and the sound to which we listen is now loud and again soft. But these phenomena, classed as fluctuations of attention, are really only fluctuations in sensational intensity, due to the periodic exhaustion of the functioning brain-cells; and sense-inten-

[1] Cf., for example, James, *op. cit.*, Vol. I., p. 420; Titchener, "Outline," § 41.　　[2] Cf. Titchener, "Primer," § 36.

sity differs utterly, as we have seen, from clearness, the attention-element.

We have thus distinguished, first, the attention-element, clearness, second, the narrowness of the experience to which this element attaches itself, and third, two results of the clearness: the relative intensity, and the relatively long duration of the clear or attended-to experience. There are two more important results of the clearness of an experience. An idea which is clear, or attended-to, does not merely persist in consciousness immediately after it occurs, but it is likely to be recalled again and again. It is, furthermore, peculiarly suggestive both of sensational facts and of relational experience. As suggestive of relational experiences, one says that the interesting object is "thought about." This suggestiveness, of whatever type, distinguishes the interesting from the uninteresting experience. It should be noticed that these results of the clearness of an experience, its aptness to be recalled and its suggestiveness, differ from the results first mentioned, in that they cannot be fully realized till long after the moment of attention.

It may be worth while to verify this description of attention with its accompaniments and results, by the study of a typical instance of each sort of attention. Suppose, in the first place, that one attends to an electric light in a dark room. This is evidently a case of primitive or natural attention. It involves, first of all, the attention-feeling of clearness or distinctness. This feeling, furthermore, attaches only to a limited part of the total object of consciousness. The idea attended-to has in itself sense-intensity, but, more than this, if the light is stationary, the impression has the clearness of outline due to good fixation, and if it swings to and fro, the impression is relatively prolonged, for one follows the light with one's eyes. Undoubtedly, this experience is more likely to be recalled than the other parts of the room-idea, for example the consciousness of the darkness,

the faint sounds, and the odors.   The idea as attended-to
is, finally, suggestive both of sensational facts — for example, of a locomotive headlight or of the moon — and of
relational experience, as when one thinks of the electric
light as *unlike* a gas jet, or as *caused by* the contact of a car-
bon filament with an electrically charged platinum wire.

We may now proceed to analyze a vivid fact of the other
type, that is, an instance of acquired or secondary attention.
Let us suppose the case of a little schoolboy who attends
to a page of his spelling book.   His consciousness of the
printed words has, in the first place, the attention-feeling of
relational clearness; and this feeling is evidently combined
with a limited part only, the printed page, out of the rich
total of sound and color and movement within the schoolroom.   The word-images have not, of course, any sense-
intensity, but they do possess the visual distinctness due
to good fixation; not until he grows inattentive does the
page grow blurred and dim before his eyes.   The sight of
the page is, moreover, prolonged, not only because the boy
follows the words from left to right with his eye-movements, and because he checks the movements of his head
and eyes in other directions, but because he has after-images
of the words, as he closes his eyes, and because the words
persist in his memory.   The later results of clearness are
as easily discovered, in this instance of attention and its
consequents.   The words of this spelling lesson, so far as
they have been attended-to, will, in the first place, be recalled when the ten thousand other impressions of the
moment, the buzzing of the flies, the singsong recitations
and the teacher's shell comb, have been eternally forgotten.
The words of the spelling lesson are, furthermore, richly
suggestive, both of the concrete objects which they describe, and of other words with which they are compared
and related.

To complete the verification of our definition, let us
finally consider the case in which the secondarily attended-
to fact is an image, not a percept.   Our schoolboy, grown

in years and in discretion, is attending, let us say, to an imagined triangle in demonstration of Euklid's fifth proposition. The experience, of course, includes the attention-feeling of clearness, and the idea, of which this is a part, is a limited portion of the boy's total consciousness, a mere speck upon a variegated background of colored, sounding, fragrant objects to which he has learned to be inattentive. The outline of the imagined triangle may be visually indistinct, but if the boy has a strong visual imagination, or if he closes his eyes and stops his ears to shut out conflicting sensations, the outline is likely to be distinct. (Of course the adjustment of eye-muscles, so important in securing visual distinctness, is lacking, yet there are certain motor accompaniments of secondary attention, both inhibitory movements, such as closing the eyes and stopping the ears, and an upward movement of the scalp, first described by Fechner, but verifiable by almost anybody.[1]) The imaged triangle is evidently, in the second place, prolonged, not through any motions of eye or head or hand, but through the persistence of the image. The attentive schoolboy keeps on thinking of his triangle; the image of it is no mere fleeting shape in a kaleidoscopic shifting of scenes, but an object of consciousness which is relatively stable and fixed. This continuance of the image is, in fact, the most obvious characteristic of secondary attention. To hold the thought to a given subject is the great problem of acquired attention, and the wandering mind and roving thought are justly become synonyms of inattention. Evidently, therefore, the imaged triangle is a clear, narrow, and prolonged fact of consciousness. The fact that it is also readily recalled and suggestive, both of mere images and of thoughts, is too obvious for further comment.

We have, up to this point, regarded attention as a simple relational experience, that of clearness, with certain signifi-

---

[1] Cf. James, *op. cit.*, Vol. I., pp. 435 *seq.*

L

cant results, first, relative intensity and duration, and second, 'revivability' and suggestiveness. It is, however, important to add that the term 'attention' is often used, in a very broad way, to cover not only the attention-feeling, clearness, but the characteristic results and accompaniments of the feeling. This widening of the term is due, of course, to the great significance in practical life of the results, especially the remote results, of 'attention' in its narrow sense. Practical interests almost always dominate discussions of attention, and from the practical point of view attention certainly is significant, not for what it is in itself, but because it is followed by memory and thought; in other words, it is distinguished for its effect on the later life.

BOOK I

PART II

CONCRETE CONSCIOUS EXPERIENCES

PART II

CHAPTER XII

CONCRETE CONSCIOUS EXPERIENCES

THE analysis of consciousness into its barest elements is a highly artificial process, undertaken merely for the scientific purpose of exhaustively enumerating the fundamental features of the psychic experience. There could be, however, no more hopeless error than the supposition that this enumeration completes the account of the conscious life. On the contrary, consciousness, as we ordinarily know it, is significant, not for its simplicity, but for its complexity, its richness, its confusion; and it is only, as we have seen, by an effort that we 'tease out' of it, with the psychological scalpel of attentive introspection, the minute fibres of which it is interwoven. We have now, however, concluded this 'post mortem' study, as James calls it, of those 'artificial abstractions,' the structural elements of consciousness, and we turn, therefore, to the consideration of our "entire conscious states as they are concretely given to us."

We shall study these concrete experiences from two points of view. In the first place, we shall regard each one of them without reference to any self, as an idea, a fact of consciousness, occurring in a series of ideas. We shall next, however, consider each experience as relation of a self to other selves, and shall distinguish it from different forms of consciousness by the nature of this relation.

I

Every conscious experience, in the first place, may be considered without explicit reference to any self, as an

149

idea, a content-of-consciousness, a percept, emotion or volition, belonging to a shifting series of ideas. When we study psychology solely from this point of view, we isolate the experiences from the self who has them, somewhat as a botanist may pick a leaf and examine it under his microscope, without, at the moment, considering the branch or tree from which he has picked it. I study a percept, for instance, or a memory, without laying any stress on the fact that it is my experience. I analyze it with as impersonal an attitude as that with which the chemist heats his potassium chlorate that it may give off oxygen.

Scientific acquaintance with an idea, thus defined, includes two factors: first, the complete analysis into the structural elements, sensational, attributive and relational, of which it is composed; second, the explanation of the fact by connecting it with some preceding fact, psychical or physiological. My image, for instance, of Rossetti's great picture, "Dante's Dream," is analyzed into structural elements of rich color and graceful form; and is explained in two ways: by connecting it with my immediately preceding percept of a red-bound copy of Dante's "Vita Nuova," and also by referring it to the excitation of nerve-cells and connecting fibres in the visual brain-centres.

At this point it will be well to call attention to the use, in this book, of certain common expressions. The word 'idea' is applied to any complex experience regarded as one term in a succession. The word 'feeling' is used, in a very general way, of any conscious experience; it may, therefore, be applied both to the complex idea and to the simple element of consciousness.[1]

II

The conception of consciousness as a mere series of ideas connected with each other is a perfectly consistent doctrine of the widest application. There is no founda-

---

[1] Cf. James, *op. cit.*, Vol. I., pp. 185–186.

tion for the opinion, sometimes expressed, that only percepts and images may be regarded from this point of view.
On the contrary, every conscious experience, emotion, and
volition, as well as percept and image, may be looked at as
an 'idea,' that is, a member of an idea-series, without any
reference at all to any self. Yet such a treatment of conscious experience loses sight of the truth that every idea
is, after all, the experience of a self who is conscious.
Even when, as students of the mere idea, we have neglected
the self and taken no notice of it, yet all the time we have
been dimly conscious of it as underlying all our feelings.
In other words, we have realized that a perception, an
imagination or an emotion does not exist independently,
but that it is my perception, your imagination or his emotion. As James says:[1] "Every 'state' or 'thought' is
part of a personal consciousness. . . . In this lecture-
room, . . . there are a multitude of thoughts, yours and
mine. . . . They are as little each-for-itself and recipro-
cally independent as they are all-belonging-together. . . .
My thought belongs with my other thoughts, and your
thought with your other thoughts. The only states of
consciousness that we naturally deal with are found in
personal consciousnesses, . . . selves, concrete particular
I's and you's." This means that besides realizing my
conscious experiences, or feelings, I am also conscious
of my conscious self, as in a sense including, but not as
identical with, the perceptions, the emotions or the thoughts
of any given moment.

What, now, is this intimate consciousness of self which
underlies and includes, though it does not consist in, the
moment-by-moment ideas and experiences? What, in
other words, do I mean by the 'I' which is conscious or
has experiences? The effort to answer this question discloses the fact that, with the exception of the analysis into
structural elements, the only description of self-conscious-

[1] " Briefer Psychology," p. 153.

ness is, first, as consciousness of myself contrasted with
other selves, and second, as consciousness of my varying
relations or attitudes to these other selves.

We have thus made the important discovery of the essentially social nature of the self. The self underlying the
conscious experiences, which we have been studying, is not
a single, lonely self, but a self related to a group of selves.
Every self is, in other words, a social self, that is, a self
in inextricable relation with many other selves,

> "a chain of linked thought,
> Of love and might to be divided not."

I, who read this paragraph, for instance, simply cannot
be conscious of my own self except as related in the most
varying ways to a vast number of other people. Let one
try to drop out of the consciousness of oneself the realization, however vague, of some or all of these relations, the
consciousness that one is son, brother, member of a fra-
ternity, student at a university, citizen of the United
States: such an imagined elimination of the consciousness of his social relationships leaves a man, in truth, with
nothing which he can recognize as himself.

Our study of psychology has, in fact, proceeded so far
as a sort of play of Hamlet with Hamlet left out. We
are now at last calling this neglected hero, the self, before
the footlights. But, behold, our leading character will not
appear alone, but comes before the curtain leading his
company after him. For our Hamlet is no solitary figure;
he is the lover of Ophelia, the friend of Laertes, the son of
the murdered king. Take away these related persons
and Hamlet also has disappeared with them; some other
man, but no longer precisely this Hamlet, is left. In the
same way, the self of the psychologist is always a related
self.

The discovery of the social nature of the self at once
discloses to us two fundamental phases of self-conscious-

ness, an egoistic, imperious phase which lays emphasis upon the 'central, everyday self' or 'myself,' and an altruistic, adoptive phase, an emphasis upon the other self, the you, not the me. It is true, as we have seen, that the one implies the other, just as the north-pointing pole of a magnet is connected with the south-pointing pole; but it is also true that one's conscious experience may lay special stress upon the narrower, central self, or may be specially concerned with the other, the related self.

These terms, 'egoistic' and 'altruistic,' are, of course, to be interpreted in a strictly psychological, not in an ethical, sense. We are apt to confuse 'egoistic' with 'selfish' and 'altruistic' with 'unselfish,' and so to regard the one as wrong, the other as right. As psychologists, however, we have no business at all to make these distinctions, and in saying that consciousness is fundamentally egoistic or altruistic, we mean only that we emphasize either ourselves or the not-ourselves, of our experience. When I hand the morning paper, unopened, to my father, I am subordinating myself to him; when I send out the chops because they are underdone, I am laying stress on my own desires; even if I only listen idly to the violin practice in the music room, I realize it as a fact of common experience; and if I resent it, for the unbearable squeak of the bow on the strings, I am setting myself against it. Always, if I am conscious at all, I am asserting with special emphasis either myself and my concerns, or the relatively-other-than-myself.

There are other important distinctions, we shall find, between the typical forms of consciousness, regarded as the experience of related selves. We shall consider only two, postponing to the chapters which follow a detailed account of them. Experiences may be contrasted as they refer to unparticularized other selves, that is, to any or all selves, or as they refer to definite and particular selves. In perceiving, for instance, I am vaguely conscious that other people might see what I am seeing, but in hating I do not hate anybody in general, but some very special and definite person or persons. Conscious experiences are often also characterized as relatively 'passive' or 'active.' Perception and will are examples of the two extremes of this distinction, which will later be more carefully considered.

It might not be unreasonable to speak of the egoistic and altruistic, the particularizing and generalizing, and the passive and active phases of consciousness, as its elements. The term 'element' is, however, almost always used of what we have called the structural elements, sensational, attributive, and relational. It is wisest, therefore, not to extend the application of the term.

III

If now we compare these ways of looking at a psychic fact, we find two main contrasts. The study of consciousness as experience of a related self takes account of certain facts with which the study of ideas is not concerned ; these facts are, first, the self which 'has' ideas, or is conscious, and second, the relations of this self to other selves and to ideas. On the other hand, the study of ideas, disassociated from conscious selves, is distinguished by a method which is not applicable to the other forms of psychology. For ideas are, by hypothesis, psychic events, which are distinct yet closely linked together. Now, to look at experience as a mere series of psychic events enables us to study it causally, that is, to consider an event of one moment as necessarily connected with that of the preceding and with that of the following moment. A psychology which considers only psychic events or consciousnesses is, therefore, a causal science ; whereas psychology, in so far as it studies selves in their relations, does not treat its facts as causally related to each other, because, strictly speaking, only phenomena in time are causally connected, and selves are, to say the least, not primarily regarded as realities in time. Anybody may verify this by his introspection. One thinks of one's body as beginning and ending at distinct moments; one thinks of one's ideas and feelings as occurring yesterday or to-day — at quarter of twelve or at half-past three; but one does not primarily regard oneself as 'in time,' and one, therefore, does not think of selves in causal relations to each other. They are related, of course, by virtue of the imperiousness, the demands, the acknowledgments, and the adoptions which make up, as we have seen, the very nature of a self; but these relations are not the causal ones which connect ideas.[1]

But though these conceptions of consciousness are so distinct, they have yet a common ground. Whether one regard a given thought or emotion as idea, without reference to a self, or as a conscious relation of one self to another, in either case one looks upon it as a complex consciousness analyzable into structural elements, sensational, attributive or relational. This has already been shown in the case of the mere idea, which is indeed definable only by analysis into its elements. But the structural element is as truly a factor of the personal consciousness: emotion is a happy or an unhappy relation between selves; perception is a consciousness of sensational experiences in common with other selves. In a word, every structural element may be regarded either as one part of an idea, or as one way in which a self is conscious.

Each of the following chapters, therefore, which discusses a distinct and concrete conscious experience, will first consider it briefly as idea, and will next describe it as personal attitude, but will ordinarily devote most space to the discussion of the experience from the common point of view, as complex of structural elements.

It is only fair to observe, finally, that some writers deny the right of the science of selves to the name 'psychology.'

---

[1] Cf. Münsterberg, "Psychology and Life," pp. 210 *seq.*; Grundzüge, S. 117.

Such a study of the nature of selves is philosophy, they say, or else it is sociology, but it has no part nor lot in psychological science. We shall here reply briefly to the first of these objections, leaving to a later chapter [1] the distinction of the psychology of selves from sociology and from ethics. A reference to our introductory chapter will remind us that we defined philosophy as the study of the self-dependent, inclusive whole of reality, or of limited facts of reality in their relation to this whole. On the other hand, we defined science as a study of facts or phenomena, that is, of limited bits of reality, taken for granted without investigation of their relation to the whole of reality. Now it is certain that consciousnesses, or ideas, regarded without reference to a conscious self, may form the material of a scientific psychology; and some psychologists have limited the science to the study of these momentary contents of consciousness, not regarded as the experiences of a self. But it is equally evident, in the opinion of the writer, that selves also may be treated as facts or phenomena, because they are certainly taken for granted by everyday people, without inquiry about their relation to ' reality.' The most ordinary division of our experience is indeed into the two classes 'selves' and ' things'; and everybody, whether or not he speculates on the ultimate nature of selves, assumes their existence and compares them with each other. Selves, in other words, though they may be objects of philosophical study, are not merely the concern of the philosopher, but form also an important class of phenomena. As such, they may both be observed from an uncritical, everyday standpoint, and systematically compared and classified from the point of view of the scientist.

[1] Cf. Chapter XXIII., pages 333 and 346.

CHAPTER XIII

FORMS OF SYNTHESIS: FUSION AND ASSOCIATION

A GENERAL problem still remains for discussion before we turn to our detailed study of the concrete conscious experiences. This problem concerns the nature of psychic synthesis or connection. There are two entirely different ways of regarding synthesis in psychology. It may be subjectively or introspectively considered as a peculiar psychic fact, an immediately observed content of consciousness. As such, it is, as we have seen, a relational and probably elemental experience — what we have called the 'feeling of connection' and what James calls the 'feeling of *and.*' This consciousness of connection is prominent, as will later appear, in judgments and in general notions, because the feeling of a connection is precisely what gives these experiences their essential character; in such complex contents as simple percepts, emotions and images, on the other hand, the feeling of connection is 'swamped' in sensational and affective elements.

But there is another, an 'objective' sense as it were, in which we may treat of synthesis in psychology. Every science, and therefore psychology, assumes facts of two sorts: substantive facts — or facts in the ordinary sense — and connections. Chemistry, for example, deals with elements and their combination, and physics treats of forces and their composition. This composition, connection or synthesis need not be metaphysically explained, but may be taken for granted by chemistry, by physics and by psychology also. In this sense, the connection is not a peculiarly psychic phenomenon, but is a general fact, common to every science. Connection, moreover, thus

regarded, is not immediately realized, but is reflectively
' known about ' the connected facts of consciousness. The
types of combination, thus objectively regarded, of elements and complexes of consciousness, form the topic of
the present chapter.

The first of these is fusion, the synthesis of peripherally
excited, conscious elements. The combination, for example,
of the C and G, the loudness and the volume of a given
chord, is a case of fusion ; and so is the combination of the
feelings of redness, yellowness, colorless light, brightness,
bigness, odor, coolness, pressure from joint and skin
stimulation and pleasure, from an orange which one is
rolling about in one's hand. The distinguishing characteristic of the fusion is physiological : each one of the
combined or fused elements must be directly excited by
the stimulation of an end-organ, and not merely indirectly
excited through the stimulation, by connecting fibres, of the
corresponding brain-centres. Evidently, therefore, fusion
is the exact psychic counterpart of the connection between
the physical stimulations to the end-organs. Nevertheless,
great care must be exercised not to confuse the psychical
with the physical combination. For, though the two may
correspond exactly, they may also be distinct. For example, a combination of ether vibrations of all wave-lengths is
the condition, not of a complex, but of a simple psychic
phenomenon, the sensational element of colorless light.

Fusions differ from each other only in the degree of
closeness with which the diverse elements are connected,
and this is tested by the difficulty of the analysis in different cases. The closest fusions which we know are those
of the different elements invariably connected in a sensation, the quality, intensity and extensity. Almost, if not
quite, as close as this fusion is that of a color with the colorless light : this is the closest combination which we know
of different qualities. Other examples are the fusion of
taste and smell in many so-called tastes, of pressure and a
feeling of temperature in what is named touch, and of the

consciousness of extensity and pressure in the experience of smoothness or of roughness.

The study of clangs [1] affords an illuminating instance of the fact that ability to analyze a fusion of elements may depend on training as well as on individual capacity. By a clang, we mean a combination of tones produced by atmosphere vibrations of two different rates. All musical instruments, for example, produce clangs, and not simple tones, because all vibrating bodies, such as masses of air, strings and metal rods, vibrate not merely as wholes but also in sections. Now this complexity of vibration invariably conditions, even in the untrained observer, the consciousness of what is called the characteristic timbre of the tone — the element which we have named its volume or bigness. The trained observer can furthermore distinguish, even within the simplest clang, different tones, the fundamental and the overtone. The easiest way of proving this is to strike a piano key, middle C, for instance, at the same time very gently pressing the key which corresponds with one of its overtones — say, the octave, C, or the major fifth, G. In this way, the damper will be removed from the wire of this higher key, yet the wire will not be directly struck. If now the key of the fundamental, C, be released, this tone, C, will no longer be heard but the overtone, G, will be heard by itself; and this shows that atmospheric vibrations corresponding to it must have set its wire vibrating, when the key of the fundamental was struck. Experiments with strings, which vibrate in sections, lead to the same result. In fact, by practice, almost any one can train himself to analyze the fusion of tones in a simple clang as well as in a chord.

Association, the second form of synthesis, demands more detailed consideration. It is the connection of elements or complexes of consciousness, occurring simultaneously or

---

[1] For experiment, cf. Sanford, 87 a and 88; Titchener, § 45.

successively, of which at least one (in successive association, the second) must be centrally excited. Here are
plainly three distinctions between fusion and association:
the connected factors may be complexes as well as elements; they may be successive as well as simultaneous;
and at least one (the second if there is a temporal difference) must occur without peripheral stimulation. This
last distinction is evidently the essential one.

The following table summarizes all these forms:—

PSYCHIC SYNTHESIS[1]

I. Fusion (of peripherally excited elements).
II. Association (of terms, one or both of which are centrally excited).
   a. Simultaneous.
     1. Assimilation (of elements).
     2. Complex simultaneous association.
   b. Successive.

The simplest form of simultaneous association, assimilation or the connection between elements, closely resembles
fusion. Every image and almost every percept affords an
example of it. As I look at a rose or a bronze or a fur
rug, I get, besides color and form, in each case, a distinct
impression of texture. This, of course, is without stimulation of end-organs of pressure, and is thus a centrally excited
and simultaneously associated or 'assimilated' sensation.
The more complex form of simultaneous association is
usually due to the persistence of a successive association;
and to the study of this form of combination we must therefore turn.

There is no more significant attribute of our mental life,
regarded as a series of ideas, than the swift succession of
percepts, images and emotions of which it is made up.
Homer's phrase, 'swift as thought,' is no mere figure of
speech, and we may well say of our ideas, what Shakespeare
says of our minutes:—

[1] Cf. Bibliography.

"Like as the waves make towards the pebbled shore
  So do our minutes hasten to their end;
  Each changing place with that which goes before,
  In sequent toil all forwards do contend."

But between these swiftly succeeding facts of consciousness we nevertheless observe, as we look back upon them, links and bonds of connection. I wake up from a revery to find myself leagues distant from my remembered starting-point, yet I am able to retrace my way, step by step, and I may find each idea 'associated' with the preceding. Not every observed succession, to be sure, is an association. I look out, for example, from the window of an English railway carriage, and one object of consciousness follows in quick succession upon another: railway station, hidden under its thatch of advertisements, green meadows divided by holly hedges, flocks of plump sheep, stone towers rising from a mass of trees. But I do not think of these as associated ideas, for they all occur through peripheral stimulation of the retinal processes. Suppose, however, that the sight of the stone towers is followed by the following series of images: Rugby Chapel (an image of words on a page) — "The chapel walls in whose bound, Thou, my father! art laid" (an image of the words as spoken) — Matthew Arnold (an image of him as he reads the poem). Here we have, between each of these images and that which precedes it, a case of association, since no one of them is peripherally excited by an object which is present.

This example shows us also another way, besides the physiological one, in which we account for cases of association. We refer them to the connection, in actual past experience, of certain contents of consciousness with which we assume that the present contents are identical. The sight of Rugby Chapel, for example, is associated with the image of Matthew Arnold because I once heard him read the poem, "Rugby Chapel," that is, I once had simultaneously the visual percept of his figure and a visual image of the building. Similarly, the sight of a dog associates the

M

image of his owner because I have seen the two together; and the sound of the word 'stop' associates the image of its frequent companion-word 'thief.'   In all these cases, I know, of course, upon reflection, that my immediate facts of consciousness, the present percept of chapel or of dog or of the word 'stop,' and the present image of Arnold or of master or of the word 'thief,' are not actually identical with those past experiences, from which, on the contrary, they are separated by great stretches of time; but unquestionably I assume this identity of present with past facts of consciousness, and base upon it my explanation of the association.

The most important and obvious classes of association may best be described by the terms 'total' and 'partial.'[1] 'Total association' is that between complex facts of consciousness which are distinct and complete in themselves, ideas of things or of events.   It is an external and prosaic sort of association, evidently accounted for by the reference to past related objects of experience.   Most of our illustrations have been of this type; the association, one after another, of the notes of a melody, the words of a poem or the implements of a trade are other examples of this common form of association which may be readily symbolized by the following diagram : —

(Past percept or image of dog) with (Past percept or image of master)

$$X^n \text{———} Y^n$$

$$X \text{———} \longrightarrow y$$

(Present percept of dog)   (Present image of master)

In this diagram, the small letter (y) stands for 'centrally excited' and the capitals stand for 'either peripherally or centrally excited'; the arrow designates the fact and the direction of the association, and the line connecting X^n and Y^n indicates that the two experiences occurred either simultaneously or successively; the dividing line and the index both suggest that X^n and Y^n are past experiences.

[1] These terms were suggested by James. The expression 'total' must not, of course, be interpreted as if it required that the entire fact of consciousness

Partial association is the association of elements of consciousness or of groups of elements. Its most extreme case, which James aptly calls 'focalized association,' is the observed connection between one single element and another elemental or complex fact of consciousness. It is more varied in form and less obviously explained by reference to past related facts of consciousness, and must therefore be considered in more detail.

First of all, let us assure ourselves that the partial association is indeed accounted for by the assumed identity of its terms with past experiences, which were either simultaneous or successive. We may select, as an extreme instance, the association implied in these verses of Shelley:—

> "And the hyacinth, purple and white and blue,
>   Which flung from its bells a sweet peal anew
>   Of music, so delicate, soft and intense,
>   It was felt like an odor within the sense."

Now, it is in the highest degree improbable that Shelley had so often or so vividly experienced together the fragrance of hyacinths and the sound of bells that the one should suggest the other. At first sight, therefore, this seems to be a case of association, which cannot be accounted for by an assumed identity of the connected terms with past psychic phenomena occurring together. But on closer scrutiny we discover that the actual connection, for Shelley, between sound and fragrance, was the bell-shape of the flower. None of the other elements of the hyacinths, their color, their height, their texture, have any connection with the sweet peal of music. But this connecting link, the form of the flowers, is not associated with the image of sounding bells as a whole, for it is itself one element of this image; in fact the only association involved is that between (1) the element 'bell-shape,'

of a given moment should be associated with a following one. On the other hand, it covers cases in which the first term of the association is very limited in extent, in which, for example, the first term is a single word.

common to both the percept of the fragrant hyacinth and the image of the pealing bell, and (2) the remaining features of the bell as imaged, the auditory image of pitch, intensity and volume of tone, and the visual image of the color and form of the bell. This will be made clearer through the following diagram:—

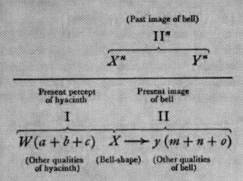

Here the Roman numerals, I. and II., represent the total, concrete facts of consciousness, the hyacinth-percept and the bell-image; X is the element common to both (the shape); y represents the group of imagined elements, pitch, intensity and the like (m, n and o), associated by X and forming with it the image of the pealing bell; whereas W groups together those elements, the color, height and so on (a, b and c) of the hyacinth percept, which have no part in the association. Comparing this, therefore, with the concrete associations, we find that it has the following distinguishing characteristics: first and foremost, (1) the starting-point of the association is a very narrow one, either a single element or — as we shall see — a group of elements, but never a concrete total. This first term (X) of the association is furthermore (2) a part both of the first and of the second of the successive, concrete ideas (the hyacinth percept, I., and the image of the bell, II.); and (3) the association, therefore, is entirely within the second of these ideas, the image of the bell. It follows

(4) that only this second one (II) of the concrete, conscious totals need be regarded as identical with any former experience; in the present case, for example, Shelley need never before have seen a hyacinth, but he must already have seen and heard a pealing bell, in order to have the association. Finally, (5) it is evident that, in cases of successive association, the first of the associated elements or groups of elements (X) necessarily persists in consciousness, whereas the elements combined with it in the earlier complex (I.) fade gradually away; and that the persisting element is then surrounded by the added elements (*m, n, o*) of the second concrete (II.). This persistence of the earlier fact of consciousness, though occurring in concrete association, is especially characteristic of the 'partial' type.

The connecting term of a partial association (the X) may include more than a single element. We have then an instance of what may be named 'multiple association.' When Shakespeare, for example, sings of love:—

"It is the star of every wandering bark,"

the star reminds him of love, not merely by the steadfastness of the 'ever fixed mark' but by the unapproachableness of that "whose worth's unknown although his height be taken." Or, to take a more prosaic illustration, if a football game on college grounds calls up an image of a Roman arena, the association is not between football game and Roman contest as total experiences, for I surely have not been conscious of them at one time or in immediate succession on each other. But neither does this association start from any single feature of the perceived game. Rather, a highly complex combination of elements (falling short, however, of a concrete total)—the amphitheatrical form of the grounds, the multitude of spectators, the straining forms of the young athletes—is common both to the perceived and to the imagined contest; and these images, common to both psychic facts, are associated with the other images, cerebrally excited, of Roman figures and costumes, which complete the consciousness of the gladiatorial contest. This is represented by the following diagram, which differs from the last, in that the X is a complex of the factors (c, d and e) already enumerated, which are common to percept and to image.

$$\overset{\displaystyle \mathrm{II''}}{\overbrace{\underset{X''}{\qquad\qquad}\quad\underset{Y''}{\qquad\qquad}}}$$

$$\overbrace{\underset{\mathrm{I}}{\qquad}\quad\underset{\mathrm{II}}{\qquad\qquad}}$$

$$W(a+b)\ X(c+d+e) \longrightarrow y(n+o)$$

It has thus been shown that the partial, like the total, association is accounted for by the assumed identity of associated facts of consciousness with earlier facts; but that these recurring facts, instead of being concrete wholes, are either elements or groups of elements, which have been combined in former percepts or images — of pealing bells and of Roman combat, for example. An association should always, therefore, be analytically studied. The important point is the determination of its first term, and the common error is the supposition that a complex content of consciousness is invariably to be taken as a whole in tracing the associative connection. On the other hand, as we have seen, all the subtler associations of our conscious experience are instances of association between more or less elemental parts of total conscious facts. Undoubtedly the greater number of associations in anybody's experience are of the total sort — associations between objects and their uses, between people and their names, and between the terms of verbal and motor series. But the associations which distinguish the imaginative from the prosaic type of mind, which are the essence of all metaphor and the very heart of humor, belong, all of them, to the ' partial ' type of association. No opposition is too fixed, no separation of time or place too wide, to be bridged by this sort of association.

We have, therefore, the following types of association : —

ASSOCIATION

(Successive or Simultaneous)

I. *Total* or *Concrete* Association, of complete ideas (with or without persistence of the first term).
II. *Partial* Association, of persisting elements of consciousness : —
    a. Multiple Association (starting from a large group of elements).
    b. Focalized Association (starting from a single element or from a small group of elements).

We have so far left untouched the practical questions: is it possible, in any sense, to determine the actual associations of one's conscious life ; is it possible to predict which one of the percepts or images of a given moment will form the starting-point of a train of associated images; and — given the starting-point — is it possible to determine what one of the numberless images, which might conceivably follow, will actually be associated? These questions, it will be observed, concern what may be named the associative suggestiveness and suggestibility of facts of consciousness. The most general answer to be made to them is this: psychic facts are both suggestive and likely to be suggested in proportion as they are interesting or attended-to ; and they are attended-to, in the main, because they are either (1) frequent or (2) recent in occurrence, or because they are (3) vivid, that is, instinctively attended-to or else rich in emotional elements.[1]

These distinctions, forming what are sometimes called the 'secondary laws' of association, may be readily illustrated from everyday experience. If the suggestive part of my percept of my desk is a battered old Liddell and Scott lexicon, this is because I consult the book so frequently; if, on the contrary, my train of images follows on the percept of a commonplace yellow pamphlet, this is perhaps because the pamphlet arrived by the last

[1] For experiments, cf. Titchener, § 52. Cf. M. W. Calkins, "Association."

mail; if, finally, a polished bit of brass or a little Veneti
water color is the suggestive part of the desk, it is assoc
tive because it is a vivid, an instinctively noticed, perce
The forms of associative suggestibility may be illustrat
in a parallel way. The lexicon may suggest the bo
table on which it commonly lies; or it may remind me
its precipitous fall, only yesterday, from desk to floor;
again it may suggest a verse of Homer or of Sophokl
an æsthetically vivid experience. It is fair to conclu
that the explanation of every definite instance of assoc
tion is through the application of one of these three pr
ciples, of frequency, recency, and — widest and vaguest
the classes — vividness. Experiment has shown the
expected importance of frequency among these, especia
as a corrective influence. Granted a sufficient number
repetitions, it seems possible to supplement, if not actua
to supplant, associations which have been formed throu
impressive or through recent experiences. This, of cour
is a fact of utmost pedagogical value, a justification of t
'line upon line and precept upon precept' method of repl
ing harmful or troublesome associations by helpful ones.

We have now to consider the physiological condition
association. In a general way, it may be described as t
excitation of a given brain-area through nervous impul
conveyed, by intra-cortical fibres, from another brain-ar
The larger these brain-areas, the more nearly 'total' is t
association; and the more continuous the cerebral exci
tion, the more persistent is the consciousness. It is a
natural that connecting fibres which have been frequen
or recently or strongly excited should offer little resistar
to the excitation; and in this probability we have the s
gestion of a physiological basis for the secondary laws
associative frequency, recency and vividness.

CHAPTER XIV

PERCEPTION

I

THE conscious experience of any given moment is, as we have seen, a complex of elemental feelings and may be regarded from one of two standpoints, either as experience of a self, or as one idea in a series of associated ideas. In this chapter, we shall first consider the percept, the psychic event or idea regarded without reference to any self; we shall next treat perceiving as a form of consciousness, realized as shared with other selves; and, finally, we shall discuss both percept and perceiving, mere idea and experience of a self, as complex forms of consciousness to be analyzed, classified and physiologically accounted for.

From the first of these points of view, perception means merely the occurrence of percepts. A percept is a complex idea or fact of consciousness, analyzable into elements, chiefly sensational; and of these elements some, as we shall see, are excited from without. Besides sensational elements, moreover, perception in all probability includes certain unemphasized relational elements. We shall try to justify this analysis in the second division of this chapter.

Perception, however, may be looked at in another way, not as mere succession of percepts, but as perceiving, a consciousness of experience shared with other selves. From this point of view, it is a personal attitude, not a mere idea, connected with other ideas. Perceiving, thus regarded, is, in the first place, recognized as in some sense a passive experience, and, in this aspect of it, is sharply distinguished from will and faith, our active personal attitudes. This means that we cannot help perceiving what we actually see

and hear. As Bishop Berkeley says, "When in broad day-
light I open my eyes, it is not in my power to choose
whether I shall see or no, . . . and so likewise as to hearing and the other senses." [1] That is to say, in bare perception, we do not impose conditions, but we accept and
acknowledge the independence and significance of what is
outside us.

This acknowledgment of something outside ourselves,
usually described as the consciousness of external things,
has long been admitted as the essential distinction of perception from imagination. It implies, in the first place,
that our perceiving consciousness is, or may be, shared by
other people than ourselves. At this moment, for instance,
I perceive lowering heavens, pouring rain, bare trees and
drenched sparrows, but I imagine wide horizons, brilliant
sky, blossoming apple trees and nesting orioles. The main
difference is this: in the one case, I assume that my experience is shared by other people, and that everybody who
looks out sees the same dreary landscape; but my imagination of the sunny orchard I regard as my private and
unshared experience.

It thus appears that even perception, the consciousness,
as we call it, of outer things, is a consciousness of other
selves as sharing our experience, a relatively altruistic, not
an exclusively egoistic, mode of consciousness. This is the
reason why we usually speak of sight and hearing and smell
as higher senses — and in the order named — than taste
and the dermal sense-experiences. Vision is the experience
most readily shared by any number of selves: for example,
everybody within a very wide area may see the mountain
on the horizon or the Milky Way in the evening sky. Next
to vision, sounds are the most frequently shared experiences; millions of people hear the same thunder, and thousands may share the same concert. Even odors, though
shared by fewer people, may be common to very many,

[1] "Principles of Human Knowledge," § 29.

whereas tastes and pressures and pains, which require actual bodily contact, and warmth and cold, whose physiological stimulation depends on conditions of the individual body, are far less invariably shared experiences. But the shared experiences are those that are described, discussed, repeated, measured, — in other words, those which are creatively reëmbodied in works of art and in scientific investigations. Vision, therefore, is a higher sense than the others, only in so far as it is more often shared, and hence more often discussed and described, measured and verified. This is the reason why it is a more significant social material of intercourse, art and science. Pressure and warmth, on the other hand, are less valued because they are less often actually shared and, therefore, less easily verified and less frequently described.

The fact that perception is common experience explains, also, why we always test the externality of things by inquiring whether other people have shared our consciousness of them. Am I really seeing this light or hearing this sound, I ask myself, or am I simply imagining it? And the test which I always apply is comparison with other people's experience. I must actually have perceived the table tipping, I say, because all these others felt it; I saw the ghost and did not conjure him up by my terrified imagination, for these others also saw him; I really feel the heat, for other people's cheeks are flushed. On the other hand, I admit that I imagined the bell and did not hear it, if everybody else remains unmoved; and I grant that the burglar is an imaginary one if none of these others heard his footfall. Professor Royce suggestively illustrates this from the development of our ideas about the rainbow. Primarily, the rainbow seems to me and to everybody as external or objective a phenomenon as the sky itself or the sun. When, however, I discover that my rainbow springs up from one point of the horizon and yours from a different point, and when I finally complete this observation and conclude that everybody sees a rainbow which is spatially a little different from every other, then my rainbow loses its externality, and is classified no longer as actual perception, but as illusion. Such a test of perception would never be applied, if perceiving did not mean to us the community of experience with other people — not with any special person, — but with any or all people.

There can, indeed, be no doubt that we all reflectively mean by perception, experience shared, actually or possibly, with any other selves. That is to say, looking back on our perception, and seeking to distinguish it from other forms of consciousness, we actually do define it in these terms. It is harder to decide whether, in the very moment of perceiving, we are immediately conscious of these other selves. The writer is inclined to the opinion that this is at least often true. We are walking, let us say, along a village street, looking idly about from stone-heap to passing carriage, gaunt telegraph pole and gabled house. We are not, to be sure, conscious of any particular person, yet we vaguely realize that this is a shared, a common, a public experience, not a private one, that the other people, actually or conceivably present, are seeing the same sights, house and carriage and stone-heap.

It should be carefully emphasized that this acknowledgment of other people, as sharing our experience, is not of necessity a conviction of their actual presence. Alone in my room, for instance, I none the less perceive, and do not merely imagine, crackling fire and book-shelves and lighted lamp, since I acknowledge, immediately or reflectively, that if others were present, they would share in what I see and hear. In other words, though the perceiver be actually alone, his experience is immediately realized or reflectively described as a social one.

But perception, the consciousness of externality, in the developed form in which we know it, includes not merely the altruistic consciousness of selves who share our experience, but a notion of something independent of consciousness and distinct from it. What is common to all selves

must be, it is argued, independent of any self. This conviction of something independent of ourselves need not,
however, be studied in detail, for it unquestionably is not
an immediate experience, but a later reflection, attained
in all probability by the effort to account for the fact of
common experience. From the standpoint, therefore, of
psychology as a study of selves in their relation, perception is the altruistic, passive experience shared by any
number of unparticularized other selves.

II

Perception, whether looked at as mere idea or as the
shared experience of a self, is in any case a complex fact
of consciousness. In other words, perception, like imagination, thought, emotion and volition, is no single element,
or even sensation, but a complex of elements; it is no
mere abstract awareness of blue or sweet, but a concrete
consciousness, for example, of 'blue gentian' or of 'sweet
apple.' The perception, therefore, must be further described by analysis into its parts. Now, all complex experiences are in one way 'sensational,' that is, all contain
sensational elements. No emotion is so lofty and no
thought so sublime that it does not include within itself a
sensational factor, a verbal image, for instance, or a core
of organic sensations. Certain complex experiences are,
however, so largely sensational, so nearly lacking in other
elements, that they may well be named sensational complexes. These are perceptions and imaginations, which
are, as everybody realizes, mainly composed of sensational
elements, of colors, tones, pressures and the like, among
which there doubtless lurk certain unemphasized relational
elements, both the attention-element, clearness, and a feeling of 'holding together,' or combination. My perception
of a lamp, for example, besides sensational elements of
color, shape, smoothness and warmth, probably contains a
vague feeling of the combination of these elements and of

their distinctness from all the rest which I see. It is,
however, very hard to observe these elusive relational elements, and they defy experimental verification.

Even the bare mention of these relational feelings suggests two important general problems. The first of these
is the question, How does the relational feeling of clearness come to be attached to particular portions of one's
sense-experience? At any moment of the normal waking
life, the retina, the basilar membrane of the ear and, in
truth, a great number of the bodily end-organs are simultaneously stimulated. The result is a rich sensational
complex, a mass of colors and sounds, of pressures, tastes
and odors. Primitively, as we have every reason to think,
this sensational mass is undiscriminated, a mere 'blooming buzz,' as James has called it. So Kaspar Hauser, who
was imprisoned for many years in a darkened room, could
not distinguish, when first he looked from his window, on
a sunshiny day, the village spires, the trees, the meadows
and the hills of the landscape before him, but saw only a
mass of color, so confused and indistinct that he compared
it, long afterward, to the colors as they are mixed on a
painter's palette. At our present stage of development,
on the other hand, a feeling of clearness is combined with
distinct groups of these elements, and we have different
percepts within the total complex: bird-notes and hand-
organ clangs in the mass of sounds; and trees, houses
and human figures within the mass of color and form.
Our questions are: how does this differentiation of complex perceptions within the total complex of consciousness
come about? Why, for example, does the feeling of distinctness attach to the limited complex of colors and forms
which make up the visual image of a rug on the floor,
instead of being combined with a greater complex of the
visual elements of my present experience.

In answer to these questions, we may point out, in the
first place, that elements like those contained within a
limited perception have often before occurred together,

with very varying accompaniments, whereas a sense complex, in its totality, is not like any preceding one. I have never, for example, experienced at Trafalgar Square precisely this moment's combination of people, carriages, street cries, horses' hoof-beats and city odors; but my percepts of the National Gallery, the Nelson Monument, the crowded Tottenham Court Road omnibus and the noisy newsboy crying the *Times* and *Chronicle* are, to all intents and purposes, exactly like many past percepts.

Professor Münsterberg has pointed out another way — the only way, as he and many psychologists hold — in which we come to distinguish perceptions within a total consciousness. Limited portions of our environment normally call out definite reactions; and an important reason for distinguishing different perceptions, as of man and horse and plant and bicycle, is that I shake hands with the man, seize the horse's reins, dodge the bicycle and pick the flower; in other words, I react in a definite way to each.

From both these points of view, it is comprehensible that percepts and images may vary greatly in extent. At this moment, for instance, I may either perceive my desk and all the things on it as a single object, or I may perceive watch, pen, paper, blotter, ink-bottle, package of letters and books. For though I have never before seen my desk in this particular degree and manner of disorder, yet there are certain constant features — mahogany color, 'rising-sun' carving, serpentine pigeon-holes, rows of books — similar to those of previous desk perceptions, and there is, furthermore, a relatively fixed reaction to the perception desk-as-a-whole, namely, the movement involved in beginning to write. My perception, on the other hand, may be of one of these objects only — say of my watch or of a letter scale — because I have often perceived this object, in various surroundings, and because it has always called out the same characteristic movement of my hand.

The second of the general considerations, suggested by the mention of the relational elements in perception, is the following: though a perception probably includes a certain feeling of combination, it is none the less true that we are only very vaguely conscious of the complexity of our perceptions. A reflectively analyzed perception is really, as we shall later see, a judgment; and a perception, in the strict sense of the term, does not appear to us as a combination of sharply distinguished elements or parts. I have, for example, an unanalyzed, unitary experience of the tree at which I chance to look or of the violin note which I hear. The perception of the tree is not, as immediately experienced, a complex idea, realized as containing the distinct ingredients, tallness, conical shape, dull green, spikiness, but it is just 'this tree,' and most of its elements are distinguished by reflection only; and the note is not primarily a recognized compound of high pitch, moderate loudness and scraping noise, but is a simple experience — analyzable, to be sure, but not necessarily or originally fully analyzed. Each perception of the tree and of the note is a unit of consciousness, and the discrimination of its elements is for practical, theoretical or æsthetic purposes. I notice the tree, for instance, in order to avoid it if I am a bicycler, or in order to classify it if I am a botanist, or in order to account for the charm of its outline if my interest is æsthetic. To quote from James,[1] who has laid special stress on the comparative simplicity of the percept: "To a child, the taste of lemonade comes at first as a simple quality. He later learns both that many stimuli and many nerves are involved in the exhibition of this taste to his mind, and he also learns to perceive separately the sourness, the coolness, the sweet, the lemon aroma, etc., and the several degrees of strength of each and all of these things, — the experience falling into a large number of aspects, each of which is abstracted, classed, named, etc., and all of which appear to be the elementary sensations into which the original 'lemonade flavor' is decomposed. It is argued from this that the

[1] "Principles," Vol. II., p. 2, note.

latter never was the simple thing which it seemed. I have already criticised this sort of reasoning. The mind of the child enjoying the simple lemonade flavor and that of the same child grown up and analyzing it are two entirely different conditions. Subjectively considered, the two states of mind are altogether distinct sorts of fact. The later mental state says 'this is the *same flavor (or fluid)* which that earlier state perceived as simple,' but that does not make the two states themselves identical. It is nothing but a case of learning more and more *about* the same topics of discourse or things."

This is, in truth, a highly important, though a negative, characteristic of the conscious complex. Because it has been overlooked, two curious metaphysical theories have crept into the doctrine of perception: the teaching of the associationists, that conscious elements add themselves to form the percept, and the opposite theory of the spiritualists, that the mind unites the elements into the percept. Both theories are psychologically inadmissible because they make philosophical implications; the former is further objectionable because it involves the invalid metaphysical doctrine of ideas as permanent realities; but, more than all, both are unnecessary, for they incorrectly assume that the original experience is that of the single elements, and that there is, therefore, need to explain the later union of these elements within a percept. On the contrary, the original experience is of undistinguished and undiscriminated complexity, and it is simply explained as due to the complexity of the physical environment and thus of the physiological excitation, that is to say, as due to the fact that retina and basilar membrane and end-organs of skin and mucous membranes are simultaneously stimulated through the outer world.

Several sorts of connection, therefore, have to do with the perception. Two of these are forms of complexity with which psychology has, strictly speaking, no concern: the combination, or occurrence together, of the physical stimuli,

N

and the physiological excitations of the percept.   The other forms of complexity are within the psychologist's domain.   These are, first, the fusion or association of elements which is reflectively observed, not immediately felt, in the perception; and second, a very vague and unemphasized feeling of combination, which is perhaps a part of our perceptions.

It will be convenient, at this point, to consider the physiological conditions of perception.   These have really been described in our study of the elements of consciousness, but one important fact must be emphasized, because it serves, as we shall see, to differentiate perception from imagination.   The perception always includes sensations which have been peripherally, not merely centrally, stimulated; that is to say, in perception, not merely sense-centres of the brain in the occipital and temporal lobes and the Rolandic area, but retina, cochlea and dermal end-organs are excited.   Often, to be sure, a perception includes centrally excited, as well as peripherally excited elements; that is to say, the excitation of some brain-centre, which has been stimulated from the outside, spreads to other brain-centres, which are thus excited from within and not from without.   But though many parts of a perception may, in this way, be centrally excited, some part of it is always conditioned by external stimulus acting on end-organs.   Probably, also, there occur excitations of certain of the so-called 'association-centres,' the physiological correlates of what we have called the feelings of combination and of distinctness.[1]

Perceptions are thus described as limited complex experiences, which are mainly sensational, and partly due to peripheral excitation, yet inclusive of the relational feelings of clearness and of combination.   They may be classified in

[1] Cf. Appendix, Section I., I.

two main groups, distinguished by three parallel sets of characteristics. The following outline makes this clear : —

PERCEPTION

Percept (mere idea)		Perceiving (shared experience)
Fused Percept	I. Pure Perception (Peripherally excited)	Completely shared
Associated	II. Mixed Perception (Peripherally and centrally excited)	Partly shared

As this outline indicates, pure perception may be defined from three points of view. In the first place, all the sensations which it includes are peripherally excited by external stimuli, and it contains absolutely no sensations which are not directly aroused by objects immediately present. For example, the pure perception of a russet apple, out of reach, is the consciousness of something brown and round, but does not include the consciousness of smoothness and of taste, because the untouched apple does not immediately stimulate the end-organs of pressure and taste in skin and in mucous membrane.

The pure perception, in the second place, may be regarded as a fusion, and this distinction, as we have seen,[1] is most often made from the standpoint of idea-psychology, in contrasting the fused with the associated percept. The percept of the apple is a fusion of the feelings of brownness, roundness and the like.

The pure perception, in the third place, if looked upon, not as mere idea, but as personal attitude, is an experience which we regard as completely shared with other people. For example, every normal person within sight of a russet apple perceives that it is brown and round.

The mixed perception has the opposite characteristics. With reference, first, to its physiological condition, it may be described as including both peripherally and centrally

---

[1] Cf. Chapter XIII.

excited elements. This means, of course, that in mixed perception we perceive far more than what is actually present. Our mixed perception of the russet apple includes the consciousness of its smoothness, even though we do not touch the apple; and in the same way we are rightly said to perceive the varying textures of the leading lady's gowns at the play; and we are even said to hear the street-car bell, though the only sensation peripherally aroused is that of the sound, and the accompanying consciousness of 'street-car' includes only centrally excited sensations.

The mixed perceptual experience, regarded as percept, that is as idea, is, in the second place, distinguished from the pure percept in that it is 'associated' and not merely fused. The centrally excited feeling of smoothness is associated with the peripherally excited feelings of color and shape in the percept of the russet apple, and the consciousness of the unseen colors, form and movement of the street-car are associated with the consciousness of the sound actually heard.

Mixed perceiving, finally, the consciousness of shared experience, differs from pure perceiving in that it includes, along with the consciousness shared by all normal persons, a more or less individual experience. Your percept and mine of the street-car bell which we hear from behind us, as we stand on the same windy corner, are assumed to be alike so far as the mere sound is concerned, but may differ very widely in the 'street-car' part of the experience, since you may be conscious of 'blue-Meetinghouse-Hill-car-bell,' whereas I may be conscious of 'green-Crosstown-car-bell.'

It is evident that the pure perception, unmixed with centrally excited, associated elements, can occur only in primitive or in half-unconscious states. The indistinct awareness of light and sound to which one sometimes wakes from a sound sleep, the baby's consciousness of any wholly novel object — of railroad train or ocean — and the savage's first view of a steamboat are examples of pure percepts. In these experiences, the sleepy person is conscious of mere light and sound without any consciousness of their source, and the child or the savage sees precisely what is before him, for example, an oblong, moving object from which puffs of smoke arise, without any consciousness of the inner mechanism or the purpose of boat or of train. Such pure perceptions are, of course, replaced by the mixed perceptions which make up by far the greater part of our adult experience.

Mixed perceptions may differ very widely in the relation of their centrally excited to their peripherally excited elements. In the first class, the centrally excited elements are no more important than those peripherally excited, but are quite as constant, and indeed form, with the peripherally excited elements, the perception of a single object, scene or event. For example, the centrally excited sensations of the coolness and smoothness of a statue belong less essentially, or at any rate no more essentially, than the sensations of color and form to our visual percept of the statue; the centrally excited sensations of color, form, internal pressure and jerk are combined with a clanging sound actually heard, to make up the perception of a street-car; and the visual and odor-sensations roused by an orange, which is beyond one's reach, combine closely with the associated impressions of its rough, cool surface and its taste. In such cases, it may be observed, the association is of the close kind, called 'assimilation,' and the centrally, as well as the peripherally, excited experience is likely to be common to most observers; for example, we are practically as unanimous in our consciousness of the roughness of the orange as of its color.

In the second class of mixed perceptions, the centrally excited part is far more variable, and often more significant, than the part peripherally excited. For example, your percept of a copy of the Hermes of Praxiteles may include a distinct consciousness of Homer's description of Hermes

binding his sandals upon his feet; whereas I, who stand
at your side and regard the figure with equal interest, may
perceive nothing save the outline, color and background of
the statue.   Again, you and I may hear the same violin
obligato, without seeing the player; your perception of
the rich harmonies may be supplemented by a consciousness of Kneisel holding the violin and drawing the bow,
whereas my perception may include the centrally excited
consciousness, not of Kneisel, but of Loeffler.   These constituents of the perception are, it will be noticed, more
remotely associated and far more individual, less common
to all observers, than the fused, peripherally associated,
common elements with which they are combined.

One sub-class of these remotely associated and individual
mixed perceptions is of such significance that it merits
especial notice.   This is the class of symbolic perceptions,
in which the peripherally excited elements are entirely
unimportant in themselves, and significant only as connected with the centrally excited parts of the perception.
A diagram is a good illustration of the symbolic perception.   The peripherally excited, the actually seen, elements
of a diagram are extremely insignificant; the important
part of it is, not the actual color or form, but the meaning, in other words, the image associated with it.   It is
of no consequence, for example, in a curve representing
the average heights of school children of different ages,
whether the curve be black or red or blue, whether vertical
or horizontal lines represent heights, whether the scale
be drawn a millimetre or a centimetre to the year of age.
Not what we actually see but what we imagine — in other
words, not the fused, peripherally excited, but the associated, centrally excited part of such a percept — is significant.

All these forms of perception — the pure perception, the
unsymbolic and the symbolic mixed perception — are admirably illustrated from the word-consciousness at different
stages of development.   To an animal, to a savage or to
a little child, a word is a pure percept, a fusion of periphe-

rally excited elements, a mere succession of sounds or an irregular outline. To the educated person, however, a word, even if it is not understood, so long as it is written in familiar letters or pronounced in familiar sounds, in fact if it is known to be a word, is a mixed percept. The words *casa* and *οἰκία*, for example, even to those who do not know their meaning, are more than irregular, black quirls on a white background. These fused, peripherally excited visual elements are combined with an assimilation of centrally excited sensations, the imaged sound of the word and the throat-sensation required to pronounce it.

A word, finally, to the man who understands it, is a symbolic percept in which the actual sensations, peripherally or centrally excited, included in the mere word-consciousness, are significant merely as they suggest others. In fact, this word-consciousness is in itself so unimportant that it may be replaced by the consciousness of any one of half a dozen words, *casa, οἰκία, Haus, maison, domus* and still others, and yet the essential part of my experience in reading the word 'house'—the concrete image of a building—remains unchanged through all this permutation of the fused and the assimilated elements. Different people, reading the same word, will, however, have different images of the concrete object which it suggests, though their experience of its peripherally excited elements, sound and shape, must be common to them all.

In conclusion, mention must be made of illusory percepts. The illusion is a percept which does not directly correspond with any outer object, though it contains peripherally, as well as centrally, excited sensational elements. It is contrasted with the hallucination, which contains only centrally excited sense-elements. The dream or delirium image of a ghost, for example, is a hallucination, because it is not excited by any external object, whereas the traditional confusion of window curtain with ghost is an illusion.

There are two types of illusion, as of ordinary perception,

the 'pure' and the 'mixed.' The phenomena of contrast, which have already been named,[1] are probably examples of pure illusions containing only peripherally aroused sensational elements. So also a rotated circle looks gray, though the physical stimuli are the black and white sectors of the circle, because of the persistent retinal stimulation. Most spatial illusions — for example, the consciousness that the upper curve of an S is equal in size to the lower curve, the overestimation of large angles and underestimation of small ones, and the distortion of parallel lines by drawing oblique lines through them [2] — belong, also, to the class of pure illusions. In these cases, it is probable that tactile sensations, usually from the unobserved motions of the eyeballs, are fused with visual sensations and produce these illusions. Such illusions, on the other hand, as that of the proof-reader who overlooks the omitted letter or reads the incorrectly printed word as correct, obviously belong to the class of mixed illusions, for centrally aroused sensations are here mixed with those peripherally excited. The illusional character, it should be added, is not a part of the illusion, as immediately experienced, but a later reflection about it.

We must now summarize the most important results of this chapter. A perception is, we have found, a complex and limited experience, which may be regarded as one of a series of ideas or as a consciousness, shared with any number of unparticularized selves. It is analyzable mainly into sensational elements, but contains also certain relational feelings of clearness and of combination. It is due in part to peripheral stimulation and may be classified as pure or mixed.

[1] Cf. Chapter II., p. 30, and Appendix, Section III., II.

[2] For experiments, cf. Sanford, 187–203; Titchener, § 44. Cf. James, *op. cit.*, Vol. II., p. 249; and see Titchener's Bibliography, " Laboratory Manual," I. (Instructor's), p. 305.

CHAPTER XV

IMAGINATION

WE regarded perception from two points of view, and in the same way we may study imagination, first, as mere occurrence of images, and second, as imagining, the experience of a related self.

I

We shall first consider the image, and shall at once discover by introspection that the image, like the percept, is a complex idea, mainly sensational, but including also the relational elements of connection and distinctness. So far, however, we have not distinguished the image from the percept, and our immediate aim must be the discovery of such a distinction. Three differences at once suggest themselves, as one closely regards almost any image. If, for instance, I close my eyes and ears, to isolate myself from my perceptual environment, and examine the resulting image of a book on the desk before me, I find that it differs from my percept of the book, first, in that its brown color is far less intense, second, in that certain features of the perceived book — the gilt lettering and the stains on its surface — are lacking, and finally, in that it is far more evanescent than the percept, that is, more readily displaced by other images. In a word, the percept has, ordinarily, more intensity, more detail and more stability than the image.[1]

Yet if one carefully reflect on one's imagined experience,

---

[1] Cf. Fechner, " Elemente der Psychophysik," II., XLIV.

one is sure to find occasional images which lack one or
more of these characteristics. The percept of one's bodily
attitude, for example, may be less intense, less accurate
and less permanent than a visual image of a face or an
auditory image of a melody; one's percept of an unknown
substance, which one merely tastes or smells, may be less
vivid, also, than one's visual image of a bowl of strawberries
or of a roasted duck. All this proves that intensity, detail
and stability are merely common and not necessary characteristics of perception; and the failure to discover a difference in constitution and duration between the percept
and the image throws us back upon the well-known distinction in physiological conditions. This is the fact that
some sensational elements of the percept are peripherally
excited, whereas all elements of the image are centrally
stimulated. When I imagine the Blue Grotto at Capri,
only my occipital lobe is excited, but when I look out at
the Grand Central Station my retina is excited as well;
when I imagine the break in the second movement of the
Unfinished Symphony, only my temporal lobe is excited,
but when I hear the street band outside my window the
inner organs of my cochlea are in vibration.

The distinction between percept and image is often
stated in another way: it is said that the objects of perception are real, whereas the objects of imagination are unreal
and that I perceive the real hydrant or cow or sunset,
whereas the imaged obelisk or parrot or cloud is unreal.
The chief objection to this division is the fact, that it is
based on a philosophical distinction, that of reality as opposed to unreality, and not on any characteristic of psychic
or of physiological facts as such. It should be noted that
this distinction is, however, almost exactly parallel to that
between peripherally excited and centrally excited ideas.
For peripheral excitations come from what we call real
objects, and even the illusory percept is at least occasioned
by a real object.

In holding that psychology is not concerned with reality

and unreality, we of course do not have reference to the feelings of 'real' and 'unreal' which are frequent factors of our experience. A feeling of realness may well, however, attach to an image as well as to a percept though, on the contrary, the image may contain the feeling of unrealness. Most often the image lacks either feeling.[1]

This brings us to the study of the physiological basis of imagination. In all probability, this differs from the physiological condition of perception only in the ways already suggested: in the first place, by the lack of excitation of the peripheral end-organs, retina, taste-bulbs and the rest; and usually, in the second place, by the slighter degree, duration and stability of the cerebral activity. The differences, to recur to our former example, between the cerebral accompaniment of ink-bottle percept and of ink-bottle image, are these: first, and fundamentally, the cerebral discharge is fainter and therefore less stable; and furthermore, it is less diffused, that is, fewer cerebral cells are excited. An experiment performed and described by Külpe[2] supports the view that the physiological conditions of percept and of image are essentially alike. On the wall of a dark room, at irregular intervals, he threw a very faint light. His subjects, required to indicate the recurrences of the stimulus, often supposed themselves to see the light when it was not present — that is, they confused the imaged with the perceived light, the centrally excited with the faint, peripherally excited sensation.

It has been held by some psychologists that an image is distinguished from a percept, not merely by the different degree and duration, but by the different locality of its cerebral excitation. Flechsig argues from the vagueness of some memory-images that they may occur when merely association-centres, not the sense-centres, are excited,[3] whereas the sense-centres must, of course, be active in per-

---

[1] Cf. Chapter IX., p. 125.
[2] "Grundriss der Psychologie," § 28, 2.   [3] "Gehirn und Seele," p. 60.

ception. James Ward bases a similar argument on the case of patients who are able to recall familiar objects, but totally unable to recognize them when they are seen. He concludes that the centres for percept and for image must differ, however little, in locality.[1] But both these arguments are insufficient. The people who could recall and describe objects named to them may have had purely verbal images, and need not have visualized the objects at all. And every image, however 'vague,' contains sense-elements and must, therefore, be conditioned by the excitation of sense-centres.[2]

Certain experiments, interesting in themselves, performed years ago by G. H. Meyer, have a slight bearing[3] on this question and confirm the theory already stated. Meyer succeeded in getting negative after-images of colors which he had only imagined, not perceived. This may mean that his retina was excited, not through external physical stimulation, but by excitation transmitted by out-going nerves from the brain; this has suggested the possibility of a direct connection, during imagination, between brain and end-organs, and a consequent activity of the sense-organs. Modern physiologists, however, tend toward the purely cerebral account of such phenomena.

The image-consciousness may, of course, be regarded as personal attitude, instead of being treated as mere idea. From this point of view, we speak of 'imagining,' not of the 'image,' and recognize that imagination, unlike perception, is a private and unshared experience. The world of perception is the external world which is common to every one alike, but day-dreams and reveries are private property peculiar to a single individual. The life of imagination is, in fact, marked off as a sort of private domain in the

[1] Ward, "Assimilation and Association," *Mind*, October, 1894.
[2] Cf. Külpe, *op. cit.* § 33. 6 *seq.*; Donaldson, "The Growth of the Brain," p. 34; James, "Principles," I., p. 592, *et al.*
[3] "Physiologische Untersuchungen usw.," quoted by James, *op. cit.*, Vol. II., p. 66.

midst of the public lands of common perceptual experience. Once within this enclosure, one may turn one's back upon the common lot, and feast one's eyes and delight one's ears on sights and sounds which are not for other people. For one is powerless to give entrance to anybody. One may long desperately to share these private experiences, but it is not possible to communicate them fully; nobody ever perfectly follows another person's descriptions, and no artist ever finds colors so glowing as those of his imagination, or ever reduces his image music to a written score.

This privacy of imagination, which marks it off from perception and from thought, is never realized while we are imagining. On the contrary, we are absorbed in the imaged colors and outlines, in the tones and in the harmonies, or in the kaleidoscopic shifting, the ceaseless changes of our images; we do not say to ourselves, at the time, "This is my experience, mine, I cannot share it; it belongs to me; other people see and hear what I see and hear, but they do not imagine what I imagine." Only in our after reflection about imagining, do we assert its privacy, its unshared nature.

Primarily, therefore, imagining, unlike perceiving, is an unsocial experience, since it denies the relation of myself or of my experience to other selves. Indirectly, however, it is after all a social experience. For, though we cannot assert the privacy of our imagination without denying that other selves have a share in it, yet this very denial is a negative acknowledgment of the existence of these other selves.

Imagining, the personal attitude, like the image or mere idea, is of course also a complex experience, including both feelings of distinctness and combination, and sensational elements, centrally excited.

II

We shall now proceed to the closer description and classification of imagination, whether regarded as image or as imagining, as personal attitude or as idea, basing our discussion on the following outline: —

IMAGINATION
(Complex of elements)

The Image   Imagining

A. (Classified by sense-order)

I. Concrete
   a. Simple
      1. Visual
      2. Auditory
      3. Tactual-motor,
         etc.
   b. Mixed

II. Verbal
   a. Simple
      1. Visual
      2. Auditory
      3. Tactual-motor,
         etc.
   b. Mixed

(Classified also by form   B. (Classified by novelty)
   of association)

In total association......I. Reproductive   Like ⎫
                            a. Inaccurate   ⎬ the
                            b. Accurate : Memory   ⎪ experience
In partial association...II. Creative   Relatively ⎪ of others
                                             unlike   ⎭

The most obvious of these divisions is the classification
according to content, that is, according as the imagination
is mainly of colors and shapes, of sounds, of pressures, of
tastes or of odors. First of all, from this point of view,
concrete imagination, that is, imagination of objects, scenes
and events, must be contrasted with verbal or symbolic
imagination; and then, within each of these classes, the
varying sense-types must be enumerated.

Concrete imagination may belong to any sense-order,
but it is in the main either visual, auditory or tactile, or
else it belongs to a 'mixed' type including elements of
several kinds. There is, in truth, no particular in which
individuals differ more than in just this prevailing sense-
type of their imagery. In recalling, for example, the

balcony scene in Romeo and Juliet, some people see with the eye of the mind the shadowy form of Romeo and the figure of Juliet, clear-cut against the lighted window, the 'stony limits,' the cypresses, statues and fountains of the Italian garden, and the "blessed moon . . . that tips with silver all these fruit-tree tops;" others, like Juliet, may "know the sound of that tongue's utterance," and may hear, in imagination, Romeo's deep-voiced love-making and the "silver-sweet sound " of Juliet's replies "like softest music to attending ears." Still others, finally, may image Romeo's movements as "with love's light wings" he "did o'erperch these walls."

The study of an imaginative writer often reveals the predominant sense-order of his imagination. His pages may glow with color or thrill with music or quiver with rhythmic motion. For example, in the poem which follows, of the blind poet, Philip Bourke Marston, there is but one color-image, but the verses are full of striking images of sound and odor:—

"All my roses are dead in my Garden —
        What shall I do ?
Winds in the night, without pity or pardon,
        Came there and slew.

"All my song birds are dead in their bushes —
        Woe for such thing !
Robins and linnets and blackbirds and thrushes
        Dead, with stiff wings.

"Oh, my Garden ! rifled and flowerless,
        Waste now and drear ;
Oh, my Garden ! barren and bowerless,
        Through all the year.

"Oh, my dead birds ! each in his nest there,
        So cold and stark ;
What was the horrible death that pressed there
        When skies were dark ?

"What shall I do for my roses' sweetness
    The Summer round —
For all my Garden's divine completeness
    Of scent and sound?

"I will leave my Garden for winds to harry:
    Where once was peace,
Let the bramble vine and wild brier marry,
    And greatly increase.

"But I will go to a land men know not —
    A far, still land,
Where no birds come, and where roses blow not,
    And no trees stand —

"Where no fruit grows, where no Spring makes riot,
    But, row on row,
Heavy, and red, and pregnant with quiet
    The poppies blow.

"And there shall I be made whole of sorrow,
    Have no more care —
No bitter thought of the coming morrow,
    Or days that were."

There is but one touch of color in this garden, the conventional red of the poppies; its summer-time charm is 'its divine completeness of scent and sound'; and its autumn cheerlessness does not consist in dull and faded coloring, though there is a mere mention of dark skies, but in winds, and cold, and in 'the horrible death which pressed there.'

It is easy to discover by introspection the prevailing sense-order of one's concrete imagery. One has only to imagine or recall, in succession, certain definite scenes or objects, and to ask oneself whether the resulting image is of colors and forms, of sounds, of pressures, of odors or of tastes, or a mixture of some or all of these elements. The visual is probably the most common type of concrete imagery, for, in spite of great differences in vividness and accuracy, there are few people who cannot imagine objects in some vague outline or dull color. Visual images are, however, in almost every experience, supplemented by percepts of pressure and of sound, as when we 'localize' a touch by imagining the look of wrist or of forehead on which it falls, or a sound by imagining the shape and position of the piano-key which occasions it. Every sculptor, painter or architect who sees his vision before he embodies it has visual imagination. The inventor also 'sees' his engine or his dynamo in all its parts and connections, before he enters upon the actual construction of it; and the well-dressed woman sees the end from the beginning, the completed gown within the shapeless fabric. Above all, visual imagination is the endowment of geometrician and astronomer. There is no more vulgar error than the everyday supposition that the mathematician is *ipso facto* unimaginative. On the contrary, there is no more lofty order of imagination than that which sees the planets moving in their courses, and which images the projections and intersections of lines and planes 'produced to infinity'!

Yet in spite of the value of visual images to artists, inventors and mathematicians, it must be at once acknowledged that even to them the visual type of imagination is not indispensable, but that it may be replaced by what we know as the tactile type, the imaging of the movements necessary to the production of sculpture, machine or figure. A well-known statistical inquiry, carried on by Francis Galton, led unmistakably to this conclusion. Galton's questions concern one's image, on a given day, of that morning's breakfast table.[1] The questions refer to —

"1. *Illumination.* — Is the image dim or fairly clear? Is its brightness comparable to that of the actual scene?

"2. *Definition.* — Are all the objects pretty well defined at the same time, or is the place of sharpest definition at any one moment more contracted than it is in a real scene?

"3. *Coloring.* — Are the colors of the china, of the

[1] "Inquiries into Human Faculty," p. 84. For a very detailed questionary on image-types, cf. Titchener, § 51, p. 198.

o

toast, bread crust, mustard, meat, parsley or whatever may have been on the table, quite distinct and natural?"

As result of this investigation, Galton found that "men who declare themselves entirely deficient in the power of seeing mental pictures . . . can become painters of the rank of Royal Academicians." And James says of himself, "I am a good draughtsman and have a very lively interest in pictures, statues, architecture, and decoration, and a keen sensibility to artistic effects. But I am an extremely poor visualizer, and find myself often unable to reproduce in my mind's eye pictures which I have most carefully examined."[1] In these cases, a quickness to recognize and to discriminate colors and forms is combined with the inability to imagine them. Evidently, the visual images are here replaced by tactile images — the images of the motions necessary to the production of sculpture, machine or figure: a sculptor of this type reproduces in imagination the movements of his chisel, and the geometrician draws his figure or indicates by imaged movements the sweep of orbits and the intersection of lines.

Külpe discovered, experimentally, the same lack of visual imagination.[2] He tested the color-imagery of several students by pronouncing in a darkened room the names of colors and requiring them to describe the resulting experiences. One of these young men proved utterly incapable, with the strongest effort, of imagining any color whatever. Another historic example is Charcot's patient, a man whose visual imagery was impaired through nervous disease. "Asked to draw an arcade, he says, 'I remember that it contains semicircular arches, that two of them meeting at an angle make a vault, but how it looks I am absolutely unable to imagine.' . . . He complains of his loss of feeling for colors. 'My wife has black hair, this I know; but I can no more recall its color than I can her person and features!'"[3]

[1] *Op. cit.*, II., p. 53.   [2] *Op. cit.*, § 27, 9.   [3] Cf. James, *op. cit.*, II., p. 59.

The auditory image-type is unquestionably less common than the visual, and it is almost always closely combined with imagery of the motor-tactual sort. It is the image-type of the great musicians, of Beethoven, for example, who composed his symphonies when totally unable to hear a note of them. But though less significant to most of us than the visual images, the concrete auditory imagination belongs, at least in some degree, to all people who are able to recall voices and melodies. The prevalence of auditory imagery is suggested by the ordinary ruse of violin players, who produce the effect of a *diminuendo*, lengthened beyond the actual sound, by continuing the drawing motion of the bow when it no longer touches the string.

The tactile type of imagination is, as we have noticed, ordinarily 'motor,' that is, the most significant pressure-images are those of the internal pressures occasioned by bodily movements. The image of the feel of 'velvet' or 'silk,' of the consistency of dough, of the resistance of the water when one is swimming, of one's shortened breath as one is wheeling up a hill, are examples of pressure-images.

Images of the other 'dermal' sense-types, that is, images of pain, of warmth and of cold, seldom if ever occur. They seem to be supplanted by the corresponding peripherally aroused sensations. The vivid account of a wound or a physical injury may excite, through the connection of sensory cells with motor-cells and fibres, the actual, visceral pressure-sensations which constitute the feeling of faintness, and it may even excite the pain end-organs. In the same way, I grow actually hot over a remembered mortification and I shiver with cold at a revived fear.

Smell and taste images are so infrequent that their existence is often denied. It is said that when we imagine objects fragrant in themselves, such as roses or cheese or coffee, we imagine their look or their feel without imagining their odor; and that when we suppose ourselves to imagine tastes, we are really imagining the vivid colors or the graceful outlines of a repast, not the actual taste of the food. So when Eve 'on hospitable thoughts intent' bestirs her to make ready a feast for Raphael, we are told that : —

> "fruit of all kinds, in coat
> Rough or smooth rined, or bearded husk, or shell
> She gathers, tribute large, and on the board
> Heaps with unsparing hand.   For drink, the grape
>
> *   *   *   *   *   *
>
> From many a berry, and from sweet kernels pressed
> She tempers dulcet creams."

There are tactile images in plenty but not a single definite taste-image in this picture;[1] and the description which follows [1] is full of rich color but lacks imagined tastes.

> "There, on a slope of orchard, Francis laid
> A damask napkin wrought with horse and hound,
> Brought out a dusky loaf that smelt of home,
> And, half-cut down, a pasty costly made,
> Where quail and pigeon, lark and leveret lay,
> Like fossils of the rock, with golden yolks
> Imbedded and injellied."

But it must be remembered that the absence of taste and smell descriptions may be due, wholly or in part, to our lack of taste and smell words.   Francis, for example, could hardly have described the taste of the brown and fossil-shaped quail or of the golden yolks, had he been so inclined.   And though smell and taste images are relatively infrequent, it is certain that many persons sometimes imagine tastes and smells.   A recent inquiry among fifty college students, somewhat trained in introspection, disclosed the fact that thirty-one are sure that they can imagine certain odors, such as the smell of tar, burning sulphur, furnace gas and mignonette.   Several observers, also, who have carefully observed and recorded their dreams,

[1] Quoted by Grant Allen, "Physiological Æsthetics."

are certain that they have occasional dreams of unequivocal tastes and smells. There is a simple biological reason
for the comparative infrequency, in the civilized consciousness, of olfactory and gustatory images. In the primitive
stages of life, the sense of smell plays an important part
in the discovery of approaching dangers, and processes
of eating have relatively greater importance than in civilized life. Accordingly, we have every reason to think that
the smell and taste images are well developed among
savages.

More common, than any of these classes of concrete
imagery, is that to which we have already referred as the
'mixed type.' The image of any object is likely, in other
words, to include elements of more than one sense-order:
it is not wholly visual and still less is it entirely auditory
or tactile. Either the visual or auditory elements may
predominate, but an image — of a dinner-party, for example — is rarely a mere complex of the colors and forms
of dresses, faces, candles, flowers, foods, nor yet of the
sounds of conversation, laughter and service, but it includes both visual and auditory images, perhaps with a
tactile image also of the 'feel' of linen or of silver, and
a gustatory or olfactory image of the taste of lobster or
the odor of jonquils. Excluding, therefore, a very few individuals, who may have imagery of one sense-type only,
the great majority of people have either a mere predomi-
nance of one sort over another, or else the strictly mixed
type of image, in which several sense-types are combined,
and no one of them is especially prominent.

Contrasted with all these classes of concrete imagery are
the word-types, which are far more prevalent than any one,
save the psychologist, realizes. In the experience of many
people these altogether crowd out the concrete images.
We suppose ourselves to be imagining the Roman Campagna, the Sistine Madonna or the ninth symphony of
Beethoven, when, as a matter of fact, we are simply say-

ing to ourselves the words 'campagna,' 'madonna,' 'symphony.' Of course this is an artificial state of affairs. Words are conventional symbols, not instinctive reactions; they play no part at all in the imaginative life of animal or of baby, and little part in that of the savage. The civilized being, however, is born into a world of people whose most characteristic activity is neither eating, walking nor fighting, but talking. At first, through pure imitation, and afterwards because he recognizes the utility of language, he largely occupies himself with words, first heard and spoken, and later read and written. And as habits fall away through disuse, so, little by little, in the experience of most of us, word-images take the place of concreter images of color, sound and the like. It is unnecessary to dwell on the immense utility of verbal images, for we are already victims of what Mr. Garrison calls 'the ignorant prejudice in favor of reading and writing,' and, he might have added, 'of talking.' Words serve not only as the means of communication, and thus as the surest method of social development, but — by their abstract, conventional form — as an aid to rapid memorizing and to clear reasoning; they are indispensable parts of our intellectual equipment; yet they are in themselves but poor and insignificant experiences, and they work us irreparable harm if they banish, from the life of our imagination, the warm colors, broad spaces, liquid sounds and subtle fragrances which might enrich and widen our experience.

We have ample proof that this is no purely fictitious danger. Galton's most significant conclusion is that the "faculty of seeing pictures, . . . if ever possessed by men of highly generalized and abstract thought, is very apt to be lost by disuse." Many of the 'men of science,' whose imagination he tested, had "no more notion" of the nature of visual imagery "than a color-blind man . . . has of the nature of color. 'It is only by a figure of speech,'" one of them says, "'that I can describe my recollection of a scene as a mental image that I can see with my mind's eye, . . . I do not see it . . . any more than a man sees the thousand lines of Sophokles which under due pressure he is ready to repeat.'" Every mixed figure is in truth a witness to the common lack of concrete imagery. The earnest preacher who exhorted his hearers to fill their lamps at the fountain of knowledge, and the fervid orator who bewailed the cup of Ireland's misery as 'long running over, but not yet full,' were, of course, without the visual images which their words should suggest. Doubtless, most of their hearers received these astounding statements without a quiver of amusement — not, primarily, because they lacked a sense of humor, but because they were without visual imagination.

The study of the varying forms of verbal imagination discloses the fact, that, like the forms of concrete imagination, they belong usually to a visual, an auditory, a tactile or a 'mixed' class, though they may conceivably be of other sense-types. The good visualizer images his words as they are printed on a page, reading them off, sentence by sentence or verse by verse, recalling the precise part of the page on which a given word or sentence appears. Galton tells of a statesman who sometimes hesitates in the midst of a speech, because plagued by the image of his manuscript speech with its original erasures and corrections. Even musicians may be helped by symbolic imagery and may play by mentally reading their scores. Again, verbal images may be of words as heard; and such masters of musical verse as Sophokles, Tennyson and Swinburne must have auditory verbal imagery. One may 'hear' words spoken by oneself or by others, one may listen in imagination to conversations between different people, or one may recall whole scenes of a play in the characteristic intonations of different actors. "'When I write a scene,' said Legouve to Scribe,[1] 'I *hear* but you

---

[1] Quoted by W. James, *op. cit.*, Vol. II., p. 60, from Binet.

see. In each phrase which I write, the voice of the personage who speaks strikes my ear. *Vous qui êtes le
théâtre même*, your actors walk, gesticulate before your
eyes; I am a *listener*, you a *spectator*.' 'Nothing more
true,' said Scribe; 'do you know where I am when I
write a piece? In the middle of the parterre.'"

One's verbal imagery, finally, may be of the tactual-
motor type; one may imagine oneself as speaking, or, less
often, as writing the words. A simple proof of the frequent occurrence of these motor-images was suggested by
Dr. Stricker:[1] the attempt to imagine a word containing
several labials — such a word as 'bob' or 'pepper' — without the faintest imaged or actual movement of the lips.
Most people will be unsuccessful in such an experiment,
which brings to light the presence, in many word-images,
of these centrally excited motor-sensations, the consciousness of those movements of throat and lips which accompany our actual pronunciation of words. Even the distinct
effort to visualize words results, for people of the tactile
type, in motor-images. James, for example, "can seldom
call to mind even a single letter of the alphabet in purely
retinal terms. I must trace the letter," he says, "by
running my mental eye over its contour." This tactile
(or tactual-motor) and the mixed tactile-auditory type, in
which one most often has the image of both hearing and
'feeling' oneself talk, are perhaps the most common forms
of verbal imagery.

The various phenomena of aphasia, the cerebral disease
affecting the word-consciousness, confirm these results of
introspection. They show that verbal imagery is impaired
by injury to the visual, to the auditory or to any tactual-
motor centre, or by injury to the fibres connecting these
areas, and that corresponding with these different pathological conditions, there may be independent loss of words
as read, as heard, as spoken or as written.[2]

[1] "Studien über die Sprachvorstellungen." Cf. James, Vol. II., p. 63.
[2] Cf. Appendix, Section II.

Several general conclusions follow from the study of the sense-orders of our images: the impossibility, first of all, of supposing that any normal person is unimaginative. Since imagination is not of necessity an artistic impulse, a lofty soaring in empyrean isolation from the everyday life, but merely, as we have seen, the possession of images of colors, sounds, pressures, odors, tastes or even of words, it follows that everybody who is conscious of anything whatever, in its absence, is in so far imaginative. When I am conscious of the hat which I yesterday bought or of the dinner which I shall eat to-day, no less than when I muse upon the picture I shall paint or of the world I shall discover, I am possessed of mental images, that is, I am, in a strict sense, imaginative. Our study, furthermore, makes it clear that almost everybody is capable of rousing, within his consciousness, vivid and accurate images of one sort or another. If, try as he will, the colors are washed out and the outlines indistinct in his visual images of an opera or of a country outlook, he may hear, in imagination, the varying parts of strings and horns in the orchestral prelude, the melodies of the songs and the harmonies of the choruses, or the liquid bird-notes, lapping waves and murmuring leaves of the summer afternoon. Even the minor image-types may be well developed, as the experiences of many defectives show. Recognition is not, it is true, an invariable test of imagination,[1] yet the blind woman who recognized garments, fresh from the laundry, by her sense of smell, and who sorted in this way the fresh linen of a whole institution, presumably also had images of many different odors. Helen Keller, who has been blind and deaf from earliest childhood, so that she can have neither visual nor auditory images, has, nevertheless, peculiarly vivid and detailed mental images of pressures, movements and even of tastes and smells.[2]

[1] Cf. p. 194.
[2] Cf. Perkins Institute Annual Report, 1891, p. 90.

The foregoing classification of imagination, first according to sense-types and then according to novelty, is possible
whatever our fundamental conception — whether, in other
words, we start from a theory of the image, the mere idea,
or from the standpoint of imagining, the personal attitude.
The terms 'imagining' and 'image' have, therefore, been
used indiscriminately in the description of the classes of
imagination.   We must notice, however, that the distinction of reproductive from productive imagination is more
readily stated in terms of the personal consciousness than in
terms of mere successive ideas.   For reproductive imagination, though it is indeed, as imagination and not perception, peculiarly my own, none the less usually resembles
other people's experience; whereas creative imagination is,
by its very nature, essentially unlike the perceptions and
imaginations of others.   The distinction between fancy
and universal imagination is even more definitely made
from the point of view of the relation of one self to
others.

A final distinction of importance requires the conception
of the image-consciousness as succession of ideas.   This is
the classification of images, according as they are associated
with a preceding percept or image, as totality, or with a
persisting element or group of elements of consciousness;
that is to say, according as they occur in 'total' or in 'partial' association.   People whom we call unimaginative are
those whose association is of the relatively total type, to
whom the present scene or object, as a whole, suggests the
succeeding image.   The imagery of the 'imaginative'
person, on the other hand, is characterized by focalized,
associative synthesis; some infinitesimal feature of the
present scene or object suggests the succeeding image.   An
unimaginative child, for example, bidden to write a compo-

'Mechanical Imagination' he calls 'Composition, not Imagination.'   'Organic
Imagination' he names 'Penetration,' and what we have called 'Universal
Imagination' is his 'Contemplation.'

our emotions, not in virtue of any rarity or surprisingness of the images themselves;" and Ruskin says that "the virtue of originality that men so strain after is not newness (there is nothing new), it is only genuineness." For the novel image, if it is not also truthful, is mere distortion, and the reproduction, if distinct in outline, intense in color and accurate in characteristic detail, is an image of far higher type. To quote Lewes once more : "The underlying principle of the true poet is that of 'vision in art,' and his characteristic method is great accuracy in depicting things . . . so that we may be certain the things presented themselves to the poet's vision and were painted because seen."

Two main forms of creative imagination are ordinarily distinguished : the mechanical and the organic. The mechanical image is a complex, not of qualities, but of relative totals, of experiences complete in themselves, as if a painter were to combine the hair of del Sarto's Caritas, with the flesh of Rubens's Magdalene and the figure of Raphael's Madonna della Sedia. The organic image is a complex, not of totals, complete in themselves, but of single elements or of fragmentary aspects of different objects, which fuse into a new whole of organically related parts. Within the class of organic imagination, one may distinguish, also, the fanciful from the universal imagination, on the ground that the first lays stress on unessential qualities which accidentally interest an individual, the second on essential, universally appealing qualities. Ruskin's comparison of Milton's description of the 'pansy freaked with jet' with Shelley's verses about the daisy, 'constellated flower that never sets,' clearly indicates the difference between the evanescent, individual, trivial nature of the 'fanciful' and the abiding, universal charm of the essentially imaginative.[1]

---

[1] This classification closely follows Ruskin's, though his terms differ from ours. 'Reproductive Imagination' he names the 'Theoretical Faculty.'

The foregoing classification of imagination, first according to sense-types and then according to novelty, is possible whatever our fundamental conception — whether, in other words, we start from a theory of the image, the mere idea, or from the standpoint of imagining, the personal attitude. The terms 'imagining' and 'image' have, therefore, been used indiscriminately in the description of the classes of imagination. We must notice, however, that the distinction of reproductive from productive imagination is more readily stated in terms of the personal consciousness than in terms of mere successive ideas. For reproductive imagination, though it is indeed, as imagination and not perception, peculiarly my own, none the less usually resembles other people's experience; whereas creative imagination is, by its very nature, essentially unlike the perceptions and imaginations of others. The distinction between fancy and universal imagination is even more definitely made from the point of view of the relation of one self to others.

A final distinction of importance requires the conception of the image-consciousness as succession of ideas. This is the classification of images, according as they are associated with a preceding percept or image, as totality, or with a persisting element or group of elements of consciousness; that is to say, according as they occur in 'total' or in 'partial' association. People whom we call unimaginative are those whose association is of the relatively total type, to whom the present scene or object, as a whole, suggests the succeeding image. The imagery of the 'imaginative' person, on the other hand, is characterized by focalized, associative synthesis; some infinitesimal feature of the present scene or object suggests the succeeding image. An unimaginative child, for example, bidden to write a compo-

---

'Mechanical Imagination' he calls 'Composition, not Imagination.' 'Organic Imagination' he names 'Penetration,' and what we have called 'Universal Imagination' is his 'Contemplation.'

sition about a cup, informs us that a cup is for drinking, that it has a saucer, that some cups are made of tin and some of china. In the eyes of the imaginative child, on the contrary, a cup is not primarily a vessel of clay, but a prize, the reward, perhaps, of some champion in a wheeling contest. To the literal child the cup is just a cup, suggesting, as a whole, the saucer in which it rests or the material of which it is made. The keener imagination seizes upon one fragmentary aspect of the cup, one only among its various uses, and this becomes the starting-point of some tale of thrilling adventure. In the same way, the image by total association is characteristic of the garrulous storyteller, who cannot name a man's father without detailing the family genealogy, nor mention a town without recalling the period of its settlement. The true poet or artist, on the contrary, the creative scientist or mathematician, the seer in any domain of conscious life, has visions linked together by the subtler connections of the partial or focalized association.

It is evident that the value of images through partial association will depend upon the selection of elements, in a total fact of consciousness, as starting-point of the association. If the artist's attention is absorbed in the accidental markings of the flower and not rather in its outline, in the variegated figures of the gown and not in the expression of the face, in the brilliancy of the conversations and not in the development of the characters, his imagery is fantastic, realistic, brilliant, but does not belong to imagery of the highest order or the most abiding value.

This division into 'totally associated' and 'partially associated' images is very nearly, though not completely, parallel, as will be observed, with the distinction of reproductive from productive imagination. Our outline[1] indicates the results of a comparison of the two forms of classification. It is evident at once that the image in total

[1] Cf. p. 190.

association is always reproduced, since a given subject, as a whole, if it suggests anything, must remind me of something connected with it in my own experience. On the other hand, an object in partial association may be either reproduced or novel (though of course each separate part of it is reproduced, since only combinations, never elements of consciousness, are novel).

All these distinctions are illustrated, in a very striking way, by a comparison of Shelley's "Sensitive Plant" with Cowper's "Winter Garden." "Who loves a garden," is Cowper's prosaic beginning, —

> ". . . loves a greenhouse too.
> Unconscious of a less propitious clime,
> There blooms exotic beauty, warm and snug,
> While the winds whistle and the snows descend.
> The spiry myrtle with unwith'ring leaf
> Shines there, and flourishes. The golden boast
> Of Portugal and western India there,
> The ruddier orange, and the paler lime,
> Peep through their polish'd foliage at the storm,
> And seem to smile at what they need not fear.
> Th' amomum there with intermingling flow'rs
> And cherries hangs her twigs. Geranium boasts
> Her crimson honors, and the spangled beau,
> Ficoides, glitters bright the winter long.
> All plants, of ev'ry leaf, that can endure
> The winter's frown, if screen'd from his shrewd bite,
> Live there, and prosper. Those Ausonia claims,
> Levantine regions these; th' Azores send
> Their jessamine, her jessamine remote
> Caffraia; . . . ."

No one can read this list of flowers without the conviction that Cowper is either 'reproducing' the rows of plants as he saw them one after another in a greenhouse, or else that he is framing an image after the most mechanical fashion. There is certainly little that is individual in the entire description, and the images, regarded from the standpoint of association, are connected as undifferentiated totals, instead of being broken up into more remotely suggestive elements.

Shelley also enumerates the flowers of his garden, but in a very different manner.

> "The snowdrop, and then the violet,
>   Arose from the ground with warm rain wet,
>   And their breath was mixed with fresh odor, sent
>   From the turf, like the voice and the instrument.
>
> "Then the pied wind-flowers and the tulip tall,
>   And narcissi, the fairest among them all,
>   Who gaze on their eyes in the stream's recess,
>   Till they die of their own dear loveliness;
>
> "And the Naiad-like lily of the vale,
>   Whom youth makes so fair and passion so pale,
>   That the light of its tremulous bells is seen
>   Through their pavilions of tender green."

We have here neither a reproduction nor a mechanical composition, but an organically related, individual experience. Almost every one of these exquisite images is connected in partial association with that which has preceded it: the mingling of earth-fragrance with the odors of the flowers suggests the interpenetration of voice and instrument; the early fading of the narcissi, mirrored in the stream, rouses the fancy that they "die of their own dear loveliness;" the tall lily leaves suggest sheltering pavilions. And, side by side with Cowper's superficial and fanciful comparison of Ficoides with the spangled beau, Shelley's images of music, of beauty and of passion fairly throb with life and with meaning.

The classification of images, by the type of their associative connection with other psychic facts, takes no account of the possibility of 'free,' that is of psychically unconnected, images. Ordinary experience furnishes many apparent illustrations: the unexpected images which spring up contrary to the trend of one's thought — the ludicrous image,

for example, which upsets one's gravity on a solemn occasion, or the sudden apparition, without warning, of a long-
forgotten face or scene. Many of these images, it is true,
are not really free, that is, unassociated, but are actually
connected by some common, but unattended-to, feature
with the preceding fact of consciousness. The sudden
image of Michael Angelo's Fawn, for instance, athwart a
religious service reverently followed, may really be induced
by an accidental and almost unnoticed glimpse of a grotesque profile; and the forgotten name which rises to my
lips, in the midst of my reading, may be itself suggested by
the rhythm of a word on the page before me. There still
remain, however, instances of images which seem utterly
unconnected, and incapable of connection, with the preceding facts of consciousness.

One way of accounting for these free images is a mere
restatement, in metaphorical terms, of their occurrence: a
forgotten idea is said to exist below the threshold of consciousness, an associated idea is defined as one which has
risen to the threshold of consciousness through the help of
another idea, and a free idea, finally, is described as one
which, quite unaided and solely by its own power, reap-
pears in consciousness. The assumption, on which this
associationist theory is based, is the continued existence of
psychic facts of which no one is conscious.[1] This conception, however, is logically and psychologically impossible,
for a psychic fact is by definition a fact of consciousness,
and an unconscious fact of consciousness is as impossible
as a straight curve. The only explanation of the 'free
image' is, indeed, in cerebral terms; it is due to a functioning of fibres, connecting different brain-areas, and
perhaps also to the excitation of association-centres in the
brain; but this cerebral activity is unaccompanied by
consciousness.

This long chapter will be concluded by a practical remark

[1] Cf. Chapter XXVIII., p. 438.

upon the means of fostering and of enriching the life of the imagination. The development of imagination is primarily an education of perception. To gain clear and vivid images, one must first possess accurate and vivid percepts. For, since the central nervous excitation is originally brought about by the peripheral, since the image, in other words, follows upon the percept, unless one has intense and clearly outlined percepts, satisfactory images are impossible. I am, therefore, deliberately cultivating my imagination when I shut myself away from distracting objects, fixate keenly, and prolong as far as I can the object of perception. A classic example of this method is given by Wordsworth in his " Daffodils " : —

> "I gazed — and gazed — but little thought
> What wealth to me the show had brought,
> For oft, when on my couch I lie
> In vacant or in pensive mood,
> They flash upon the inward eye
> Which is the bliss of solitude."

This at once suggests the justification of the effort to develop the life of the imagination. For imagination is more than the 'bliss of solitude' and the light of monotony; its bright colors may overlay the sordid discomforts of one's actual environment, and its music may drown the discordant cries of the present reality. By imagination, in truth, every man may create a world of his own; and to widen and vivify his imagination is to widen and enrich this world of his inalienable possession.

P

CHAPTER XVI

IMAGINATION (*continued*): MEMORY

MEMORY has been defined already as accurate, reproductive imagination, and its essential feature is, therefore, the exactness of the repetition. In framing this definition, we must not ignore the fact that the word 'memory' is often used, with entirely different meaning, in the sense of recognition or consciousness of familiarity. Since, however, the two conceptions, 'repetition' and the 'feeling of familiarity,' are not perfectly parallel, it is wisest to use the term 'memory' in the former sense, and not to make it equivalent to recognition.

Memory is distinguished, merely as complete or incomplete. My memory of a friend, for example, may include a consciousness of his name and history; I may know that we travelled to Olympia, ten years ago, in the same party; that we next met at a musicale in New York; that his ancestors came over with William the Conqueror; that he has studied in Berlin; that his wife is a blonde; and that he now belongs to the diplomatic corps in Vienna. On the other hand, I may say that I remember a man when I have merely a correct verbal image of his name, or a vague, yet accurate, image of the scene of our meeting. Strictly speaking, a memory is incomplete unless it resembles all conceivable details of the past; and absolutely complete memory is certainly very rare. The usual test of the completeness of memory is the ability to name an object, but, important as the name-image is, it is not sufficient to constitute a memory complete. In itself, indeed, the name of person or of object is the least important of details, and is significant only as peculiarly suggestive of other facts. The plot of a novel, the interests and achievements of one's companion at dinner, the way to reach one's destination —all these are of more importance than the bare verbal images of the names of book, of man, or of street.

This chapter will concern itself especially with the conditions of what is called a good memory, and with the means of strengthening the memory, or tendency to accurate reproduction. The conditions of memory certainly deserve especial study, for everybody knows the importance, in all callings and walks of life, of images exactly resembling previous experience — precise reproductions of name, scene, event and verbal sequence. It is true, to be sure, that the importance of memory may be overestimated. There are many things which we may rediscover as easily as we may recall them; and there are countless details which it is perfectly useless to remember. Memory should never, therefore, be an end in itself irrespective of its content, and James is quite right in his observation [1] on the farmer who remembered the kind of weather on every day of forty-two years, — " pity that such magnificent faculty could not have found more worthy application." As a basis for other sorts of experience, reproductive imagination is, however, of great significance. Emotional life is the more vivid the more one relives past experiences, and intellectual achievement is conditioned by the readiness and accuracy with which one recalls results already gained. The commonest and most effective method for stimulating memory is repetition of the fact to be recalled. Given a sufficient number of repetitions of a percept or image which is not too complicated, and any normal person may recall anything! The difference in individual memories may, in fact, be tested by discovering the different amounts of repetition required for memorizing the same material under similar conditions.

Repetition is one of the most important pedagogical

[1] *Op. cit.*, Vol. I., p. 661.

methods, precisely because it is always at hand. No amount of fixation or narrowing can give intensity to certain experiences, but one may repeat stimuli until they are, willy-nilly, recalled. The comparative value of this heavy labor of repetition has, however, to be considered. Is the play worth the candle? we must ask ourselves. Is the reproduction worth the expenditure of time and energy by which alone it is secured? This is a question to be decided afresh for almost every type of experience, by every individual. Some things, such as the multiplication table and the senseless spelling of English words, one simply must be able to recall, however wearisome the repetition. Other details, such as the names of one's students or the dates of Greek history, one may be sorrowfully resigned to lose, for lack of time to drill oneself often enough in them.

Very valuable and painstaking experimentation has concerned itself with the more exact relations between repetition and reproduction. Most important is the work of Dr. Hermann Ebbinghaus,[1] whose experiments on himself were carried on through two periods of more than a year each. As material he used twenty-three hundred meaningless syllables, of three letters, arranged in series of varying length. The immediate aim of each experiment was the discovery of the number of readings necessary to the correct, unhesitating reproduction of the series from first to last syllable. The experiments, in the first place, confirm ordinary experience, showing, among other things, (1) that the time of learning increases with the length of series, and (2) that the greater the number of repetitions the shorter the time in which a series can be relearned. The experiments also supplement everyday observation in several particulars. They show that more is forgotten, in the first fifteen minutes after learning such a series, than in the month which follows the quarter-hour; and that one can reproduce as much of it after a month as after two days.

---

[1] "Über das Gedachtniss," Leipzig, 1885.

Another method of facilitating reproduction is of incomparably greater significance in the life of consciousness. It consists in the association, or relation, of the fact to be recalled with other facts. As James says, "The secret of a good memory is the secret of forming diverse and multiple associations with every fact we care to retain." There are three ways in which this multiplication of associations facilitates memory. It contributes to a completer first-hand knowledge of the fact to be recalled; it increases the number of topics which are likely to recall this one; and it connects the fact to be remembered with other facts, into a system so close that only one central fact, in place of a multitude of different ones, has to be recalled. In illustration of the effectiveness of the multiplication of relations, let us suppose that I wish to recall the year, 1861, of my cousin's birth, and that I cannot directly remember it. I proceed to associate the year with other events, the admission of Kansas as a free state and the firing on Fort Sumter. The effort to recall the date is now likely to be successful, through first reminding me of one or more of the historic dates. The experiments of Ebbinghaus, already described, incidentally corroborate this conclusion. A comparison of the repetitions, necessary to memorize his meaningless series, with those required for certain stanzas of Byron — series of words directly connected in meaning and rich in other associations — showed an enormous reduction of time in the later experience.

The mere multiplication of suggestions is, however, far less effective than the systematic grouping of facts to be remembered by some fundamental likeness. I am studying, we will suppose, the fall of Constantinople and the consequent dispersion of scholars and renaissance of learning; I connect this intellectual awakening with the contemporaneous invention of printing; I observe the analogy of this mental progressiveness with the outbreak of the adventurous spirit of travel and the consequent discovery of America; and thus I bind all these events to the well-known date of the landing of Columbus, remembering them, not in their detail, but as an organic unity. To remember Greek verb-forms by their connection with a common root, or poems by their adherence to a certain verse-scheme, are illustrations of the same method. Most mnemonic devices, on the contrary, merely multiply unrelated associations, or else combine the facts to be remembered in artificial systems of insignificant facts. The fundamental memory-method is thus the unification or grouping or, as it has been called by Herbart and Wundt, the apperception of facts in a whole of related parts. This, however, as we have seen, is what we mean by judgment and reasoning, and characterizes all effective intellectual achievement. We are justified, therefore, in the assertion that successful memorizing must be thoughtful; and in the consoling conclusion that even the physiologically 'unretentive' individual can strengthen his memory, by persistent seeking for fundamental similarities, by constant widening of his thought-systems to include more and more details. Facts thus intimately interwoven with the very 'warp and woof' of one's mental life simply cannot be unravelled or forgotten.

The next and last of these rules for the cultivation of memory involves the principle of selection: the memory is more effective when the fact to be remembered belongs to the natural image-type; the visualizer, for example, has most accurate, complete and readily suggested visual images. So far as possible, therefore, one's memorizing should use this natural sense-material; and one should visualize, or repeat, or listen to the words to be remembered, according as one's memory is visual, 'motor,' or auditory; indeed, one should ordinarily employ all three methods, since most people's images are of what is called the mixed type. This is one of the principles underlying many so-called modern methods of education. The child no longer studies his spelling lesson merely by glaring at the open page, but he repeats it and writes it and listens to it. And one learns to read one's Greek not merely 'at sight,' but 'at hearing,' that is, one familiarizes oneself with the sound as well as with the sight of the words. The most universally effective application of this principle is in the effort, so far as possible, to replace the verbal by the concrete memory image.[1] Almost without exception, everybody remembers concrete experiences more readily than bare words, and very naturally, since the words are ordinarily insignificant in themselves, and only useful when they serve to suggest these same concrete things. This is one great reason why it is better to travel for oneself than to read descriptions of foreign lands, and better to watch a machine in motion than to hear an account of its movements. It is a reason, also, why it is absolutely essential to practise oneself in translating the words one reads into concrete images, so that one never leaves a page without 'seeing' the faces or scenes which have been described.

Many word-series, it is true, are significant in themselves, as well as representative of concrete meanings. These are the words of the great poets ánd the masters of æsthetic prose, word-series with a music of their own, a liquid modulation of sound, a swinging metre or a winning alliteration. The value of an exact verbal memory for great poetry and for majestic prose is, therefore, simply immeasurable. It widens and invigorates the life of imagination, enriches the literary style, increases the mental effectiveness. The ability to recall, word for word, Hebrew psalms, Homeric descriptions, Roman oratory, Shakespearian drama and German lyrics means the sure possession of what the greatest artists have wrought, and the potent means of enriching and ennobling one's life of æsthetic enjoyment and intellectual aspiration. It follows, of course, that every child should be trained to commit to memory poems and prose works of literary beauty. Yet

[1] Cf. Kirkpatrick, *Psychological Review*, Vol. I., p. 602; cf. also "Short Studies in Memory and Association from the Wellesley College Psychological Laboratory," *Psychological Review*, Vol. V., p. 452.

a caution is needed. All forms of memorizing are intellectual exercises of secondary importance, since memory,
as we have seen, is subsidiary to the life of thought, of
emotion, and of will. Now, there are many people, whose
verbal memory is so abnormally dull and inaccurate, that
they might better devote themselves to problems in arithmetic, experiments in chemistry or study of Greek syntax,
than to memory exercises of any sort. Many a child has
been hunted and harried into a condition of abject misery
by the requisition of so many poems per week, and many
an older student has devoted time to memorizing his three
hundred lines of Shakespeare which might better have
been applied to understanding their meaning. In a word,
then, a good verbal memory is an intellectual luxury, not
a capacity indispensable to vigorous mental life. Great
pains should, therefore, be taken to stimulate and to cultivate it, but when an individual is almost utterly devoid
of it, he should not be condemned to a life of ceaseless
and all but useless repetition.

The physiological conditions of memory, as distinguished
from mere imagination, perhaps demand more extended
consideration. It is evident, in the first place, that the
efficiency of memory is in part affected by what has been
called the retentiveness of brain-substance, that is, its
tendency to reëxcitation. This ' tenacity,' as James calls
it, differs enormously in different individuals, and ordinarily decreases from youth to age. It is probably increased,
to some degree, by the prolongation of intense stimuli in
attentive perception, and also by the repetition of stimuli
in voluntary memorizing. Differences in the physiological
retentiveness of distinct brain-areas are regarded in the
selection of natural memory-material for memorizing.
But, though it is likely that this neural tendency to re-
excitation may be strengthened, especially by the repetition of stimuli, it must nevertheless be admitted that, as
James has pointed out, the effect of repetition is a limited

one, strengthening the memory for particular facts or words only, instead of promoting a general ability to recall all sorts of facts. " No amount of culture," James says,[1] " would seem capable of modifying a man's general retentiveness." " This," he adds, "is a physiological quality given once for all with his organization, which [an individual] can never hope to change," except as he betters it by generally helpful bodily conditions. Evidently, therefore, the most important physiological results of memory-methods are the origination, the multiplication, the strengthening and the unification of connections among the different brain-centres, and are brought about by the systematic development of associations.

[1] *Op. cit.,* Vol. I., pp. 663, 664.

CHAPTER XVII

THOUGHT : GENERALIZATION

I

In this chapter, we shall discuss the experience usually known as thought, from the two points of view already familiar to us. We shall study ' the thought,' the temporally distinct idea, without explicit reference to any self, and we shall also consider ' thinking,' the experience of a self. According to the first of these conceptions, a thought is described merely as a complex idea, in which untemporal, relational elements are prominent. In other words, a thought is the immediate consciousness of a synthesis or unity which is not temporal. It is contrasted, on the one hand, with association and fusion, forms of unity of which one is not immediately conscious, and on the other hand, with memories, beliefs and volitions, which are, as we shall see, ideas of temporal unity, of the relation of present to past or to future.[1]

But though we may regard thought as a mere succession of temporally distinguished thoughts, yet it also means more than this; we are always conscious of thinking selves as well as of succeeding thoughts. Thought, in this sense, is like perception, which has been defined as social experience, that is, as consciousness shared with other selves. For generalization, judgment and comparison, the more important forms of thought, are experiences which we suppose ourselves to share with an indefinite

[1] For instances of this common theory of thought as consciousness of unity, cf. Wundt, "Physiolog. Psychologie," 3ᵗᵉ Aufl. p. 495; Ladd, "Psychology Descriptive and Explanatory," p. 432, and Höffding, "Outlines of Psychology," Eng. trans., p. 173.

number of unparticularized other selves. There is something private and particular about our reveries and our day-dreams, but our thoughts are never regarded as personal property. Our castles in Spain are private dwellings, but the great halls of thought swing wide to every comer. This is most readily illustrated from the more abstract sorts of thinking, and the most striking of all examples are from logic and mathematical science. No man appropriates the multiplication table or the axiom that 'things equal to the same thing are equal to each other,' or the theorem that the sum of the angles of a triangle equals two right angles, as an experience peculiar to himself. One would as soon lay special claim to the stars in their courses or to the law of gravitation. But in spite of the fact that the abstract sciences most brilliantly illustrate the social character of thinking, any generalization or judgment, however concrete, is also as conceivably a common experience. Not merely one's conception of 'numeral' or of 'triangle,' but one's general notion of 'food' or of 'animal' is always acknowledged as sharable or public, as in no sense a particular experience of one's own. It makes no difference to our psychological analysis, whether or not we are correct in this assumption that our conceptions and judgments are shared. As a matter of fact, we are often most wofully mistaken, and arguments usually arise from the unrealized difference in the concepts marked by the same word. But, none the less, we do always in our thinking assume the conceivable universality of the experience, we acknowledge that other selves have, or may have, the concepts which we possess, and that they make or might make the same judgments on the same subjects.

From imagination, or the hypothetically unsharable experience, and from emotion, will and faith, the acknowledged relation to strongly individualized selves, thinking, like perceiving, is thus distinguished as a common experience of 'any,' that is of unparticularized, selves. In the case of most forms of thinking, the recognition of this community of experience is usually an after reflection, not an immediate constituent of the thought. In the moment of comparing or in that of judging, one may not realize the actual or possible conformity of another's consciousness. One may note the difference between two chords or one may reason about the outcome of the Spanish War, without any conscious acknowledgment of the possible agreement of everybody else. Conception, or generalization, on the other hand, is a form of consciousness in which, as in emotion, the consciousness of other selves is an inevitable and a significant part of the experience. The very word 'any,' the characteristic epithet, as we shall find, of the general notion, has a sort of personal aroma. 'Any cat,' 'any triangle,' 'any truth,' — these expressions always mean to us not merely the presence, in these facts of consciousness, of a relational factor, but their reference to an indefinite number of unindividualized selves. 'Any triangle' is the triangle in which the features which I chance to imagine, the size and color and degree of obliqueness, are quite unimportant, whereas the triangularity (the part experienced by everybody who thinks of the triangle) is altogether essential.

Since thinking, then, like perceiving, acknowledges the common experience of unparticularized other selves, the question arises, How is it to be distinguished from perceiving? From the purely social standpoint there is in fact no distinction between the two, but they are contrasted from another point of view. It has been shown that developed perception takes account of 'external things'; and that physical externality involves two factors, (1) admitted reference to any selves, and (2) assumed independence of all selves. The thought, as distinct from the thing, lacks precisely this second element of physical externality. Comparison, concept and judgment, the facts of thought, are never supposed, as 'things' are, to be independent of the selves who think. Multiplication table and geometrical figures and laws of thought, in spite of the certainty and universality which sharply distinguish them from the lawless and capricious and private objects of our imagination, are yet regarded as conscious experiences, psychic phenomena, not physical things; in other words, they are never cut loose from selves; and this is their great distinction from objects of perception.

II

In whatever way one regards thought, whether as a thought or as thinking, as mere idea in a series, or as shared experience of selves, it is a complex consciousness which may be analyzed into elements, and which includes always a relational element without temporal reference. We shall proceed to the closer analysis and description of the most important forms of thought. Obviously, there are as many types of thought as there are relational elements without temporal reference. We shall, however, confine our discussion to the three sorts of thought most often considered: conception, judgment and reasoning, referring incidentally also to comparison, the thought-complex distinguished by feelings of likeness and of difference.

a. GENERALIZATION

By generalization (or conception) we may mean both generalizing, the personal experience, and the general notion, or concept, the idea regarded without reference to any self. Both alike are complex experiences including the relational feeling of generality. In what follows, we shall, it is true, most often consider the 'general notion,' that is, the complex idea; but all that we shall say will be perfectly applicable to generalizing, the personal experience.

We must first discuss the nature of the feeling of generality. My consciousness of 'a rose,' for example, is a case of concrete perception, mainly a complex of sensations; when, on the other hand, I am conscious of 'rose,' my experience includes not only the image, probably blurred or dull, of a rose (very likely of more than one rose), but another feeling, quite different from any sensational or affective experience. We may call this supplementary experience the feeling of generality, and we shall probably find that it includes two simpler experiences, that of likeness and that of wholeness. In other words, the feeling of generality involved in my consciousness of 'vase' or of 'justice' seems to me to include both the feeling with which I observe similar objects and the feeling with which I observe a group of objects. In actual experience, however, I seldom attend to the feeling of likeness and that of wholeness, as distinct from each other, but rather to the fused feeling of generality.

This attempted analysis of our feeling of generality labors, of course, under the difficulties attending all merely introspective analysis of relational elements. But it should be observed that this account of conception is, in its general features, explicitly or virtually the view of many psychologists. Wundt definitely adopts it[1] by the expression 'characteristic concept-feeling (eigenthümlicher Begriffsgefühl)'; Ladd clearly implies it[2] by the statement, "the individually similar becomes the universally identical"; and it is the most important teaching of James on this subject. He calls the "sense of sameness . . . the very keel and backbone of our thinking,"[3] and means by this almost exactly what has been expressed in the statement, that the feeling of generality is the consciousness of the likeness of a group, or whole, of facts.

We must now recur to the assertion that the idea of generality may be combined with any content of consciousness. It follows that general notions will be most readily classified as (1) simple, when the feeling of generality is combined with an element of consciousness, as in

[1] *Op. cit.*, Vol. II., Chapter XVII., p. 477.
[2] "Psychology, Descriptive and Explanatory," p. 434.
[3] *Op. cit.*, Vol. I., Chapter XII., p. 459.

the concepts 'blueness,' 'loudness,' 'pleasantness,' 'one-ness,' and (2) complex, when the idea of anyness is combined with a combination of elements as in the concepts 'animal,' 'fear,' 'comparison.' Such a classification sharply opposes a traditional view of the general notion, the doctrine that generalization differs *in toto* from every other conscious experience, so that when we are generalizing we cannot be at the same time perceiving or imagining, and that conversely, when we are perceiving or imagining, we are not at the same time generalizing. The general notion, on this view of it, is, in fact, a not-sensation, a not-image and the like. John Locke has given a famous example of the absurdity to which this doctrine leads, by his attempt to illustrate it in the case of a concrete, complex concept. The general notion of a triangle, he tells us,[1] must be the consciousness of a 'triangle — neither oblique nor rectangle, neither equilateral nor equicrural nor scalenon, but all and none of these at once.' This illustration of a complex general notion, which is not at the same time an image or percept, sufficiently disposes of the theory that generalization is an exclusive sort of consciousness; for everybody realizes, with Bishop Berkeley, that it is impossible "by any effort of thought [to] conceive the . . . idea above described."[2] The truth is, as we have seen, that the generality of an experience is a supplemental feature of it, attaching itself as readily to a complex as to an element. An experience, in other words, is not debarred from being image or percept because it is a general notion; rather, as a general notion, it is also sensation, affection, relational element, image or percept. Its generality or conceptual quality consists, indeed, merely in the addition of the 'feeling of generality' to some element or combination. We have, therefore, particular experiences, described as 'the pink of the apple blossoms in this water color,' or as 'your

[1] "Essay concerning Human Understanding," Bk. IV., Chapter VII., §§ 9 *seq.*

[2] "Principles of Human Knowledge," Introduction, §§ 6-20.

desk,' 'my memory of Edward Everett Hale in Faneuil
Hall,' but we have also general sensations and images,
such as 'Pompeian reds,' 'the sight of your desk realized
as one of many like it,' or the general image 'orator.'
(There are no general emotions, volitions or beliefs, for
these, as we shall find, are intensely particularizing experiences.)

Psychologists do not invariably teach that a percept, as
well as an image, may form the groundwork of the general notion. A percept, to be sure, because of the nearly
equal vividness of its parts, is less likely to become 'abstract,'
or partially attended-to ; but it is quite conceivable that
the shape or name or use of the perceived desk, as well
as of the imagined one, should be attended to and supplemented by the feeling of generality. This is the teaching
of James in the chapter already quoted.

The doctrine that generalization excludes imagination
and perception may fairly be said to be disproved. Like
all persistent errors, however, it is based upon an important truth, the observation that all general notions are
abstract. We are thus led to discuss the nature of abstraction. As we shall see, the subject would more consistently
be studied under the head of 'attention,' but it is here included because of its close connection with generalization.

Abstraction is simply attention, with emphasis upon the
narrowing aspect of it. The abstract notion is thus the
attended-to part of any complex content of consciousness.
It may be of greater or less extent, just as attention may
be less or more narrowing ; and there may be as many
abstract notions as there are elements of consciousness.
The determining consideration is simply this, that the
whole of one's experience should not be equally interesting, but that some part of it should be in a sense shut out,
unattended-to and uninteresting.[1]

This simple doctrine, that the abstract notion is merely

[1] Cf. Chapter XI.

any part attended-to of a complex idea, disposes of two ordinary theories about it. 'Abstract,' in the first place, is often supposed to mean 'unsensational.' Most intelligent persons, therefore, if asked to give examples of abstract notions, would select some such ideas as those of 'identity,' 'beauty' or 'virtue,' under the impression that the consciousness of color or sound or smell and the like must be ruled out of the class of abstract notions. But 'blueness,' 'pleasantness,' 'four-footedness' are as much abstract, that is partial experiences, as the supposedly unsensational ideas already suggested. Every element, sensational, attributive or relational, is, therefore, abstract, and every complex of elements short of a complete percept or image is also abstract.

It is even more important to observe that an abstract notion is not necessarily a general notion. This conclusion is quite contrary to the ordinary assumption. Almost everybody, psychologist or layman, quite regardless of the meaning of English, uses 'abstract' and 'general' as synonymous terms.[1] But the truth is, that when I am conscious of 'this blueness,' 'the sweetness of this pear,' 'the warmth of this room,' I am abstracting, that is, attending to a part only of my total experience, yet I am not generalizing because my idea is of *this* or *that* element, not of *any similar* element.

But this error, like others, is based on a truth. Though abstraction does not involve generalization, so that abstract notions are not necessarily general, yet, on the other hand, generalization does involve abstraction, and every general notion is abstract. This is a fact of common observation.

---

[1] Cf. Höffding (*op. cit.*, p. 167) : "General ideas exist, therefore, in the sense that we are able to concentrate the attention on certain elements of the individual idea." This assertion, inaccurate as it stands, would be perfectly correct if made about the abstract idea. The same confusion of abstraction with conception occurs in James's discussion of the subject, side by side with the adequate view of the relation, expressed in the following statement (*op. cit.*, Vol. I., p. 461), "Each act of conception results from attention singling out some one part of the mass of matter for thought which the world presents."

Q

sake, but differing widely in the bodily movements required, the implements used and the costumes worn. From this point we may well quote again from Huxley's account of the matter : —

"When several complex impressions which are more or less different from one another — let us say that out of ten impressions in each, six are the same in all, and four are different from all the rest — are successively presented to the mind, it is easy to see what must be the nature of the result. The repetition of the six similar impressions will strengthen the six corresponding elements of the complex idea, which will therefore acquire greater vividness; while the four differing impressions of each will not only acquire no greater strength than they had at first, but, in accordance with the law of association, they will all tend to appear at once, and thus will neutralize one another.

"This mental operation may be rendered comprehensible by considering what takes place in the formation of compound photographs; . . . all those points in which the six faces agree are brought out strongly, while all those in which they differ are left vague; and thus what may be termed a *generic* portrait of the six, in contradistinction to a *specific* portrait of any one, is produced."

Most psychologists call attention to the fact that the concept or general notion lacks distinctness. Ladd calls it pale, less lifelike and sketchy; Baldwin speaks of its vagueness and indefiniteness; Külpe says that "it lacks definite determination"; and Wundt's idiomatic statement is the following, "es verliert an Anschaulichkeit." The tendency of associationists, like Hume and Huxley, is to treat this vagueness as the essential feature of the general notion. The difference in degree of definiteness is, however, an insufficient ground of distinction. We have many images, in drowsy revery, for example, which are very indistinct but which we never call general.

Another frequent, but not invariable, characteristic of the general notion we may call its compositeness, if we use this term to indicate the fact, that a general notion very often includes within itself several similar elements or combinations to which, taken together, the generality-feeling attaches. My general notion 'dog,' may be, for instance, the indistinct image of a group of dogs of different shapes and sizes, and my general notion of 'blue' is very likely an image of one blue on a background of several others.

It might be supposed that this duplication is necessary, that if, for example, my consciousness of 'rose' includes the feeling of generality, already analyzed into the feelings of 'likeness' and 'wholeness,' it must include at least two rose-images. For — it might be insisted — one thing is always like a second, and a whole implies at least two parts. Of course, this is true; yet the feeling of 'like,' though unquestionably due to the observation of at least two things, and leading to the recognition of two things, is not identical with the consciousness of 'two,' and may conceivably be present when one of the ideas which gave rise to it has disappeared from consciousness. The same assertion may be made concerning the feeling of 'whole.' The general notion, therefore, may be, but need not be, 'composite.'

This compositeness is closely related and readily confused with the final characteristic of the general notion, the fact that it is associative of similar ideas. It will be observed that this mark of the general notion, its associativeness, is not a constituent feature but a function of it — not a part of it, but a result of it, as it were. There can be no doubt that a general notion does, as a matter of fact, suggest a series, longer or shorter, of images of objects said to belong to a class. The general image 'tool,' for example, suggests a panoramic series of axes, saws and hammers; and the general notion 'rat' is followed by a rapidly-shifting, imaged procession of —

"Great rats, small rats, lean rats, brawny rats,
   Brown rats, black rats, gray rats, tawny rats."

In this function of associating a class of similars, the general notion is sharply contrasted with the ungeneralized content of consciousness. My image of one particular volume of Montaigne is likely to associate an image of the odd little book-stall, on the Parisian quay, where I bought it, and this, in turn, may be followed by an image of a lecture-room in the neighboring Sorbonne, and this by an image of the Grecian city about which the lecturer spoke. The images, following upon the initial image, may thus be absolutely different from their starting-point and from each other. It is quite otherwise with the general notion. This is, as we know, an 'abstract,' that is, it does not contain the special features which make up 'my Montaigne,' and it associates a series of book-images, each resembling all its predecessors in the possession of certain common qualities. Both 'particular' and 'general' notions are associative, but the associates of a general notion are similar to each other and are known as a class or group.

The study of the general notion, as associative of similars, introduces very naturally a question of detail, What sorts of general notion are most common? In attempting to answer the question, we must constantly bear in mind that the presence of what we have called generality-feeling is the one unfailing test of the general notion. For, true as it is that the general notion is ordinarily 'blurred' or vague, and often complex, and always associative of similars, yet an image with all these characteristics would not be 'general' if the feeling of generality did not occur.

Two especially significant types of general notion have been pointed out by psychologists. The first of these is the name-idea, that is, the verbal image supplemented by the feeling of generality and suggestive of a series of similar ideas. There is no doubt that every word in a language, exclusive of its proper nouns and its expletives, if it stands for anything at all, and is not merely a set of meaningless sounds or scrawls, is a general term suggestive of a great many ideas similar to each other, at least in so far as they have the same name. It is easy to test this assertion. Let any one pronounce to himself any series of words, for example, the first three or four of the " Æneid." ' Arma ' will suggest an image-series including 'sword,' 'helmet,' 'spear'; ' virum ' readily associates an imaged procession of Greek and Trojan heroes; ' que ' vaguely suggests connections of several sorts; and the word-image ' cano ' will be followed by the representations of various vocal activities. What is true of these words is true of any others; all words, in fact, may represent a group of like ideas, that is, may be suggestive of a series of similar images. But this, as we have seen, would not turn a verbal image into a general notion, and it is difficult to decide introspectively, in what cases a given verbal image is accompanied by the feeling of generality. Often, certainly, the feeling is absent even when the word-image performs its function of suggesting similars. I may read the word ' candle,' for instance, and it may suggest to me a series of tapers of different shapes and sizes, and yet I may not be conscious of any generality-feeling. In this case, though the spoken or written word ' candle ' may be called a ' general term,' the verbal image ' candle ' is not, according to our doctrine, a ' general notion.' It is probable, in fact, that psychologists who have laid most stress on general name-ideas have confused these two, the general term, a word associative of similars, and the verbal general notion, a verbal image, not only associative of similars, but inclusive of a certain feeling of generality. Such genuine verbal concepts, or general notions, do probably occur in our experience, though it is not easy to be introspectively certain about any one of them. For example, many unsensational general notions, such as 'truth,' 'identity,' ' tariff,' probably consist, in part at least, of a verbal image accompanied by the generality-feeling.

A more important type of general notion is that which contains the idea of motor reaction. Such an idea forms a common feature of many images, which in other respects are very diverse, and it is naturally, therefore, suggestive of long series of similar ideas. The generalized feature of our notion 'chair,' for example, is not that of material, of color, or even of form, because no one of these is common to our ideas of the innumerable, widely different objects known as chairs. Between the Westminster Abbey coronation chair and the unsteady support provided at parlor lectures, there is in fact little in common except the characteristic motor reaction called forth by each. The chair is thus the ' to-be-sat-down-on,' and this imaged bodily reaction is probably the part of my image 'chair' which is accompanied by the feeling of generality and followed by the series of images — of throne, stuffed arm-chair, rush chair and milkmaid's stool — very different objects, similar in this one respect, that they are things to be sat down on. In the same way, foods differ in every conceivable particular of color, form and consistency, but agree in calling forth a common system of bodily movements. The generalized feature of the general notion, food, is thus the image of it as the 'to-be-eaten.' In the same way, the pen is the ' to-be-written-with,' the flower is the ' to-be-smelled ' or ' to-be-picked,' the hat is the ' to-be-put-on-one's-head.'

An interesting proof that the idea of our motor reactions is a significant feature of the general notion is found in the fact that we commonly suppose ourselves not to 'know' objects, that is, to be incapable of generalizing and classifying them, when we do not know what to do with them, in other words, when they involve no imaged motor reaction. Somebody shows me an oddly shaped stone and I exclaim, "I don't know what it is." But all the time I am perfectly aware that it is irregular in shape, gray in color, cold to the touch. I know many things about it, but I don't know what to do with it, and I, therefore, have no general notion of it until some one tells me that it is a pre-

historic battle-axe. At once, the image of attacking movements becomes part of my consciousness of the bit of stone,
and is accompanied by a feeling of generality and followed
by a series of imaged weapons, very different in most respects from this bit of stone, yet similar to it because including the notion of movements of attack. Such a general
notion is, in the words of Professor Royce, 'an idea of the
way to do that.' Careful consideration of the actual meaning of most of our general notions of concrete objects will
show that they are of this type. The concrete thing means
to us what we do with it, and our general notion of it is
an image of our reaction to it, supplemented by the feeling
of generality, and actually followed, as is later discovered,
by a series of similar ideas.

It is not, however, true, as some psychologists imply,[1]
that this is the only type of general notion. The idea of
motor reaction surely forms no distinguishing part of our
unsensational, general notions. No common motor reaction, for example, characterizes all forms of 'cause' or of
'science.' The consideration of these two historically
important forms of general notion brings us, in fact, to the
conclusion that there is no element or complex of consciousness, sensational, attributive or relational, verbal or
concrete, which may not be attended by the feeling of
generality, and which may not become, by virtue of this
accompaniment, a general notion. In the general notion of a
concrete percept, this generality-feeling often indeed supplements the idea of a common motor reaction; in an elemental
general notion, such as redness, it may either be directly
attached to the element, or to the verbal image, 'redness';
in an affective concept, it is probably combined, not merely
with a verbal image, but with a weak throb of the affection
itself. In all forms of concept, the perceptual or image
experience is usually vague, and is followed by a series of
similar images. The similarity of these images consists in

[1] Cf. Baldwin, *op. cit.*, pp. 325 *seq.*, and Royce, as quoted by Baldwin.

their common possession of the generalized feature, motor idea, sense-element or affection.

The relational experience of generality, which alone distinguishes the general notion from the elements and ideas already discussed, has, of course, no regular physical stimulus. Our incomplete knowledge of cerebral conditions forbids, also, the attempt to describe exactly its intracortical excitation. In general, we may say that the feeling of generality is conditioned by the activity of connecting fibres and probably also of cells in the 'association-centres.'

There is another theory of the general notion, so consistent and so plausible that it must be briefly outlined. It is virtually the doctrine of the scholastic nominalists and of English associationists, but the clearest statement of it, known to the writer, is that of Dr. Dickinson Miller.[1] According to this theory, the 'generality' of an experience consists simply in the fact, so often noticed, that it associates similar images. In other words, this theory denies the existence of any 'feeling of generality,' and holds that generality is not a constituent of the particular content of consciousness, but a function of it. As immediately experienced, the general notion is not, on this view, different from any other, but it proves to have suggested similar images, instead of diverse ones, and it is called 'general' therefore, not for what it is, but for what it does.

The positive part of this doctrine is, of course, indisputable. General notions are, as we have over and over again discovered, suggestive of similar ideas. The negative teaching, that the general notion is distinct in function only, and that it has no peculiar consciousness characteristic of it, contradicts, in the opinion of the writer, the plain witness of introspection to a distinct feeling of generality.

[1] *Psychological Review*, Vol. II., pp. 537 *seq.*

CHAPTER XVIII

THOUGHT: JUDGMENT AND REASONING

b. THE SIMPLE JUDGMENT

LIKE conception or generalization, judgment is a complex consciousness distinguished by the presence of an untemporal, relational experience, the feeling of wholeness. This consciousness of 'whole' is accompanied by a discrimination of parts within a whole. Judging is, therefore, the shared consciousness of a whole, with especial attention to one or more of its parts; and 'a judgment' is a complex of elements of consciousness, containing one or more emphasized parts, and yet realized as a whole. A judgment, like a general notion, is, therefore, a percept or image *plus* a relational experience, in this case, the feeling of wholeness. It is, of course, useless to attempt a close description of the cerebral conditions of judgment. Excitation of connecting fibres and of cells in 'association-centres' probably, however, occurs.

Let us first try to make clear to ourselves the shifting distinction between the judgment and the mere percept or image. I look off at a gray church spire, half a mile below me, and have a consciousness of grayness, form, roughness, oneness and limitedness. I do not reflect upon this experience nor analyze it; and no one part of it — grayness or tapering height — impresses me more than another. So far, then, this experience is a mere percept. But now, for some reason, the grayness of the spire draws my attention; I lay little stress on its form, but I am interested in its color, — in other words, I have an 'abstract notion' of the color. Finally, however, I am conscious of the grayness as a part of the spire, as belonging to it, as forming with its shape and other features one whole; and now for the first time I am judging, conscious of a complex as a whole inclusive of an emphasized part. Perception and judgment alike are distinguished, first, from the abstract notion by their complexity, and second, from the total sensational complex by their limitedness. But judgment is distinguished from perception by the added feeling of wholeness, and by the invariable emphasis of some part within its total. The three sorts of experience, percept, abstract notion, judgment, may be represented in words, by the expressions 'gray spire,' 'grayness,' 'the spire is gray.' The propositional form of the last clause is an indication of both aspects of the judgment, the feeling of wholeness and the attention to one part.

There are two basal types of judgment: we shall call them 'analytic' and 'synthetic.' They differ in the manner of their formation, not in their essential nature; that is to say, they are distinguished genetically, not analytically. Our church spire example is an illustration of the analytic judgment, which is formed by the persisting vividness of one part of any complex experience, supplemented, of course, by the feeling of its connection with the other parts in a 'whole.' Any object or scene which is thought of as a whole of discriminated parts is, therefore, a judgment; and it is probably true, that most of the undifferentiated percepts and images of a child's consciousness are later replaced by analytic judgments. 'The birch leaves are yellow,' 'the whale is a mammal,' 'Europe includes Germany,' are propositions which represent these analytic judgments (unless, indeed, they stand for mere percepts, and mean no more than the expressions 'yellow leaves,' 'mammalian whale,' 'European Germany'). From Professor Titchener,[1] we may quote several examples of these

---

[1] "Outline of Psychology," § 54.

analytic judgments, and the way in which they are formed. "The best illustration," he says, "is the connection of auditory ideas in the sentence. The whole 'thought,' *i.e.* complex of ideas, which the sentence expresses must form part of our consciousness, however vaguely, before we begin to speak, otherwise we could not carry the sentence to its conclusion without hesitation and mistake." "Suppose," he continues, "that I say to myself: 'That chord contains the notes C, E, G.' The chord is given as a total impression; it is a complex of simultaneously sounding tones. But the attention fixes for some reason upon one of the constituent tone-complexes, the note C. This is rendered prominent and distinct, while the remaining constituents are blurred and weakened. The impression is thus split up, its components dissociated. The attention soon relaxes from its first object, and the other two notes receive, in turn, their share of notice. The whole complex is thus reviewed, part by part, and put together again in the sentence: 'It contained the notes C, E, G.'"

It should be added that Titchener replaces our term 'analytic judgment' by the expression 'association after disjunction,' and that he makes no mention at all of the class of synthetic judgments. A more serious difference is his neglect of the distinguishing feature of the judgment, its 'feeling of wholeness.' It is noteworthy, however, that he suggests the wholeness-feeling by the observation that the judgment has the 'character of completeness or finality.' This definition of judgment as association overlooks the fact, already emphasized,[1] that association is an objective synthesis of ideas, that is, a connection on which one later reflects, not a unity of which one is immediately conscious. But judgment and reasoning are characterized by precisely this immediate consciousness of unity. Association, or the after reflection on connection, cannot, therefore, be identical with judgment, or the intimate feeling of

[1] Cf. Chapter XIII., p. 157.

wholeness; and, indeed, association may occur when judgment, in this sense, is absent. For example, the ideas whose combination is indicated by the proposition 'heat is a form of motion' may be merely associated, that is, they may be later observed to be connected; but such association is utterly different from the immediate feeling of wholeness which distinguishes the judgment.

Within the class of analytic judgments, we may further distinguish the abstract from the concrete. It will be noticed that the third of our illustrations, at the end of page 235, is different from the others, in the completeness and independence of its discriminated part. That is to say, the image of 'Germany' may occur without that of 'Europe,' whereas the consciousness of 'yellow' always forms a part of another complete whole — of 'leaf' or 'wall' or 'gown'; and in the same way the idea 'mammal,' though more complex than the sensation 'yellow,' is present to consciousness only as constituent of some larger idea, as 'whale' or 'cow' or 'human being.' Judgments, in which the discriminated feature occurs only as part of a larger content, are called 'abstract'; judgments in which the discriminated parts are conceivably independent are named 'concrete.'

Contrasted with the whole class of analytic judgments, whether abstract or concrete, is the second fundamental class, that of synthetic judgments. This type of judgments may be illustrated in the most diverse ways. 'Napoleon burnt Moscow,' 'Browning played the organ,' are clear examples of it; 'platinum is ductile,' or 'some water-lilies are pink,' are less obvious instances. The distinction is the following: an analytic judgment is formed, as we have seen, by the emphasis of part of an undifferentiated, though limited, complex; it therefore involves nothing new except the feeling of wholeness. A synthetic judgment, on the other hand, arises by the association of new facts of consciousness to the fact already present; and old and new are then regarded as parts of a whole. In other words, a percept or image, gained by the association of one fact of consciousness with another, is supplemented by a feeling of whole-ness, and forms, thus, a synthetic judgment. The synthetic judgment is, therefore, a judgment of discovery. It differs from the analytic judgment only in the manner of forma-tion, not in nature, for, in both cases, the judgment is con-stituted by the included 'feeling of wholeness.'

The synthetic judgment, also, has the two classes, 'ab-stract' and 'concrete.' There is, however, no way of indi-cating by words the difference between an analytic and a synthetic, abstract judgment. To recur to one of our ex-amples: 'platinum is ductile' is a synthetic judgment only to the person whose concept of platinum does not already include the idea of ductility. In this case, the idea of ductility is added to one's initial image of a light, silvery metal, to form one complete total-image of platinum as a light, silvery, *ductile* metal. Only introspection can decide, in any special case, whether an abstract judgment is analytic or synthetic.

The terms 'analytic' and 'synthetic' are Kant's, and his use of them, from the standpoint of psychology, is sim-ilar to ours. It should be observed that the expressions cannot be replaced by the words 'discriminative' and 'asso-ciative,' since even in an analytic judgment there is associ-ation, that of discriminated part with whole, and even in a synthetic judgment there is discrimination, that of the rel-atively independent part in a whole. For illustration of the use of the term 'abstract,' in the sense 'incomplete' and in contrast with 'concrete,' that is, 'relatively complete' or 'self-sufficient,' we may refer to certain statements of James.[1]

It should be added that a judgment may conceivably include more than one emphasized part. Since, however, our attention is very limited, it is probable that the greater number of judgments include, psychologically as well as logically, but a single predicate. The experience, for instance, expressed by the sentence, 'McKinley stands

[1] Cf. especially *op. cit.*, Vol. II., p. 337.

for imperialism and sound money,' though expressed in a single proposition, is, for most of us, two judgments, in which the feeling of wholeness attaches successively to the complexes ' McKinley — sound money,' and, ' McKinley — imperialism.' This suggests once more the important truth that the proposition is a mere form of words, subject and predicate, and that it may as well express a series of associated images as a judgment. When the French soldiers and Napoleon first realized that 'the Russians burned Moscow,' the experience probably was a judgment, that is to say, the feeling of the event as a whole of distinguished parts was presumably present to them. But the words, as we repeat them, may stand to us for a mere succession of images, verbal or concrete.

An important instance of a proposition which does not express a judgment is the so-called negative judgment, " No cats are two-legged," or, " No Frenchmen are Teutons." These are negative propositions, but the experiences for which they stand involve the relational feeling of exclusion, not the feeling of wholeness ; psychologically, therefore, they are quite distinct from judgments. But though a negative proposition does not express a judgment, it undoubtedly implies a judgment. One must have the consciousness of a whole before one can think of anything as excluded from that whole, and the negative proposition is essentially, as we have seen, the assertion of a feeling of exclusion.

We must notice, in conclusion, that many psychologists regard judgment as identical with belief. This belief-theory is first found in Aristotle's observation that only propositions, never mere terms, can be true or false. In modern times, Brentano [1] coördinates judgment with will and perceiving, as fundamental activities of consciousness ; and Stout adopts the same view,[2] defining judgment as the ' yes — no ' experience, and treating it as a distinct

[1] " Psychologie," Chapter VII.
[2] " Analytic Psychology," Vol. I., pp. 97, 99.

attitude of consciousness. Traces of this doctrine are found in many other modern discussions of judgment. The theory is really founded on a confusion of judgment with proposition. For the proposition-form of words is often used to express, not a judgment, but a belief, as in the asseveration, 'This music *is* wretched.' But a judgment, a conscious experience, is not identical with a proposition, a form of words; and this use of the term 'judgment,' as synonym for the unobjectionable word 'belief,' leaves unnamed the characteristic experience of wholeness. It seems wisest, therefore, to content ourselves with one name for 'belief,' and thus to leave the term judgment as name for the consciousness of a whole.

c. REASONING

Judging is best known in the form of reasoning. We seldom reflect upon the single judgment, the mere consciousness of discriminated wholeness in our immediate perception and imagination, but we notice the continuous judging which we call reasoning. A reasoning, or a demonstration, is a succession of judgments, so related that the ideas combined, in the realized whole of the final judgment (or conclusion), have already been combined, in the preceding judgments, with another idea or with several others, which do not form an emphasized part of the conclusion. We may illustrate this definition by any instance of reasoning. Suppose, for example, a succession of experiences, describable by the following propositions:—

This drawer will not open.
This drawer which will not open has a loose handle.
The looseness of the handle lessens the force of my pull.
A lessened pull keeps the drawer from opening.

Here, the first judgment is the consciousness of the drawer as a whole, with emphasis on the fact that it will not open. The second judgment follows upon the accentuation of still another feature of the experience, the loosened handle, and consists in the consciousness of the drawer, a realized whole, with this part of it especially vivid. In the third judgment, most parts of the drawer-percept are unattended to, but the consciousness of the loosened handle is very vivid, and is supplemented by a new idea, the consciousness of a diminished pull, with which it forms a conscious whole. Finally, in the conclusion, the idea of the handle loses its vividness or even fades away utterly, but the two ideas successively connected with it, (1) that of the sticking drawer and (2) that of the wĕakened pull, are vivid and are realized as discriminated parts of a whole. Thus, the concluding judgment is the realized connection of the terms of two preceding judgments; each of these terms was previously connected with a third term, now unemphasized; and the whole experience is properly called reasoning or 'mediate judgment.'

Reasoning, it must be observed, may consist of all types of judgment in all sorts of combinations. The judgments which it includes may be analytic or synthetic, abstract or concrete. In our example, for instance, the first and second and fourth are analytic judgments, due to the emphasis of ideas already present, but the third is, or may be, synthetic, that is to say, the consciousness of my pull may have been added, instead of being present from the beginning. The following argument, on the other hand, probably consists throughout of 'analytic' judgments, in other words, the conclusion is gained by mere reflection on the judgment with which we start, and includes no absolutely new features : —

> These boots are very heavy.
> Very heavy boots are durable.
> These boots are durable.

Here the idea of durability is probably present throughout, though it does not become vivid until after the idea of the heavy material has been emphasized.

This last illustration is an instance, also, of abstract reasoning, that is to say, the emphasized parts of the successive judgments, heaviness and durability, are qualities of objects and not regarded singly, or by themselves. But many examples of reasoning have to do with perfectly concrete experiences. The following example illustrates this concrete reasoning: —

> The Athenians claimed jurisdiction over Delos.
> Delos contained the treasure of the allies.
> The Athenians claimed jurisdiction over the treasure.

In this succession of judgments, there are evidently no abstract terms except the ideas of 'claiming jurisdiction' and of 'containing'; the other ideas — of 'Delos' and 'treasure' — are concretes, added successively and forming part of the final whole, 'Athenians — claiming jurisdiction over — treasure — in — Delos.'

It has thus been shown by our illustrations, that what we know as reasoning is, indeed, mediate judging, that is, a consciousness of the wholeness of discriminated experiences, previously connected with one or more 'suppressed' ideas. We have made clear to ourselves, also, that the connected judgments may be of any type. In spite of all this variety, however, only two forms of reasoning need be specially considered. These are first, 'purely synthetic reasoning,' in which every judgment is gained by the association of a new idea to the unanalyzed idea with which one starts. It is hard to give a plausible example, for effective reasoning is never of this type. A random instance is, however, the following: —

> Stephen Phillips wrote 'Herod.'
> 'Herod' was published by John Lane.
> Stephen Phillips's publisher is John Lane.

It is obvious that such reasoning seldom, if ever, occurs, and that it is useless at the best; one would be likely, for

example, to think of the publisher without the intermediate
idea of the book; and such immediate association would be
better, if only because swifter, than the mediate reasoning
process, which requires at least three such associations.
If there were, in fact, no type of reasoning except the
'purely synthetic,' composed by association without analysis, then reasoning would be nothing less than a peculiarly
toilsome way of attaining results, which might be reached
at a bound, by immediate association.

There is, however, a second form of reasoning, the
analytic, of so much greater significance, that psychologists usually treat of it to the exclusion of synthetic
reasoning.[1]   It consists of the following order of judgments: there is, first, an analytic judgment, in which
some one feature of an idea is singled out and brought to
the foreground of attention; second, a synthetic or supplementing judgment, which adds a previously unthought-of
idea to the emphasized part of the first judgment; and
then, finally, the combination of the initial, originally unanalyzed idea with this new feature.   An analytic judgment
may thus be defined, in the words which James applies to
judgment in general, as 'the substitution of parts and their
implications or consequences, for wholes.'   One concerns
oneself, for example, with the question of Porto Rican tax-
ation.   One's idea of Porto Rico is highly complex and
very vague; it includes visual images of tropical scenes
and images, largely verbal, of economic conditions.   If any
conclusion is to be reached, it must be, therefore, by the
emphasis of some one feature of the complex idea, Porto
Rico — its connection, let us say, with the United States.
" Porto Rico," one observes, "is a United States territory."
At once, this simpler idea, 'United States territory,' suggests, what the more complex one had failed to do, the idea
of exemption from import duty on United States products; and, finally, this idea of exemption is added to the

---

[1] Cf. James, *op. cit.*; Titchener, *op. cit.*

idea of Porto Rico, with which one started, and is realized as forming with it a whole. So one has, as expression of this reasoning, the syllogism : —

Porto Rico is a territory of the United States.
Territories of the United States should be exempt from import duty on United States products.
Porto Rico should be exempt from import duty.

The peculiar value of reasoning is thus, as James has said, its ability to 'deal with novel data' and to discover the functions and possibilities of new situations and objects. It attains this end by means of the analysis involved in its first judgment. For this judgment, since it is analytic, emphasizes a quality or an attribute within a whole object or situation; and, because this discriminated part is less complex than the total in which it belongs, it has fewer possible consequences; and, because it has certain definite consequences, it is likelier than a more complex experience to form the nucleus of a second judgment. When, for example, I judge that a certain mosslike substance is 'animal,' not 'vegetable,' that is, when I emphasize its animality as contrasted with its other features, I readily reach conclusions about it, impossible by mere observation of it as a whole. 'Animal' at once suggests to me all the properties, irritability, motivity and sensitivity, which distinguish animal life. So, if I analyze my neighbor's attitude and judge that his reserve includes deep shyness, I may correctly infer the further consequences of this as yet unsuspected characteristic. All this is clearly taught by James.[1] "Whereas the merely empirical thinker," he says, "stares at a fact in its entirety and remains helpless or gets 'stuck' if it suggests no concomitant or similar, the analytic reasoner breaks it up and notices some one of its separate attributes. This attribute he takes to be the essential part of the whole fact before him. This attribute

[1] *Op. cit.,* p. 330.

has properties or consequences which the fact, until then, was not known to have, but which, now that it is noticed to contain the attribute it must have. . . . The art of the analytic reasoner will consist of two stages: first, sagacity, or the ability to discover what part, M, lies embedded in the whole, S, before him; second, learning, or the ability to recall promptly M's consequences, concomitants, or implications."

This study of analytic reasoning enables us to understand why thinkers of all schools and all ages have laid such stress on reasoning. For, beginning back at least with Aristotle, who defined man as a reasoning animal, reasoning ability has been assumed as a fundamental character of effective thought. Purely synthetic reasoning does not, as we have seen, live up to this reputation, but certain definite values can be assigned to analytic reasoning. It is significant, in the first place, because it widens our knowledge, enabling us to reach, by means of a judgment already formed, a result which would not have been immediately suggested. John Locke has well set forth this function of reasoning. "When the mind," he says, "cannot so bring its ideas together as by their immediate comparison, and as it were juxtaposition or application one to another, to perceive their agreement or disagreement, it is fain, by the intervention of other ideas (one or more, as it happens) to discover the agreement or disagreement for which it searches; and this is that which we call reasoning. Thus the mind, being willing to know the agreement or disagreement in bigness between the three angles of a triangle and two right ones, cannot by an immediate view and comparing them do it; because the three angles of a triangle cannot be brought at once and be compared with any one or two angles; and so of this the mind has no immediate, no intuitive, knowledge. In this case the mind is fain to find out some other angles, to which the three angles of a triangle have an equality; and finding those equal to two right ones, comes to know their equality to two right ones."

It must, however, be admitted that analytic reasoning is not the only method, though the usual one, of enabling us to reach new results. For it is always possible that immediate judgment may replace even analytic reasoning in any given case. One man may gain by a flash of intuition the same result which another attains only by the closest reasoning; and the bare result is as valuable in the one case as in the other. There is thus a kernel of truth in the observation of a modern character in fiction, "that if you reason a thing out, you're always wrong, and if you never reason about it at all, you're always right." Few of us would admit this, yet it certainly is true that one sometimes is wrong when one reasons and sometimes is right in unreasoned judgments, and that one sometimes reaches, without analysis and reasoning, correct results in complicated problems. But granting that the mediate method of analytic reasoning is not the only way of attaining the adequate solution, there still remain several unassailable advantages with the analytic reasoner. His results, in the first place, are readily repeated. Intuitions, that is, immediate judgments or mere associations, occur we know not how; and we cannot reproduce them at will. The result which a man has reached by an unexplained association, once forgotten, is beyond his voluntary control. On the other hand, he can repeat at will the reasoning founded on close analysis. A student has forgotten, let us say, the accusative singular of the Greek word, ἐλπίς. He remembers, however, the reasoning process by which he first fixed in his mind the fact, that third declension nouns in -ις, when accented on the last syllable, have the lengthened accusative, to avoid the abrupt stop. Thus the accusative ἐλπίδα, forgotten in itself, is remembered as one link in a chain of reasoning. In the same way, one can repeat a geometrical demonstration, though one has forgotten it, by beginning with the close analysis of the figure; one can recover the lost date, by reasoning from one of the facts associated with it, by arguing, for example, that, since crossbows were used in the battle, the period must antedate the discovery of gunpowder. It behooves, therefore, even the person of quick intuition and of ready memory to train his reasoning power. The flash of inspiration may be more brilliant, but is surely far less steady, than the light of reason. The Aladdin rôle in the mental life is no sustained part; the genius which appears at one's first bidding may well forbear to come at a second summons. In plain English, the power to analyze and to reason is relatively stable, whereas unreasoned association is capricious and untrustworthy. It is, therefore, the part of wisdom to secure a reasoned theology or scientific system or practical philosophy, precisely because one thus has the chance to review and to recall it.

This suggests another advantage of reasoning over immediate association: the opportunity which it offers to the candid person to revise and to amend his results. The most dogmatic and unyielding of individuals is the man who has jumped at his conclusions. He is naturally tenacious of them, because he has no idea how he came by them and no hope of gaining any others if he lets them go. So the most ardent sectarian is the one who doesn't know the *raison d'être* of his own sect, and the most zealous political partisan can give you no reason for his vote beyond the utterance of a talismanic name or symbol. It would be too much, of course, to claim, for the other side, that every reasoning person is open-minded; but it is quite fair to say that only persons who reason are open-minded. For nobody can revise his decision who cannot review it, and, as we have shown, one can only accept without question one's immediate conclusions, and can only review one's results by retracing the steps of deliberate reasoning.

The reasoner has, finally, still another unique advantage. He can share his results with other people. The lucky man who guesses correctly may be brilliant and inspiring, but he cannot well be convincing. He may be absolutely

sure that one presidential candidate is far and away
ahead of another, or that Thackeray is greater than
Dickens, or that the lyric is the highest form of poetic
art; he can even temporarily impose his enthusiastic beliefs
on other people, but he cannot work permanent change in
their convictions. We are constantly hearing that argument is useless, and its futility in many cases must be
admitted; yet it certainly is the only method by which
one can effectively share one's intellectual convictions.

The student of logic has noticed, throughout the discussion of judgment and reasoning, the divergences of the
psychological from the logical treatment of the subject.
The differences are inherent in the nature of logic and of
psychology. In the first place, logic distinguishes valid
from invalid reasoning, whereas psychology has to do with
the nature of reasoning, correct or incorrect; logic, in other
words, is a normative science, whereas psychology is an
analytic science. To the logician, for example, the following series is no syllogism : —

> Many Frenchmen are fickle.
> Jacques Bonhomme is a Frenchman.
> Therefore Jacques Bonhomme is fickle.

The logician points out the fallacy in this argument and
excludes it from consideration, but the psychologist recognizes it as a genuine case of reasoning and mediate judgment. From certain specific rules of formal logic, the
psychologist has also cut loose: the conventional require-
ment, of exactly two terms in a proposition and exactly
three propositions in a syllogism, is an artificial abbrevia-
tion of the powers of analytic and synthetic judgment,
and its only justification is the observation of the limited
range of attention.

A brief consideration of language as related to thought
will conclude this chapter. The nature and origin of

language will later be discussed in more detail,[1] but our present problem is urged upon us by certain thinkers, notably by Max Müller, who insist that thought is impossible without language, that language and thought are, in fact, two sides merely of the same phenomenon. Now, this theory is certainly based on a very ordinary experience. When we catch ourselves in the act of reasoning, we do usually find that we are imagining *sub silentio* the words of our argument; and in generalizing, also, the verbal image is very apt to form the centre of our concepts, so that, for instance, the general notion 'dog' is apt to include the verbal image 'dog.' But beyond this assertion of the frequent occurrence, in our thinking, of verbal images, we have no right to go. Language, as we know, is a system of signs, composed of certain images, usually auditory, motor or visual. Thinking, on the other hand, necessarily includes a consciousness of untemporal unity. It is absurd to assert that this feeling of unity is absolutely dependent on one's possession of any specific set of images.

Certain experiences of the deaf and dumb furnish interesting testimony on exactly this point. D'Estrella, an educated deaf-mute, has given a detailed account of his moral and theological reasoning in the very early years of his neglected childhood.[2] He had never attended school, knew nothing of the conventional gesture-language, and possessed, in fact, only a few rude signs, none of them standing for abstract ideas. Yet, during this time, he not only gained a belief that the moon is a person, — a conclusion carefully reasoned from facts of the moon's motion and regular appearance, — but, by meditating on other nature-facts, he found for himself a god, a Strong Man behind the hills, who threw the sun up into the sky as boys throw fireballs, who puffed the clouds from his pipe,

<hr />

[1] Cf. Appendix, Bibliography.
[2] James, *Philosophical Review*, Vol. I., pp. 613 *seq.*

and who showed his passion by sending forth the wind. Mr. Ballard, another deaf-mute, describes a parallel experience,[1] his meditation "some two or three years before . . . initiation into the rudiments of written language," on "the question, How came the world into being?" Testimony of this sort, though of course it may be criticised as involving the memory of long-past experiences, confirms the antecedent probability that thinking may be carried on in any terms — concrete as well as verbal. Whenever one is conscious of an image, verbal or concrete, as identical in a group of more complex experiences, then one is generalizing. The generalized image, as we have seen, is often that of a word, but it is often, also, that of a motor adjustment, and it need not be either. Whenever one is conscious of the wholeness of a complex, with emphasized part, then one is judging. The judgment often includes an imaged proposition, but does not necessarily contain it. Whenever, finally, one is conscious of successive discriminated wholes, one reasons. Reasoning, to be sure, more often than conceiving or judging, has a verbal accompaniment, yet reasoning also may be carried on without words.

Conversely, the use of the general term, proposition or syllogism is no sure indication of judging or reasoning. For these forms of word-series have become so habitual, that one may use them without full realization of their meaning. For example, the proposition, "the apple is yellow," may not mean more to the man who speaks it than the words 'yellow apple,' that is to say, no judgment at all, no idea of differentiated wholeness, need be involved; and the propositional form of the words may be a mere unconscious reflex, due to habit. Evidently, therefore, the psychologist must be on his guard against the false supposition, that wherever proposition or syllogism is, there also is judgment or reasoning. He, of all men, must be alive to the possibility, that words do not always

---

[1] James, "Psychology," Vol. I., pp. 266 *seq.*

reveal, or even conceal, any 'thought within,' but that they may be used without any meaning, for mere pleasure in their liquid syllables, their rotund vowels, their emotional impressiveness.   In a prattling and babbling age which rolls polysyllables like sweet morsels under the tongue, the psychologist must practise himself heroically in the task of abjuring language for its own sake.

CHAPTER XIX

RECOGNITION

I

As there are two ways of regarding perception, imagination and thought, so, also, there are two possible theories of recognition. It may be described, in the first place, without reference to any recognizing self, as the occurrence of 'recognized,' that is, of familiar percepts and images. From this point of view, the discussion resolves itself in the main to a study of the nature of the feeling of familiarity. Such a study will form the second division of this chapter.

But recognition ordinarily means far more to us than the bare occurrence of familiar facts. It is the consciousness of myself, 'the constantly presupposed, central, individual self of everyday life,' in its relation to familiar past facts, psychical and physical. These facts are not impersonally and unattachedly familiar; they are familiar to me and I recognize them, I remember them, I attach them to myself, I claim them, I hold them. This essentially personal character of recognition (or memory, as it is often named) is admitted by most psychologists, and forms the basis of many philosophical theories. "What is memory?" John Stuart Mill asks.[1] "It is not merely having the idea of [a] fact recalled. It is having the idea recalled along with the belief that the fact, which it is idea of, really happened . . . and . . . to myself. Memory implies an Ego who formerly experienced the facts remembered, and who was

---

[1] Note 33 to Vol. II., Chapter XIV., § 7, of James Mill's " Analysis of the Phenomena of the Human Mind."

the same Ego then as now. The phenomenon of self and that of memory are merely two sides of the same." David Hume expresses the same relation in his statement that "memory is to be considered as the source of personal identity."[1] We are not now concerned with the philosophy of self, as it is held by Mill and by Hume and implied in these assertions, but simply with their psychological teaching of the close relation between remembering and the consciousness of self. Traces of the same view will be found, indeed, in writings more definitely psychological. Wundt, for instance, calls attention[2] to the fact that supplementary associations in recognition "belong to a group of conscious complexes, with which self-consciousness is ingrown"; and James defines memory[3] as "knowledge of an event or fact . . . with the additional consciousness that we have thought or experienced it before."

The nature of recognition as self-consciousness may be briefly considered. It is like perception, thought and imagination, in that it is a relatively passive experience.[4] It is different from them all in its greater emphasis on the self which experiences. I may almost lose myself in my absorbed perception or imagination of some scene or object, but I cannot recognize without being the more vividly conscious of myself and of the recognized object or scene as related to me. Recognition, moreover, may be either like perception and thought, or like imagination, in its reference to other selves. I need not be immediately conscious of other people as sharing the familiarity of an experience, but, on the other hand, my sense of familiarity may take in a consciousness of other selves. In other words, one's memory-world is both, like one's revery-world, a private domain of feelings all one's own, and it is also a public world of communicable experiences. This consciousness of other selves, however, like that of

---

[1] "Treatise," Bk. I., Pt. IV., § 6.
[2] "Physiologische Psychologie," 4te Aufl., II., p. 489.
[3] *Op. cit.*, Vol. I., p. 648.   [4] Cf. Chapter XXI., p. 306.

thought and perception, is relatively indirect. As we shall see, direct relations to people are those of emotion, will and faith : we always love or hate them, subordinate or follow them, compel or yield allegiance.[1] When, therefore, we speak of recognizing people, we really mean that we recognize their names or their faces ; and this recognition is merely a factor of our directly personal relation to them.

But recognizing, viewed as personal attitude, no less than as recognized idea, includes, as characteristic element, the feeling of familiarity. The close description and classification of recognition as complex experience is, in great part, therefore, an analysis of this familiarity-consciousness.

II

Recognition, from whatever point of view we regard it, is of two main types. It is either perception or imagination, combined with the feeling of familiarity ; in other words, either a percept or an image may be recognized. For example, one recognizes the man whom one meets, face to face on the street, or the friend, at this moment in Labrador, of whom one is thinking. Our present problem is the consideration of the obvious difference between familiar and unfamiliar consciousness of person, object or scene. We are to study the nature of this familiarity, to ask ourselves, for example, what makes only one figure familiar in the crowd which seethes through a great railway station, or why one's image of the Jungfrau is familiar and one's image of Mount Shasta unfamiliar.

The feeling of familiarity has already been referred to as a relational experience. This account of it must now be justified in more detail. For, as has been shown, the very existence of relational elements is denied or ignored by most psychologists, and we have, therefore, no right to take them for granted without consideration. We shall

[1] Cf. Chapters XX. and XXI.

begin by discussing those accounts of the feeling of familiarity, which reduce it to sensational or to affective elements. The first of these is most easily stated in terms
of idea-psychology, though it could be formulated after
the other fashion. It is the theory that familiarity consists in the presence, within percept or image, of associated images, supplementing the bare, unfamiliar percept
or image, of object or event. On this view (that associated images must form a part of all 'familiar' ideas), my
image of a yellow omnibus with three white horses associates, first, the visual image of a crowded square and of
the Doric portico of a great church, next the complex auditory image of trampling horses' feet and street cries, and
finally, a verbal image, and along with this last image comes
the familiarity as I say to myself, "the *Filles de Calvaire*
omnibus, starting out from the Madeleine." Or, let us
suppose the case of a familiar percept, in place of a familiar memory-image : my recognition, for example, of a long-
lost copy of " In Memoriam " which I find, behind a row
of tall volumes on a bookshelf. The bare percept of the
worn, old, brown leather volume, with its dulled gilding and
its yellow pages, is followed by a perfect rush of images.
Among them, perhaps, are the visual image of the dormer
window in my father's study and of myself, a mere child,
curled up in it, looking up from this old book to watch the
doves as they circle about the neighboring, gray church
spire, the auditory image of the voice which used to read
aloud from the poem, and finally, the verbal image of the
words, " My old ' In Memoriam ' ; " and with these images
comes the gush of familiarity-feeling which pervades the
experience.

There is not, then, the faintest reason to doubt, that the
familiar percept and image usually include associated
images of name and of former environment. But two
important facts forbid the conclusion that the recognition
or familiarity consists of these supplementary images. In
the first place, it is highly probable that percepts and

images are sometimes familiar without the occurrence of supplementary images. Such cases are doubtless very rare, and need to be carefully tested, for one may often suppose oneself to recognize an object, without knowing name or date or attendant detail, and yet later introspection may discover the presence of some supplementary image, however insignificant, some imaged movement or odor or intonation. In spite of this difficulty, certain good observers are convinced that percepts and images are occasionally familiar, without supplementary images. The Danish psychologist, Harold Höffding, holds this view, and instances an unaccustomed and unnamed, yet familiar, tint in the sky, and an unlocated organic sensation. In these cases, he says, "we know nothing about the former setting of the experience; we know neither the time nor the circumstances of its former occurrence, we do not know even the name. The objects are, nevertheless, 'familiar,' though introspection shows not the faintest trace of other representations, awakened by the recognized phenomenon." [1]

More important than this general testimony is the result of certain experimental observations made by Lehmann, another Danish psychologist.[2] He tested several observers, with a series of sixty-six odors, and found, in seven per cent of the tests, that the odors were familiar, and that the persons tested were, nevertheless, unable to name them or in any way to connect them with other experiences. A repetition of Lehmann's experiment, under more careful conditions in the Wellesley College laboratory, has corroborated these results.

In the end, however, every one must decide, by introspection, whether or not the feeling of familiarity consists in the presence of supplementary images. To the writer it seems perfectly certain that these images, when they are present, are accompaniments, not constituents, of the famil-

---

[1] "Vierteljahrschrift für Wissenschaftliche Philosophie," XIII, p. 425.
[2] Wundt's "Philosophische Studien," Bd. VII.

iarity-feeling. The familiarity of a face, for example, does not consist in a verbal image of the name, or of a scene, nor in any combination of images. The familiarity may, to be sure, attach to these supplementary images, and not to the original percept or image; for instance, not the face, but the name which it suggests, may be familiar; and because the feeling of familiarity arises along with the image of name or of former scene, it is natural to confuse them. But, in the experience of the writer, the feeling of familiarity itself is individual and distinctive, it persists in varying experiences, and it clearly is something besides the supplementary images which accompany it.

Abandoning this theory, we therefore consider a second: the conception of familiarity as consciousness of the relaxed or 'easy' bodily attitude characteristic of recognition. We have all observed the change from the strained position of sense-organs and limbs, in puzzling over an unrecognized object, to this relaxed and unstrained attitude of recognition. Titchener describes this complex of organic sensations, set up by an easy bodily attitude, as in fact simply 'a weakened survival of the emotion of relief.' "To an animal," he adds, "so defenceless as was primitive man, the strange must always have been cause of anxiety. The bodily attitude which expresses recognition is still that of relief from tension."[1]

This is doubtless an accurate account of the bodily sensations which accompany the feeling of familiarity — sensations, in other words, of bodily relaxation, more constant in our moods of recognition than we realize. Yet nobody can well suppose that it is precisely the same thing to be conscious of the easing of one's bodily attitude and of an object's familiarity. At the most, these organic sensations can form only a part of the feeling of familiarity. This conception is, therefore, combined with another, and familiarity-feeling is defined as the mood of pleasantness com-

[1] "Outline," § 70.

bined with sensations of bodily relaxation. Now, it certainly is often true that recognition is a pleasant experience. But when I call an object or a scene 'familiar,' I mean by that term something more than 'pleasant and productive of bodily relaxation,' and when I say that the familiarity of a landscape is pleasant, I mean that the landscape is 'familiar and pleasant,' not that it is 'familiar, namely, pleasant.' This relation becomes clearer by comparison with pleasant sensational experiences. Brilliant color is usually pleasant, as familiarity is, but the color is accompanied by the pleasantness, not identical with it, and in the same way the familiar is pleasant, though the pleasantness is not a part of the familiarity.

Moreover, it is not perfectly certain that the familiar always is pleasant. The ordinary experiences of tiring of amusements and growing weary of one's surroundings, in other words, the everyday feelings of tediousness and of *ennui*, seem to be illustrations of familiar experiences, which are unpleasant, not in themselves, but precisely because of their familiarity. At the same time, too great stress must not be laid on this argument. For, in opposition, it may be urged that these apparently unpleasant, yet familiar, experiences are felt as familiar for only a brief time, and that when they later lose the evanescent pleasantness, they lose, with it, the sense of familiarity.

The familiarity-feeling is, then, neither a group of supplementary images, nor a consciousness of bodily attitude, nor a feeling of pleasantness, though ordinarily, perhaps even always, accompanied by all these experiences. In no one of these phenomena, however constant their appearance, and in no combination of them, does the feeling of familiarity consist ; and since virtually no other account of it has ever been given, in terms of mere sensational and attributive elements, we have a right to say, if our careful introspection accords with that of this book, that the feeling of familiarity does not consist in such sensational and attributive elements. We are fairly driven, therefore, to the doctrine that familiarity-feeling is fundamentally a relational experience. Beyond this indefinite statement it is difficult to proceed, for relational experiences, as we have seen, present grave difficulties to the analyst. It is hard to analyze them, in the first place, because it is impossible to regulate their physical and physiological conditions, and consequently to apply experimental tests, and in the second place, because the relational elements so closely fuse with each other. It is quite possible, therefore, to realize the distinctiveness of familiarity-feeling and also its complexity, and yet to be unable to analyze it further. Like some sensational complexes, humidity, for example, it is so intimate a fusion of elements as to have an individuality of its own. But like that, too, it is, after all, capable of analysis into simpler parts, the relational feelings of 'same' and of 'past.' In other words, the recognition of an object seems to mean, when reflected on, the consciousness 'same with a past thing,' and the recognition of an event means the awareness of 'this event identical-with-something-past.' Closely observed, therefore, every feeling of familiarity is analyzable into these factors. This does not mean that we necessarily think of the words 'same' or 'past,' but that we have special sorts of feeling expressed by these words. The feeling of the 'same' is relatively simple. The analysis of the 'feeling of past' is far more difficult. It involves, like all consciousness of temporal relation, a realization of the 'moment,' that is, of the fact which is linked with other facts in two directions. But the 'past' is the irrevocable, unrevivable moment. The feeling of the past may, therefore, be roughly described as the consciousness of an irrevocable fact, linked in two directions with other facts.[1]

At the present stage, however, of our training in psychological method, it is idle to pursue too far an analysis, incapable of verification and precise formulation by experi-

[1] Cf. p. 301.

mental methods. We have seen that the feeling of
familiarity is a relational, not primarily a sensational or
an attributive experience, and that familiarity-feeling is
analyzable into simpler relational experiences : (1) the
feeling of 'same,' and (2), the feeling of 'past' (probably
involving a feeling of linkage, or connection). Furthermore, we have observed that familiarity is almost always a
pleasant experience, including the consciousness of a relaxed bodily attitude ; and that the familiar, or recognized,
percept or image is almost always, though not invariably,
accompanied by supplementary images, concrete and verbal, to which the familiarity often attaches.

It should be noticed that the feeling of familiarity often
accompanies experiences, which are not reproductions or
repetitions of the past. This false recognition goes by the
inaccurate name of paramnesia, or false memory. Its commonest form is the 'been-here-before' feeling which sometimes overwhelms us when we enter places which are strange
to us and scenes which are new. This is a case of false
perceptional recognition, and is paralleled by experiences
characteristic of many forms of insanity : a man's delusion,
for example, that he has himself written the articles which
he reads in the daily papers. A second sort of paramnesia
is false image-recognition. Many of our dream-imagina-
tions and many experiences of the mentally deranged are
of this type, but even commoner illustrations of it are
the inaccurate testimony and the fictitious 'recollections'
of perfectly honest people. Nicolay and Hay, the biogra-
phers of Lincoln, are quoted [1] as saying, from their experience in editing recollections, that " mere memory unassisted
by documentary evidence is utterly unreliable after a lapse
of fifteen years" ; and a French writer, Le Bon, says explicitly, " Works of history must be considered as works of
pure imagination — they are fanciful accounts of ill-ob-

[1] Burnham, " Memory," *American Journal of Psychology*, Vol. II., p. 435.

served facts. Had not the past left us its monumental works, we should know absolutely nothing in reality with regard to bygone times." Without going to this extreme, we certainly must admit that we have countless experiences of false recognition, in which, as we have said, the 'feeling of familiarity' attaches itself to some novel percept or image.

In conclusion, a fresh reference must be made to the widely different uses of the words 'recognition' and 'memory.' In this book, memory is defined as the faithfully reproduced imagination. On this view, a memory may or may not be a recognition. One may be dreamily conscious, for example, of an imaged figure, before one wakes up to the consciousness of its familiarity, exclaiming, "It is Murillo's St. John in the National Gallery." Yet all the time the imaged picture, if a reproduction of the real one, is remembered, though it is not recognized. Opposed to this view, is the conception of memory as the imagination-form of what we have called recognition.[1] On this hypothesis, an image, however faithfully recalled, is a mere reproduced image, not a memory, unless it is known as familiar; and the familiar image, however false the familiarity, is 'remembered.' From this point of view recognition means merely 'familiar perception,' and memory means 'familiar imagination.'

The physiological basis of recognition, as consciousness of familiarity, has never been experimentally determined. According to the ordinary theory, the physiological condition of familiarity-feeling is a function of the fibres connecting the different brain-areas. But this is not a sufficient physiological explanation of recognition, for all centrally aroused images depend on the excitation of connecting fibres, yet not all centrally aroused images are recognized.

[1] Cf. Titchener, "Outline," § 74.

It is far more likely that the excitation of cortical cells conditions recognition ; and this view accords with analogy,
for cell-activity of nerve-centres is supposed to condition
sensational and affective consciousness.   Probably, therefore, the excitation of certain cells in the so-called association-centres is the condition of recognition.

Many physiological explanations of paramnesia have
been attempted, of which the best known attributes it to
the functioning, in quick succession, of the two sides of
the brain.   This conception runs athwart the strong probability that one side only of the brain is normally active.
Other psychologists explain paramnesia as due to the succession, because of weariness, of ordinarily overlapping
brain processes; still others believe that it is due to un-
wontedly prompt cerebral activity.   No one of these
explanations is physiologically established.

CHAPTER XX

EMOTION

I

THERE are, of course, two points of view from which we may regard the emotional consciousness. An emotion may be considered, in the first place, as a complex fact of consciousness (or idea), which forms one link in a series of conscious experiences. From this standpoint, an emotion is defined as any complex fact of consciousness, of which either pleasantness or unpleasantness is an important feature. To quote Titchener, in emotion, the perception or image "is swamped in the affection." Briefly, then, an emotion is an affective complex, and since there are precisely two affections, pleasantness and unpleasantness, there are, as we shall see, two main types of emotion, those of happiness and those of unhappiness. A secondary constituent of emotions must now be mentioned: the consciousness of bodily changes, of warmth or chill, of quickened or retarded heart-beats, of respiratory movements, as in laughing or sobbing, and of movements of the limbs, such as trembling or clinching the fists. Probably all emotions, and certainly most emotions, contain these ideas of bodily change. It will be most convenient to discuss them later, in connection with our study of the physiological conditions of emotion.

But emotion is not adequately described as a mere idea, containing affections and consciousness of bodily change. For love and hatred, pity and envy, jealousy and contempt are intensely personal experiences, and are not fully known

while they are looked on as mere ideas without any
reference to the selves who 'have' the ideas.   Indeed,
we cannot think of love, sympathy and contempt, without
taking account of the selves who love and are loved, who
sympathize and are sympathized with, who despise and
are despised.

Emotion — now regarded not as mere idea, but as experience of a self related to other selves or to things — is like
perception, thought, imagination and memory, the experiences which we have so far studied, in that it is recognized as passive relation of one self to another.   This
characteristic, passivity, will stand out more clearly as
contrasted, in the chapter which follows, with the activity of
will and of faith.   From perception, thought and the rest,
emotion, however, is also distinguished.   For emotion is
the relation of a happy or unhappy self to particular other
selves or to other things, to ' this person ' or to ' that landscape,' not to ' people in general ' nor to ' any scene.'   In
perception and in thought, we assume, as we have seen, our
agreement with all selves or with any selves, that is, with
an undifferentiated mass of selves.   Emotion, on the other
hand, narrows and particularizes.   The criminal fears, not
authority in general, but the personified executors of the
law ; the *nouveau riche* envies, not society in the abstract,
but the living, concretely successful men and women ; the
true philanthropist loves, not humanity in general, but
actual, suffering, striving human beings.   And because
we realize, all of us, this concrete personality of emotion,
we so quickly detect the false note of pretended feeling,
and so quickly suspect that 'affection for childhood,'
' love of the animal world,' ' sympathy with the masses,'
are pseudo-sentiments and pretended emotions.   The real
emotions are particularizing, never abstract or generalizing, and the resentment, with which every vigorous man
receives public charity or mere institutional aid, is a witness to the universal conviction that emotion is the relation of individual with individual.

This individuating power of emotion is well suggested in Matthew Arnold's description of the meeting of Sohrab and Rustum. Father and son come forth to do battle in the level plain on the banks of the Oxus, between the Tartar and the Persian hosts. They are not known to each other, and Rustum, the father, has denied his own name; but Sohrab, in spite of this protestation, vaguely realizes the presence of his father, and exclaims:—

> "Thou sayest thou art not Rustum; be it so!
> Who art thou, then, that canst so touch my soul?
> Boy as I am, I have seen battles too, . . .
> Have . . .
> . . . heard their hollow roar of dying men,
> But never was my heart thus touched before.
> There are enough foes in the Persian host
> Whom I may meet, and strike and feel no pang,
> But oh! let there be peace 'twixt thee and me."

Sohrab has heard the cries of battle, but they have not touched his heart, for they have assailed his ears as the sounds of mere undifferentiated 'dying men'; he has met and struck, without a pang, undistinguished Persian champions; now, at last, he meets one whom he no longer knows as 'Persian,' as 'warrior' or as 'foe,' but as 'thou,' and with this acknowledgment of personal relation his heart is softened and his arm unnerved.

II

We have now to describe the emotions in more detail. And, in the effort to be true to the distinctions of actual experience, we shall find, as will appear, that the most significant classes of emotions, as commonly recognized, are based on the varying relations of different selves to each other. The significant contrast between unhappy and happy emotions is, however, common both to idea-psychology and self-psychology. Our description of emotional experiences is based on the following outline:—

A. PERSONAL EMOTIONS

I. Egoistic or Unsympathetic Emotions:—
  a. Primary.
    1. Happiness, realized as due to others . . . Liking.
    2. Unhappiness, realized as due to others . . Dislike.
  b. Developed.
    1. Happiness, realized as due to others . . . Gratitude.
    2. Unhappiness, realized as due to others,
      Who are
      (*a*) Greater than oneself . . . . Terror.
      (*b*) Equal to oneself . . . . Hate.
      (*c*) Inferior to oneself . . . . Contempt.

II. Altruistic or Sympathetic Emotions:—
  a. Happiness through shared happiness . . . . *Mitfreude.*
  b. Unhappiness through shared unhappiness . . Pity.

III. Mixed Emotions:—
  a. Happiness through another's unhappiness . . Malice.
  b. Unhappiness through another's happiness . . Envy.

B. IMPERSONAL EMOTIONS[1]

We recognize, first, the distinction between personal emotion, the passive and particularizing relation of happy or unhappy self to other selves, and impersonal emotion, a similar relation not to other selves, but to events or to things. Of these classes, that of personal emotion is most primitive and most significant, and we shall first consider it.

a. PERSONAL EMOTION

Personal emotion appears in the two well-marked phases which underlie all consciousness, the imperious or egoistic and the sympathetic or adoptive. Imperious or unsympathetic emotion is sometimes described as if it were a mere recognition of one's own self without reference to

[1] For amplification, see p. 276 *seq.*

any other. If this were true, it would not be personal emotion at all, for that demands the relation to a particular other self, and exists only in so far as it emphasizes and individuates the other self or other selves. Like and dislike, fear and gratitude and all the rest are obviously expressions of one's attitude to other selves, but these 'others' are not realized as themselves caring and hating and fearing, but only as the conscious, yet unfeeling, targets or instruments to one's own emotions.

It follows from this distinction that many kindly, good-natured feelings are rightly classed as unsympathetic. Mere liking, for example, is as unsympathetic and egoistic an experience as dislike. Toward this particular realized self one reacts with pleasure; from this other, one turns away. But the pleasure is as distinctly individual and unshared as the dissatisfaction. The other selves are means to one's content or discontent, and are thought of as subordinated to one's own interests.

We have, therefore, two distinct types of unsympathetic emotion. On the one hand, there is the moroseness, the discontent, the hostile fear or hate or contempt, of the man who realizes himself as unfavorably related to other selves. Quite as significant, on the other hand, is the unruffled good-nature, the sunshiny content, the unaffected liking, or even gratitude, of the individual who feels that he is happy in his relations with other selves. The common temptation is, of course, to give to these genial feelings an ethical value, and to contrast dislike, as selfishness, with liking, as if that were unselfish. The truth is, however, that the one attitude is as 'egoistic' as the other. To like people is to realize them as significant to one's own happiness, not to identify oneself with their happiness. And, in truth, a great part of what is known as 'love' of family or of country is of this strictly egoistic nature. Dombey loved his son because the boy was 'important as a part of his own greatness'; Victor Hugo is credited with the sublime egoism of the assertion " France is the world; Paris is France;

I am Paris"; and many a man loves family, church or
country merely as the embodiment of his own particular
interests and purposes.

It is even possible to secure other people's pleasure and
to avoid paining them, not in the least to gain their happiness, but because their cries of grief assault our ears as
their happy laughter delights us. The most consummately
heartless figure of modern literature, Tito Melema, is so
tender-hearted that he turns his steps, lest he crush an in-
sect on the ground, and devotes a long afternoon to calm-
ing a little peasant's grief. "The softness of his nature,"
we are told, "required that all sorrow should be hidden
away from him." But this same Tito Melema betrays wife
and foster-father and country, in the interests of his own
self-indulgence: other people's emotions are insignificant
to him in themselves; he regards them only as the expression of them rouses him to delight or to sorrow; he never
for an instant enters into them, identifies himself with them,
or makes them his own.

The avoidance of another's pain does, it must be added,
require what is sometimes called sympathy, the involuntary
tendency to share the organic sensational consciousness of
other people. The pain which one feels at the sight of
somebody's wound is an illustration of this experience,
known as 'organic sympathy.' We are discussing, however, the emotion of sympathy, not the sympathetic sensation, and it is certain that one may further the pleasure or
pain of others with purely egoistic emotion.

Besides this fundamental difference between the personal emotions, liking and gratitude, which involve pleasantness, and the opposite ones, dislike, terror and hate, which
are unpleasant experiences, we must take account also of
another difference, which marks off the primary from the
developed form of these feelings. In all these experiences,
our happiness or unhappiness is referred, as we have seen,
to other selves, and is realized as connected with them.
When the consciousness of this relation becomes explicit,

that is, when other people are clearly and definitely realized as affecting us and as sources of our happiness or unhappiness, then those vaguer personal feelings of like and dislike give way to emotions, in which the realization of others is more sharp-cut and more exactly defined. We may study these developed egoistic emotions in more detail.

The egoistic, imperious emotion which refers our own happiness to other selves is gratitude. This definition, it must be admitted, is inadequate to the ordinary conception of gratitude. For gratitude is more often regarded from an ethical than from a psychological standpoint, and is usually classed as 'virtue,' not as mere 'emotion.' There is, none the less, an emotional experience of gratitude which is utterly unsympathetic, albeit the natural basis of sympathy. I feel grateful, when I am happy over the furtherance of my interests by somebody else, realizing definitely, at the same time, my dependence, in this happiness, on my benefactor. This is gratitude, surely, but it is none the less the imperious emphasis on my own happiness, and need not be in any sense a sympathetic, shared experience. The constant characteristic of gratitude, as of mere liking, is a sort of hugging of one's own pleasure, which is supplemented, not obscured, by definitely attributing it to somebody else. It is true that the transition is easy from gratitude to sympathy. A natural outgrowth, from the realization of my own happiness as influenced by some one else, is the interest in his experience, that is, the acknowledgment of his emotional interests. These, however, are distinct, not identical experiences, however closely they are connected. The benefactor toward whom I entertain undoubted gratitude may be temperamentally uncongenial. It may be literally impossible for me to sympathize with him, to make his happiness and unhappiness my own, even while I unequivocally realize him as influencing my happiness. Truth to tell, everybody knows people to whom he is grateful, without feeling the remotest sympathy with them, indeed, without ever understanding them or getting their point of view. And almost everybody knows people who are, he believes, grateful to him without in the least sharing in his own life, in his feelings, or in his ideals. We are justified, therefore, in classing gratitude as imperious or unsympathetic emotion, an exclusive concern in one's own happiness, with a recognition of other selves as merely instruments to one's own satisfaction. Gratitude is, therefore, an egoistic experience, though it naturally adds to itself the genuinely sympathetic emotion.

The egoistic, or imperious, emotion of dissatisfaction is the realization of other selves as means to one's unhappiness. It assumes the characteristic attitude of all these unsympathetic experiences, regarding others, not as independent individuals, but as significant only in their relation to oneself. It is a curious fact that these unpleasant experiences are far more elaborately differentiated than the pleasant ones — or at least, that they are distinguished by many more names. Closely regarded, these distinctions are found to be based on the estimate which is formed of those 'other selves,' who are means to one's unhappiness. When these are realized as 'greater,' more powerful, than oneself, the resulting emotion is terror; when they are conceived as on an equality with oneself, the emotion is hate; when they appear, finally, as less important or significant, the feeling is 'scorn' or 'contempt.'

Every revolt from tyranny and oppression is a living illustration of this contrast of terror with hatred or rage. Why did the French peasantry, who endured the burdens of Louis Quatorze, rebel against the materially lessened impositions of Louis Seize? What is the nature of the emotional contrast between the two generations, only a century apart: in the earlier period, hapless suffering from disease, starvation and exaction of every sort, without the stirring of opposition; a hundred years later, fierce and furious resentment against oppression and misery? There is only one answer to questions such as these. The peasants of the older period were still bound by the traditional belief, that court and nobles were naturally above them, loftier and more powerful than they. Their feeling to these superior beings, realized as instruments to their own undoing, was of necessity, therefore, the paralyzing emotion of terror. From the standpoint of the inner life, terror is, of course, what has been named unsympathetic or egoistic emotion. That is, it involves no adoption of another's life as one's own, but regards all others in their relation to one's own experience. So these French peasants regarded court and nobles without sympathy or understanding, merely as their own oppressors and taskmasters; but the feeling remained impotent and futile, and led to no effective reaction so long as the nobles held, in the minds of these peasants, their position of lofty isolation. The French Revolution was, in fact, directly due to the spread of the doctrine of social equality. Rousseau's teaching of the essential likeness of man to man, once it took root in the mind of the French people, grew of necessity into the conviction that peasants and nobles were no longer separated by an impassable barrier. And with this conviction of their equality, the unnerving emotion of terror gave way to the invigorating, infuriating feeling of anger. So it is with all. Men rage against their equals, are angry with them and hate them: against the gods in Olympus, or the Fates with spindle, thread and shears, men have never rebelled so long as they have regarded them as unapproachable deities: they have feared, not hated them. Only the demi-gods, the Titans and the heroes of Greek mythology, beings of divine descent who were proudly conscious of their high birth, ever made battle against the gods; and no ancient writer would attribute to mere mortals even the impotent hatred of the gods which inspires the Chorus of Swinburne's "Atalanta":—

> "Lo, with hearts rent and knees made tremulous,
> Lo, with ephemeral lips and casual breath,
> At least we witness of thee ere we die

> That these things are not otherwise, but thus;
>   That each man in his heart sigheth, and saith
>   That all men, even as I,
>   All we are against thee, against thee, O God most high."

Such antagonism is possible only to men who realize in some dim way that, in spite of their pitiless strength and their wasting scorn, the gods are not beyond the range of human hate.

Apparent exceptions are really illustrations of this principle, for the outburst of fury against one's superior always turns out to be a momentary denial of his superiority, a temporary tearing of the god from its pedestal. The fear of the superior beings readily, however, reasserts itself, and this explains the temporary nature of many revolts and the easy resumption of authority. A handful of soldiers may check the violence of a mob, because the vision of brass buttons and uniforms inspires an unreasoning conviction of the superiority of military force, and transforms destructive rage into futile fear. The insubordinate fury of usually obedient children is like mob-violence, a temporary assertion of equality with their old-time superiors; and like mob-fury, the anger of children readily gives way to the old acceptance of authority.

The emotion of scorn, finally, involves the conviction of another's inferiority. It is evidently impossible to despise a man, so long as one regards him as one's own superior, or even as one's equal. Contempt is, thus, the dissatisfaction involved in one's relation to an inferior person. The inferiority may be real or imagined, and of any sort; but just as gratitude may be regarded as a virtue, so contempt is readily considered from the ethical standpoint, and it is rightly rated as morally unworthy if it takes account of the superficial inferiority of fortune or of station.

The experiences, which we have so far described, have all been characterized by their egoistic narrowing of consciousness, their heavy emphasis on one's own concerns and interests, their incurable tendency to regard other selves merely as ministers to one's own individual satisfactions and dissatisfactions. The sympathetic emotions are manifestations of the adoptive phase of self-consciousness, the widening embrace of other people's interests, the sharing of other people's happiness and unhappiness. In one's sympathetic relations with other people, one regards them as possessing a significance of their own, quite aside from their relations of advantage or disadvantage to oneself, and one lays hold upon these new interests and ideals in such wise as to enlarge the boundaries of one's own experience.

Emotions of personal sympathy are of two main types: we are happy in another's happiness or unhappy in his grief. There is no English word to express the sharing of joy, and we are forced to borrow from the Germans their exact and perfect word, *Mitfreude*. The poverty of the English language expresses, unhappily, a defect in human nature. We certainly are quicker in sympathy with people's sorrow than in delight in their happiness. It is easier to weep to our friends' mourning than to dance to their piping, easier to share their griefs than to share their amusements, infinitely easier to console them than to make holiday with them.

The greatest distinction in these simple feelings of sympathy is in the narrowness or the wideness of them. There may be but one individual whose experience I actually share, whose joys and sorrows I feel as mine. In the presence of this one other self my strictly individual happiness is disregarded, and the boundaries of my self-consciousness are enlarged. I live no longer my own life, but this other life — or rather, my own life includes this other life. Yet my relations to all others save this cherished one may remain narrowly egoistic: I may still be concerned only for myself, and interested in these others only as foils to my emotions. Life and literature abound in examples of sympathy within the narrowest limits, of egoistic emotion giving way at one point only.

Aaron Latta is a modern illustration of this attitude:
he lives his self-centred life undisturbed by the wants, the
hopes, the cares, of the village life about him, but he is
quick to notice the shade on Elspeth's brow and the
merest quiver on her lip. With a true intuition, indeed,
the novelists and the dramatists have united to represent
the most unsympathetic of mortals as vulnerable at some
point. Dickens, the keen anatomist of the emotions, has
only one Scrooge 'quite alone in the world . . . warning
all human sympathy to keep its distance,' and represents
even the Squeerses as possessed of 'common sympathies'
with their own children.

Closely following upon the narrowest form of sympathy,
which recognizes the claims and adopts the interests of
one individual only, are family-feeling, club-feeling, col-
lege-feeling, church-affiliation and all the other sympathies with widening groups of people. For sympathy is
normally of slow growth. The more primitive emotions
are naturally self-centred, and they give place only gradually to the identification of oneself, first with the joys and
griefs of one's mother or nurse or most intimate playmate,
then with the emotional experiences of the whole family
group, later with the hopes and fears and regrets and
delights of a larger circle. It is interesting to observe
that, with every widening of one's sympathy, the limiting
circumference of one's own self is pushed further outward.
The sympathetic person has always a richer, concreter
personality than the self-centred one. He has actually
shared in experiences that are not immediately his own ;
he has seen with other's eyes and heard with their ears,
and his pulses have beat high to their hopes and joys :
his experience has been enlarged by his sympathies.

There is something abnormal, therefore, in the checking
at any point of this outgrowth of sympathy. People whose
sympathies embrace only the members of their family,
their cult or their class are only incompletely human, for
a lack of emotional comprehension, or sympathy, marks a

stunted personality. Even patriotism, so far as it limits
sympathy to feeling with the inhabitants of any one corner
of the globe, deprives a man of his birthright: communion in the joys and sorrows of life with 'all nations of
men,' or rather, with that which Tolstoi calls 'the one
nation.'

We have, finally, to consider the mixed emotions: happiness through realization of another's unhappiness, that is,
malice, and unhappiness through consciousness of another's happiness, that is, envy. By common consent,
these are morally undesirable emotions, yet there can be
no question that they are sympathetic, as well as egoistic,
that is, that they require a genuine sharing of another's
experience. I cannot envy you, if I am so deeply occupied with my own emotions that I do not realize you as
happy. And I cannot really know that you are happy
without, in some degree, experiencing or sharing your
happiness. This, to be sure, is often denied: we are said
to possess the idea of an emotion without experiencing the
emotion itself. But, surely, to be conscious of emotion
means nothing if it does not mean to have the emotion.
I may, of course, have the purely verbal images, 'happy,'
'unhappy,' 'emotion,' without any affective consciousness
and without any realization of myself in relation to others;
but nobody's emotion can influence my own without my
experiencing or sharing it to some degree. The resulting
relations to other selves are, therefore, as has been said,
mixed emotions. Not only do they combine happiness
and unhappiness, but they supplement a sympathetic by
an egoistic emotion: the happiness which we faintly
share with another, in our envy, is swamped in the egoistic unhappiness which it arouses, and the unhappiness
of our fellow, dimly felt in our maliciousness, is swallowed
up in a surging happiness that is quite our own.

It would be a mistake, however, to suppose that malice
and envy exhaust the nature of this emotional experience
of mingled sympathy and egoism. Barrie has shown us

a perfect embodiment of mixed emotion in the figure of Sentimental Tommy. Never was anybody more sympathetic than Tommy, boy and man. He entered into the feeling of friend and of foe alike: divined and shared in Elspeth's loneliness, Aaron's bitterness, Grizel's passion and scorn, and Corp's loyalty. He never could have been what he was to all of them, had he not, up to a certain point, shared actually in their feelings; had he not believed in himself as Elspeth and Corp believed in him, hated himself as Aaron hated him, alternately loved and despised himself as Grizel loved and despised him. And yet all this sympathetic communion with others was merely a stimulus to his own private emotions, a ministry to the luxury of his self-occupation, whether delicious pleasure or equally delicious misery. Such sympathy, as element of one's egoistic and unshared happiness or unhappiness, is mixed emotion.

b. IMPERSONAL EMOTION

We have so far concerned ourselves with personal emotion, the conscious relation of happy or unhappy self with other selves. But one may like or dislike the furnishings of a room as cordially as one likes or dislikes its inmates, and one may be as desperately frightened by a swift-rolling automobile as by a haughty despot. This means that emotion, though primarily a realized relation of one self to other selves, may be also a relation of oneself to ideas and to things.

Some emotions, to be sure, are necessarily personal. Every form of sympathy presupposes our realization of other selves, and gratitude, like contempt, is felt toward selves and not toward things. Hate, also, is a personal emotion — since, although we often feel a certain irritation, more than bare dislike, for inanimate objects when they thwart our purposes, yet in these cases we probably personify the things at which we are angry. Such personification of inanimate objects is ridiculously clear in a child's anger at the blocks which refuse to be built into forts, or at the doors which resist his efforts to open them; and even grown-up resentment against obdurate buttons, creaking hinges, and smoking lamps involves a personification of the offending object. "Oh, you are a stupid old donkey!" Bella exclaims, as she knocks the "Complete British Housewife" on the table; and most perverse, inanimate objects are similarly apostrophized.

After all these eliminations, there none the less remain certain impersonal emotions. We shall not attempt to discuss, or even to enumerate all of them, but shall consider only certain representatives of the class. These we may group together in the following summary, distinguishing these impersonal emotions not only from the standpoint of self-psychology as egoistic or altruistic, but also from the analytic point of view, common to both methods of psychology, as pleasant or unpleasant, sensational or relational :—

IMPERSONAL EMOTIONS

I. Egoistic	II. Altruistic (sentiments)
a. Sensational: Like. Dislike.	*a*. Sensational: Æsthetic pleasure.
b. Relational: Enjoyment of the familiar. *Ennui,* etc.	*b*. Relational: Sense of humor, etc.

Impersonal emotion, the conscious relation of happy or unhappy self to event or to thing is, like personal emotion, a narrowing and particularizing experience. Just as I love or hate, pity or envy, this particular person or these people, and do not impartially and indiscriminately care for 'anybody,' so, also, I like or dislike this special thing or these things, am bored by this monotony, and pleased with that familiar experience; and my æsthetic pleasure is always an absorption in this pastoral symphony, this western outlook, or this Browning lyric, not an indiscriminate delight in sense-experience.

We have already instanced impersonal like and dislike for things, not people. We have many experiences, also, of satisfaction or dissatisfaction with the relational aspects of things or events. Our outline names only two of these: enjoyment of the familiar, and the parallel distaste for the repeated or monotonous. Both feelings are well known: the cosey comfort of the old slippers and the old pipe, even when one can find a thousand flaws in both; and, on the other hand, the flat, stale profitlessness of the well-known scene and the everyday objects. We, poverty-stricken, English-speaking people, have no noun by which to designate this latter experience: we may call it tediousness, or may speak of ourselves as 'bored,' but we are often driven to borrow one of the adequate, foreign expressions, *ennui* or *Langweile*.

Both like and dislike and the relational emotions are distinctly egoistic, laying special stress on myself and my condition. Among the impersonal emotions, however, are certain highly significant ones which are embodiments of the other phase, the adoptive, self-effacing phase of consciousness. The first of these, æsthetic enjoyment, we must consider briefly: a full treatment of it would require another volume, and would lead us far afield into domains of philosophy and of art. Æsthetic enjoyment is the conscious happiness in which one is absorbed, and, as it were, immersed in the sense-object. No words describe æsthetic emotion better than Byron's question: —

> "Are not the mountains, waves, and skies a part
> Of me and of my soul, as I of them?"

For the æsthetic consciousness, as truly as sympathetic emotion, is a widening and deepening of self — not a loss of self — by identification of the narrow myself, not with other selves, but with sense-things: with wide outlooks or with forest-depths, with up-springing Gothic arches or with glowing masses of pictured color, with thrilling harmonies or with measured rhythms.

It is important to dwell on the consciousness of self involved in the æsthetic feeling, because there is, as we have seen, a sense in which the æsthetic consciousness, because it refers to things, not to people, is rightly called impersonal. But absorption in the beautiful is never a loss of self. Most of that with which one is usually concerned is indeed lost: one's practical needs, one's scientific interests, even one's loves and hates and personal relationships are vanished, but in place of these, there is the beauty of this or that sense-thing, which one adopts, accepts, receives, acknowledges, widening thus the confines of one's personality. There is an easy introspective verification of this account of the æsthetic consciousness. Let a man scrutinize closely the feeling with which he emerges from one of those 'pauses of the mind,' in which he 'contemplates' an object 'æsthetically'; he is sure to experience a curious feeling of having shrunken away from a certain largeness and inclusiveness of experience, and though he has regained interests which he had temporarily lacked, he has also lost something from his very self.

From this general description of æsthetic enjoyment as an adoption and acknowledgment of sense-objects, an immersion of oneself in the external and objective, we enter upon a more detailed consideration of its characteristics. The æsthetic consciousness is, first and foremost, enjoyment, not dissatisfaction, a mode of happiness, never of unhappiness. This follows from the completeness of absorption in the æsthetic object, for unhappiness and dissatisfaction involve always desire, aversion or resentment, the effort to escape from one's environment. This means, of course, that the æsthetic experience is a consciousness always of the beautiful, never of the ugly. Ugliness is not, therefore, a term of æsthetics: it is not a positive term at all, but a reflective description of an object as unæsthetic, an epithet which can only be applied after one has

had experience of the beautiful.[1] The æsthetic consciousness, furthermore, involves a high degree of attention, the
clear, or vivid, experience, which is narrowed, prolonged
and readily revivable. This, indeed, is definitely implied in
the description of æsthetic pleasure as absorption of oneself in the sense-object. Now this conception of æsthetic emotion, as involving attention, helps us account for
the things which people call beautiful. It is an open question whether simple experiences, such as single colors or
tones, have any beauty ; but if we do attribute beauty to
them, it is certainly by virtue of their intensity or distinctness : as when we admire the bright color or the distinct
sound. But intense and distinct experiences are, as we
know, ready objects of attention, so that it is fair to conclude
that sensational experiences are beautiful, if ever, when
easily attended to.[2] A careful scrutiny of complex objects
of beauty shows that they, too, are easily attended to, though
for another reason. The sense-object which is beautiful is
always a whole of sense-experience, and both by the unity
in which its details are united, and by the individuality of
the combination, it is readily attended to. Every beautiful
object is an illustration of the principle. Thus, curves are
beautiful, and broken lines are ugly, in part because the
curve is a whole, readily apprehended, whereas the broken
line is a series of unessentially connected sections, with
difficulty grasped as a whole; and rhythm is beautiful
because it binds into a whole, expectantly apprehended,
the successive movements, tones or words of the dance,
the melody, or the poem.

The more complex the parts which are bound together,
if only the complexity does not overstrain the attention,
the more organic the unity and the greater the beauty.

[1] Cf. George Santayana, "The Sense of Beauty," § 11, for a statement
of this theory of the nature of ugliness. The opposite view is held by many
writers.

[2] Cf. Ward, "Psychology," *Encyclopædia Britannica*, 9th ed., Vol. XX.,
p. 70.

This explains the thrilling beauty of Swinburne's meters and certain of Browning's. One need not understand the words to have one's heart beat high to such rhythms as that of Swinburne : —

> "Bind on thy sandals, O thou most fleet,
> Over the splendor and speed of thy feet ; "

or of Goethe : —

> *" Es schlug mein Herz*
> *Geschwind zu Pferde."*

By this principle, also, we may explain what we call the development of our æsthetic sense. To a child, the couplet or the quatrain may well give more æsthetic pleasure than the sonnet, precisely because he can attend to the one and not to the other, as harmonious whole.

Our consciousness of the beautiful is, in the second place, direct and immediate, not reflective and associative ; that is, the beautiful is always an object of direct and immediate perception. An object may gain interest, significance and value, but never beauty, by its suggestiveness. This is an important point, for sentimental moralists and even sober psychologists are constantly contrasting what is called the beauty of expression, or significance, with immediately apprehended beauty. We are told, for instance, that the gnarled, misshapen hands of a devoted mother are 'beautiful' because they have toiled for her children, or that an ill-proportioned, wooden building is beautiful because it is a house of worship. These are misleading metaphors : nothing can be beautiful which is not a direct and immediate object of sense-perception ; the hands are ugly, though the mother's life is an inspiration ; the church is hideous, though it serves a high ideal. Nothing is gained, indeed, by confusing every value with the distinct and well-defined value of the beautiful. What we mean by æsthetic consciousness is a direct experience ; and, as Münsterberg teaches,[1] only the unconnected, the 'isolated fact in its singleness,' can be beautiful — can bring about, in other words, the complete absorption of self in sense-object.

The third feature of the æsthetic consciousness has already been suggested; it is a characteristic emphasized by Kant, by Schiller, by Schopenhauer, and indeed, by all the great teachers: the entire disinterestedness of æsthetic pleasure. This means that the contrast between one self and other selves is all but vanished in the æsthetic experience, and that one becomes, as Schopenhauer says, 'a world-eye,' a perceiving and enjoying, not a grasping or a holding self. To enjoy a bronze or a painting because it is mine, or to delight in a view because it stretches out before my window, is thus an utterly unæsthetic experience, for the sense of beauty admits no joy in possession, and beauty does not belong to any individual. This disinterestedness of the æsthetic consciousness explains the mistaken opposition, sometimes made, of the 'beautiful' to the 'useful.' It is quite incorrect to hold that a useful object may not also be beautiful: and, indeed, men like Morris and Ruskin have fairly converted even this Philistine age to the possibility of welding together use and beauty, in the practical objects of everyday life, in buildings, furnishings and utensils. But it is true that one's consciousness of the utility banishes, for the time being, one's sense of the beauty, so that one cannot, at one and the same moment, appreciate the convenience of the Morris chair and the severe simplicity of its lines, or realize the beauty of a sky-line and the durability of a roof. While, therefore, objectively regarded, the union of beauty and utility is the end of all the arts and crafts, subjectively considered, the consciousness of utility cannot be fused with the sense of beauty, precisely because the æsthetic sense demands the subordination of narrow, personal ends.

By this same principle, also, we may explain the common

---

[1] " Psychology and Life," p. 201.

distinction of æsthetic from unæsthetic sense-experiences. The organic sensations, such as satisfied hunger and thirst, bodily warmth, active exercise, — all these are pleasant but they are not 'æsthetic' pleasures, because they are, of necessity, sharply individualized and referred to my particular self. Tastes, also, and smells, are experiences not readily objectified, but serving narrow and definite personal ends of bodily sustenance. They are seldom, therefore, artistically treated as objects of æsthetic pleasure. For the beautiful object is cut off as utterly from my narrow needs and interests as from the associative connection with other facts · in the words of Schopenhauer, it is 'neither pressed nor forced to our needs nor battled against and conquered by other external things.' Thus the world of beauty narrows to include one self, absorbed in one object of beauty.

Two other forms of altruistic or adoptive impersonal emotion must be mentioned. The first of these is the enjoyment of logical unity, often discussed under the name 'intellectual sentiment.' Every student knows the feeling, and counts among the most real of his emotional experiences the satisfied contemplation of an achieved unity in scientific classification or in philosophical system. The feeling should be sharply distinguished from another characteristic pleasure of the student, the excitement of the intellectual chase, the enjoyment of activity in even unrewarded search. The feeling which we are now describing follows upon this tormenting pleasure of the chase, as achievement follows upon endeavor. It clearly resembles æsthetic emotion, not only in its absorption and disinterestedness, but also in the characteristic harmony, or unity, of the object of delight. For this reason, the enjoyment of logical unity is sometimes reckoned as itself an æsthetic experience. The writer of this book, however, approves the ordinary usage which restricts the application of the term 'beautiful' to sense-objects. This limitation, of course, forbids the treatment of enjoyment of logical unity as a form of æsthetic pleasure.

We shall, finally, therefore, touch upon a third form of impersonal and adoptive emotion: the sense of humor. For our present purpose, it is most important to dwell upon the self-absorbing, externalizing nature of the experience. Just as we are said to forget ourselves in our apprehension of the beautiful, so also we forget ourselves, that is, our narrow individuality, our special interests and purposes, in our appreciation of the humor of a situation. What Professor Santayana has well said of the æsthetic consciousness we may equally apply to the saving sense of humor: there is hardly a "situation so terrible that it may not be relieved by the momentary pause of the mind to contemplate it æsthetically," or humorously. It is because we have such need of pauses, in the arduous business of living, that we value the sense of humor so highly, and for this same reason we find the most estimable people, if devoid of humor, so inexpressibly tiresome.

There are as many theories of the comic as of the beautiful, but virtually all of them agree in defining the sense of humor as enjoyment of an unessential incongruity. Narrowly scrutinized, every 'funny' scene, every witty remark, every humorous situation, reveals itself as an incongruity. The incongruity between one's ordinary freedom of movement and the mechanical jerks of a Jarley waxwork figure make the comedy of that situation; and in the incongruity between the two clear meanings of the word 'illustration,' lurks the wit of that celebrated introduction of Freeman, as 'the historian who had most brilliantly illustrated the barbarous manners of our ancestors.'

This incongruity must be, as has been said, an unessential one, else the mood of the observer changes from happiness to unhappiness, and the comic becomes the pathetic. A fall on the ice which seemed to offer only a ludicrous contrast, between the dignity and grace of the man erect and the ungainly attitude of the falling figure, ceases utterly to be funny when it is seen to entail some physical injury; and wit which burns and sears is not amusing to its victim.

The study of these typical impersonal emotions of the altruistic type—æsthetic delight, enjoyment of intellectual harmony and the sense of humor—leads us to reaffirm the conclusion of our study of sympathy, the adoptive personal emotion. It shows us the significance of a widened personality and the importance of a relaxed hold on the things which concern only the narrow 'myself'; it teaches us the value of self-objectivation in the apprehension of beauty, of logical unity and of harmony, three highways of escape from the petty tyrannies of life.

III

We have postponed to the end of this chapter the study both of the feelings of bodily change, included in emotion, and that of the physiological basis of emotion, for both subjects are closely related and are full of detail and of difficulty. The emotion includes, as we have seen, two significant features: the affection or affections, and the feelings due to bodily change. The affections are of two sorts: first, the immediate affection, which is not always present in emotion, and second, the affection—conditioned, as we shall see, by the bodily changes—which is characteristic of emotion and essential to it. For example: I may dislike a very pretty woman. A glimpse of her occasions therefore an immediate feeling of pleasantness, but my dislike of her includes a feeling of unpleasantness, and this unpleasantness is the essential affection in the dislike.

The bodily changes, involved by emotion, are also of two main classes. They are: first, internal changes, especially changes of heart-beat and arterial pressure, directly concerned in the circulation of the blood; and second, the movements of head, limbs and trunk, including respiratory movements. An emotion of fear, for example, includes the consciousness of quickened heart-beat, and may include a realization of one's trembling limbs; the emotion of joy includes the sensation of bodily warmth, and may include the consciousness of one's involuntary gesticulations of delight. We must lay stress on the fact that the feelings due to the internal changes, the consciousness of heart-beat, of warmth, of cold and the like, are probably always a part, even if an unemphasized part, of emotion; whereas the feelings of external changes, of altered breathing or of actual movements of the body, are frequent, but probably not invariable, constituents of emotion. My amusement, for example, often includes my consciousness of my smile, yet I may be amused without smiling; and though the realization of my dancing feet may be part of my emotion of delight, I may yet be happy without dancing.

We have now to assign a physiological condition for each of the distinguishing factors of emotion — for both sorts of affection, and for both forms of the consciousness of bodily change. Affection has already been explained,[1] as conditioned by the more than adequate or the inadequate reaction of the frontal lobes of the brain, directly stimulated by radiation of nerve impulse, through connecting fibres, from the region about the fissure of Rolando, the brain-centre of bodily movements and feelings. The series of bodily changes is probably the following: when the nervous end-organs are excited by any external object, the excitation is conveyed by ingoing nerves to sensory cells of the brain. The excitation of these sensory cells, in whatever part of the brain they are, probably always spreads to the brain-centre of bodily feelings and movements, that is, to the region forward and back of the fissure of Rolando, and there excites motor cells. The excitation of the motor cells of the Rolandic region may be carried to the frontal lobes, whose reaction occasions pleasantness and unpleasantness. But this affection — conditioned by the immediate spread of the nerve-excitation from some brain-centre, through the Rolandic area, to the frontal lobes — is not, as we have seen, the sort of pleasantness or unpleasantness

[1] Cf. Chapter IX., pp. 117 *seq.*

especially characteristic of the emotion. To explain this second, essential affection, we must consider that the excitation of these motor cells, of the Rolandic area, is not only often carried forward, but is probably always carried downward. It is carried in the first place to lower brain-centres in the *medulla oblongata,* which control the unstriped muscular coatings of inner organs of the body, such as blood-vessels, heart and intestines. In this way, internal changes are brought about, and among these, the circulatory changes are most important: the heart-beat and pulses are checked or increased, and the arteries (not the big ones near the heart, but the smaller, thin-walled vessels in outlying parts of the body), are dilated or constricted, thus occasioning either a flush and rising temperature or pallor and chilliness. The exclamation of an observant old man, who figures in a recent novel, suggests that the significance of these changes in circulation is commonly recognized. "Passions," the old man complains, "are bred out nowadays. I don't believe the next generation will be shook to the heart with the same gusts and storms as the last. We think smaller thoughts and feel smaller sentiments; we're too careful of our skins to trust the giant passions; our hearts don't pump the same great flood of hot blood."

These internal bodily changes might conceivably be unconscious, but as a matter of fact some of them, at least, are felt in our emotional states. This consciousness of bodily change is brought about in somewhat the following way. The internal changes, such as altered heart-beat or pulse, and the skin-changes, occasioned by expanding and contracting blood-vessels, stimulate the end-organs of pressure, warmth and cold, in different parts of the body; the excitation of these end-organs is carried upward by ingoing nerves to the sensory cells of the bodily-feeling-and-movement-centre (the Rolandic area); and the excitation of these sensory cells conditions those sensations, due to heart-beat, pulse and bodily temperature, which are always present in emotional experience.

Two constituents of emotion have thus been explained:
the immediate affection and the feelings of internal bodily
changes. We are ready now to account for the affection
characteristic of emotion. The excitation (due to the internal bodily changes) of sensory cells in the Rolandic area,
of course, spreads to the neighboring motor cells, and once
more is carried from them to the frontal lobes, which react
vigorously or inadequately, thus conditioning pleasantness
or unpleasantness.

But we must not forget that bodily movements of a second sort are characteristic of emotional states. These are
the external movements of face, trunk, or limbs — a smile,
for example, a laugh (which is a respiratory movement) or
a clenching of the hands. These movements are immediately due to the increased or lessened contraction of the
striped, or skeletal, muscles attached to the bones of the
body. And these muscular changes are occasioned in one
of two ways, either directly by excitation of a second set
of fibres leading downward from the Rolandic area of the
brain, or else indirectly by the changes in the blood-supply
whose origin has just been described.[1] Sometimes, as has
been said, these external bodily movements stimulate surface end-organs of pressure, ingoing nerves and sensory
brain-cells, and one is then conscious of them; but often
these external movements are unconscious.

An emotion is probably therefore conditioned by the
following cerebral phenomena: often, in the first place, by
a reaction of the frontal lobes through excitation from any
sense-centre, by way of Rolandic motor cells; invariably,
second, by the functioning of Rolandic sense-cells, due to
internal bodily changes; always, third, by an excitation of
the frontal lobes, due to the spread of excitation from the
Rolandic sense-cells, by way of motor cells; and frequently,
in the fourth place, though not invariably, by the functioning of a second set of Rolandic sense-cells, excited by the
external bodily movements of head, chest and limbs. The

[1] Cf. Lange, "Über Gemüths bewegungen," pp. 41 *seq.*, for defence of the
latter view.

diagram which follows, takes account of all these facts and of their temporal relation, but does not represent the relations between the psychic facts : —

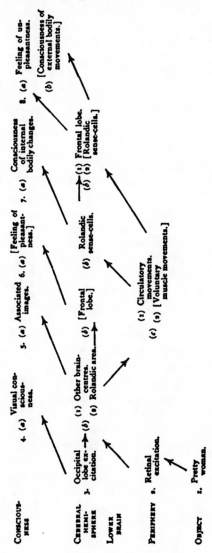

This account will be clearer, if we work it out in more detail for typical emotions. We may select as illustration the bodily conditions of the joy, with which a man hears that his dearest friend, who has been for five years absent, will reach him in an hour. Of course, no immediate affection of pleasantness or unpleasantness accompanies the reading of the telegram which brings the news; for the words in themselves are neither agreeable nor disagreeable. The bodily conditions of the joy are, therefore: —

First, (*a*) the spread of excitations from the sense-centres, excited by reading the words, to motor cells in the Rolandic area ; and (*b*) the excitation of downward, motor fibres.

Second, stronger heart-beat and pulse, and dilation of the smaller arteries which results in bodily warmth and in reddening of the skin.

Third, increased muscular contraction, manifested not only by movements of the limbs — by hand-clappings and leaps of delight — but by the rounded face and the smiling lips, due to contraction of the facial muscles.

Fourth, (*a*) excitation of end-organs of pressure, occasioned by the internal bodily movements which always occur, and by the external muscular contractions when they occur ; and (*b*) the upward spread of these excitations to sense-cells of the Rolandic area. The excitation of one group of these sense-cells occasions the feelings of internal warmth and pressure, which are always a part of the emotion of joy; and the excitation of another group of these cells, when it occurs, conditions the feelings of external movement which often form a part of 'joy.'

Fifth, the spread of excitations from these Rolandic sense-cells, by way of motor cells, to the frontal lobes, followed by the adequate excitation of frontal-lobe cells. This vigorous excitation may be explained, at least in part, in the following manner: the stronger heart-beat, characteristic of joy, pumps more blood from the heart, and all parts of the body, including the brain, are therefore relatively well nourished. Furthermore, the deep breathing of the joyful state results in the oxidation of the blood, and consequently in the better nourishment of all parts of the body.

The bodily conditions of the grief, with which one hears that one's friend has perished at sea, are, on the other hand : —

First, as before, spread of excitation from sense-centres to Rolandic motor cells and excitation of downward fibres.

Second, weaker heart-beat and pulse, and contraction of the walls of the arteries. The change in heart-beat and in pulse stimulates pressure end-organs; the change in arterial pressure results in bodily chill; and pallor naturally follows. (The constriction of blood-vessels in the lungs and the consequent insufficient blood-supply may also stimulate end-organs, whose excitation indirectly conditions feelings of suffocation and oppression.)[1]

Third, lessened contraction of the voluntary muscles: shallow breathing, drooping eyelids and mouth, slow and heavy movements, bowed head, dragging step, hanging arms and weakened voice.

Fourth, excitation of end-organs of pressure, and of sensory cells in the Rolandic area.

Fifth, the spread of excitations from these Rolandic sense-cells to the frontal lobes, followed by the feeble excitation of the cells in the frontal lobes. This inadequate excitation may be explained, in part, by the weaker heart-beat which pumps out less blood into the body, and by the shallow breathing which supplies insufficient oxygen.

Every emotion is some form of happiness or of unhappiness, or a mixture of the two, hence an account of the physiological conditions and accompaniments of any given emotion must follow, in the main, the account of the conditions of joy and of sorrow. Hope, for example, is conditioned and accompanied by the bodily changes char-

[1] Cf. Lange, *op. cit.*, p. 16.

acteristic of joy, only these are less permanent and more changeable. The bodily conditions and correlates of fear are like those of sorrow, but all the internal organs, and not — as in sorrow — only or chiefly the heart and the blood-vessels, are contracted.[1] The bodily changes characteristic of fear are, moreover, less coördinated and stable, more convulsive and also more intense than those of grief. Ordinary language, as Lange has shown, constantly dis-closes this difference : one is 'bowed down by grief,' but 'paralyzed' or 'turned to stone' by fear, and one is 'silent' in sorrow but 'dumb' with fear. And, finally, fear — more often than sorrow — is followed by strong muscular con-tractions — those, for example, involved in flight.

Hate is another emotion of unhappiness, and has the fundamental physiological correlates of unpleasant emo-tion : the pallor, recognized by the proverbial expression 'white with rage,' and the characteristic slowness of move-ment. Anger is, on the contrary, in the writer's opinion, a mixed emotion, a compound of pleasurable and unpleas-ant experience, in which one's dissatisfaction with the object of one's wrath is supplemented by a distinct enjoy-ment of one's own excitement. The flush of anger is a correlate of this pleasurable factor of emotion ; and the active movements of passion may be explained in the same way or — more reasonably, perhaps — as a reaction follow-ing the emotion.

Two minor considerations may be urged, in corrobora-tion of this general theory of the physiological basis of emotion. It satisfactorily explains the fact that pleasant experiences beget still other pleasures, that pleasure, in other words, is self-propagating. For pleasantness has been found to depend on the reaction of well-nourished cerebral cells, including Rolandic motor cells, and nutrition is due to plentiful blood-supply, and a good circulation of the blood depends, in turn, on vigorous pumpings of the

---

[1] Cf. Lange, *op. cit.*, pp. 22 *seq.*

heart, and these, as we have noted, are the result of the reaction of well-nourished motor brain-cells. These physiological processes, therefore, form a perfect circle, the pleasure of one moment being accompanied by cerebral processes, which occasion those circulatory changes that supply the cells of the brain with the nutrition, required for the pleasure-bringing reaction of a later moment.

Our theory, in the second place, can readily explain the fact, that both deep breathing and vigorous movements of the limbs are usual accompaniments of joy. For it is known that venosity of the blood, supplying the centre of reflex movements in the medulla, is the main cause of deep breathing; and this venosity of the blood is occasioned by its having lost oxygen through vigorous movements of other muscles. Thus, deep respiration and strong movements of the voluntary muscles, both of which, on our theory, are correlates of pleasant emotion, are related phenomena.

We must not fail to admit that this account of physiological conditions lacks complete and unambiguous experimental verification, by either physiologist or psychologist. The difficulties of experiments on emotional conditions are easily understood. It is very hard, in the first place, to bring about any genuine emotion under laboratory conditions — to rouse keen joy or pronounced grief while one is encased in apparatus destined to measure the bodily processes. Furthermore, the frequent complexity of affective experience makes it all but impossible to distinguish the conditions of pleasurable feeling from those of discomfort. Experimental conditions, for example, designed to bring about enjoyment, may arouse the subject's apprehension by their very unfamiliarity. And, finally, those bodily changes which are the most constant conditions of emotion, the excitation of brain-cells and the altered pressure of blood in the arteries, are either, as in the case of the brain changes, unsusceptible of direct examination or else, as in the case of the blood pressure, they are registered with difficulty and inexactness by our available apparatus.

In default of conclusive experiment, and in consideration of the fact that other accounts of the physiology of emotion have been proposed, it is necessary to supplement what has been said by a brief consideration of two of these other theories. Such of them as regard the physiology of the affections only have already been discussed,[1] and need not be reviewed. We have, therefore, in the main, to consider alternative theories of the relation of emotion to bodily changes : —

The first of these is the conventional theory. It teaches that the bodily changes are ' expressions of the emotion,' in other words, caused by it; that is to say, that the emotion is felt before the occurrence of the bodily phenomena, and that it brings them about as its effects or consequents. According to this view, one is first afraid, and then one grows pale and trembles; one is first jubilant, and then one flushes and claps one's hands. This traditional theory is disproved in many ways. It is challenged, first of all, by our introspective discovery that a consciousness of these bodily changes is part of the emotion. Since the consciousness of my heart-standing-still and of my chilly hands is part of the total experience which I call ' being afraid,' the altered heart-beat and the bodily temperature cannot be caused by my fear, but must rather be partial conditions of it; and in the same way, my quickened pulse and my flushed face must be the condition of the feelings of pulse-beat and of warmth, which are part of my joy.

Two further facts, though they do not suffice to prove that the bodily changes are never expressions of emotion, none the less show definitely that the bodily changes are not invariably expressions of emotion. The first of these

[1] Cf. Chapter IX., p. 120 *seq.*

facts has been emphasized by James. He points out that it is often possible to bring about an emotion artificially, by mechanically performing the actions characteristic of it. "Whistling to keep your courage up," he says, "is no mere figure of speech.[1] On the other hand, sit all day in a moping posture, sigh, and reply to everything with a dismal voice, and your melancholy lingers. There is no more valuable precept in moral education than this, as all who have experience know : if we wish to conquer undesirable emotional tendencies in ourselves, we must assiduously, and in the first instance cold-bloodedly, go through the *outward movements* of those contrary dispositions which we prefer to cultivate. The reward of persistency will infallibly come, in the fading out of the sullenness or depression, and the advent of real cheerfulness and kindliness in their stead. Smooth the brow, brighten the eye, contract the dorsal rather than the ventral aspect of the frame, and speak in a major key, pass the genial compliment, and your heart must be frigid indeed if it do not gradually thaw!" It is true that this is not a perfectly certain way of arousing emotion : one's courage does not always come at the bidding of a whistle, and one's emotion doesn't inevitably follow the line of one's backbone. Yet the fact that we are often able to arouse emotion, in this way, shows that the usual doctrine is wrong, in supposing that bodily attitude or gesture or organic change is necessarily conditioned by the emotion and sequent upon it.

The second of the arguments, against the conventional theory, is biological in its character. It is based on the interesting and probable hypothesis, emphasized by Darwin[2] and by others, that these 'emotional' bodily changes are modified survivals of instinctive reactions of animals and of primitive men to their environment. The trembling of fear, for example, is regarded as an instinctive

[1] *Op. cit.*, Vol. II., p. 463.

[2] Darwin, "Expression of the Emotions in Man and Animals," Chapters I.–III. and XIV. Cf. Dewey, *Psychological Review*, Vol. I., pp. 553 *seq.*

movement which takes the place of actual flight from the
enemy; the snarl of hate is a modified survival of the way
in which an animal uncovers his teeth, in order to tear and
devour his prey, and the quickened breath of anger is a
survival of the labored breath of an animal or of a savage,
in a life and death contest with an enemy. But there is
every reason to believe that the primitive reactions, of
which the so-called expressions of emotion are probably
indeed survivals, must have occurred instantaneously, and
therefore unconsciously, upon sight or sound or smell of
the dangerous or hateful object. To suppose a temporally
distinct emotion of fear, between the antelope's glimpse of
the tiger and his flight, is to assure the whole race of
antelopes of destruction. Preservation of animal life, in
fact, requires what observation establishes, the instantaneous sequence of many bodily movements upon the percept of the environment. And this shows that an emotion
has not always preceded the bodily change, which is
ordinarily named its expression; and that if the movements were primitively instantaneous and unconscious,
there is no reason to suppose that an emotion is required
to occasion them.

We must therefore abandon the usual way of talking
about emotion and its bodily expression. For we have
seen, not only that the bodily movements bring about the
brain changes which condition emotion, but that the consciousness of the bodily movements is part of the emotion
itself. One does not first feel afraid, then turn pale, feel
one's heart sink and one's limbs tremble, but one's emotion of fear includes always the consciousness of chill and
of heart sinking, and often the consciousness of wavering
knees and shaky hands. Modern psychologists, led by
William James and by the Danish physiologist, Conrad
Lange, have successfully combatted this traditional theory
of emotional expressions. In so doing, they have, however, sometimes fallen into an opposite error and have,
first, treated the bodily changes as entire, and not merely

partial, bodily conditions of emotion; and then, second, they have defined emotion as nothing more than this consciousness of bodily changes. (Of course the second of these doctrines is not a necessary consequence of the first, but the two are combined by James and by Lange.) "A man's fright," says Lange,[1] "is only a perception of the change in his body." "Our feeling," James declares,[2] "of the bodily changes as they occur IS the emotion." In the opinion of the writer, these statements are clearly untrue to our introspective observation. We do, to be sure, have experiences, sometimes called by the names of the emotions, which are made up solely of the consciousness of bodily changes. The best example is the experience of 'being startled' at a loud sound from which one apprehends no danger. One certainly is conscious of one's trembling at the banging of a door or at the explosion of an empty gun, without at the same time having any other feelings characteristic of emotion. The writer, however, appeals rather confidently, to the reader's introspection, for confirmation of the view that this experience of being startled is radically different from emotional fear; and that fear, grief, hope and joy are, as actually felt, something more than that awareness of beating heart, warmth or cold, and smile or sob, which unquestionably forms a part of them.

The conclusions of this long chapter may be briefly summarized as follows: Emotion may be regarded either (1) as complex fact of consciousness, idea, or (2) as consciousness of oneself, in passive relation to particularized people or things. From either point of view, it is an experience which includes pleasantness or unpleasantness (or both), and which includes, also, the consciousness of bodily phenomena, especially of those due to circulatory changes. Its cerebral conditions are probably the follow-

---

[1] *Op. cit.*, p. 51. [2] *Op. cit.*, Vol. II., p. 449.

ing: first changes in sensory Rolandic cells, due to the bodily movements already mentioned, and second, the vigorous or weak reaction of the frontal-lobe cells. Emotions are first classified as happy or unhappy; they are then best described, from the point of view of the conscious relation of one self to other selves or to things, as personal or impersonal, and as imperious or sympathetic.

CHAPTER XXI

VOLITION AND BELIEF. WILL AND FAITH

I

a. VOLITION

In the first section of this chapter the discussion will be confined, as strictly as possible, to what has been called the idea-psychology, that is, we shall consider the succession of ideas, and so far as possible keep out of sight the selves who have the ideas. We shall thus discuss, not will and faith, the relations of self to selves, but volitions and beliefs, distinguishable parts in the stream of successive consciousnesses. In discussing volitions, we shall follow the usual division which distinguishes 'the outer' from the 'inner volition,' the volition to act from the volition to think, the volition to sign a cheque or to fire a gun or to make an electric contact, from the volition to attend to the elusive analogy, to remember the forgotten name or to work away at the unsolved problem. The outer volition will first be discussed.

The outer volition may be defined, provisionally, as the image of an action or of a result-of-action, which normally precedes this same act or result. In other words, the volition is the image of an action or of a result of action, which is normally similar and antecedent to this same action or result. My volition to sign a letter is either an image of my hand moving the pen or an image of my signature already written, and my volition to purchase something is an image of myself in the act of handing out money or an image of my completed purchase — golf stick or Barbédienne bronze.

But the volition is more than this bare antecedent image. Experience furnishes each of us with countless examples of movement preceded by idea of movement, which we never think of calling voluntary. I imagine an operatic air, for instance, and am surprised to find myself humming it, or I listen to an orchestra and my waving fan moves unconsciously to the rhythm of the symphony. These are instances of movement preceded by idea-of-movement, yet nobody calls the antecedent images — of operatic air or of musical rhythm — volitions; and one names these movements ideo-motor, not voluntary. For, just as an image of the past is not of necessity a recognition, so an antecedent image is not of necessity a volition ; and just as the image of the past becomes a recognition, only when it is characterized by the factor 'familiarity,' so the antecedent image is not a volition, unless it includes a certain realized 'anticipatoriness,' which we may describe roughly as the 'thought of a real happening.' The volition is not merely, therefore, an image which is later realized as having been anticipatory: rather, the anticipation is part of the content itself, and one is conscious of anticipation in being conscious of a volition. That is to say, the complex volitional idea includes a conscious reference to a real future linked with the present image, somewhat as the recognition includes a reference to the past.

Before we treat of the factors or elements of this feeling of anticipation, we must emphasize the chief obstacles to this analysis. The first of them is an old difficulty : the impossibility of direct experimental verification, since the physiological organs of the anticipation-feeling are within the brain. The second is the difficulty, which will grow more evident as we proceed, of keeping consistently to the point of view of idea-psychology. With this proviso, we may enumerate, with brief comment, three features of the realized anticipatoriness : —

First of them all is the idea of the future, itself highly complex. For this idea involves a consciousness of the connection of one moment with other moments. Every moment, past and present as well as future, is realized, whenever one is conscious of it at all, as that-which-is-always-linked-in-two-directions, with its past and with its future. But the idea of the future is distinguished, from that of past and of present, by lacking the sense of irrevocableness which belongs to them. Past and present are felt to be beyond all control or change, whereas the future seems to be relatively undetermined.

In the second place, the feeling of anticipatoriness, the characteristic of every volition, involves the feeling of realness. This has already been defined as an element of consciousness, an irreducible experience. It 'feels like itself,' and cannot be described, but it can be indicated — as distinguishing, for example, my inspection of Gobelin tapestries from my image of the richly wrought draperies of Tennyson's "Palace of Art." This feeling of realness is a very significant part of every volition. The object of volition is always a something to be realized : in other words, what we will we always will to be real. We may recall any volition whatever — the determination to hit the bull's eye, to snatch the Elzevir edition from rival bidders at the book auction, or to resist a temptation to speculation — and we are sure to find, within the experience, the consciousness not merely of a future, but of a future real. In fact, this is the precise distinction between the volition and the wish. The wish, no less than the volition, refers to the future, but whereas I may entertain a wish for a castle in Spain or for a trip to Mars, I have volitions for such objects only as seem to me attainable.

The feeling of anticipatoriness contains, finally, a consciousness of the linkage not merely of any present with any future, but of this particular event with the future reality — movement or result of movement. Here is the distinction between the volition and the belief of the future fact. The difference, between the belief that my market man will give me a green goose for my Christmas dinner and the intention that he shall do it, is not in the reference to future reality, for that is common to both, but in the occurrence, within the volition, of a realized linkage of this particular image of mine with the future result.[1] It must not be forgotten that we are discussing, not a logical distinction, but an actual psychological ingredient of the volition. When we are conscious of volition, we are actually conscious of a present image linked to an imagined reality. The consciousness of realness and of what we have called linkage, or connectedness, are actual parts of our experience; we are just as much conscious of them as we are conscious of the imagined movement.

We must, finally, make it very clear to ourselves that a volition exists quite independently of any specific result. The fact that I am prevented, by bodily incapacity or by external circumstance, from carrying out my purpose, does not alter the volitional nature of the purpose itself. The volition is the image of an act or of its result, including the feeling of anticipation, the consciousness of the necessary connection of this definite idea with a future real. Its physiological consequence certainly is the excitation of motor cells and of outgoing fibres. But this nervous impulse may exhaust itself before the contraction of any muscles occurs; or the contraction may indeed take place, but insufficiently; or, finally, my successful action may miss the needed support of other actions. I may address the ball with infinite pains, but top it ingloriously; I may raise the pitch of my voice, but fall short of the high C; or I may sign the paper, but it may not rescue my friend from financial ruin. In all these cases, whatever the reason of external failure, the volition remains what it is by virtue of its essential nature.

The inner volition may be passed with mere mention. It is an antecedent image involving the idea of anticipatoriness, that is, the consciousness of its definite connection

---

[1] Cf. Münsterberg, "Die Willenshandlung," for statement of a different view.

with a future which is real. The future real is, however, in
this case, another image, not a physical action or situation,
but a psychic fact. The volitions to remember the forgotten
name or date, to guess the riddle and to understand the working of the intricate mechanism are examples of what we mean
by inner volitions. Comparing them with outer volitions, it
is evident that they do not so closely resemble their results.
The volitional image of an act may be, in detail, like the act
as performed; but the object of inner volition is itself an
image, and to have an anticipatory image of an image, precisely similar to it yet not identical with it, is impossible.
Inner volitions may, therefore, be defined as anticipatory
images, including the idea of linkage with a future real, and
normally followed by partially similar images, not by acts.

Both outer and inner volitions are further distinguished
as either simple volitions or choices. The difference is
this : in the case of the choice, a fluctuation of opposing
images precedes the volition itself. This distinction will be
illustrated in a later section of this chapter; but it is well
to notice here that there is no difference, at the moment of
volition, between the simple volition and the choice. Each
is an antecedent image realized as 'anticipatory.' The
difference is merely that the choice is preceded by the
restless, shifting fluctuation of alternating images.

It should be added that volition always includes some
consciousness of bodily movements. In outer volition, the
movement is toward the outer object or act which one wills :
one finds one's fingers moving to a tune or one's eyes turned
in the purposed direction. Even in inner volition — the
effort, for example, to solve the problem or to remember the
forgotten date — one is apt to wrinkle one's forehead, to
clench one's fingers or to hold one's breath. Psychologists
have sometimes mistaken this vague consciousness of bodily
movements, for an elemental and unanalyzable consciousness which they have called 'conation' or 'volition.'[1]

---

[1] For criticism of this view, cf. Titchener, "Outline," § 37.

b. BELIEF

The relation of the belief to the volition has already been suggested. The belief is an idea which contains the feeling of realness, and which refers to another idea or to an event. In these respects, it is like the volition, but it differs from the volition in three particulars: in the first place, it does not necessarily contain a reference to the future. One may believe a past or a present as well as a future event, as when, for example, one believes that the Egyptians fought at Carchemish, or that some one is at the front door. In the second place, when the belief does refer to the future, it lacks the consciousness of the linkage of this especial image with the future. My belief that dinner will be served at seven differs from my volition that it shall be served, because the belief lacks, what the volition has, a sense that this antecedent image has a certain bearing on the result which will follow.

The belief, finally, differs from the volition by a more positive characteristic. In the belief, the feeling of realness always attaches itself to the relational feeling of harmony, or congruence. Nothing seems 'real' to us which does not also seem harmonious. It follows that beliefs, complex contents of consciousness containing the feeling of realness, are of the most varied sort, but that they all agree in being realized as congruent. When our percepts are called 'real,' by contrast with our images, they are [1] known as harmonious both with other people's experience and with each other: the clock-tower which I see accords with the heavy railway station which supports it, the campanile which I imagine is contradicted by every architectural feature of this New England town; the electric bells which I hear are congruent with the habitual experiences of the city streets, the strains of Gounod's Sanctus which I imagine are unrelated with my entire surroundings.

[1] James, " Principles," Vol. II., p. 300.

From this it follows that a given idea may seem from one point of view real and from another unreal, according as it is compared with one set of facts or with another. James has brilliantly illustrated this truth under the heading "The Many Worlds of Reality," and has suggested seven such worlds,[1] including the worlds of sense, of science, of abstract truths, of fiction and of individual opinion. The motion of the sun, which is real in the sense-world, is thus unreal in the world of science; Goethe's Lotte, though unreal in the sense-world, is so real in the world of poetry, that we sharply contrast with her Thackeray's parodied Charlotte, whom we unhesitatingly pronounce unreal. And these distinctions mean merely, that the motion of the sun is a phenomenon, congruent with the facts of our everyday observation — sunrises, moons and twilights — but contradicted by the Copernican conception, of our earth and the other planets of our system, in revolution about the sun; and that the romantic Lotte is a figure congruent with the life and environment of Goethe's Werther, whereas Thackeray's prosaic Charlotte is utterly unrelated to the Werther world of Goethe's creation.

The belief is, thus, an idea distinguished both by the feeling of realness and by the feeling of congruence. Beliefs, like volitions, may be 'inner' or 'outer,' that is, they may refer to ideas or to external events, and they may be deliberative or simple, that is, they may or may not be preceded by a fluctuation of alternative images.

II. Will and Faith[2]

We have so far proceeded on the basis of idea-psychology, that is, we have regarded volition and belief, each as the idea of a particular moment, connected with the other ideas which make up the stream of consciousness, and without

---

[1] *Op. cit.*, Vol. II., p. 292.

[2] The discussion which follows is in substance, and sometimes verbally, identical with that of a paper, by the writer, in the *Philosophical Review*, IX., 490.

x

definite reference to any self or selves. But this treatment,
of the consciousness which we ordinarily call willing or
choosing or determining, must strike every one as a little
forced and artificial. The experience of aiming at a target
or selecting a book or adhering to a creed is more naturally
expressed by the words, ' I will, I choose, I believe,' than
by the parallel statements, 'a volition — a choice — a belief.' In other words, just as we have not merely ' percept' and 'image' and 'general notion' but 'perceiving'
and 'imagining' and 'thinking,' so we have not only 'volition' and 'belief' but 'will' and 'faith.' One and the
same experience may, therefore, be regarded as an idea in
a series, relatively distinct from a self, or it may be regarded
as an attitude or relation of a self.

Our first question is this: how are will and faith,
regarded as relations or attitudes of a self, distinguished
from emotion, thought and perception? The difference
seems to be this: perception, imagination, thought and
emotion are, in a sense, passive experiences, whereas will
and faith are recognized as active. There is no need to
justify the statement that perception is a passive experience,
for everybody admits that we cannot help seeing and hearing and smelling, that is, that we have no direct control of
perceptual consciousness. It is evident, also, that we are
victims of memory and imagination. Insignificant word-
series repeat themselves with wearisome iteration, gruesome
scenes thrust themselves upon us, and bitter experiences
unroll themselves before our unwilling eyes. It is not so
obvious that thought is a passive experience: on the other
hand, it is often regarded as active, in contrast with perception as passive. But closer observation will disclose
that thought, like imagination and memory, can be called
active only when combined, as it often is, with will. In and
for itself, comparison or generalization or judgment is as
unavoidable as perception or memory; and the truths of
geometry thrust themselves upon us with as firm a front as
the things of the sense-world. Emotion, finally, is com-

monly recognized as a passive sort of consciousness, in which we are influenced by people and things, a prey to them, 'prostrate beneath them,' as Goethe somewhere says.

Sharply contrasted with these passive relations of the self—with perception, thought, emotion and the others,—are two supremely active experiences, will and faith.

a. WILL

Will is a consciousness of my active connection with other selves or with things, an imperious relation, a domineering mood, a sort of bullying attitude. It is thus distinctly untrue that we stand in the will-relation to people or to things, only when some bodily change or activity is the object of our will. To be sure, that effect on the acts of others is the inevitable and most practically significant accompaniment of will; but not only may external conditions prevent any action of another, in accordance with my will, but I may not even contemplate any such action on his part, yet I am actively related toward him, if I inwardly assert him to be subordinate to me, a means to my self-realization. Similarly, I may not have in mind any specific change to be brought about in my material environment, yet I am actively, assertively, related to it, if I am conscious of my superiority and my independence of it, or if I conceive of it as existing mainly for my own use or gratification.

Every leader or captain among men is thus an embodiment of will: his domain may be great or small, spiritual or physical, civil or literary; he may be king or shoe-maker, archbishop or machinist, inventor or novelist; whatever his position, if he consciously imposes himself on others, if he moulds to his ideals their civic functions, their forms of worship or their literary standards, their electrical furnishings or even their boots, he stands to them in the relation of imperious, domineering, willing self.

The rebel and the stoic are even more striking embodi-

ments of the will-relation than the mere leaders of men.
For stoicism and rebellion are instances of imperiousness,
in the face of great or even overwhelming natural odds, —
assertions of one's independence in the very moment of
opposition or defeat. The stoic, in spite of his conviction
that apparent success is with his opponent, is unflinching
in the assertion of his own domination. "I am like the
promontory," he declares, "against which the waves continually break, but it stands firm and tames the fury of the
water around it." The rebel, in Promethean mood, defies
the very gods who are torturing him. "Can you tear me
from myself," he challenges. "They ask to share with
me," he cries again, "and I will give them naught." [1]

It is this attitude of mind, not any specific direction
of consciousness toward a definite result, which constitutes what we call will, in the most intimate meaning of
that word : a realization of one's independence of people
and of things, a sense more or less explicit, of the subordination of one's environment to one's own use, active or
spiritual, — such a possession of one self as is, in its completest development, a subjugation of every outlying circumstance and of every opposing self. In this broadest sense,
will may be the very heart of defeat, as the splendid
defiance of this modern outburst of the stoic mood makes
evident : —

> "Out of the night that covers me,
>   Black as the pit from pole to pole,
>   I thank whatever gods may be
>   For my unconquerable soul.

---

[1] Cf. Goethe's " Prometheus " : —

Prometheus. Vermöcht Ihr zu scheiden
            Mich von mir selbst?

          *   *   *   *

Epimetheus. Wie vieles ist da dein?
Prometheus. Der Kreis den meine Wirksamkeit erfüllt

      *   *   *   *   *   *   *

            Sie wollen mit mir theilen, und ich meine
            Dass ich mit ihnen nichts zu theilen habe.

"In the fell clutch of circumstance
    I have not winced nor cried aloud.
Under the bludgeonings of chance
    My head is bloody, but unbowed.

"Beyond this place of wrath and tears
    Looms but the Horror of the shade.
And yet the menace of the years
    Finds and shall find me unafraid.

"It matters not how strait the gate,
    How charged with punishments the scroll,
I am the master of my fate:
    I am the captain of my soul."

There are two fundamental forms of will, simple will and choice, that is, will after deliberation. Deliberation is the fluctuation of tendencies or directions of one's self-assertiveness, a sort of clashing and warring of different self-activities. We shall later illustrate it, and consider it in more detail.

Will, it should be noted, is originally, like all consciousness, personal, — a relation of self to other selves. Later, however, when we have made the distinction between selves, on the one hand, and things and feelings on the other, these psychic and physical facts, also, are thought of as subordinated to the willing self. The most fundamental formulation, of this imperious tendency in relation to external things, is the anthropocentric theory of nature. This doctrine regards nature as existing solely for man, and explains natural phenomena merely by showing how they subserve man's interests. Animals, it teaches, live to furnish man food and clothes and sport, the earth revolves to afford him darkness in which to sleep, sunsets and oceans and birds of paradise exist to provide him means of æsthetic pleasure, and cork trees grow, as Hegel suggests in scornful paraphrase, to furnish corks for his wine bottles. In a word, the universe is regarded solely as 'owing man a living,' and is pronounced satisfactory, in so far as it fulfils this obligation.

We have now to analyze into its elements will, as active relation of a self to other selves and to things. The analysis will be parallel, except in one particular, with the analysis of a volition into its elements. Will, the active relating of one self to another, certainly includes the consciousness of reality and the consciousness of the linkage of subordinated self or thing to imperious self. But, in so far as will is a relation of self to other selves, it does not necessarily include a consciousness of time. This follows from the truths already emphasized, that the consciousness of selves does not primarily take account of time, whereas the consciousness of a temporal order is fundamental to idea-psychology, the study of the series of connected ideas. We may, however, and often do, regard will from a combination of both points of view, that of self-psychology and that of idea-psychology, and may treat it as imperious attitude of the self to future event, inner or outer. Such a future event is seized upon, emphasized and dominated by the willing self. This form of willing includes all the elements of volition, the feeling of futurity, as well as the consciousness of realness and of linkage. Its two forms are the will to act and the will to know.

The will to act consists in the compelling relation, the dominating, active attitude of a self, toward an imaged, outer event. This imaged event or situation is, of course, no private affair of one's own, but a 'public,' shared, communicable experience. In other words, the will to do is an explicitly social experience, an imperious relation to other people's perception. The will to hit the target, to secure the book, or to march at the head of one's legions always involves the consciousness of the onlooking other selves, and is always, thus, an imposition of oneself upon them.

The will to know, to remember or to attend is a similar domination of the inner or psychic event. Both the will to know and the will to act may, furthermore, be distinguished as either simple or deliberative.

b. FAITH

Faith, as distinct from will, is an adopting or acknowledging, not an imperious, demanding phase of consciousness, laying emphasis not on myself but on the 'other self.' In the attitude of will, I subordinate others to myself; in that of faith or loyalty, I submit myself to others. In the mood of will, I am 'captain of my soul'; in my faith, I acknowledge another leader. Yet faith, like will, is an active, not a passive, attitude of one self to other selves. It is no emotional sinking beneath the force of opponent or environment but a spontaneous, self-initiated experience, the identification of oneself with another's cause, the throwing oneself into another's life, or the espousal of another's interests. Men of faith have always, like the heroes of Hebrew history, "subdued kingdoms, wrought righteousness, obtained promises, stopped the mouths of lions," and this, through the active identification of themselves with great selves, great ideals and great theories.

Primarily, of course, this attitude of acknowledgment and adoption is a relation to other selves. And it is in this form only that we call it faith. When, later, the notions of external thing and of event, outer or inner, are gained, our adoption of these is called no longer faith but belief. A man has faith in his father, his teacher, his business associate, his God; he believes the efficacy of the gold standard, the doctrine of evolution, the dogma of the inspiration of the Bible. The difference between this term 'belief' (used without the article), as describing a relation of selves to events or to doctrines, and the term 'a belief,' which refers to the belief-idea, should be carefully marked.

This doctrine of faith is most often obscured by confusing it with the bare consciousness of reality. A certain consciousness of reality is, it is true, essential to the active attitude toward selves and toward things, that is, both to faith and to will. But the mere awareness of reality is a very subordinate part of the experience of faith, or belief, despite the fact that it is chief constituent of beliefs, regarded as mere ideas. Faith is always an active, personal attitude toward another self; belief is always an active, personal attitude toward things, events or truths; and both faith and belief involve, but are not exhausted by, a consciousness of the realness of selves or of things.

It is interesting to notice that the opposite confusion of terms sometimes occurs, that is to say, that the consciousness of realness is sometimes described as if it were a personal attitude. So James says[1] that the "quality of reality is a relation to our life. It means our adoption of things, our caring for them, our standing by them." And with a similar suggestion, Baldwin[2] speaks of our 'personal endorsement' of reality.

The relation between faith and the mere awareness of reality is most often discussed on an ethical basis. We receive, from great teachers of righteousness, fervid exhortations to have faith and to believe. But still other teachers warn us, as solemnly, that it is alike irrational and immoral to proclaim an obligation to hold opinions. These moralists insist that it is meaningless to assert the ethical superiority of one idea to another, and they teach that the alleged duty, to hold this or that view of reality, is in opposition to the only intellectual obligation — unswerving honesty in investigation.

This revolt against the 'duty to believe' would be justified, if it did not presuppose a wrong interpretation of the exhortations to faith. The truth is, that the great moral teachers always regard faith as personal acknowledgment of great selves and of great personal ideals. Such acknowledgment may involve, it is true, a certain consciousness of reality, and is never possible toward self or toward cause which is held as definitely unreal. On the other hand, such a personal acknowledgment does not presuppose any reasoned conclusion or any philo-

---

[1] *Op. cit.*, Vol. II., p. 569.   [2] "Feeling and Will," p. 158.

sophic conviction about reality, and may even exist along with an unemphasized or a fluctuating consciousness of the reality of the self or the cause, with which one allies oneself. The duty to have faith is always, therefore, the obligation to identify oneself with the persons or the causes which seem the highest; and the exhortation to faith is always, on the lips of the great teachers, an incentive to loyalty. Thus, the New Testament commands to believe emphasize, always, the need or the duty of an affirming, consenting, personal attitude toward a divine self, and do not require that one hold an opinion about him; and the great creeds, also, are expressions of a personal relation. For, from this point of view, a conception of the duty of faith may clearly be held, since personal relations, not convictions of reality, are the objects of obligation, and since faith is the active, adoptive relation of one self with another.

III

We are ready now to consider, in more detail, the different forms of these experiences which, regarded from one point of view, are called will and faith, whereas, from the other standpoint, they are known as volitions and beliefs.

Our discussion will follow the course of the following classification : —

WILL AND FAITH		VOLITION AND BELIEF
I. Will to Act (and Belief).	*a.* Simple.	I. Outer Volition (and the Belief).
	1. With resident end.	
	2. With remote end.	
	b. Choice.	
	1. Without effort.[1]	
	2. With effort.[1]	
II. Will to Know (and Belief).	*a.* Simple.	II. Inner Volition (and the Belief)
	b. Choice.	
	1. Without effort.	
	2. With effort.	

[1] With resident or with remote end.

The chief distinction which is found, between the forms of the active relations of one self to other selves, is that between the simple will-relation and the choice. In addition, we shall consider only the will to act and the will to know, which are will-relations of selves to things and events, not to other selves. We shall not, on the other hand, attempt a formal scheme of the delicately varying relations of self to selves.

In discussing volitions, we found them distinguished as 'outer' and 'inner,' and in considering the imperious relation of a self to things and events, we contrasted the will to act with the will to know. A similar division may be made, we observed, among beliefs or forms of belief. This distinction we shall now illustrate and discuss in greater detail.

Outer volition, or the will to act, may be either a consciousness of bodily movement or a consciousness of the result of movement. In the expression of James, it may be of the 'resident' or of the 'remote' end. It is thus a consciousness of straining muscle or of moving hand, or else a consciousness of the effect of these movements, of the note to be sounded, the button to be fastened, or the outline to be drawn. This consciousness of the remote end may be visual, auditory, or, in fact, of any sense-type whatever. The movements necessary to gain this remote end are, however, not voluntary but merely reflex, since the image, which precedes them, is of result not of movement. This conclusion accords with the certainty,[1] that a given bodily movement, without preceding image, may be performed, not only with entire unconsciousness (as an unconscious reflex), but with accompanying, though not antecedent, consciousness (as a conscious reflex). The movements, by which a 'remote end' is attained, belong to either class of reflex acts, that is, they are either unconscious or conscious, but they are involuntary. A man's volition, for example, is to reach the railway station,

[1] Cf. Appendix, Section VI.

and involuntarily he breaks into a run toward it; he has a visual consciousness of the platform, which means that a centre in his occipital lobe is excited; this excitation spreads along fibres which lead to the Rolandic centres of leg-muscle activity, and by the excitation of these centres his movements of running are excited. He is conscious of the running, but only after it has begun, and he is even unconscious of some of the leg-contractions involved in the running. His definite volition-image is merely ' railroad station,' not ' movement of running '; or, in terms of self-psychology, he actively relates himself to the railroad station, not to his leg-muscles, and the movements follow as reflexes, without being specifically willed.

In truth, the development of the life of consciousness always tends to suppress the direct motor volitions. Almost all bodily movements are better executed when our aim is directed toward the result to which they lead, that is to say, when the object of volition or of will is an ' outer object,' not an imaged bodily movement. A reduction in the number of one's detailed voluntary movements is thus a work of psychic advancement : only the amateur musician needs to decide the exact curve of his finger, only the child thinks how he will twist the obstinate button.

A still more fundamental distinction — applying equally to inner volition, or the will to know, and to outer volition, or the will to act — is that between the simple volition (or willing) and the choice, the volition (or willing) after deliberation. As has been said, the essential feature of this situation is a fluctuation of experiences. From the standpoint of idea-psychology, this fluctuation is of images ; from the standpoint of self-psychology, it is a fluctuation of different active attitudes of one self toward other selves or things. I choose, let us say, to hear Tannhaüser instead of Lohengrin, but my choice is preceded by what is called deliberation, a sort of mental see-saw of Tannhaüser and Lohengrin consciousness : now the ' Pilgrim Chorus ' sounds clear and sweet in my imagination, but its music is drowned by that of the bridal music; again, the swan-boat is vivid before me, but it is blotted out by a vision of the festival scene. The whole experience is attended by feelings of perplexity and unrest, the characteristic discomfort of 'making up one's mind.'

The alternating images are not always of the definite ends of action. The imaged accompaniments and results of these rival acts may play leading rôles in my deliberation. If I am deciding between a year of travel and a year of graduate study, the thought of the culture which may come from travel will be confronted by a reflection on the definite attainments of the university courses. If I am wavering between a new rug and a set of books, the vision of my glorified floor will be crowded out by an image of the tooled leather backs of the Molière volumes, in a prominent corner of my bookshelves. That is to say — in terms now of the consciousness of self — I relate myself, now to one, now to another of these rival images.

The great dramatists lay bare before us the crises of deliberation in their heroes' lives. A classic example is the conflict of pity and honor with patriotism and personal ambition in the heart of Achilles' son, Neoptolemos, face to face with the sufferings of the hero, Philoctetes, whom he may betray for his own gain and for the interest of the Hellenes, or save and befriend for loyalty's and for friendship's sake. Another illustration is found in the soliloquies of Hamlet, in whom

> "the native hue of resolution
> Is sicklied o'er with the pale cast of thought."

Sometimes, as in the experience of Hamlet and of Werther, the deliberation is never concluded, but becomes a fixed habit of irresolution, a perpetual vacillation. Normally, however, it is ended by the decision, or choice. The choice, it will be remembered, may be regarded from two points of view. In terms of idea-psychology, it is that one of the alternating images to which, finally, the feeling of anticipatoriness is attached. Thus, the image of himself, as conquerer of the Trojans, gives place in the mind of Neoptolemos to the image of his father's friend, the injured Philoctetes, rejoicing to regain his bow; and this last image, supplemented by a consciousness of necessary connection with a real future, is a volition, not a mere antecedent image. Or, to translate into terms of self-psychology, Neoptolemos no longer vacillates between the imperious and the loyal attitudes toward Philoctetes, but definitely acknowledges and adopts the interests of the wounded Greek.

In considering the different sorts of choice, we shall do well to follow the lead of James, distinguishing 'choices without effort' from 'choices with effort.' For idea-psychology, the difference is simply this: in the choice without effort, the victorious volition, or will, drives its rival off the field, whereas, in the choice with effort, a man chooses one alternative in full view of the other. The choice without effort, however prolonged and restless the deliberation which has preceded, is an easy choice, because at the exact time of making it no other act or result is contemplated.

The choice without effort usually conforms with our habits of thought, inclination and action. I am deliberating, let us suppose, whether to eat the green bon-bon or the pink. The green one is larger, but the pink one is prettier; the green one looks as if had nuts in it, but the pink one looks as if it were creamy. So far I am undecided, but now the green suggests pistachio, which I do not like, and at once, quite without effort, I choose the pink. Or I am trying to decide whether or not to buy this volume of Swinburne. The paper is poor and the print is fine, but the price is low and the poems are complete. "I really must have it," I say to myself. "But the print is impossible," I reflect. My indecision, however prolonged, is ended by the discovery that the book is an unauthorized

American reprint. Now I long since decided to buy only authorized editions of English books, and my actual decision, to reject the book, is made without effort, that is, without even a thought of the advantage of the book.

When confronted, therefore, with what seems a new decision, it is wise, as James has taught, to consider its relation to former choices, to fundamental inclinations and to habitual actions. The result of such a 'classification,' as James calls it, is usually a decision without effort. An action, clearly realized as essential to the fulfilment of a choice already made, will promptly be chosen. The advantage of what the old psychologies called 'governing choices' is precisely this, that they make 'subordinate choices' easy. When, for instance, I have chosen a college or a society, I have limited the range of my subordinate choices, and I can no longer consider seriously courses of study which my college does not recognize. One of the reasons why it is so necessary to make these inclusive, governing choices is simply, therefore, that one may economize the time and energy required by deliberation. For the same reason, the more developed the consciousness, the fewer always are the decisions. Just as the acts at first performed with definite purpose become mere reflexes, so actions once performed by deliberate choice tend to follow from simple volitions. When I am reading, for instance, in an utterly desultory way, I may have to choose between "Eleanor" and "Unleavened Bread," but if I have entered on a "Modern Italy" course of reading, I take the first without hesitating, whereas if I am studying American society, I turn to the second.

The choice with effort is not, of necessity, preceded by longer or more painful deliberation (that is, vacillating consciousness) than the effortless choice. The essential difference is simply this, that the choice is made with full consciousness of the neglected alternative. "Both alternatives," James says, "are steadily held in view, and in the very act of murdering the vanished possibility, the chooser realizes how much he is making himself lose." George Eliot has suggested this experience in the story of Romola's meeting with Savonarola, as she sought to escape from Tito and from Florence. "*She foresaw that she should obey Savonarola and go back.* His arresting voice had brought a new condition to her life, which made it seem impossible to her that she could go on her way as if she had not heard it; *yet she shrank as one who sees the path she must take, but sees, too, that the hot lava lies there*." [1]

This book follows the usage of James in making the term 'effort' describe simply the 'unhappy experience of fluctuating consciousness.' The word, however, is used by others, with at least two other meanings. It is sometimes employed as synonym for 'conation,' to designate the alleged element of consciousness which is found in volition. It is also used, by Titchener [2] and by others, for the complex consciousness of the bodily movements which accompany all volition.

It must be added that the accounts of deliberation, formulated in terms of the psychology of ideas, are far less convincing, that is, less adequate, than descriptions of deliberation as opposition of distinct tendencies of a self. Such doctrines of conflicting ideas often, indeed, win their credence, because we unconsciously add to the conception of alternating ideas the more fundamental one of warring self-activities. We may illustrate this from our former examples. We do not naturally represent to ourselves the struggle of Neoptolemos, as a mere fluctuation of images, — a picture of himself, the triumphant possessor of the bow of Philoctetes, striding as victor through the walls of Troy, alternating with a picture of Philoctetes, calmed and consoled, the holder of his own bow. We rather think of this deliberation, as a struggle between will — the tendency to subordinate Philoctetes despoiled of his weapons — and faith — the loyal acknowledgment of the rights

---

[1] Italics, mine.   [2] Cf. "Outline," § 37.

of Philoctetes and the active adoption of his cause. Romola's deliberation, also, is essentially the vibration between these two fundamental tendencies toward self-assertion and self-effacement, toward the satisfaction of her own craving for a new life and the acknowledgment of a higher authority than her own desire. Both these are instances of an alternation, not between one willing tendency and another, but a fluctuation between will and faith, the egoistic and altruistic tendencies, the imperious and the acknowledging moods, the decision to lose one's life for another's sake or to save it.

Deliberation may, furthermore, be a struggle of faith with faith. Antigone's loyal love for her brother in opposition to her obedience to the state, the jealousy of Brutus, for Rome, rising up against his grateful love to Cæsar, Robert Lee's allegiance to his state in conflict with his love for the Union, — are classic examples of an experience to which nobody is a stranger. A final form of deliberation is the conflict of will with will, the alternating impulses to subordinate now one, now another, person or thing to oneself, — for example, to possess oneself of this object or of that, to suppress this inclination or that other.

The most strenuous deliberations of all these types are those of the moral life: the fluctuations between good and evil, right and wrong, desire and obedience. Lifelike descriptions of deliberation are, for this reason, almost always accounts of moral choices. Of this fact, the dramatists and the novelists give abundant illustration; and even on the pages of the moralists, one may find vivid suggestions of the warring of personal tendencies in deliberation. "I see another law in my members," St. Paul exclaims, "warring against the law of my mind." "Clearly there is," says Aristotle, "beside Reason, some other natural principle which fights with and strains against it."

CHAPTER XXII

TYPICAL PERSONAL RELATIONS

THE RELIGIOUS CONSCIOUSNESS

I. TYPICAL PERSONAL RELATIONS

FROM the conception of psychology as study of related selves, it follows that every concrete social relation may be the basis of a psychological study: my relation to this friend and to that, to brother or father or wife or child, to my employer or to my cook — every one, indeed, of the relations, in which my life consists, may be reflected on, analyzed and explained after this manner of the psychologist. The truth is, however, that a very healthy instinct prevents us, ordinarily, from this sort of analysis of our personal relations. We are too deeply absorbed, in living the relations, to reflect about them from the dispassionate scientist's point of view. We hesitate, and rightly, to pluck out the heart of our own mysteries; we prefer to love and to have faith, to sympathize and to enjoy, to command and to yield, without rendering up to ourselves a balanced account of our attitude to other people. But though we rarely expose our own experience to the dissecting knife of the psychologist, there is yet no reason why the text-book in psychology, in so far as it treats of the relations of selves, should not supply the lack of scientific analysis in our own lives, by furnishing us with a series of studies of typical, personal relations — studies, for example, of the filial, the fraternal or the civic relation, or even more general studies, after the fashion of Hegel's analysis of typical moods of youth — the romantic, the

Quixotic and the Byronic. But there is a practical reason
why the text-book on psychology does not, ordinarily,
include such studies of typical and universal relations.
The novel and the drama have already usurped this function of the psychological treatise, and just because their
characters, however typical, are also particular and highly
individual, therefore, the psychology of novel or of drama
is more absorbing and closer to life, than that of any
treatise. It follows that the novel has become, in some
degree, the popular introduction to psychology. For just
as it is true of beauty that

> "we're made so that we love
> First when we see them painted, things we have passed
> Perhaps a hundred times nor cared to see, — "

so we may first have taken notice of our own tendencies
and attitudes, as embodied in a Shakespearian courtier or in
one of George Eliot's scholars.

The novel or drama is, of course, a study in the psychology of personal relations only. With the enumeration of
structural elements of consciousness and the assignment of
each to a physiological condition, it is only incidentally concerned; but the complexity and richness of the relations of
its *dramatis personæ* are the very soul of it. The interest of
a Shakespeare play does not centre in the scene — the
witches' heath or the field of Agincourt — nor in the rhythm
and melody of the verses, but in the developing and contrasting relations of the central figures to each other and to
the lesser characters. Thus, the plays of which King
Henry the Fifth is hero are a study of a youth of promi-
nently active nature, in whom the emotions are undeveloped and unaccentuated. The love scene is sufficient
proof of this: King Henry complains that he has 'no
genius in protestation,' and that he "cannot look greenly
nor gasp out his eloquence,' but though he doubtless himself believes that he lacks only expression, the discriminating reader realizes that he is not capable of deep emotion,

and that even while he laughs and plays pranks with Falstaff, and makes love to Kate, he is never carried out of himself, never a prey to feeling, in a word, never in passive emotional relation to anybody, even to his sweetheart. Always, therefore, on the battlefield or in the court of love, he is the plain soldier, actively and imperiously related to men, whether he hand them their death warrants or give them his gloves as favors, whether he boast of his army's prowess or hearten his soldiers in their discouragement.

So — to take a very different example — "Red Pottage" is not primarily a story of certain tragic happenings. The plot, to tell the truth, strikes most of us as melodramatic and unessential, and we forget it promptly. The book is significant mainly because it introduces to us two characters, and because it lays bare their relations to other people. These characters, alike for all the difference of costume and setting, are Lady Newhaven — who rehearses every situation with herself as central figure, who regards every person as minister to her desires or as foil to her charms, and who treats every incident as stage-accessory — and Mr. Gresley, who occupies the foreground of all his own canvases, and who never looks at any event or thing or person from any other than his own self-centred point of view.

But though, for the most part, we are content to leave in the hands of dramatist and of novelist the treatment of concrete personal relations, there is one such relation so universal, so significant and so misapprehended, that we shall venture to consider it. This is the relation of human to divine self.

II. THE RELIGIOUS CONSCIOUSNESS

Many definitions of the religious consciousness may be found, but simplest and most adequate, in the opinion of the writer, is the conception of religion as the conscious relation of the human self to a divine self, that is, to a self regarded as greater than this human self or any of its fellows.

If there were space to argue in detail for this conception

of the religious consciousness, one would first of all point out that it lies at the base of all historical forms of religion. As is well known, living beings and nature phenomena are the objects of the primitive religious consciousness. Ancestor worship is the most important form of the worship of conscious beings; fetichism and the worship of the heavenly bodies are the extreme forms of the nature religions. Now it is obvious that the worship of the dead warrior or patriarch, and indeed the worship of any person, or even of any animal, living or dead, is a conscious relation of the worshipper to another self. But it seems, at first sight, as if the worship of a nature phenomenon could not be in any sense a conscious relation to a greater self. A fetich is an insignificant object, a bit of bone or a twig or a pebble, not a living being; and sun, moon, air and water, the gods of the nature religions, are inanimate beings. A closer study, however, shows that these objects, fetiches as well as sun and moon and stars, are worshipped, not for what they are, but because they are looked upon as embodiments of conscious selves. No savage is so ignorant that he fears and reverences a bit of bone, as mere bone; he worships it because he looks upon it as, in some mysterious way, the instrument or symbol of a powerful, though unseen, self or spirit. And no Aryan, we may be sure, ever bowed down before the sun, feeling that his god was a mere flaming, yellow ball. He worshipped the sun as a being, apart from him and infinitely greater than he, yet none the less a self, however vaguely conceived. Nature souls, in the words of Pfleiderer, a well-known historian of religion, "are originally nothing but the livingness and active power of the phenomena of nature, conceived after the analogy of animal and man as willing and feeling beings."[1]

If this were a book about religion, instead of being a book about psychology, it would go on to show that the

---

[1] "Philosophy of Religion," Vol. III., p. 237. Cf. E. B. Tyler, "Primitive Culture," Vol. II., pp. 185 and 294.

systems, which seem to diverge from this conception, are no true exceptions. It would show, also, that the history of religion chronicles, in a sort of pendular succession, a reaction of two motives, one upon the other. A given religion, while it must include both factors, emphasizes either the superior power of its gods or else their essential likeness to human beings. In the lower forms of animism, for example, there is little difference between god and worshipper; and the gods of the Hellenes, who live among men, feasting, plotting, making love, come perilously near to losing the divine attribute of power. The higher nature-deities, on the other hand, are revered as immeasurably greater than human beings.

The history of religious rite and ceremonial furnishes another proof of the personal nature of the religious consciousness. Prayer is, as Tyler has said,[1] "the address of personal spirit to personal spirit . . . simply an extension of the daily intercourse between man and man." The prayer, often quoted, of the Samoyed woman on the steppes, shows very clearly how simple may be this communication of the human with the divine. In the morning, bowing down before the sun, she said only, 'When thou risest, I too rise from my bed,' and in the evening she said, 'When thou sinkest down, I too get me to rest.'[2] Here we have neither petition, confession nor explicit adoration, but mere intercourse, that is, acknowledgment of common experience. Prayer may be, indeed, a mere request for material good like the Gold Coast negro's prayer, 'God give me rice and yams, gold and agries, give me slaves, riches and health,"[3] or it may be a prayer for forgiveness, like the Aryan's cry, "Through want of strength, thou strong and bright God, have I gone wrong; have mercy, almighty, have mercy;"[4] but whatever its form, prayer, like

---

[1] *Op. cit.*, Vol. II., p. 364.
[2] Tyler, *op. cit.*, Vol. II., pp. 291, 292.
[3] Tyler, *op. cit.*, Vol. II., p. 367.
[4] Quoted by Tyler, *op. cit.*, Vol. II., p. 374, from the Rig Veda, VII., 89, 3.

sacrifice, is always the communion of the human with the more-than-human spirit.

This introductory reference to the history of religions and of religious rites prepares us for our specific problem, the nature of the religious consciousness. The conception which we have gained enables us, in the first place,[1] to limit the essentials of the religious experience. Ritual and ceremonial, theories of heaven and hell, and even hopes of immortality are religious only in so far as they grow out of the consciousness of God or grow up into it; in the realization and immediate acquaintance with God, the religious experience has its centre and its circumference. We shall gain a truer understanding, therefore, of the religious consciousness, if we do not regard it as an experience radically different from the other personal relations of our lives. For if God be just a greater self, then one's attitude toward him cannot be utterly unlike one's attitude toward a powerful human friend or chief. In our study of the religious consciousness, we must thus be guided throughout by the analogy of human relationships.

Now human beings are, first of all, liked or disliked, feared or thanked, loved or hated, and in the same way the religious experience is always, in part at least, emotional. At its lowest emotional terms, it includes at least the feeling of the dependence of the human on the divine. But ordinarily the religious experience is far richer in emotion, and there is, indeed, no significant phase of human feeling, which may not as well characterize the relation of man to God as that of man to man. Abject fear, profound gratitude, bitter hatred or devoted love may be factors of the religious experience. The savage, who bribes his gods through fear of them, and the rebels who cry out, " All we are against thee, against thee, O God most high," are as truly religious in their emotion as the humblest and most self-forgetful worshippers.

[1] This sentence and a few of those which follow are quoted from a paper, by the writer, in the *New World*, 1896.

We have found, however, in our analysis of personal relations, that there is an active as well as a passive attitude to other selves, a relation of faith or will, as well as an emotional relation of fear or gratitude. This active acknowledgment of loyalty or faith is the second characteristic phase of religious experience. It may be touched by emotion, yet it is sometimes an utterly unemotional acknowledgment of the divine self, a submission to what one conceives to be his will, an adoption of what one looks upon as his ideal, a resolute loyalty unlighted by emotion, supported only by a sober and perhaps rather dreary conviction of duty. It may be questioned whether there is a more heroic type of religious experience, than just this cold adoption of what one conceives to be the right relation to God.

We are thus brought, face to face, with the significant problem regarding the connection between the religions and the ethical experience. Our definition of religion, as relation of the human self to the divine, provides us with a standard by which to test the frequent claim that morality is religion. This claim is often strongly opposed on historical grounds. It is pointed out that primitive religions are full of positively immoral customs and rites, that the Borneans, for example, gain new spirits by headhunting, and that the Oceanians have a god of thieving, to whom they offer a bit of their booty, bribing him to secrecy with such words as these: "Here is a bit of the pig; take it, good Hiero, and say nothing of it."[1] Such an argument, however, is inadequate, no matter how firmly established the facts on which it is based. For though Borneans and Oceanians and all other savage people perform acts, which we call wrong, as parts of their religious observance, it may be that they do not thereby violate their own moral codes.

The opposition between religion and morality lies deeper. The religious experience is fundamentally a consciousness

---

[1] Cf. Ratzel, "History of Mankind," Vol. I., p. 304.

of God or of gods, a realized relation of the worshipper to
a spirit or to spirits, who are greater than he and greater
also than his fellow-men. The moral consciousness, on
the other hand, is, as we shall see, a form of the social
consciousness, a man's recognition of his place in the whole
inter-related organism of human beings. Now, just as any
human relation is incomplete and unworthy, if it lacks the
moral experience, that is, the consciousness of obligation
toward another self, so the religious consciousness is superficial, unhealthy and fragmentary, if it does not include the
acknowledgment of duty toward God. But though religion without morality is ethically degrading, it is none the
less religion. Any conscious relation to God, however
low and lifeless, however destitute of moral responsibility, is
religion ; and no morality, however sublime, no life, however noble, is religious, if it lack this conscious relation to
God. It follows, of course, that a bad man may be religious and that a good man may lack the consciousness of
his relation to God. Undoubtedly, therefore, certain ethical
systems are better and safer guides than certain religious
creeds. Religion, however, is not and cannot be morality, simply because religion is, and morality is not, a conscious relation of human self to the divine.

The æsthetic, almost as frequently as the moral, experience is mistaken for religion. The profound emotion, with
which one falls upon one's knees with the throng of worshippers in a great cathedral, is named religious awe, though
it is quite as likely to be what Du Maurier calls mere 'sen-
suous *attendrissement.*' The stately proportions of nave
and transept, the severe beauty of pillar and arch, the
rich coloring of stained glass, the thrilling sounds of the
organ and the heavy odor of the incense may hold one's
whole soul enthralled, and leave no room for the realization of any personal attitude, to a God who is in or behind
all this beauty. In the same way, the absorbed study of
nature beauty is a self-forgetful, but not, for that reason, a
religious experience.

This teaching, it must be admitted, is in opposition to the modern tendency to class experiences as religious if they do not deal directly with material needs and conditions. But the very breadth and comprehensiveness of these conceptions make them, in the writer's opinion, valueless. It is indeed true that the religious, the ethical and the æsthetic consciousness are alike, in that they are, in a greater or less degree, altruistic rather than merely egoistic experiences. It is, however, misleading to confuse relations which, though similar in one respect, are none the less sharply distinguished.

Our study of the religious experience has not yet even named what is ordinarily accounted its most important factor: the conviction of God's reality, or — as it is commonly called — belief. The truth is that belief, in this sense, is not a part of any personal experience, that is, of any relation of one self with another. We are not occupied, in our personal relationships, with reflections upon one another's reality: we merely like or dislike each other, and are loyal or imperious. We may, to be sure, be conscious of the reality of God and of our human fellows, but this reflection upon reality is usually a phase of the philosophical consciousness, and not even an ingredient of the religious experience. Certainly, a bare conviction of the actual existence of another self, human or divine, by whom one does not feel oneself affected, to whom one is utterly unrelated, is not a personal experience at all. A belief of the reality of President Steyn of the Orange Free State is no personal relation with him; and the mere persuasion that there exists a Supreme Being does not constitute a religious experience.

But though the conviction of reality does not enter into the immediateness of the personal experience, it is evident that no relationship with God is possible, to one who is distinctly convinced that there is no God. Some degree of the conviction of God's reality must, therefore, form the background of every religious experience, except the primitive personal relation in which one neither questions nor

believes.[1] But this sense of God's reality has unsuspected
gradations of assurance, lying between the extremes of
doubt and reasoned conviction. The consciousness of
God's reality may attain the completeness of philosophical
dogma, but it may, on the other hand, be incomplete and
illogical; it may be firmly held or it may be feeble and
vacillating. For the truth is, as we have seen, that this
consciousness of reality is, at most, a secondary and unemphasized part of religious experience; and religion is, as we
cannot too often repeat, a relation with God, like our relations with our fellow-men.

A crabbed Devon peasant, who figures in a recent novel,
has expressed this conception of religion in striking and
unconventional terms: "As to the A'mighty, my rule's
to treat Un the same as he treats me — same as we'm
taught to treat any other neighbor. That's fair if you ax
me. . . . If God sends gude things, I'm fust to thank Un
'pon my bended knees, and hope respectful for long continuance; if he sends bad, then I cool off and wait for better times. . . . No song, no supper, as the saying is.
Ban't my way to turn left cheek to Jehovah Jireh, after
he's smote me upon the right. 'Tis contrary to human
nature. . . . When the Lard's hand's light on me I go
dancin' and frolickin' afore him like to David afore the
Ark . . . but when He'm contrary with me and minded to
blaw hot and cold from no fault o' mine, — why, dammy, I
get contrary too . . ."

Such a religious experience may well be criticised, on
the ground that it makes no distinction between human
and divine, but it does not lack what the *soi-disant* religious
consciousness, æsthetic or ethical, always misses, a robust
personal experience of God. "Herein," as Fichte says,
"religion doth consist, that man in his own person and
not in that of another, with his own spiritual eye and not
through that of another, should immediately behold, have
and possess God."

[1] Cf. Chapter IX., p. 126.

CHAPTER XXIII

THE SOCIAL CONSCIOUSNESS

In this chapter, as in the last, self-consciousness is discussed, not primarily from the standpoint of one's own subjective attitude — active or passive, imperious or adoptive — but with special regard to the nature of that other self, with whom one feels oneself related. The 'other self,' whom this chapter considers, is no single self, but a composite self or group of selves. To the recognition of a group or circle of selves, the term 'social consciousness' is usually applied, in a narrower and more technical sense than that in which we have heretofore called the consciousness of any other self, even of a single self, a social consciousness.

All social groups are characterized by their imitativeness, so that a modern sociologist, Tarde, has defined society as a circle of imitation. We shall later find reason to supplement this definition: let us for the present reflect on the truth which it contains. If we try to discover how many of our daily acts are repetitions of those of other people, we shall perhaps be surprised at our conclusion. We rise, breakfast, travel by car or by train, enter workroom or office or shop, work behind machine or counter or desk, lunch, work again, return to our houses, dine, amuse ourselves and sleep; and innumerable other people, near and far, are also breakfasting, travelling, working, dining and sleeping.

Yet we are in error if we reckon all these repeated activities as imitations. An absolutely isolated individual, without opportunity to imitate any one, would nevertheless

331

eat and sleep and move about. An imitation is an act or
a conscious experience, conditioned by another, or by
others, similar to it. Repeated activities are not, then, of
necessity, imitations, but may be independent expressions
of an individual, though common, instinct.

When, however, we weed out from the tangle of our
repeated acts, those acts which are mere instinctive or else
accidental repetitions, a goodly growth of these imitative
actions still remains. For example, though we sleep, not
because others do, but because of the conditions of our
individual bodies, yet we sleep on the ground or on beds,
and from eight o'clock till five, or from dawn till noon,
simply because the people who educated us and the people who surround us do the same. So we eat, not because
others eat, but to satisfy individual needs, yet we eat
tallow or rice or terrapin, we eat with our fingers or with
chop-sticks or with forks, and we eat from the ground,
from mats or from tables, partly because people have
taught us these ways, and partly because these are the
manners of those about us. Again, our wanderings from
place to place are un-imitative, instinctive activities, but
the manner of our travelling, on horseback, on bicycles
or by automobile, is, oftener than we think, a caprice of
fashion.

The list of our imitative acts is scarcely begun. The
root words of a language, except such as are instinctive
vocal outcries, are imitations of nature sounds,[1] and language is always acquired by imitation. People speak
English or Dutch or Portuguese not accidentally—as the
child suggested, who feared that his baby brother might
speak German, in place of English — but through imitation of the people about us. Our handwriting is an imitation of our teacher's, and the earliest handwriting was
abbreviated from the pictured imitation of natural objects.
We bow to each other instead of rubbing noses, we lace

[1] Cf. Bibliography.

on calf boots instead of binding on sandals, we read and write short stories instead of three-volumed romances, we revel in sociological heroines in place of romantic ones, and we study psychical research and no longer burn witches. But all these acts, ideals and tendencies are directly due to custom or fashion, that is, to imitation. We do and think all these things and scores of others, because others act and think in these ways.

I. FORMS OF SOCIAL CONSCIOUSNESS

This preliminary illustration of the wide extent of imitation is a fitting introduction to our study of the social consciousness. The social consciousness has two forms or stages, of which the first is fairly well described as the mob-consciousness; for the second, there is no adequate name, and we shall somewhat awkwardly call it the reflectively social consciousness. The crowd, or mob, is a group of selves, of whom each one imitates the external acts and the unreflective consciousness of the others. The mob, however, in so far as it concerns the social psychologist, is consciously imitative. It is probably true, to be sure, that mob-actions may be unconsciously performed. The most serious-minded may be carried out of bounds at an exciting football game, and may wake up to find that, quite unconsciously, he has himself joined lustily in ear-splitting yells during several mad minutes. But this unconsciously active mob is the concern of the sociologist. The social psychologist's interest is limited to the group of people who realize their imitativeness, who are conscious, however vaguely, of shared experiences and actions, who know that they are joining the shout of a thousand voices, or that they are rushing on in a great, moving mass of people. Such vague social consciousness the people of the mob almost always possess.

We have next to remark the strict limitations of the mob-consciousness. The individuals who compose it share each other's perceptual and emotional experience, but their actions are too precipitate to admit time for thought, and they are too deeply swayed by emotion, to be capable of loyalty or of deliberate will. The mob-consciousness is not only fundamentally imitative, but utterly lacking in deliberation and reflection, and it is therefore capricious and fantastic. For this reason, the acts of a mob are absolutely unpredictable, since they spring from the emotions, notably the most temporary of our subjective attitudes. The fickleness of the crowd is, therefore, its traditional attribute; the mob which has cried aloud for the republic rends the air with its *Vive le Roi*, and the Dantons and Robespierres, who have been leaders of the crowd, become its victims.

What is sometimes called the insanity of a mob is in reality, therefore, a psychological, not a pathological, phenomenon. Every emotion and passion gains strength as it is shared, and is characterized by reactions of increasing vigor. The accelerated force of primitive emotions, shared by scores and hundreds of people, is for a time irresistible, the more so, because both emotions and the acts which go with them are unchecked by reasoning or by deliberation. No one supposes that the crew of the *Bourgogne* deliberately trampled women down, in an effort to reach the boats. No one imagines that the Akron mob would have set fire to the public buildings, when they knew that the man whom they sought had escaped, had they reasoned the matter out. Seamen and citizens alike were a prey to elemental passions uncontrolled by deliberation.

The activities of a mob may, none the less, be constructive as well as destructive, ideal as well as material. Gustave le Bon, a brilliant French writer, lays great stress on the capacity of a mob to perform capriciously generous deeds as well as cruel ones; and he instances the crusades as example of a great altruistic mob-movement. "A crowd," Le Bon says, "may be guilty of every kind of crime, but it is also capable of loftier acts than those of which the isolated individual is capable." It is, however, perfectly unequal to any logical conclusions, any reasoned acts, any purposed, planned or deliberately chosen performance. Whether it drive the tumbril or rescue the Holy Sepulchre, its action is purely emotional and capricious, and it takes its cue unreflectively from the leader of the moment, for "a man . . . isolated . . . may be a cultivated individual; in a crowd he is a barbarian."

The suggestibility of a crowd is so well marked, that it is regarded by certain writers[1] as a form of hypnotization. This suggestibility extends even to the sense-experiences of the crowd, which is, therefore, subject to actual sense-illusions. Le Bon brings forward instance after instance of these collective illusions, for example, the phantom raft, seen by the whole crew of the *Belle Poule*, and the St. George who appeared on the walls of Jerusalem to all the crusaders.

Many modern writers, Le Bon among them, believe that the crowd or mob is the only social group. They thus completely identify the crowd with 'society,' teaching that the mob-consciousness is the only type of social consciousness. From this doctrine, we have good reason to dissent most emphatically, for we clearly find in human experience what has been named the reflective social consciousness. We shall try to illustrate and later to define it. We may compare, for example, the reflective national consciousness with mob-patriotism. We are all familiar with the mob-activities of so-called patriotism: the shouts, the fire-crackers, the flag-wavings. They are all a part of the contagious feeling and action of a lot of consciously, but unreflectively, imitative selves. A reflective national consciousness is an utterly different sort of experience. The possessor of it has certain deep-seated social conceptions, ideals and purposes; these have their significance to him as shared with a group of selves, who are consciously

[1] Cf. Boris Sidis, "The Psychology of Suggestion."

related with himself and with each other. These principles and ideals would be meaningless to the reflectively social individual, if they were merely his own. Yet he individually adopts and promulgates them, and he acts them out at the primaries, at the polls and in public office. Such a reflective national consciousness may well be emotional, but it is not purely emotional, and its emotional attitudes are constant, not temporary and capricious.

Different forms of college spirit illustrate the same distinction. To cheer oneself hoarse at the athletic meet, and to join the men who carry the hero of the games in triumph from the field, may be a mere manifestation of mob-consciousness, an unreasoned, unpurposed wave of feeling, which carries one off one's feet in the contagion of a great enthusiasm. But there is also a deliberate college spirit. The student is profoundly conscious that his pursuit of a well-shaped, academic course, of a life of close social affiliations, and of an honorable college degree, is the aim of hundreds of other students. He realizes that he is imitating and, in some ways, leading them, and that they are both imitators and leaders of each other and of him. He more or less clearly recognizes that his advance is an alternate imitation of his teachers and his fellows, and a reaction against them. His degree has a purely social value dependent on other people's estimate of it. In a word, his college life is consciously and reflectively social.

Our illustrations have paved the way for our definition of the reflectively social consciousness, as (1) the reflective adoption of, or domination over, the external activities and the conscious experience of other selves, who (2) are regarded as forming a social group. Such a group of reflectively social persons may be called 'society' in contrast with the crowd or mob.[1]

The best way, in which to bring out the meaning of this

[1] Cf. Baldwin, "Social and Ethical Interpretations," Chapter XII.

somewhat abstractly worded definition, is to contrast the reflecting social consciousness with the mob-consciousness, in more detail. The most fundamental characteristic of the reflective social experience may be thus described : the reflectively social person realizes that his own consciousness and his acts are imitations of the other members of his social group or are models for them; he realizes, also, that the consciousness and the actions of every other member of the group are, similarly, either patterned on the feelings and deeds of the others or else suggestive of their experiences and activities. One consciously imitates, opposes or leads others, with the consciousness that they are similarly related to oneself and to each other. This recognition of social relations is evidently a reflective and deliberate affair, and forms no part at all of the mob-consciousness. The individual in the crowd, though he may indeed have the vague feeling of companionship, does not know that his acts are the result of social contagion. If you ask him why he shouts, or rescues, or kills, he tells you that he cannot help it; and he is right, for imitation is an unreasoning instinct, and although his acts are influenced by those of the group to which he belongs and by the acts of their common leader, yet he does not reason about this imitativeness or clearly realize it. The reflectively social individual, on the other hand, is profoundly conscious of the influences, the imitations and the counter imitations, of the social organization. The reflectively social consciousness may be, in the second place, deliberate as well as immediate, thoughtful as well as emotional. This is its most obvious distinction from the mob-consciousness, to which it is likely at any moment to give place. The legislative assembly or committee meeting, as it should be, is a manifestation of the reflective social consciousness, not swayed by the feeling of the moment, but carefully reasoning, deliberately adopting this or that recommendation, and passing motions only after long consideration. The assembly or meeting, as it actually is, is often enough a frenzied mob in which passion excites passion, and deliberation is an unattainable ideal.

The reflective social consciousness is, finally, no longer merely imitative. The reflectively social person is aware of his power to lead, as well as of his capacity to follow. This tendency of the developed social consciousness has been greatly underemphasized. Tarde, for example, as has already been said, believes that the essential nature of society is imitativeness. "Socialité," he says,[1] "c'est l'imitativité." It is perfectly evident that this definition leaves out of account the characteristic attitude of the leader of society. Even those who have confused society with the mob have been the first to acknowledge the leader as related to the mob, yet not a member of it. " A crowd," Le Bon declares,[2] " is a servile flock — incapable of ever doing without a master." In truth, however wide the place we make for imitation as a social function, it can never displace spontaneity and leadership. The charge is lost when the officer falls, and the mob disperses when its leader wavers. Customs and conventions and fashions are imitations which are dominated by invention, and every institution is, as Emerson said, 'the lengthened shadow of a man.'

Nobody can deny that these masters of men, these captains of industry, these world conquerors, are men possessed of social consciousness. We certainly cannot attribute social feeling to the Old Guard and deny it to Napoleon. We cannot assert that the doers of the law have a realization of a public self, society, and that the makers of the law are without it. The sense of moulding the common purpose, of inflaming the public feeling, and of inciting a group of selves to imitative action, is as truly a social consciousness as the realization that one is imitating the thoughts and feelings and acts of a group of similarly imitative selves, at the inspiration of the same leader.

[1] Cf. " Les Lois de l'Imitation," p. 75.
[2] " The Psychology of the Crowd," p. 113.

This dominating phase of the reflectively social consciousness does not belong to the great leaders and masters only. On the contrary, every reflectively social individual may assume the dominating, imperious attitude, as well as the imitative, acknowledging attitude. Anybody may, moreover, adopt this position not only toward individuals but toward society — the reflectively social group whose members are realized as either imitative of each other or as dominating each other. The consciousness of this imperious attitude lies at the basis of what is known as the realization of one's moral influence. One may go to religious services and observe church festivals, not as a personal duty, but because one believes the observances socially valuable, and is conscious of one's actions as likely to influence other people's. More than this, as our study of will has suggested,[1] a dominating, not an imitative, attitude toward society is entirely possible when one is not master of a situation, and when, rather, one is leading a forlorn hope or, single-handed, defying a mob. Thus, the experience of Sokrates was profoundly social when, in the Heliastic Court, he stood alone for a legal trial of the generals of Ægospotami, while the Athenians, beside themselves with horror over the unburied crews, were crying out for quick vengeance on the leaders of that luckless sea-fight. Certainly Sokrates was conscious of himself as opposing, not a single man nor any fortuitous aggregate, but all Athens, a composite, group-self, whose members were being swept on in a universal passion to a common crime.

II. IMITATION AND OPPOSITION

It is vitally important, as has been said, to keep in mind that imitation and opposition are no newly discovered tendencies, which hold true only of the social, not of the individual, experience. On the other hand, they are mere

[1] Cf. Chapter XXI., p. 308.

manifestations of adoptiveness and imperiousness, which are the underlying attitudes of all self-consciousness. This will become clearer if we study the two, imitation and inventiveness, in more detail, regarding them not only as relations of an individual to a social group, but as relations of one individual to another.

Two forms of imitation are socially significant: fashion, or imitation of the present, of contemporary selves and facts, and tradition, or imitation of the past, of one's ancestors, their thoughts and their acts. In Paris, for instance, dress is regulated by fashion, which changes with every season, and every woman therefore dresses as her neighbor does. In Brittany, dress is a tradition, and every woman dresses as her great-grandmother did; the pay-sanne, who moves from one province to another, tranquilly, and as a matter of course, wears a coiffe which is as tall as that of the neighborhood is broad, as pointed as that is square, as unadorned as that is richly embroidered. This adherence to tradition as opposed to custom is the real distinction between conservative and radical. The latter need not himself be original and inventive, but he is friendly to innovation and receptive of the customs of his contemporaries; he breaks with the past and allies himself with the present; whereas the conservative clings to the past and imitates the traditional observance.

The second of the ordinary distinctions is that between physical and psychic imitation, imitation of movement and imitation of emotion or idea. Uniformities of movement — for example, those of a military drill — are illustrations of the first class, and fashions in creed or in theory, such as the evolution hypothesis or the modern theory of training children on lines of their own spontaneous interest, are instances of the second sort. The usual order is from outward to inward imitation. One adopts a tight sleeve, for example, or a fad in visiting cards, in mechanical imita-tion of the people about one, privately believing that the sleeve is hideous and that the custom is senseless. Little by little, however, one follows the fashion of thought as well as the outward custom, and comes to believe sincerely that the dress which seemed grotesque is a model of the beautiful, and that the convention which appeared absurd is a bulwark of society.

The truth, however, is that conscious imitation is only secondarily of idea or of act. Primarily and fundamentally, it is a richly personal experience, the imitation of other self or of other selves, of individual or of social group, — a conscious attempt to make oneself into this fascinating personality or to become one of this attractive circle. So the child imitates his father's stride, because it is his father's, not from any intrinsic interest in the movement in itself, and he is fiercely Republican because his father belongs to the Republican party, not because he himself inclines toward these principles rather than toward others. The life of the child shows most clearly, indeed, the intensely personal nature of imitation. The development of his own personality is, as Royce has shown,[1] by the successive assumption of other people's personality. Now, he imitates, or throws himself into, the life of the adventurer, he adopts the rôle of the cow-boy, not merely in his plays, from the back of his spirited rocking-horse, but in his daily walk and conversation. A little later, his ideals are incarnated in the persons of military heroes: you will find him gallantly defending the pass at Thermopylæ behind a breastwork of pillows, or sailing into the harbor of Santiago on a precarious ship of chairs; he adopts a military step, organizes his companions into a regiment, attempts military music on his toy trumpet, cultivates in himself, and demands from others, the military virtues of obedience and courage. And, in all this, he is primarily imitating people, and is imitating specific acts and ideals, only as they are characteristic of these people.

One need not turn, indeed, to the life of childhood, for

[1] *Century*, 1894.

illustration of the fundamentally personal nature of imitation. For there surely are few adults whose aims are not embodied in human beings. Whether one's ideal is that of the student, the physician or the business man, it stands out before one most clearly in the figure of some daring and patient scholar, some learned and sympathetic physician, some alert and honorable business man. One's effort is often explicitly, and almost always implicitly, to be like this ideal self, to realize in oneself his outlook and his achievements; and one is consciously satisfied with oneself when one has completed an investigation, made a diagnosis, or launched a business enterprise as this ideal self might have done it. Our moral life, perhaps, offers the most frequent illustration of the personal character of imitation. Our ethical ideals live in the person of some great teacher, and our moral life is a conscious effort to be like him; our aims, also, are set before us as a supreme personal ideal, and we are bidden to "be perfect as our Father in Heaven is perfect."

Leaving imitation, let us briefly consider the main forms of the contrasted tendency. We have already named them: mere opposition to act, idea or self, and domination, expressed or unexpressed, of act, idea or self. In its simplest form, 'opposition' manifests itself as the desire to be different. Professor Royce is probably right in insisting [1] that this tendency has been underrated, in consequence of the almost exclusive interest of the sociologists in the function of imitation. In all save the most servile forms of the social consciousness, there is, as we have seen, alongside of the impulse to follow one's neighbors, the instinct to show oneself unlike them, or — as the impulse is sometimes formulated — to show one's own individuality. We are most likely, of course, to find opposition 'writ

[1] *Psychological Review*, 1898, p. 113. Cf. a letter quoted by Baldwin, "Social and Ethical Interpretations," p. 233.

large' in the actions of children. But the mischief of a child which prompts him quite wilfully to say 'dog' or 'cow' when he knows well that he has spelled c-a-t, to run when he is expected to walk sedately, and to talk when silence is demanded, is merely a more obvious expression of the opposition instinct, which lies at the basis of all eccentricity in dress, repartee in conversation and inventiveness in science or in art. Throughout these varying manifestations, we may descry the tendency to be different, to attain what Royce calls the 'contrast effect,' quite for its own sake and without effort to influence other people. In this way, 'opposition' is distinct from the kindred form of domination, or command, the spirit of the leader of crowds and the organizer of societies.

But whatever the stage of its manifestations, this assertive tendency is never to be designated as 'individual and therefore unsocial.' As truly as imitation, it is a social attitude. One cannot be 'different' unless one realizes the selves from whom one differs, one cannot show oneself off as a man 'of rare wit,' a novelist of 'unusual and elusive subtlety' or a philosopher of epoch-making originality, without a realization of the commonplace social background, against which one's meteoric brilliancy is displayed.

One final observation is of great importance. It is quite inaccurate to separate imitation and invention, as if some people and some achievements were imitative and others inventive. The truth is that every normal person unites in himself, in varying proportions, these two fundamental tendencies of consciousness. Nobody could be absolutely original, if that means unimitative; and conversely, one could hardly be a self without some trace of opposition to one's environment. Thus, the most daring inventor makes use of the old principle, and the most original writer is imitative, at least to the extent of using language. On the other hand, few copies are so servile that they are utterly undistinguishable from the model.

The intimate union of the two tendencies is shown, also, by the fact that the usual road to inventiveness is through imitation. Sometimes, indeed, inventiveness consists solely in the selection of unusual persons or ideas for imitation. So, Marie Antoinette and her court ladies, in the Petit Trianon, invented a brave sport, when they gayly imitated the milk-maids ; and the novelty of a recent Newport season was a glorified sort of haymakers' dinner. But we need not seek our illustrations so far afield. Any honest effort to imitate intelligently must result in transformation rather than in mechanical copying. The healthy mind simply cannot follow copy, without the spontaneous and unexpected occurrence of suggestions for change — hot air instead of steam, an iambic meter in place of a trochaic, burnt umber rather than sienna, or zinc solution in place of chloride. It matters not whether we work at machinery, at poetry, at painting or at chemistry : we all become inventive by trying to imitate. A curious, yet common, result of this relation is the inventor's inability to realize the extent of the changes which he brings about. Fichte, for example, supposed that he was merely expounding Kant, until Kant disclaimed the exposition and stamped Fichte's doctrine as an injurious and heretical system of thought.

It may be shown, finally, that successful inventions are always based on imitation, and that effective imitations are always touched with inventiveness. The well-dressed person neither defies fashion nor follows it to its last extreme ; in general outline he conforms, but in well-chosen detail he is law unto himself. In the artistic dinner, the procession of the courses does not deviate from the traditional order, and one is able to identify the dishes of which one partakes, yet, here and there — in a rare combination of delicate flavors or in an unconventional arrangement of the flowers — the skill of the inventor betrays itself. So, the successful conversationalist is neither slavishly imitative nor eccentric to the point of wearying his friends. For though one can barely survive an hour, in company with the amiable person who echoes all that one says, yet one retreats, battle-sore, from an encounter with the original talker, who is wont to treat the most commonplace remark as a challenge to mortal combat or, at the least, as a target for repartee.

We have seen that only the inventive imitation and the imitative invention are valued and appreciated. It is also true that the practically successful, that is, the permanent innovation, is the one which can be readily imitated. The inventor of machinery, so complicated that the common man cannot use it, will not succeed in introducing his machines, and the promulgator of doctrine, so profound that few men can apprehend it, will not greatly influence contemporary thought. This is the reason why the most original thinkers are so seldom leaders of their own age; why, for example, the teachings of Sokrates, of Jesus, of Galileo and of Spinoza exerted so little influence on contemporary thought. On the other hand, the brilliantly successful man almost always has that highest grade of commonplace mind which strikes out nothing essentially new, but which is yet keenly susceptible to most suggestions, selecting from these, with unerring good judgment, the readily imitable features. "Too original a thought is," as Baldwin says, "a social sport." Neither Rousseau nor the French Revolution, he points out,[1] could make a democracy of France, for centuries under absolute rule had unfitted the French to imitate and to adopt ideals of *liberté, égalité, fraternité*. For a like reason, Constantine could not christianize his legions by baptizing them; and indeed nobody ever yet foisted on a group of people any ideal which they were unprepared to imitate.

It is not altogether easy to summarize our results. We began by considering the 'social consciousness,' in the narrower sense of that term, an individual's consciousness

[1] *Op. cit.*, p. 469.

of a group of other selves. We found two stages of it:
first, the mob-consciousness, conscious imitation of the un-
deliberative acts and experiences of others; and second, the
reflective consciousness of oneself as follower or leader of
an interrelated group of selves. We proceeded to identify
the two tendencies, imitation and invention (or opposition),
with the self-assertive and adoptive tendencies underlying
all self-consciousness.

In conclusion, it will be well to contrast the moral with
the social consciousness. The moral consciousness, whatever else it is, is certainly a form of reflective social experience, a recognition of one's own relation to a group of other
selves. All ethical systems, with the one exception of that
form of hedonism which teaches that individual pleasure is
the chief good of life, unite in the admission that the moral
life involves an altruistic recognition, by one individual,
of the claims and needs of others.

By some writers, indeed, the moral consciousness in its
social phase is not distinguished at all from the reflective
social consciousness, and any reflective realization of oneself, as member of a group of related selves, is regarded as
a definitely moral experience. In the opinion of the writer,
there is, however, a difference between the merely social
and the ethically social attitude: any group, however small,
of related selves, can be the object of a genuinely social
consciousness, but the moral consciousness keeps in view
the relationship, not of any single group, but of all human
selves, with each other. The purpose of ethical conduct,
therefore, is the realization of complete union between one
self and all other selves. In other words, when I am acting morally, I am not aiming at my own pleasure or profit,
I am not working to secure the ends of my friend, my
family, my society, or even of my state: I am inspired by
a wider purpose, an ideal of the harmonized claims and
needs and desires of all individuals.

This fact, that the moral law is a recognition of the universe of selves, explains, in part, the common definition of moral experience as the consciousness of a moral law. For a law, from the standpoint of science, is the widest of generalizations; and what we know as the moral law is the demand for universal acknowledgment of the inter-related rights and needs of all men, a demand which toler-ates no over-emphasis of individual desires or of narrowly social purposes.

BOOK II

COMPARATIVE PSYCHOLOGY AND ABNORMAL
PSYCHOLOGY

CHAPTER XXIV

DIVISIONS OF PSYCHOLOGY

OUR study has so far been limited to the problems of introspective, normal psychology. It is high time to break over these barriers and to take at least a general survey of the outlying fields of psychology. We shall do well to preface our discussion by summarizing the chief divisions of psychology, as suggested in our introductory chapter. There are, of course, many other principles on which the classification might be carried out. In the summary which follows, the bracketed titles indicate divisions which, though logically possible, are actually seldom or never recognized; and the middle column includes sub-heads common to 'idea-psychology' and to 'self-psychology.'

A. INTROSPECTIVE PSYCHOLOGY

I. Psychology of   II. Psychology of
    Ideas.   Conscious Selves.

a. Normal.
  1. Individual.

[2. Social.]   2. Social.

b. Abnormal.
  1. Individual.
  [2. Social.]

B. INFERENTIAL OR COMPARATIVE PSYCHOLOGY

a. Normal.
  [1. Not genetic.]
  2. Genetic.
    (*a*) Individual.
      (1) Of animals.
      (2) Of children.
      (3) Of primitive men.
  [(*b*) Social]
b. Abnormal.

The division on which all our study has been based is the contrast between introspective and inferential, or comparative, psychology. Introspective psychology is, as we have seen, the direct study, by the civilized adult (who only is capable of introspection), of his own conscious experience. In the study of comparative psychology, one first observes the words or the movements of other human beings or of animals, one then introspectively reflects on the consciousness which accompanies such words or acts in one's own experience, and finally, one infers, on this basis, the consciousness of the animals, children or savages whom one is studying.

Next after this division, comes the familiar contrast between the study of successive ideas and the study of the consciousness of related selves. This distinction, of course, is most significant and most readily studied in introspective psychology.

In considering the opposition of normal and abnormal psychology, we must first notice that abnormal psychology is both introspective and comparative. Certain conscious phenomena, such as dreams and waking visions, so far diverge from everyday experience that we call them abnormal, and yet they may be studied by the direct introspection of those who have the experience. The most pronounced varieties of the abnormal consciousness must, however, be studied by the method of comparison. It should be added that every subdivision of normal psychology is logically possible in the abnormal. Abnormal psychology, for example, may concern itself not only with adults, but with children and with animals, since both are subject to abnormal experiences, as for instance, dreams, hypnotic influence and insanity.

In distinguishing 'individual' from 'social' psychology, it must be observed that we use the second term in its narrower meaning of 'psychology of the social group,' although, as we have seen, the psychology of selves is itself a social psychology, in the wider sense of the term, since it treats of the self as 'social,' or related to other selves. 'Social psychology,' as the scientific study of the social group, may be a branch of the psychology of ideas, in so far as it is logically possible to consider an image, an emotion or an impulse as common to a group of people, and as manifested in their collective action, without considering the group of selves who have the ideas and the emotions. This, however, is a particularly unnatural and artificial procedure, and all fruitful studies, which have actually been made, of the social consciousness, are investigations of the action and reaction of selves upon each other. Social psychology may, finally, be inferential.

We have next to formulate the conception of genetic or developmental psychology, the comparative study of conscious experiences, at different stages of the development of individuals or of social groups. Primarily, this conception of development is certainly biological, and concerns merely the stages of bodily growth. Later, it is applied to selves, regarded from a temporal point of view. It can never be applied to the succeeding facts of consciousness, for the idea or emotion of one day or month is different from that of another day or month, even if exactly similar to it; and nothing can be said to develop which has not a certain permanence of its own. There is, therefore, no genetic study of ideas, because they are too evanescent to have a development, but in its place there is a study of similar ideas, at different periods of bodily growth. The close connection, at this point, of biology with psychology, occasions a final contrast between the genetic study of children and that of animals. The former concerns itself with the development of a human body, the latter regards the development of a race. Thus, the problem of child psychology is ontogenetic, and concerns the connection of characteristic groups of conscious facts, with different ages of the individual; whereas the problem of animal psychology is phylogenetic, and considers the correlation of phases of consciousness with animal species of greater or less development.

2 A

We come, finally, to the distinctions between human adults, children and animals, as objects of psychological study. In the first place, we must notice that adult psychology may be pursued from the genetic standpoint, if one regard the characteristic consciousness of the adult periods of bodily development: youth, early and late middle age, old age and senility. And yet, as our summary indicates, the ordinary study of adult psychology assumes a sort of typical individual experience, and does not concern itself with different stages of growth. On the other hand, the psychological study of children and of animals has the genetic interest at heart. So, though the study of children might logically limit itself to the study of conscious experience at some particular age, yet child psychology is practically most significant and theoretically most interesting, when it contrasts the conscious phenomena of one age with those of another, and draws conclusions about the rate and the direction of development. And similarly, though the study of animal psychology might content itself with the investigation of animals of one special degree of development, it finds its chief interest in the phylogenetic study of animal consciousness, at different periods of the evolution of species.

From this discussion of logical possibility and actual usage, in the mapping out of fields of psychology, we must proceed to a closer study of those divisions of psychology, which we have so far disregarded. In so doing, we shall distinguish, for practical convenience, between comparative and abnormal psychology, although, as has been pointed out, the comparative method is important in the study of abnormal consciousness.

PART I

COMPARATIVE PSYCHOLOGY

CHAPTER XXV

THE PSYCHOLOGY OF THE ANIMAL CONSCIOUSNESS

WE have already faced the difficulty which lies, like a barrier, across our very entrance upon the study of animal psychology. Psychology is an introspective study, and one can be conscious of one's own experience only. It follows that every man must be his own psychologist, in other words, that he must put every statement, of book or of teacher, and every statistical result, to the test of his own introspection. The discovery, through spoken or written communication, that other people's introspection agrees in a general way with our own, does give us, it is true, a certain right to refer to other people the results of our own introspection, and in this way the introspective psychology of the adult human consciousness is formulated. But study of the consciousness of animals and of babies utterly lacks the confirmation of spoken communication. Neither animals nor babies can reflectively observe their own experience, nor report it to us in words. Our only resource is, as we have seen, to infer their states of mind from their actions; but a given action may be interpreted in so many ways, that we cannot hope to escape entirely the dangers of mistaken inference. No psychologist, therefore, has greater need of caution than the student of animal consciousness. He should never forget that he is observing, not the consciousness, but the movements of animals, and that he can frame no more than an intelligent guess at their real experience.

The ideal student of the animal consciousness is both biologist and psychologist: he is not merely trained in introspection and in the analysis and classification of consciousness, but he understands the structure and development of the animal body, and he has a first-hand acquaintance with the life and habits of the animals themselves, supplementing close and patient observation by experimental methods. The writer of this book possesses none of these special qualifications, and the chapter which follows is little more than an annotated summary of the results of other people's study. It aims merely to present an outline of the main features of animal psychology.

I. Structural Elements of the Animal Consciousness

a. sensational consciousness of animals

The occurrence of a given sensation, in an animal's life, is argued in two ways: first, from the fact that the animal reacts to stimuli, for example, that it approaches a light or starts at a sound; and second, from the discovery of corresponding sense-organs. Neither argument, we must remind ourselves, is without ambiguity. The response to a stimulus, if an unvarying movement, may be an unconscious reflex act; and, as we shall see, the function of the different end-organs is not definitely made out. Yet the study of end-organs and the observation of bodily movements remain our only sources of information about the sense-consciousness of animals.

The phylogenetic evolution of animal life as a whole resembled, we have reason to think, the ontogenetic development of the individual vertebrate. The skin was certainly the primitive sense-organ, for all the sense-organs, except the retina in vertebrates, are developed from the skin. An undifferentiated consciousness, through constant stimulation of the skin, must therefore have been the primitive type of sensation, unless we suppose that animals, at this low stage of development, are unconscious. The earliest differentiated sensations must have been those of pressure, taste and smell, for the end-organs of these sensations are first developed. It is not certain at what stage sensations of warmth, cold and pain arose, but sensations of hearing and vision were evidently later than the others. These general statements, regarding the development of sense-consciousness in the animal kingdom, are, roughly speaking, true, as has been said, of the individual animal consciousness, but an important exception concerns sensations of warmth and cold, which are very evident in many young vertebrates immediately after birth.

From this preliminary account of the rise of sense-consciousness in animals, we shall go on to study the different classes of sensation, discussing them in an unsystematic manner, and not even attempting to consider all orders of animal life. Of pressure-sensations, least need be said, since, as we have seen, all animals, even those lowest in the scale, react to pressure-stimuli. Such reactions may conceivably be unconscious reflex movements, yet they suggest, if they do not prove, the universality of pressure-sensations. In the more developed forms of animal life, the pressure-organs, of course, become differentiated, and we find, in general, that the more mobile parts of the body have to do especially with pressure-stimuli; for example, the hairs which pierce the tough covering of the crustaceans and of certain insects, the cat's whiskers, the hairs of a rabbit's lips, the elephant's trunk, the horse's lips and the man's fingers are, in a sense, pressure-organs.

The invertebrates have no olfactory or gustatory organs, and they probably have, in place of taste and smell, a so-called 'chemical sense,' that is, sensations which enable them to distinguish, first, different sorts of food, second, different animals of the same species, foes or mates, and finally, the purity or pollution of the medium in which they live.[1] Well-known observations prove that insects are affected by olfactory stimuli: for example, one of Lubbock's ants stopped short when she came to a scented object; and another observer checked a fight, among a group of pavement ants, by placing a cologne-saturated paper near them. Lower in the scale, medusæ, and probably even unicellular animals, react to olfactory stimuli.

Taste and smell have, together, the biological importance of the 'chemical sense'; for both smell and taste test the chemical constitution of food, and smell has still other primary functions, of which the most important is the detection of foes and of mates. Therefore, animals who are deficient in taste and smell sensations are likely to fall a prey to their foes or to their own indiscriminate appetites, or else to fail of securing mates; and in either case, they will not propagate their species. The careful experimental observations of Professor Wesley Mills, on young vertebrates, have shown that, next to pressure, taste and smell are their very earliest sensations. In chicks and in young guinea pigs, Mills noticed smell and taste sensations in the very earliest hours. The great sensibility of rabbits' lips to pressure-stimuli made it hard to test their sensibility to taste, but there were signs of reaction to taste-stimuli on the first day. The dogs were later in their taste and smell discriminations, but mongrel puppies developed more quickly than terriers, and the terriers, in their turn, were more precocious than larger dogs, St. Bernards. "On the seventh day," according to Mills,[2] "when aloes is placed on the finger, the latter is not long sucked," by the St. Bernard puppy, and "the facial movements indicate disgust"; the mongrel performs the same actions on the second day. Both smell and taste are in general earlier in the cat[3] than in the dog, but cats, unlike dogs, rabbits and pigeons, seem earlier to have smell than taste sensations. There is little

[1] Cf. Zwaardemaker, "Physiologie des Geruchs," Appendix X.
[2] "Animal Intelligence," p. 119.   [3] *Op. cit.*, p. 222.

doubt, as every one knows, that vertebrates have a more delicate consciousness of smell than that of human beings, though the odors which they most closely discriminate may be different from those whose variations we best distinguish. A dog, for example, must recognize a greater variety of animal smells than his master distinguishes, but it is possible that the man discriminates more rose-fragrances than the dog does. Every reader of sporting tales knows the pains which the hunter has to take to cover his scent from the wild creatures; and nobody can be long in the society of a dog, without realizing that his interest is centred in the smells of his environment. So a dog traces people through crowded streets by their footsteps, that is to say, by the odor of their boots, even when the boots have been soaked in anise; and it is likely that a room full of people, significant to most of us for its colors and sounds, is regarded by an intelligent dog as a bewildering complex of smells, combined with a few dashes of color and, here and there, a sound. Readers of Kipling's Jungle Books will remember, how often the story turns on the keen smell-discriminations of the animals, the ' hair-trigger-like sensitiveness of a jungle-nose,' as it is called; and admirers of Ernest Seton Thompson's animal heroes have laughed at the discomfiture of the trapper who, wearing a pair of gloves steeped in the blood of a heifer, encased poison in a capsule and then inserted it in lumps of fat, only to find his bait avoided by the wolf, whose nose defied even these precautions.

A comparison of the brain and nostrils of a mammalian animal, with the human brain and nose, shows an anatomical basis for the animal's superiority in smell-discrimination. The olfactory lobes of the human brain are merely small protuberances on its lower median surface, whereas the olfactory lobes of a dog's, a sheep's, or a calf's brain, protrude far forward and form a distinct division of the brain. The mammalia are not, however, the only vertebrates who have smell-sensations, though smell-sensations seem to be unimportant in birds and in reptiles. Vultures, for example, do not discover food which they cannot see.[1] On the other hand, fishes appear to smell, though the smell-stimulus must, of course, be in solution. They certainly detect their food from afar, and though they have no brain and therefore no olfactory lobe, yet within their nasal cavities is a sensory epithelium with olfactory cells.

It has already been implied that many kinds of animals are not proved to have sensations of warmth and of cold. But it is very evident that vertebrates experience both cold and warmth. Nobody who has lived with a cat really doubts that cats, at least, have sensations of warmth, and that they revel in them. The cat's unerring choice of an abiding-place on the sunny window-sill, on the narrow path of the sunlight across the carpet, or on the section of the floor which conceals hot-water pipes is clear enough proof of this. The huddled cattle on a bleak prairie also seem to be feeling the cold. Mr. Mills, in his diaries of early animal life, notes that cats, dogs, rabbits and pigeons are sensitive in the first days of life to warmth and cold. Of pigeons, Mills says:[2] "One can quiet the most disturbed and pugnacious young one by gently holding the warm hand, a warm cloth, etc., over it. A single cold day is liable to kill young pigeons if their parents do not sit on them constantly, and sometimes even when they do. The essential vital processes of the body seem to be deranged by cold."

We come, finally, to the higher sensations, so-called, of hearing and vision. First of all, it is important to notice that response to light-stimulation is no clear evidence of visual sensations. Earthworms, for instance, have no kind or description of eye, yet their movements show pretty clearly that they are sensitive to light and to darkness. We cannot suppose that vision exists until there is some sort of visual organ; and we must, therefore, infer

[1] Cf. Morgan, *op. cit.*, p. 256.   [2] "Animal Intelligence," p. 254.

first, that the light presumably affects the skin of an eye-less animal (which reacts to it), by bringing about a chemical change, and second, that the consciousness, if any exist, is of contact. The earliest form of eye is a pigment-spot in the skin, an area differentiated from the surrounding skin, often provided with a sort of lens, and always affected by the change from light to dark. It is found, for example, in some forms of mollusca and in the very lowest verte-brates. The second form is the facetted eye, familiar to us in the fly and in the bee. It consists in a large number of little cone-shaped organs, each of which transmits only the ray of light which passes directly through it; oblique rays are absorbed by the pigmented material with which these cones are surrounded. The result is a miniature 'stippled,' or mosaic, reproduction of the field of vision, since each of the thousand cones transmits light from one point only. A third type of eye, found also in insects, is the ocellus — a small eye, consisting mainly of lens, retina and rods, and of use, it is supposed, in darkness and for near objects. There is, finally, the true eye, with its lens and its retina, found in crustaceans and in most verte-brates. The eyes of quadrupeds are usually larger, further apart and more effective than human eyes. The whole field of vision is larger, for there is less overlapping of the two fields. For these reasons, vision as well as smell reaches its greatest acuteness below man. The keener night vision of the beasts is explained by the fact that the pupil (which often contracts to a narrow slit) may also dilate very widely.

The mammalia are not the only animals distinguished by their keen sight. Mr. Bateson describes the vision of a fish (the wrasse) which "can see a shrimp with certainty when the whole body is buried in gray sand, excepting the antennæ and antenna plates."[1] And Morgan instances[2]

---

[1] *Journal of Marine Biological Association*, N. S., I., 2 and 3. Quoted by Morgan, *op. cit.*, p. 287. [2] *Op. cit.*, p. 256.

the unerring aim of small lobsters, who plunge from considerable heights into tiny crevices of a rock.

Sensations of color, also, are not a perquisite of vertebrate animals. Sir John Lubbock, one of the first of the enthusiastic and careful students of the animal consciousness, showed clearly that his bees distinguished blue from orange. For when he placed honey on papers of both colors, they constantly chose the honey from the blue background, persisting in this even when the position of the papers was changed. One bee, we are told,[1] "returned to the orange spot and was just going to alight when she observed the change of color, pulled herself up, and without hesitation darted off to the blue." To Lubbock we owe, also, an experiment on water-fleas (daphnias), which suggests that their susceptibility to color-stimuli may be different from ours.[2] The daphnias, placed in water on which a spectrum was thrown, at first crowded in greatest numbers into the part which was green, though some were found in each of the differently colored parts of the water. Next, however, Lubbock covered, and thus darkened, the visible spectrum, leaving the daphnias free to collect in this darkened space or in the ultra-violet part of the spectrum, which, of course, is equally dark to human eyes. But two hundred and eighty-six of the three hundred daphnias thronged the ultra-violet part, suggesting, as Morgan says, that they are "sensible to ultra-violet rays beyond the limits of human vision."[3]

The phenomena of protective coloration are an argument, if one be needed, to the wide prevalence of color-sensations among the vertebrates. The facts are these: the weaker edible animals are so colored that they resemble their surroundings; the caterpillar is dull green like the leaves on which it feeds, the plover's eggs are like the stones among which they are laid, and the brilliant coral fish

---

[1] "Ants, Bees and Wasps," p. 292.   [3] *Ibid.*, p. 295.
[2] Lubbock, British Assoc. Report, 1881. Cf. Morgan, *op. cit.*, p. 295.

is no brighter than the coral reefs among which he lives.[1] The probable explanation is the following : highly colored animals, being more conspicuous, fall a prey to stronger creatures, and have thus no chance to propagate their species. The protectively colored individuals, on the other hand, are preserved and transmit their coloration. This explanation presupposes, on the part of the animals who devour, a discrimination of the colors of their prey.

The study of the auditory consciousness of animals is rendered difficult, by the uncertainty whether certain organs are adapted to stimulation by sounds, or whether they are excitable merely by shocks and concussions. Of course, there is no doubt that mammals and birds have both a keen and a delicate discrimination of sounds. The mobility of the outer ear of many animals facilitates the distinction of sound-directions ; for example, when a dog faces suddenly about and pricks up his ears, the sounds are probably better reflected from the lifted ears, than from the normally drooping ears. The facility of birds, in imitating the calls of other birds and even human sounds, is evidence of their delicate discrimination. "No one," Morgan says,[2] "who has watched a thrush listening for worms, can doubt that her ear is highly sensitive."

But almost all animals, even those much lower in the scale, seem sensitive to sound. Even the earthworm, which has nothing like an auditory organ, appears to be affected by sound ; and most invertebrates have simple organs, apparently auditory, — either 'auditory pits,' depressions in the skin, or else closed sacs containing the small stony particles called otoliths. These supposedly auditory organs are very differently distributed in different animals : they are found near the edge of the umbrella of certain jelly-fish, in the muscular foot of the fresh-water mussel, in the antennules of lobsters, in the abdomen of locusts and in the legs of certain insects. But, as has been hinted already, it is not

[1] Cf. Morgan, *op. cit.*, pp. 82–83.   [2] *Op. cit.*, p. 264.

possible to prove that the little pits and the tubes containing otoliths are auditory organs at all. The otoliths of the human ear belong, we remember, to the semicircular canals, whose function is to condition a consciousness of bodily position; and it is not impossible that the auditory pits serve a similar end, in other words, that, although they are stimulated, like auditory organs, by the contact of the vibrating air, they serve to excite pressure-sensations. This is the more likely, because these undeveloped auditory organs are often connected with hairs; and hairs are usually organs of contact-sensations.

The comparative development of vision and hearing is most easily studied, in the case of young vertebrates. All those on whom Mills experimented were born both blind and deaf. He finds that the eyes open before the ears, but that "hearing follows sooner on complete opening of the ears than seeing on opening of the eyes."[1] For example, on the fourteenth day, a St. Bernard dog gave no sign of hearing a shrill dog-whistle, and only on the seventeenth day was there a twitching of the ears in response to the sound. But this same dog did not follow an object with his eyes till its eighteenth day. Both the cats and the rabbits saw and heard several days earlier than the dogs, and the guinea pigs and pigeons were more precocious than either. Yet, except in the case of the guinea pigs, who could both see and hear a few hours after birth, all these animals responded later to visual, than to auditory, stimulus.

From this summary, certain general results emerge. Observation of animal sensations confirms, in the first place, the teaching of evolutionists, that development is, in a measure, parallel within different animal sub-kingdoms. We do not find, for example, that the sense-experience of all vertebrates is fuller than that of certain members of other sub-kingdoms. On the other hand, the lower vertebrates — reptiles, for example — are less sensitive to light,

[1] *Op. cit.*, p. 172.

sound and smell, than many insects. As Morgan says about ants and bees, " We must be careful to avoid the error of supposing that because they happen to have no back-bone, they are necessarily low in the scale of life and intelligence. The tree of life," he adds, " has many branches, and . . . there is no reason why the bee and the ant in their branch of life should not have attained as high a development of structure and intelligence as the dog and the elephant in their branch." A different illustration of progressive development, within an animal sub-kingdom, is furnished by the mollusks. Some mollusks have no visual organ, some have only a pigment spot, and some have developed eyes. It is, therefore, perfectly evident that mollusks differ widely in the possession or in the degree of visual consciousness.

Our second general conclusion is a very obvious one: the higher vertebrates probably possess all the different sorts of sense-experience, which characterize the human consciousness, and yet they must be widely different from us, not only in the range of their sensational experiences, but also in the character of the affective consciousness, which accompanies their perceptions. Given a man and a dog in a summer meadow, and it is pretty certain that the dog will care far more for the smells and far less for the colors than the man does.

Finally, we must emphasize once more our initial warning. We know nothing, after all, and can barely venture to infer anything about the consciousness of animals of the lower orders. That earthworms, who have no visual organs, and daphnias, who have only eye-spots, are affected by visual stimuli, is definitely proved. But that their movements are accompanied by sensation, still more, that they are accompanied by visual sensation, is surely beyond the power of demonstration.

There is no doubt at all that the higher vertebrates and the insects possess sense-images, as well as sense-percepts. The dog who bounds up from his lazy drowsiness, at sound of a footstep, has probably before his mind the image 'man'; and, as Morgan observes,[1] the bird who hops about the lawn tapping, here and there, and then listening eagerly for the sound of the worm, has almost certainly been impelled to the hopping and the tapping by the image of a fat and luscious worm.

The images of animals are, of course, mainly in terms of the sensations which most interest them, and need not, therefore, closely resemble our images of the same objects or scenes. A dog's image, of Quincy Market on Christmas Eve, would be a bewildering consciousness of exciting smells; a man's image would be mainly visual, a complex of dark buildings, flaring lights, the ruddy coloring of the meat and vegetable stalls, and the green of Christmas wreaths. This wide difference, in the predominant image-qualities of animals and of men, is well suggested by a single expression in one of the Jungle Book stories. Mowgli was entering Messua's hut, "when he felt a touch on his foot. 'Mother,' said he, for he knew that tongue well, 'what dost thou here?'" Evidently the feel of Mother Wolf's tongue, which had so often lapped him in the old cave-home, was an important part of Mowgli's image of her.

Many of these images of an animal's consciousness must be accurate repetitions of past experience, that is, memory images. The dog who refuses to eat from anything save a certain cracked, brown plate, must remember either the look or the feel of the dish; the cat who leaves her post on the porch and chases about the house to the window-sill outside the dining room, must remember that this is her usual avenue of approach to the breakfast-table.

b. RELATIONAL EXPERIENCES

We have so far found reason to conclude that at least the 'higher' animals have a rich and full sensational consciousness, affectively toned. Postponing for the present

[1] "Animal Life and Intelligence," p. 350.

the further discussion of their emotional experience, we must face the question: do animals have relational consciousness? It is not strange, indeed, that the answer should be difficult, for one of the physiological tests of sensational experience is lacking here, in the nature of the case: there are no end-organs of relational elements of consciousness, and we have only, therefore, the movements of animals, from which to infer the presence or absence of these relational elements. Moreover, the bodily movements, indicative of relational experience, are far harder to interpret than the simple motor response to the sensational stimulus.

1. *Recognition*

There is and can be no evidence, for or against the fact that animals have a consciousness of familiarity. This does not mean that there is no evidence of animal memory: on the other hand, we have seen from their actions that animals must possess memory images, that is, images which reproduce their past experience. But we cannot know positively whether or not a feeling of familiarity accompanies these images, in other words, whether the dog recognizes the cracked, brown plate, or whether the cat knows the sunny window-sill as 'the familiar thing which I've met before.' Our ignorance is due, not only to the absence of any end-organs of familiarity-feeling, but also to the fact that no bodily actions are sufficiently characteristic of familiarity-feeling to distinguish it. The evidence of its existence is thus, as we have found,[1] purely introspective. Evidently, therefore, though we rightly conclude that animals remember, we simply do not know whether or not they recognize.

2. *Thought*

No problem of animal psychology is more hotly disputed than the question, do animals have thoughts? It

---

[1] Cf. Chapter XIX.

will be remembered that the test of the presence of thoughts in experience is the test of direct introspection. Our decisive question is always: have we the feeling of any-ness or of wholeness? Obviously, this test cannot be applied in a study of the animal consciousness. The only basis for argument is, as we have seen, the bodily movements of the animals; and these, it is once more evident, are not so easy of interpretation as mere motion to and from sense-stimuli. None the less, we have no resource, save to study the actions of animals, with intent to discover if they act as they could not act without thought.

This necessary limitation of our method means a limitation of the scope of our study. For no distinctive and externally observable form of bodily reaction accompanies the comparison, the general notion, the single judgment or even the synthetic reasoning. We are left then with the one question: do animals reason analytically;[1] in other words, do they perform acts which can only be explained, on the supposition that they abstract single features from total situations, and then combine these into novel conclusions?

There is, of course, no earthly doubt that the higher animals, invertebrate as well as vertebrate, act as they would act if they reasoned. People who argue the affirmative of our question heap up tale after tale, each well authenticated, and yet each more astounding than the last, of these 'rational' acts of our animal friends. They tell, for example, how a South African beetle extricated his load, from a hollow out of which he could not roll it: "Leaving the ball, he butted down the sand at one end of the hollow, so as to produce an inclined plane of much less angle, up which he then without difficulty pushed his burden."[2] Romanes has a story of birds who scatter when they light on thin ice so that their weight is divided; and

---

[1] Cf. Chapter XVIII., throughout.   [2] Morgan, *op. cit.*, p. 368.

somebody else tells the tale of a dog who calculates, in swimming across a harbor, the allowance to be made for incoming or outgoing tide. An unpublished tale shall conclude this series, which might be indefinitely lengthened. It is the story of a terrier, who has been trained to carry home the newspaper from the five o'clock train. He now goes to the train unattended, and leaves the house exactly at the whistle of the four-forty-five train. "He was never taught to do this," his owner explains, "so, of course, he reasons that this will give him just time to reach the station at five o'clock."

Writers, who believe that animals reason, do not fail to point out the probability that animals 'attend,' that is, that their percepts are clear, narrowed, prolonged and suggestive. Perceptual attention seems to be, indeed, as Ribot says, 'a condition of life.' "The carnivorous animal that had not its attention roused on sight of prey would stand but a poor chance of survival; the prey that had not its attention roused by the sight of its natural enemy would stand but a poor chance of escape." [1] Now the fact that animals appear to be attentive to some parts of their total environment, certainly suggests that they have analytic judgments, because, as we have seen, the emphasized part of an analytic judgment is always an 'abstracted' or attended-to portion of it. But we have no right to the conclusion that animals are proved to reason, in other words, to reach conclusions by mediate inference, until we have satisfied ourselves that these 'rational' acts could not have been unreasoningly performed by the immediate association, due to past experience, of some imaged act. The only conceivable criterion of the inevitably-reasoned act is, thus, the one which James suggests, its entire novelty. The dog who saw a boat full of water and, obeying his master's gestures, ran back to the house, returning with a sponge, has been regarded as a reasoning dog, because

[1] Morgan, *op. cit.*, p. 343.

24

though he was never trained to carry the sponge to the boat, he had none the less 'reasoned' that it was wanting. But James is correct in the remark that the dog may have re- membered past observations of boat cleaning. The act "might fairly have been called an act of reasoning proper," James adds,[1] "if unable to find the sponge at the house, he had brought back a dipper or mop."

In the opinion of the writer, who follows Morgan and James in this view, this test of entire novelty, as criterion of the reasoned act, has never been fully met. The most rational-appearing acts of animals may have followed upon immediately suggested images, and not upon conclusions mediately reached through analysis. The beetle, the dogs and the birds, heroes of our stories about apparent reason- ing, may have performed the acts, so admirably adapted to secure their desires, purely as repetitions of acts already performed. In accordance with this view, Morgan analyzes the act of the dog who seems to allow for the current. "The dog," he says, "has presumably had frequent experi- ence of the effect of the stream in carrying him with it. He has been carried beyond the landing-place, and had bother with the mud; but when he has entered the stream higher up, he has nearly, if not quite, reached the landing- stage. His keen perceptions come to his aid, and he adjusts his action nicely to effect his purpose. On the bank sits a young student watching him. He sees in the dog's action a problem, which he runs over rapidly in his mind. 'Velocity of stream, two miles an hour. Width, one-eighth of a mile. Dog takes ten minutes to swim one-eighth of a mile. Distance flowed by the stream in ten minutes, one-third of a mile. Clever dog that! He allows just about the right distance. A little short, though. Has rather a struggle at the end.' The dog intelligently performs the feat; the lad reasons it out."

In a similar way, we may account for the action of the

[1] *Op. cit.*, Vol. II., pp. 349–350.

little dog, who seems to have reasoned that fifteen minutes is necessary to reach the station. The shrill whistle of the earlier train excites an image of his habitual scamper, late in the afternoon, to the station; and he is off at once, because the image inevitably excites his movements, not because he has analyzed the situation and reasoned out the time between the trains.

This view of the case is sustained by the results of careful experiments, performed by Dr. Edward Thorndike, on dogs, cats and chicks. His method is the following:[1] the animals are placed, when hungry, in large boxes, from which they can "escape and so get food only by manipulating some simple mechanism (*e.g.* by pulling down a loop of wire, depressing a lever or turning a button)." Dr. Thorndike finds that a young animal usually chances to make the proper movement, in the course of its instinctive reactions, clawing, biting, attempting to squeeze through holes; that this movement, probably because of the pleasantness of the escape, tends to be remembered, and that therefore "after repeated trials, the animal will perform the act immediately on being confronted with the situation." So far, of course, the experiment seems to indicate that these animals do perform mechanical operations by merely recalling and repeating their chance movements, but the experiment does not prove that its subjects might not also perform these acts through reasoning. The disproof of this reasoning hypothesis seems to be supplied, by the discovery that "in the case of some difficult associations," the animals, "would happen to do the thing six or seven times, but after long periods of promiscuous scrabbling, and then forever after would fail to do it." Dr. Thorndike is quite correct in the remark: "If they had acted from inference in any case, they ought not to have failed in the seventh or eighth trial. What had

---

[1] Monograph Supplement No. 8, of the *Psychological Review*. Cf. *Psychological Review*, Vol. V., p. 550.

been inferred six times should have been inferred the seventh."

The theory that animals do not reason is bound to enrage their most ardent admirers. These gentle souls must console themselves with two reflections: first, the reiterated truth that all conclusions about animals are mere inference. The demonstration that animals have not been proved to reason is not equivalent, therefore, to a positive proof that they do not reason. It is even more important to bear in mind that reasoning is not essential to an alert and many-sided intelligence. As has been said so often, the immediately associated image may lead to the same result, in action, as the reasoned conclusion. In questioning the ability of the higher animals to reason, we are not, therefore, questioning their capacity to act effectively, or their possession of rich percepts and of swift-coming images. We are, it is true, denying their rationality, in the technical sense of that word, but we are freely admitting the wide scope and the wonderful adaptation of their intelligence.[1]

c. AFFECTIONS AND EMOTIONS

It is generally agreed that the sense-experience of the 'higher' animals often gives them pleasure or dissatisfaction. The presence, in their consciousness, of these pleasures and dissatisfactions is argued mainly from the persistence, with which they seek certain situations and avoid others. The emotional experience is also inferred from the observation of specific movements of expansion or depression, which in human beings have been observed to accompany the affective experience.[2]

Admitting, therefore, that many animals have pleasant and unpleasant experiences, we shall next briefly consider the indications which they give of emotions, complex states

[1] Cf. throughout, Morgan, *op. cit.*, Chapter IX.; and James, *op. cit.*, Vol. II., Chapter XXI., pp. 348 *seq.*   [2] Cf. Chapter XX. pp. 287 *seq.*

in which affections predominate. No one doubts that the higher animals experience the basal and primitive emotions, happiness, unhappiness, hope and fear. Darwin has contrasted the appearance of a dog, when cheerful, — his 'high steps, head much raised, moderately erected ears and tail carried aloft,' — with the attitude of the same animal dejected and disappointed, with his ' head, ears, body, tail and chops drooping, and eyes dull.' [1] The contrasted attitudes, in their general aspects, are exhibited by other animals, and are an evident result, of either strengthened or relaxed muscular contraction. The bodily accompaniments of fear — trembling, for example — are essentially the accentuated marks of disappointment or grief, but these are followed by violent contractions of the flexor muscles: [2] dogs, for instance, in moments of fear, like their ancestors, the wolves and jackals, 'tuck in their tails,' and often lay back their ears, instead of merely drooping them, as in grief.

We must, of course, guard ourselves carefully from too exact and assured an interpretation of these bodily attitudes of so-called joy, grief and fear. They are probably, as we have seen,[3] the developed and abbreviated forms of movements of advance and retreat, which may well have been originally performed without consciousness. Furthermore, though the capering movements or the drooping ears and tail are almost certainly accompanied by emotion, we have yet no assurance about the exact nature of that emotion. It is not, for instance, safe to conclude that the dog with tail between his legs and trembling limbs, in a heavy thunderstorm, is 'afraid of the thunder' precisely as the trembling child is afraid of it. A certain primitive fear, a thoroughly unpleasant consciousness of deafening sound and blinding light and trembling limbs, the dog may certainly be supposed to share with the man. But everything which the child has heard or learned to increase his fear,

[1] " Expression of the Emotions," pp. 57 and 122.
[2] Cf. Chapter XX., p. 292.   [3] *Ibid.*, p. 296.

every anticipation of house in flames, property lost, eyes blinded, must be lacking in the dog's experience. In other words, the emotional experience of animals is limited by the range of their imagination : the traditional past, which they do not know, and the wide future, which they cannot foresee, do not enter into their emotional life ; whereas, we human beings as often grieve and joy for the imagined as for the seen.

We have purposely neglected the discussion of the strictly social emotions of animals — their love and their sympathy, because the study of these experiences is undertaken in the following section of this chapter.

II. The Personal and Social Consciousness of Animals

We have so far considered the problems of animal psychology, from the strictly analytic standpoint, merely trying to discover the structural elements of the consciousness of animals. We have now to inquire, whether animals give evidence of a consciousness of themselves in relation to other selves. We are, of course, inclined to the belief that they do have some sort of self-consciousness, because our own consciousness is always, in some sense, a consciousness of self, so that we cannot conceive of an utterly impersonal consciousness. But we have more external evidence of the self-consciousness of animals. A study of their pairing, mating and herding undoubtedly suggests to us that they have a certain consciousness of their fellows, that is, in the wider sense of the term — a social consciousness.

The relation of the higher animals with human beings gives further evidence that they possess a social consciousness. The ecstatic leaps and barks and tail waggings with which a dog, who has watched unmoved a hundred passers-by, dashes forward to greet his master, seems to show, not merely the recognition of a familiar footfall or odor, but the acknowledgment of his master himself. No part

of the Odysseus tale is more real to us, than the story of
the faithful dog Argos who, alone, knew Odysseus, returned
after the long years of wandering. The old dog, we are
told, "wagged his tail and laid back both his ears, and was
then overtaken by the fate of black death."

As a matter of fact, then, we usually do attribute to animals a personal consciousness, beginning always with the
consciousness of a relation between ourselves and them.
We smile at the story of Dr. John Brown leaning far out
of his carriage to follow with his eyes "a dog who is one
of my friends"; but most of us number animals among our
acquaintances, and we naturally suppose them to realize
their relation to ourselves and to each other. Indeed, the
reason why we revel in Kipling's Jungle Books and in Ernest Seton Thompson's closer studies of animal life is that
both writers successfully individualize their animals, and
necessarily, therefore, treat them as conscious selves in
personal relations with other selves. "This," says Mr.
Thompson, "is the principle I have tried to apply to my
animals. The real personality of the individual and his
view of life are my theme, rather than the race in general."

But it is time to pull ourselves up, rather sharply, with
this question: have we not been proceeding, somewhat
sentimentally, to attribute our own feelings to the animals?
We have really been arguing from the fact that, when we
caress our friends or rush to meet them, we are neither following blind instincts nor mindful of any mere trick of
voice or attitude, but profoundly conscious of other selves.
It is not certain, however, that animals perform similar
acts with this same sort of personal consciousness; and we
must remember, furthermore, that we ourselves often
bestow caresses in a perfectly mechanical and impersonal
way. We should therefore scrutinize, with especial care,
our constant inference that animals love the people or the
other animals, whom they caress or fawn upon. Darwin,
for instance, vividly pictures the dog who "suddenly discovers that the man who is approaching is his master.

Instead of walking upright, the body sinks downward or even crouches, and is thrown into flexuous movements; his tail, instead of being held stiff and upright, is lowered and wagged from side to side; his hair instantly becomes smooth; his ears are depressed and drawn backward, but not closely to the head; and his lips hang loosely. From the drawing back of the ears, the eyelids become elongated, and the eyes no longer appear round and staring."[1] To this description, whose accuracy no one questions, Darwin adds a statement, which might conceivably be challenged, when he says that these movements are "clearly expressive of affection." For though there is no doubt that most of us interpret these movements as Darwin does, yet we cannot prove that they express more than impersonal satisfaction with familiar odor, look or 'feel.' A story like the one which follows strongly suggests this doubt : —

A Llama herdsman, whose cow had lost her calf, replaced the living calf by the skin of the little beast, rudely stuffed with hay. "The mamma," writes Mr. Hamerton, who tells the story,[2] "opened enormous eyes at her beloved infant; by degrees she stooped her head toward it, then smelt at it . . . and at last proceeded to lick it with the most delightful tenderness." The sequel of the story shakes one's faith in the permanence of this emotion. " By dint of caressing and licking her little calf, the tender parent one fine morning unripped it. The hay issued from within, and the cow, manifesting not the slightest surprise nor agitation, proceeded tranquilly to devour the unexpected provender."

Mr. Morgan rightly observes that the cow, "if she could think at all, was not to be reproached for her want of surprise at finding calfskin stuffed with hay. She had presumably," as he says, "some little experience in *putting* hay inside. Why not *find* hay inside?" We, however, are concerned with another difficulty. If the caresses of

[1] *Op. cit.*, p. 51.
[2] "Chapters on Animals," p. 9, quoted by Morgan, *op. cit.*, p. 333.

a cow's tongue really are what Darwin calls them, 'a striking way of exhibiting affection,' then the emotion of this
deceived mother must have been of an indescribably
evanescent character, else she would have shown some
grief at the untimely loss of her child, instead of tranquilly
replacing the satisfaction of licking calfskin by the pleasure of eating hay. The truth is, that the cow was probably
never deceived at all. She licked the stuffed calfskin because she enjoyed the taste and the feel of it, not because
she took it for her lost calf. The story, therefore, is disturbing to our preconceived ideas, not because it proves
that the cow did not love her calf and grieve for it — for
on these points the tale is silent — but because it proves
that the caresses of a cow's tongue are indications of sensational satisfaction, not expressions of maternal emotion.

The imitations of animals are urged as another evidence
of their personal social consciousness. Some observers, it
is true, do not admit that the imitativeness of animals has
been demonstrated,[1] but most of them agree that certain
acts of the higher animals are imitations. Of course, no
one claims that all common animal activities are imitative.
At one and the same moment, on a summer morning, a
group of hens will march proudly about a barnyard, cut-
cut-ca-da-cutting after the same exultant fashion. Yet
their simultaneous cluckings are not imitations, but rather
the expressions of individual instinct : each hen would have
clucked as loudly if all her sisters had fallen a prey to the
hawk or to the poulterer. When, however, both instinctive and accidental 'common' activities have been excluded,
there remain tolerably clear examples of activities, acquired
by animals through imitation. Wesley Mills, for example,
vouches for the story of a kitten which could not be taught
to jump, until it had seen its mother perform the trick, and
Morgan concludes, from experimental observation, that
ducks enter the water only through imitation of their

---

[1] Cf. E. B. Thorndike, *op. cit.*

mothers, but that, once they have touched the water, they swim instinctively. But admitting the occurrence of imitative animal activities, it is none the less impossible to regard them as certain proof of a social consciousness, a recognition of other selves. The imitativeness of animals does, indeed, indicate the existence of a social life among them, but this is not the same as a social consciousness, and does not necessarily show even a faint consciousness of 'me' and 'thee.'

We conclude, therefore, that animal caresses and animal imitations suggest, yet can never prove, the existence of a social consciousness. Our belief in the conscious social life of animals rests, however, on far more unambiguous evidence, than these imitated games and activities and these flexuous movements and impetuous tail-waggings. This stronger evidence consists in the deliberate actions of animals, contrary to their habits and to their instincts of self-preservation. The lives of animal mothers are full of illustrations of these altruistic acts. Swallows who fly into burning houses to save their young, partridges who draw the attention of sportsmen from their nests to themselves and whales who run the risk of the harpoon, that they may not desert their wounded children, give proof, we are apt to conclude, of personal feeling. The attitude of Seton Thompson's hero, Lobo, the king of Currumpaw, to Blanca his mate, forms a striking illustration of this personal relation between animals. Lobo was a wolf who, for years, guarded himself and his followers from every device of man, who detected poison in the cunningest preparations and discovered the most exquisitely hidden traps. But when Lobo's mate, the white wolf Blanca, was captured, he wandered about, recklessly following her tracks, and was caught at once by the traps which never before had deceived him. It is almost impossible to read the story, without sharing the conviction of its writer, that in some inarticulate way Lobo cared for Blanca. If his actions were not due to personal emotion, then they must have been occasioned by some intense sensational impulse, for example, by the frenzied following of an intoxicating odor. But it is hard to imagine that a mere sensational impulse of this sort could triumph over the lifelong habit, itself founded on sensational instincts, of avoiding poison. It is surely simpler to attribute Lobo's tragic end to some sort of affection for Blanca. Even more convincing a story, of a habit broken down by emotion, is the tale of Vixen, the fox, who deliberately poisoned her own child, when repeated attempts to rescue it from captivity had failed. There is, indeed, no lack of well-authenticated examples of animals, who check instinctive reactions of self-preservation or antagonism, who relinquish pleasures and seek pains, through the influence of some other self, animal or human. The frequent instances in which an animal restrains himself from biting the hand of the master, who dresses his wounds, cannot always be explained as due to the anticipation of help: very often they seem to indicate, on the part of an animal, a sympathetic consciousness, " It would hurt the man if I should bite him." This victory of personal consciousness, over merely sensational reaction, is curiously illustrated by the mock-fighting of animals. Actual fighting may be explained as conscious, yet immediate, reflex activity. But a mock fight demands restraint of one's antagonistic activities, beyond a certain point; and there seems to be no reason for this restraint save a consciousness of "the other fellow something like me, whom I do not want to hurt."

The personal consciousness of animals must, however, be very different from the personal consciousness of the developed human being, more closely connected with primitive wants, and more limited to experiences of the present hour and the immediate surroundings. Our conclusion, that many animals feel affection and sympathy, must not, therefore, pave the way for a false interpretation of their actions, as indication of vastly more complex personal experiences. The animal books are full of stories, which read into the animal consciousness emotions that are pretty certainly human. The dog with tail between his legs is pointed out as 'evidently repentant'; the animal who hobbles about as if lame is described as 'deliberately deceiving'; the monkey who has bitten his mistress is characterized as 'ashamed of himself, hiding his face in his hands and sitting quiet for a time.'[1] In all these instances, we observe directly only act or attitude, and straightway we interpret it, as we should if the actor were a human being, as indication of shame or of deceit. On the contrary, the alleged deception may be the unreflective repetition of a movement, which has been in the past rewarded by petting and creature comfort; the 'repentant' attitude may be mere shrinking from imagined punishment, or it may be, as was later found in the case of the 'repentant' monkey, pure fatigue after a fit of passion. Our only source of knowledge about the unsensational consciousness of animals is, as we have seen, the observation of their movements and their attitudes. We can never argue from these alone that animals deliberate and will, still less, that they have a moral consciousness.

Thus, we end, as we began, with frank admission of our unsatisfactory results. We have not merely, like all psychologists, substituted a study of the typical consciousness for the vivid, individual biography; but we have carried generalization still further, and have been prone to reach conclusions about 'animals,' instead of distinguishing, constantly and carefully, the different orders of animals. And we have been hampered, throughout, by the indirectness of our method — the necessity of inferring conscious experiences from a study of end-organs and of bodily movements. We cannot, then, avoid the dispiriting conclusion that we are deeply ignorant of the lives of our animal friends. The probable difference, in the scope and

[1] Romanes, "Animal Intelligence," p. 444.

in the intensity of sensation, and the obvious difference in interest make their world of observation materially different from ours. Their ignorance of the unseen universes, of history and of science, narrows their imagined world, beyond the power of our imagination to conceive. The number and precision of their instinctive acts stand them in the stead of reasoning. Therefore "we always," Mr. Hamerton says,[1] "commit one of two mistakes; either we conclude the beasts have great knowledge because they are so clever, or else we fancy that they must be stupid because they are so ignorant." We are not even able to interpret their suffering and their satisfaction, perhaps undervaluing its momentary poignancy, but, almost certainly, forgetting that they must be less conscious than we of past and of future, and that they must, therefore, miss much of the sweetness and the anguish of anticipation, of the sadness and the delight of retrospect. Still less can we venture to interpret dogmatically their social consciousness, their emotional relations to their fellows and to us. Yet perhaps we are nowhere safer in our inference, than in the conclusion that the consciousness of animals is, in some sense, like ours, a social one, and that they too may love and hate, may be treacherous or faithful.

[1] Quoted by Morgan, *op. cit.*, p. 355.

CHAPTER XXVI

THE PSYCHOLOGY OF THE CHILD'S CONSCIOUSNESS

THE study of the conscious life of children is pursued, to-day, in part only, for the light it throws on problems of general psychology.[1] This relation to adult psychology is, to be sure, always recognized. The fundamental characteristics of the conscious life appear, it is evident, in greater isolation in the earlier periods of development, and although one can never argue, with certainty, from the presence or absence of an element of consciousness in an earlier stage of life, to its presence or absence at a later period, one may better learn to know it in the earlier and simpler consciousness, and thus more readily recognize it in the greater complexity of the developed consciousness. In the same way, then, in which we train ourselves to detect the overtones of a clang by listening, first, to the same tones in isolation, we shall better understand the emotions, for example, by studying fear in the life of the child who is not ashamed to betray his feeling, or by observing childish envy, which is unadulterated by moral scruple.

The impetus toward child-study is, nevertheless, more personal than technical, and due rather to human interest than to scientific concern. One need not be a student — one has only to be father or sister or teacher or kindly human being — to be vitally interested, in the investigation of the conscious life, behind the sometimes impenetrable screen of child-eyes and child-lips, and in the interpretation of the ceaseless activity of the child's body. The

[1] Several paragraphs of Chapter XXVI., are quoted from a paper by the writer, "The Religious Consciousness of Children," in the New World, Dec. 1896.

commonly effective motive in child-study is thus the personal, the ethical, or the pedagogical, not the scientific; and the psychic life of the child is usually observed in the belief that "the greatest value of this work is" in drawing one "toward the highest object of human affection, the object most worthy of reverence, love and sacrifice, — the growing child." [1]

This claim, it is true, does not go unchallenged. Child-study, it has been objected, tends to foster an unhealthy self-consciousness in the child; it also changes the teacher from the friend, with wise and sympathetic interest, to the critical and dispassionate observer, actually crippled in his power to enter into personal relations with the child. "My children," says Professor Münsterberg, who strongly champions this view, "are for me not phenomena, not objects of perception, . . . but objects of my will, my love, my duty. . . . You may artificially train yourself," he adds, "to fluctuate between these two attitudes, to observe in one moment what you loved in the moment before, but the one will always interfere with the other." [2] At precisely this point, however, Dr. Münsterberg's assertions may be questioned. The attitude of the scientific observer does indeed differ from that of the devoted friend or teacher, but the results of previous study may quicken insight, enlarge wisdom, and add comprehension to love. A statistical or experimental study of childhood may certainly be as dispassionate and as unemotional as the study of a fossil or of an Aryan root; but the results of such a study may also minister to the needs of the personal life.

The account, which follows, of the child-consciousness is based on the records of two forms of child-study: first, upon close observations of one child in its development from birth onward, and second, upon topical studies of a given psychic phenomenon, say of anger or of imagination, as manifested in a group of children of the same age and

[1] Sara E. Wiltse, *Pedagogical Seminary*, Vol. III., p. 212.
[2] *Journal of Education*, May, 1895.

environment. These latter studies have been mainly concerned with children of school-age.

I. The Consciousness of the Baby

The study of the baby-consciousness, like that of the animal-consciousness, is through inference, first, from the stage of development of end-organs and cerebral centres, second, and most important, from the baby's bodily attitudes and movements. In the study of older children, the observation of their actions is interpreted by the observer's memory of his own childhood, and supplemented by the child's account of his own experience.

The normal baby has sensations of all sorts within the first few weeks after birth. This is inferred both from the condition, at birth, of the sense-organs, and from the early movements of the child. The structure of the organs in the skin, and of the taste bulbs, is complete before birth, and it is therefore entirely possible that the child has pre-natal sensations of pressure, pain, warmth, cold and taste. The mechanism of the eye, also, is fully developed in the embryo, but light-stimulation is, of course, possible only after birth. Smell-stimulation requires air in the nasal cavities, so that there cannot be pre-natal smell sensations, and the ear is not cleared of the viscous matter which fills the drum cavity, nor is it reached by the air for some time after birth.

Corresponding with these facts, are the phenomena of a child's early movements. Reactions to contact with the tongue, lips and palms of new-born children have been repeatedly observed. Stimulation, with quinine and sugar solutions, of the tongues of babies, in their first minutes and hours, have been followed by distinct and characteristic facial expressions. Experiments with strong odors, such as asafoetida, on babies (most of them less than a day, and some of them less than an hour, old) have occasioned uneasy movements of body and of facial muscles. Sensibility to light is shown, by turning toward it in the first few minutes of life; but coördination of the movements of the two eyes, the fixation of objects and the trick of following a moving object, with the eyes, are the results of experience, often extending over several months. To sound-stimuli, however, newly born children certainly do not at once react. Setting aside cases in which the whole body is jarred by the vibrations caused by a loud noise, we find that the "period of beginning to hear varies with individual children from the sixth hour to the third week." [1]

Very early, therefore, in his life, the child is provided with sense material of every type. His experience, however, in this very primitive stage is doubtless utterly chaotic and undifferentiated. As James says, [2] "the body, assailed by eyes, ears, nose, skin and entrails at once, feels it all as one great, blooming, buzzing confusion." The adult approximates to this experience, in the moments of recovery from a fainting fit or of gradual awakening from a deep sleep. His consciousness, in such moments, is an undistinguished conglomerate, say of colors, sounds, pressures and discomforts, a very turbulent solution, as it were, which only gradually precipitates the consciousness of distinct things and of selves. Almost everybody knows what it is, to have this confusion of undiscriminated elements give place to a consciousness of familiar objects and of well-known selves. Such a confusion of thronging feelings is somewhat like the earliest stage of the conscious life. Almost from the very first, however, some parts of this chaotic experience are emphasized at the expense of others. Certain instinctive interests soon assert themselves, the attention to intense sensations is very early developed, and any element of consciousness, repeatedly experienced in different combinations, is discriminated and attended to. Thus, the child soon gains an especial inter-

---

[1] F. Tracy, "The Psychology of Childhood," 2d ed., p. 21. Tracy presents an excellent summary of results, up to 1891, of the study of the baby's experience. See, also, Tracy's Bibliography.

[2] *Op. cit.*, Vol. I., Chapter XIII., p. 488.

2 C

est in certain parts of his environment, and learns to discriminate one color from another, colors from forms,
pitch from loudness and pressure from warmth.

It is probable that the careful study of most children
would confirm the important conclusion of a close and
accurate observer, that the so-called higher sensations,
visual and auditory, are earlier discriminated than the sensations of pressure, smell and taste, which are more immediately connected with bodily welfare. " Contrary to
accepted opinion and to my own expectation," Miss Shinn
writes,[1] " so far from finding an early dominance of taste
and smell, displaced later, . . . I found a lively attention
to sight impressions very early, slowly overtaken by attention to other sensations."

Most studies of a child's sense-discrimination are studies,
also, of his affective consciousness, his preference for certain colors or sounds or tastes. So far as one may judge
from attitude and expression, and from movements of
approach and of retreat, there is no reason to doubt that
a child very early experiences pleasure and dissatisfaction.
Sweet tastes, rhythmic movements, soft sounds, light and
warmth almost always seem to be pleasant. Bitter tastes,
jolting movements, loud sounds, darkness and cold, on the
other hand, are apparently unpleasant. And in spite of
the absence of conclusive experiments, it is fair to say that
observation tends to suggest a common preference for the
warmer colors. It is usually assumed, also, not only that a
child discriminates colors far better than forms, but that he
prefers the colors. Miss Shinn's observations, have, however, shown definitely that this is not a universal relation.
From the eleventh month, when Miss Shinn's niece began
to recognize uncolored pictures, there was never an indication of preference for colored pictures, and the independent interest in the outlines of letters, figures, trees

[1] "Notes on the Development of a Child," Pt. II., p. 177.

and flowers was very noticeable. This conclusion has since been supplemented and confirmed by the results of a test, with colored and uncolored pictures, on school children of various ages.[1] Interest and apparent pleasure, in rhythmic motions and sounds and in melody, is relatively early, and has been noticed in the fourth month.[2] It is indicated, at first, by a movement of the head toward the sound, and a little later, by imitative movements and sounds.

Darwin classes the evident pleasure in music as 'first of the æsthetic sentiments,'[3] and this generalization suggests to us the important subject of children's emotions. The confusion of bodily movement with conscious experience is as easy here as in the parallel study of animal-consciousness. The shrinking of a few-weeks-old baby at a sudden sound is often described as fear; the 'frowning and wrinkling of the skin around the eyes before crying' is interpreted by Darwin[4] as his baby's sign of anger. Darwin adds, to be sure, "this may have been pain, not anger," but he has no doubt that anger occurs in the fourth month. The truth, however, as we have seen before, is that these bodily attitudes and movements, the shrinking of so-called fear, for example, may be unconscious reflex movements. Even if they are conscious, they may accompany experiences which do not resemble what we know as emotions. For fear and anger and the rest involve a relatively developed self-consciousness; and the baby's earliest experience must therefore be unemotional. Indeed, if we recall the abject terrors of our own childhood, such as corridors which we feared to enter for dread of lurking bears or robbers, or the big policeman whom we avoided for fear of a mysterious fate named 'prison,' we shall realize that these fears were all acquired, the evident work of nursemaids or playmates or of story-books. The results, though numerically few, of

---

[1] "Wellesley College Psychological Studies," *Psychological Review*, Vol. VII., 1900, p. 580. [2] Cf. Tracy, *op. cit.*, 1st ed., p. 33.
[3] "Mind," O. S., Vol. II., p. 289. [4] *Ibid.*, p. 287.

a study of children's fears, confirms this opinion of all
thoughtful observers of children. Miss Fackenthal found [1]
that nine, out of twenty-three children under three years,
were reported by their parents to be without fear; that
only six, of fifty-two children between three and six years
old, were entirely fearless; and finally that all, save one,
of one hundred and twenty-seven school children about
twelve years old, had fears of one sort or of another, most
often the purely imaginary fear of wild animals.

It is not so easy to identify relational elements in the
consciousness of the child who does not yet speak. It is
clear that a child early has images, cerebrally excited, of
absent objects, as well as percepts of things about him.
Perez relates, for example, that a child of three months,
on hearing the word *co-co*, turned about and looked for
the bird-cage, and that a child of six months shrank back
from a hot dish which a few days before had burned him.[2]
But the occurrence of memory-images does not, as we
have seen, of necessity imply recognition, the consciousness of familiarity. Nevertheless, though it is impossible
to assure oneself that the baby actually recognizes people
or things, certain bodily movements, his outstretched hands
and his smile, at first hesitating then eager, are most
readily interpreted as recognition. There is no experimental evidence, to show that any type of experience is
better remembered than another, but an interesting observation of Baldwin suggests that a complex experience is
more readily recognized than a simple one. Baldwin's
child of six months and a half failed to recognize either
the figure or the voice of a nurse, who had been three
weeks away, but joyfully recognized the nurse when she
entered the room singing. The summation of sense-stimuli seemed to facilitate recognition.[3]

[1] "Wellesley College Psychological Studies," *Pedagogical Seminary*, Vol.
III., p. 319.
[2] Cf. Tracy, *op. cit.*, 1st ed., p. 142, for account of both cases.
[3] *Ibid.*, p. 40, referring to *Science*, May, 1890.

There is little doubt that the baby, long before he can speak, is conscious of similarities. It is incorrect, to be sure, to assume that identical reactions are a certain indication of this feeling of likeness. When, for instance, the baby holds out his arms to every man whom he sees, this action may simply show a failure to discriminate other men from his father; but the child who was taught the letter *o* in her twelfth month, and who " a little later found a large *q* on a letter card and held it out with a questioning sound," [1] was evidently conscious of a resemblance; and the child of fourteen months who was observed "to feel his own ears and then his mother's, one day when looking at pictures of rabbits," must have been impelled to this action by a consciousness of likeness and of difference.

From the pedagogical or personal standpoint, the most absorbing topic of child-psychology is the nature and growth of the child's self-consciousness. According to the theory set forth in this book, all consciousness is, it is true, in a certain sense self-consciousness, but the undiscriminated, conglomerate consciousness of one's own body, resembling, as we have seen, the sleepy adult consciousness, is only in a very vague and inarticulate way a self-consciousness, and can only faintly resemble what we know as the consciousness of ourselves. It is, strictly speaking, impossible for us to assign a period at which a child becomes definitely conscious of himself, as related to other selves, and as contrasted with things, for no actions of his can be unequivocally interpreted as requiring distinct self-consciousness. We may, however, describe with a high degree of probability, certain accompaniments of the growing self-consciousness of a child.

The growth of interest in human bodies is, in the first place, evident. From the very first, the satisfaction of the baby's hunger, his escape from pain and, in truth, all his

---

[1] "Notes on the Development of a Child," Vol. I., p. 58.

pleasures, are connected with those facts of his experience which are later known as people. Human bodies, also, present certain permanent features, of voice and of appearance, against a background of varying dress and position, and for this reason they are earlier discriminated. They are, furthermore, primitively interesting because of their great mobility. Everybody knows that moving objects are more readily noticed than quiet ones; a signal, unobserved on a quiet day, is seen at once when it floats in the breeze, and a crab, which has lain for hours undistinguished from sea-anemones and waving seaweed, is immediately recognized as it scuttles across the surface of the rock. A baby early learns to follow moving objects with his eyes, and is naturally interested in the human bodies which surround him, since they are by all odds the most restless part of his environment, constantly rising and sitting down and walking about and changing their position. Baldwin suggests still another reason for a baby's interest in people. At a very early stage, as he points out, the child recognizes vaguely the uncertainty of the experiences associated with people. "This growing sense," he observes, [1] "is very clear to one who watches an infant in his second half-year. Sometimes its mother gives a biscuit, and sometimes she does not. Sometimes the father smiles and tosses the child; sometimes he does not. And the child looks for signs of these varying moods and methods of treatment. Its action in the presence of the persons of the household becomes hesitating and watchful. Especially does it watch the face for any expressive indications of what treatment may be expected."

Along with this growing interest in people's bodies and the developing recognition and discrimination of them, it is highly likely that there goes the widening and differentiation of the child's self-consciousness. The development of his imitative activities is doubtless a second potent

[1] "Mental Development in Child and Race," p. 123.

factor in this experience. Originally, the baby must reflect on these imitations, for example, the rhythmic movements of his head and hands, and must compare them with their models; and because his imitative movements include motor as well as visual sensations, they must therefore contribute to the baby's consciousness of his own body as distinct from other bodies.[1]

It is quite true that we have not succeeded in tracing to its source the consciousness of self, in its relation to other selves and to things; and we have merely suggested certain possible factors in the development. Yet hypothetical as all this is, one negative conclusion may be emphasized. We may confidently reject the popular theory that the child first becomes conscious of himself and his body, and that later, observing the resemblance of other bodies to his own, he 'ejects' his consciousness into them, that is, infers that these bodies, so like his own, must be connected with consciousness like his own. The unlikelihood of this explanation is evident. For it is certain — if any inference may be drawn from a baby's movements to his consciousness — that he is earlier conscious of other people's bodies than of his own. Many months pass before a baby gains a knowledge of his own body, through explorations of one leg by another, and through slow discoveries of the connection between head and arms and body. Long before this result is reached, the baby has been following other people's movements with his eyes, and has shown, by other motions of his own, that he is conscious of them. Even his first imitative movements are performed with apparent unconsciousness of them, but with fixed attention to the movements which he is imitating.

We have the right to conclude that the baby's consciousness of other selves is not an inference from the observed likeness of their bodies to his own. But we are not free to conclude that the relation is precisely reversed, and

---

[1] Cf. Royce, *Philosophical Review*, Vol. III., September, 1894.

that a baby is first conscious of other selves, and thus led
to a consciousness of himself.   For the truth, as we have
already so often realized, is that one is never conscious of
others except as related to oneself, and seldom if ever conscious of oneself except as connected with other selves.   So,
whatever the date of the emergence of a definite self-consciousness, there can be no distinction of time between the
consciousness of oneself and that of other selves.   Many
observers believe that they can trace this experience back
into the later months of the first year of life, and no one,
however far-reaching his memory, has any knowledge of
a time when he was not distinctly conscious of himself, in
his relations to other selves.

II.   The Consciousness of Little Children

An exhaustive study of the consciousness of children,
beyond the age of babyhood, is plainly impossible within
the limits of such a chapter as this.   Indeed, the materials,
adequate to such a study, do not exist, for investigations
of the child-consciousness have been either observations,
often fragmentary, of a few individuals, or else they have
been incomplete statistical investigations, considering only
limited questions and involving particular ages and surroundings.   A few generalizations may, none the less, be
ventured upon.   They have the unquestionable advantage
of challenging our own introspection, that is, our memory
of our childhood experiences.   Untrustworthy as these
memories are, from the length of time which has passed,
they form our best standard, for the interpretation of
children's words and actions.

The most significant truth about the childhood consciousness is this, that no hard-and-fast lines can be drawn
between adult and childhood experience.   The greatest
error, in our ordinary estimate of the mind of a little child,
is exactly opposed to the mistake which we commonly make
about the baby's consciousness.   We are apt to conclude,

from a baby's quick movements, that he knows and feels more than he does. On the other hand, we virtually imply, by our treatment of little children, that they have one sort of consciousness and that grown people have quite another sort. Such a theory runs counter to the results of our study of even the baby-mind, for we have found strong proof that, within the first years, the child possesses all the elements of his lifetime's experience. And no one can intimately know children or vividly remember his own childhood, without the conviction that a child is equal to abstract thought and to intricate reasoning, as well as to accurate memorizing; that his heart may be not only open to the gentle emotions of love and pity, but a prey to the devastating passions of jealousy and envy; and that he is capable of great loyalties, of high determinations and of tremendous conflicts of will.

There are in truth wide differences between the childhood and the adult experience. They consist, however, not in the child's lack of fundamental forms of consciousness, but in his lack of certain specific experiences, and in his greater interest in other experiences. This is clearly shown by any sympathetic observation of the emotional life of children. We may consider, first, the delights of life which we grown people do not share with them — for example, the little child's ecstatic joy in mere running and jumping and shouting, without apparent end or purpose. Evidently, this is a result of that perfect exuberance of vigor which few adults experience, but as enjoyment, it certainly does not differ from the satisfaction which a grown person gains from a swinging walk or from a brisk dumb-bell exercise. A child's pleasure in his collections is another instance of the same sort. He eagerly amasses objects far removed from a grown person's interest, old bottles, garish advertisements or common buttons, but his delight in these possessions is the very same sort of feeling as his mother's enjoyment of her collection of rare laces or his father's eagerness to secure first editions.

The griefs and fears of the child are, in the same way, conditioned by his ignorance. It is usually held that a child is incapable of deep emotion, because he is unmoved by desolating bereavements and separations. The truth is, rather, that the child does not sorrow, because he does not know or understand. Mrs. Burnett has made this very clear, in her charming story of "The One I knew the Best of All." "Papa in her mind was represented by a gentleman who had curling brown hair, and who laughed and said affectionately funny things," but "she did not feel very familiar with him and did not see him very often"; and "when some one carried her into a bedroom and . . . held her that she might look down at papa lying quite still upon the pillow . . . she was not frightened, and looked down with quiet interest and respect." But this same little girl, incapable both of sorrow for the father whom she did not really know and of frightened awe in the face of the mystery which she did not realize as mystery, used to wake with terror at night, and tremble through the day, at the joking threat of a big policeman. She was not, then, incapable of emotion, but she could feel emotion only when she stood in a close personal relation; and she was too ignorant either to look forward to the consequences of her father's death or to estimate, at its proper value, the big policeman's threat.

The poverty of the child's experience, coupled with the vividness of his imagination, is responsible for his most abandoned delight and for his most palpitating fears. Pegasus, the Chimæra and the Golden Fleece are as real to him as the butcher's horse and the house-cat and the tiger-skin rug in the drawing-room; and he simply doesn't know enough of the ways of this world to realize that winged horses and fire-breathing dragons belong to a story-world only. So he dreads the dark, which prevents his seeing and guarding himself against the lurking monster, and he pleases himself with enchanting dreams of winged horses and of treasures rivalling the Golden Fleece.

An adult would be incapable of these special fears and pleasures; but as fears and pleasures, irrespective of their objects, the child's experiences do not differ from the adult emotions. Moreover, far more often than we realize, children share in emotions commonly supposed to be exclusive possessions of the adult. Æsthetic joy is probably one of these. One can hardly read Pierre Loti's accounts of his childhood delight—in the sunsets seen from the high windows of 'Grandetante Berthe,' in the forests of Limoise, in the blue dome of the sky, as it arched over the chateau of Castelnan—without the conviction that children may early experience that which we know as æsthetic feeling.

Quite as common as the conviction that little children are careless and rather heartless little animals, with an emotional life entirely their own, is the theory that they do not think or reason, that their vivid imaginations and their relatively ready memories really take the place of the later developed capacity to reason. Now it is highly probable, as we know, that the sensational and affective consciousness precedes the relational, in the conscious life of the baby; but there is every likelihood that the child of two years compares and recognizes; and the statements of little children, together with grown people's memories of their earliest years, tend strongly to confirm the belief that even little children reflect and reason. We are apt to deny that they reason because their actions seem to us so absurd. We forget that the premises, on which their reflection is based, are conditioned by that same poverty of experience which so affects the objects of their emotion.

These conclusions have a very practical bearing, and though, as psychologists, we have no real right to moralize, we shall nevertheless indulge ourselves in a pedagogical observation. The perverse and persistent confusion of children's undoubted ignorance of the world's ways, with their alleged incapacity for thought and for serious feeling, is responsible for most of the mistakes we make in our dealings with them. The common misfortune of a child's experience is its isolation. He early learns that he is considered a being apart. He may be royally cared for and devotedly loved, but he is not understood, and he is accounted incapable of understanding much which goes on about him. Under these circumstances, he lives his life alone. He does not recount his pleasures, because he knows that no one will enjoy them with him; he silently endures his fears, because he cannot bear to have them laughed at; he does not confide his perplexities, for he knows that nobody suspects him of thinking about the disquieting subjects. So his whole childhood may be darkened, by tormenting fears of evil spirits, who will pounce upon him if he inadvertently treads on the seam of a carpet, or by disturbing religious doubts, quite unsuspected by the parents who might readily set them at rest. The truth is, that the natural and happy development of a child is conditioned on a relation of entire confidence in older friends, who can control his emotional and reflective life by enlarging his knowledge and by correcting his ignorance. But such a relation of confidence is impossible until grown people learn to treat seriously the questions and the hesitating confidences of children, and to respect the sincerity of their thoughts and their emotional life. At the best, grave dangers of misinterpretation beset us. We have only the obscure media of children's confused words, and of our often unsympathetic hearing, through which to read their thoughts. To meet the child's bewildered expressions with indifference, with ridicule, or with reproof is to drive him back into the isolation of his own experience.

PART II

CHAPTER XXVII

ABNORMAL CONSCIOUS STATES OF PERSONS IN HEALTH

ABNORMAL Psychology, in the widest sense of the term, includes the study of the varying forms of insanity, as well as the discussion of abnormal phases of the normal consciousness. We restrict ourselves to the latter subject, considering in most detail the phenomena of dreaming, of visions and of hypnotism.

I. PHENOMENA OF ABNORMAL CONSCIOUSNESS

(a) Dreams

There is an obvious advantage in beginning here, for one may directly consider one's own dreams, instead of making inferences from the words and actions of other people. But though the student of the dream-consciousness has the advantage of studying his own experience, his knowledge of his dreams is much impaired by the difficulty and uncertainty of remembering them. The dreams of the early night are usually forgotten, and those which we recall in the morning are a small proportion of all which we have dreamed. A curious experience of the writer illustrates this danger. For some months she kept a careful record of all dreams, writing them down from memory as soon as she awoke. In this way, she accustomed herself to write legibly even in the dark. One night, a long dream was recorded with a pencil so blunted that it made mere scratches on the paper, and in the morning the disheartening discovery was made, that the dream had been completely forgotten, in spite of the fact that the dreamer had waked enough to write it down. A second danger is the likelihood of supplementing our fragmentary dream-memories, by images which did not actually occur in the dreams, but which we unwittingly supply to fill the gaps. The main requirements of dream investigation are, therefore: first, completeness in the record of them, so that one's study may be based, not on a very few striking dreams, but on a larger number of representative dreams; and second, the habit of recording dreams as soon as possible after their occurrence. Dreams, recorded immediately on waking from them, are obviously the most trustworthy materials of study. The statements which follow are based upon the writer's records, during seven successive weeks, of her own remembered dreams, and on several other records of the same type.

The dream is most simply described as consciousness during sleep. Its essential features are the sleeper's unconsciousness of his bodily state, and his fallacious consciousness of the perceptual reality of dream-objects. When, for example, I dreamed last night of floating about in a gondola, I was obviously unconscious of my body, which lay relatively motionless, under an eider-down quilt, in a room of forty degrees Fahrenheit; and I mistook my own memory, of a summer day on the Grand Canal, for an experience actually shared with other people. This characteristic dream illusion is very readily explained. The conditions of sleep make it impossible to compare our images with other people's experience, and even with our own percepts. But in the waking consciousness our images are felt to be unreal, precisely because we do compare them with the more stable, and often more vivid, objects of perception; and because we realize, originally by communication, that

other people do not share the image experience. Without
these standards of comparison, the vivid images of our
hours of revery would certainly seem as real as our dream
experiences. I imagine, for example, the ride from St.
Malo to Dinan, in the little steamboat on the river
Rance. I picture vividly the serpentine windings of the
river, the ruined chateaus and moss-grown towers of the
banks, the coiffed peasant women, three abreast, harnessed
to a boat which they drag along and, finally, the winding
streets and ruined walls of Dinan itself, built high upon its
hill. But I realize, throughout, the privacy of my imagination, because it so sharply contradicts my prosaic outlook
on American city streets, electric cars and ten-storied
buildings. If, however, I were dreaming of Dinan, my
eyes would be closed to my surroundings, and there would
be no perceived reality opposing my dream visions; the
dream experience, accordingly, would be undistinguished
from the common world of perception.

There are at least three stages in the dream illusion.
The first has been already described, as the mere absence
of any feeling of the privacy or unreality of the dream experience. In the next stage, one attributes one's own
thoughts and feelings to other individuals; for example,
one dreams of forgetting a date and of hearing some one
else give it correctly. Here, there is a failure of definite
recollection. A vivid speech image is followed by an
equally vivid consciousness of some person, and the two
are then closely associated. The dream illusion, finally,
may reach the level of what is called changed or doubled
personality: this phenomenon we shall later discuss in
some detail.

The contrasts between dream and waking are ordinarily
so strongly emphasized, that it is even more important
to consider their essential likenesses. Just as we have
found that the child has the same sorts of consciousness
as the adult, so also we discover, within our dreams, every

type of conscious material, sensational, attributive and relational.

In the experience, so far as it is known, of most dreamers, visual elements predominate: that is to say, most people dream of how things look, and some, indeed, describe their dreams as purely visual — shifting pantomimes, as it were, of colored figures and objects. Many of us, however, dream also of sounds and of dermal sensations; and conversation, which involves both auditory and tactile elements, plays an important part in the dreams of many persons. People dream far less frequently of tastes and of odors, so that dreams of banquets break off just before one actually begins to eat; and we often decide that what we at first remembered as a dream of tasting or of smelling was merely a dream of the 'look' of objects which, in waking life, would also have been tasted and smelt. In spite of their rarity, however, there is no reason to doubt that, as there may be taste and smell images, so there may be taste and smell dreams. The most accurate dream records confirm this view.[1]

The relative frequency of the different sorts of sense imagery, in the dreams of four observers, is shown by the following table, in which each per cent shows the proportion of dreams in which one class of sense-images occurred.[2]

SENSE-IMAGES IN DREAMS

OBSERVERS	VISUAL	AUDITORY	DERMAL	GUSTATORY	OLFACTORY
S. (133 dreams)	85.0%	57.1%	5.3%	.0%	1.5%
C. (165 ")	77.0	49.1	8.5	.0	1.2
W. (141 ")	100.0	90.0	13.5	12.0	15.0
H. (150 ")	72.7	54.6	6.0	2.7	2.7
Total, 589	83.2%	62.1%	8.3%	3.6%	4.9%

[1] Cf. E. B. Titchener, *American Journal of Psychology*, Vol. VI., p. 507; G. A. Andrews, *ibid.*, Vol. XI.; and see next note.
[2] M. W. Calkins, *American Journal of Psychology*, Vol. V., p. 321; S. Weed and F. Hallam, *ibid.*, Vol. VII., p. 407.

Though there are dreams which, so far as remembered, are quite unemotional, affective elements are, nevertheless, very prominent in many dreams. There is, perhaps, no point in which the individuality of the dreamer is more manifest. To one person, dreams, though seldom vividly disagreeable, are 'apt to be pervaded by a generally unpleasant feeling,'[1] but another dreamer says, " I look forward with delight to my hours of sleep."[2] Fear, shame and perplexity are frequent forms of unpleasant dream emotion; experiences of pleasure are harder to classify, yet even æsthetic pleasure occurs in one's dreams, though it is rare. It is clearly suggested in the record which follows:[3] " I went into the garden and there were all the roses beginning to open. A little bluebell rang out, and the roses began slowly to unfold. The garden was a perfect bower of beauty; every rose on every bush was opened, the bluebells were all ringing, the other flowers all opened, the birds began to sing."

Relational experiences are no less prominent in our dreams. To begin with, every constant dreamer admits the occurrence of recognition in his dreams. Sometimes he correctly recognizes events which have really happened in the waking life, but, quite as often, the feeling of familiarity attaches to imaged events which have never actually occurred. Explicit thinking and reasoning are so often reported by accurate observers, in the records of their dreams, that we may deny, quite dogmatically, the frequent assertion that dreams are characterized by entire absence of thought. Dream reasoning, though sometimes accurate, is often incorrect, and it often is based on very absurd premises. Dr. Sanford, for example, after dexterously fitting a dream-baby with a new skull,[4] discovers that the baby can talk. Dr. Sanford, in his dream, ingeniously reasons that " by getting an older skull [the baby] came

[1] M. W. Calkins, *op. cit., American Journal of Psychology*, Vol. V., p. 327.
[2] *Ibid.*, Vol. VII., p. 408.   [4] *Ibid.*, Vol. VII., p. 325, note.
[3] *Ibid.*, Vol. VII., p. 409.

into . . . the size and attainments of the previous owner of the skull. This," he observes, "puts the active and organizing principle—the soul—in the skull instead of the brain."

Will and moral consciousness, also, in spite of assertions to the contrary, certainly occur occasionally in dreams. Both are found, for example, in a dream recorded by a college student, in which she was required to make a dissection for which directions were written in Greek : " I was in distress because my instruments would not work, and I had forgotten what I knew of the Greek. I reasoned with myself about the honesty of having some one translate the directions. After much thought I decided that I would not have the directions translated, because the work was to be individual . . . and this would be deceiving." [1]

It is easy to describe in a general way the physiological correlates of dreaming. All dreams, in the first place, are conditioned by the excitation of brain-centres; and many, perhaps all, dreams are conditioned also by the functioning of some sensational end-organ. When, for example, one dreams of brilliant autumn woods, and wakes to find the sun shining full upon one's eyelids, it is evident that the excitation of retina and optic nerve has preceded that of the visual brain-centre. Very few dreams, it is true, can be traced directly to the external stimulation, and it is possible that the brain-centres may be stimulated directly through changes in the blood supply; but, on the other hand, slight sounds, like those of a flapping window curtain, changes in the pressure of one's coverings and internal bodily changes must occur frequently during sleep, and may form the starting-point of every dream.

(b) Abnormal Experiences of the Waking Life

1. *Waking Illusions and Hallucinations.* — History is full of accounts of illusions and hallucinations of waking

---

[1] S. Weed and F. Hallam, *op. cit.*, Vol. VII., p. 408.

people. The daimon of Sokrates, the blazing sword of Savonarola, the devil who used to argue with Luther, and the Madonna who appeared to Raphael are illustrations which at once suggest themselves. It is not always easy to decide from the descriptions which we have of them, whether these visions are illusions, that is, conditioned in part by peripheral excitation, or whether they are hallucinations, that is, conditioned by cerebral excitation only. Sometimes, however, the distinction is obvious. For example, the phantoms which haunted Charles IX. after the massacre of St. Bartholemew were hallucinations, but the image of Byron which appeared to Sir Walter Scott was a mere illusion, for the clothes of the figure consisted, Sir Walter discovered, of the folds of a curtain.

Far more important as materials for study than these vivid, yet often confused and unverified, stories from which we have quoted, are the massed results of an *International Census on Waking Hallucinations*, made by the Society for Psychical Research.[1] The question on which this study is based is the following: "Have you ever, when believing yourself to be completely awake, had a vivid impression of seeing or being touched by a living being or inanimate object, or of hearing a voice; which impression, so far as you could discover, was not due to any external physical cause?" To this question 27,329 answers were given, and of these 3271, or 11.96 per cent, were affirmative: in other words, one out of every twelve of the persons, reached by the investigation, asserted that he had experienced hallucinations. This percentage, however, is, in all probability, too high to be representative, for the larger the number of answers received by any one collector of these statistics, the smaller was the number of affirmative replies. It follows that if the investigation were further extended, the percentage would probably fall still lower.[2] Yet, with all

[1] *Proceedings of the Society of Psychical Research*, Vol. X., 1894.
[2] Edmund Parish, "Hallucinations and Illusions" (Scribner, 1897), pp. 85 *seq.*

allowances for overestimation, the fact remains that waking hallucinations must be commoner than many of us think. Visual hallucinations far outnumber the others: of 2232 cases completely described, 1441 included visual elements, 850 were partly auditory, and only 244 were tactile. Most of these hallucinations related to people, living or dead, but a few represented angels or supernatural beings, and a slightly larger number were grotesque or horrible figures. About one-twentieth of them were indefinite or indescribable. Persons between the ages of fifteen and thirty reported more than one-half the number of these illusions and hallucinations, and men reported only two-thirds as many as women, 9.75 per cent as compared with 14.56 per cent. The general conclusion of the Report is " that this apparent difference should, to a great extent, be attributed to the fact that men, among the pressing interests and occupations of their lives, forget these experiences sooner." [1]

Besides the involuntary hallucinations and illusions, there is the whole class of illusions which are voluntarily induced. The commonest method of bringing about illusions is known as crystal vision: the experimenter looks fixedly at a glass sphere, at a mirror surface or even at a glass of water, until there appear pictures in its reflecting surface. Crystal-gazing, it may be noticed, is an ancient custom. Oriental people, as well as Greeks and Romans, are known to have practised it with many reflecting objects, for example, with metal mirrors, beryl stones, wells, and liquids held in the palm of the hand. Crystal vision has even been observed among the uncivilized races of the South Sea Islands. In the sixteenth and seventeenth century it flourished in the English court and on the continent.[2] The images which appear within these different crystals are usually reproductions of former experiences, and often of long-forgotten objects or scenes. One sees,

---

[1] Cf. Parish, *op. cit.*, p. 84.   [2] Cf. Parish, *op. cit.*, pp. 63–66.

for instance, a forgotten date, or a garden familiar in early childhood. The images, on the other hand, may be purely imaginary, as when Mrs. Verral sees in her crystal[1] colors so vivid that they leave an after-image in complementary colors. The images seen in crystals may be, finally, veridical images of actual scenes beyond the range of the normal vision of the crystal seer. Images of this sort we shall later discuss, in considering the general subject of veridical phenomena in the abnormal consciousness.

It would be possible to include, in this account of abnormal experiences of the waking life, a description of the chief phenomena of synæsthesia, including so-called colored hearing and mental forms. Most of these experiences are, however, mere instances of ordinary imagination, and they are not therefore considered in this chapter.[2]

2. *Automatic Writing.* — One abnormal motor experience, relatively common in the waking life, must be very briefly described. It is known as automatic writing, and is of the following nature:[3] the subject, provided with a pencil and so placed that the hand which holds the pencil is hidden from his eyes, unconsciously responds to stimulation of the hand. If the hand be pressed three times, it will make three marks when these pressures are over; if the hand is guided and made to draw a single letter, it may go on to complete a word. Normal persons possess the rudiments of automatic writing, passively repeating uniform movements when the experimenter has initiated them, following the rhythm of a metronome or even outlining figures, or writing names, of which they themselves are thinking. The emphasized feature of this experience is the subject's entire unconsciousness of the movements of his own hands. In hysteria and in hypnosis the phenomena of automatic writing are very marked.

[1] *Proceedings of the Society for Psychical Research*, Vol. VIII., pp. 473 *seq*
[2] Cf. Bibliography.
[3] Cf. A. Binet, " Double Consciousness," pp. 80 *seq.*

(c) *Hypnosis*

Hypnosis differs in two general ways from the forms of the abnormal consciousness already discussed. In the first place, it is brought about by the influence of some other person or persons, instead of being explained solely by bodily or conscious changes in the life of the individual. The hypnotized subject, furthermore, almost always forgets, in his waking state, the experience of the hypnotic sleep. It follows that the hypnotic condition, unlike the dream or the vision, is studied chiefly by inference from the words and acts of hypnotized subjects. Hypnosis, therefore, is in the main a branch of comparative psychology, whereas the study of dreams, and even of visions, belongs to what has been named introspective psychology.[1] Hypnosis has been defined as a state of abnormal suggestibility. It may be described, provisionally, as the relatively complete obedience of one individual to the suggestions of another. It is brought about in many ways; but all methods unite in compelling the absorbed attention of the subject, or person to be hypnotized, and conversely in drawing his attention from every other feature of his surroundings. Often, this result is gained by requiring the subject to look fixedly into the eyes of the hypnotizer; at other times, the subject is asked to regard a brilliant object which the hypnotizer holds; again, the attention is gained by certain rhythmic movements of the hypnotizer; sometimes, finally, there is need of nothing except his spoken exhortation. In all these cases the aim is, as has been said, to direct the full attention of the subject upon the hypnotizer, and to divert him from every other interest.

The hypnotic subject, so far as his general surroundings are concerned, is, therefore, like a sleeping person. He is relatively deaf and blind to what goes on about him,

---

[1] Cf. p. 352.

and, indeed, in most stages of hypnotism he is outwardly like a sleeper, for his eyes are closed and his limbs are relaxed. In relation to the hypnotizer, on the contrary, the subject is intensely awake, and alive to every direction or suggestion. An illustration, suggested by one of the writers on hypnotism, may make this clearer. He compares the sleeping state to a chandelier with several burners dimly lighted; the waking state to a chandelier with all the burners turned on; and the hypnotic state to a chandelier with the gas turned off from all the burners save one, but issuing at full pressure from that one.

For an adequate discussion of the nature and conditions of hypnosis, the student must at once be referred to the books which treat the topic in detail.[1] This chapter will attempt an outline, only, of its most significant phenomena. It is important to notice that there are many degrees of hypnosis, in other words, that the subject follows the suggestions of the hypnotizer, to greatly varying extents. In very light hypnosis, for example, the hypnotist may be able only to prevent certain simple movements; in complete hypnosis, as we shall see, the hypnotist may influence the secretions of the body or induce complicated movements, and may bring about positive illusions, or even affect the thought and emotion of the subject.

It is not easy to classify the stages of hypnosis, for these vary greatly with different subjects and with different methods of hypnotization. A simple and comparatively satisfactory classification is suggested by Max Dessoir and adopted by Albert Moll.[2] It distinguishes two important stages of hypnosis. In the first, only the voluntary muscles are affected. The second stage is characterized both by mental disturbances, and by bodily changes due to contraction of involuntary as well as voluntary muscles. Roughly speaking, no more than a

---

[1] Cf. Bibliography. [2] "Hypnotism," p. 51.

third of the whole number of hypnoses reach this second stage.

The nature of these hypnotic phenomena will now be described and illustrated, in more detail. The hypnotic influence on the voluntary muscles must, therefore, be first considered. These may be negatively or positively affected: the subject, after the hypnotic state has been induced, may be unable to open his eyes or to raise his hand, if the hypnotizer asserts that the movement is impossible; or again, the subject extends his arm, holds it motionless and lets it drop in imitation of the hypnotist's movement. In deep hypnotic states, complete rigidity of the body may be induced so that if the subject's head be placed on one chair and his feet on the other, his body will not double up between them. Very complicated acts may also be performed: for instance, the subject lifts objects from a table or whirls several times round.[1] The subject may even imitate the delicate movements of the vocal organs. Trilby's musical achievements, for example, were due to Svengali's hypnotic influence; and, years ago, a hypnotized girl imitated the singing of Jenny Lind.

The deep hypnosis of what has been called the second stage is often characterized by involuntary muscle contractions, and thus by disturbances of pulse, secretion and bodily temperature. Such changes are readily explained by analogy with the normal life of emotion and attention; for there is no doubt, as we have found, that circulatory changes accompany emotional states. Certain other bodily phenomena of deep hypnosis are harder to explain. These are the structural bodily changes. There are, for example, well authenticated though infrequent cases, in which blisters have been produced, by a hypnotizer who assured his subject that a burning object would be applied to his skin. We may quote, in illustration, from Kraft Ebing's account of his well-known patient, Ilma

[1] Cf. Moll, *op. cit.*, p. 63.

S——[1]: "The experimenter draws with the percussion hammer a cross on the skin over the biceps of the left arm, and suggests to the patient that on the following day at twelve o'clock, in the same place, a red cross shall appear. . . . [On the next day] at eleven o'clock . . . the patient wonders that she has an itching, excoriated spot on her right upper arm. . . . The examination shows that a red cross is to be seen on the right arm exactly at the place corresponding with that marked on the left side yesterday." Later a 'sharply defined scab' is formed.

We must turn now to hypnotic disturbances of consciousness; and, first among them, we shall consider the sense illusions and hallucinations, classifying them as positive or negative. The suggestion of the hypnotizer may induce illusions or even actual hallucinations of every sort. He may point out to his subject certain black blotches on a white background, telling him that they are birds, and may thus call up to his subject's mind a vivid landscape. Or, the hypnotizer may hand to his subject a cup of water or even of ink, telling him that it is coffee. The subject drinks it eagerly, complains, perhaps, that it is warm, and shows by the expression of his face that he is quite unconscious of its real nature. Indeed, the alleged coffee may produce actual bodily effects, a flushed face, for example. For the same reason, the hypnotic subject sneezes when told that he has taken snuff, and trembles with cold when told that he is standing on ice. His eyes water as he eats an apple which the hypnotist has described as an onion, but he sniffs at ammonia with impunity if he is told that it is eau de cologne. These, of course, are instances of illusion, brought about by means of an external object. Genuine hallucinations can also be induced: a subject, for example, will hear the sounds of a piano if they are merely suggested by the hypnotist.

[1] "An Experimental Study in the Domain of Hypnotism," by R. von Krafft Ebing, translated by C. G. Chaddock (Putnam, 1889), pp. 57–60. Cf. pp. 78, 96.

So far, we have spoken of fallacious perceptions of a positive sort. The negative illusions and hallucinations of the hypnotized subject are far more difficult of explanation. The hypnotizer, for example, indicates some person who is present and says decidedly, "This man has left the room: he is no longer present." Forthwith, the hypnotized subject utterly disregards the banished individual, failing to reply to his questions and even running against him. "Part of an object," Moll says,[1] "can be made invisible in the same way. We can cause people to appear headless and armless, or make them disappear altogether by putting on a particular hat, as in the story of the Magic Cap. The situation may be varied in any way we please." In like manner, the hypnotizer may suggest to his subject that he is unable to see or to hear or to feel pain. The pain-sensations are, however, least susceptible to suggestion, and the value of hypnotism as an anæsthetic has been much exaggerated.[2]

We must next consider the phenomena of the hypnotic memory. In the lighter hypnotic states there are no abnormalities of memory, but two characteristics of the memory of deeper hypnosis should be emphasized. The hypnotized subject is able to remember both the events of former hypnoses and those of his normal experience; on the other hand, he seldom remembers, in his normal state, the events of the hypnotic state. The books on hypnotism are full of illustrations of all these phenomena. Cases are reported in which hypnotized subjects remember the events of hypnoses ten and thirteen years earlier, even when the same occurrences are utterly forgotten in the normal state. The intensification of memories of the waking life is shown by the tendency of hypnotized subjects to talk in the forgotten language of earlier years. A well-known illustration is the story of a hypnotized English officer, who surprised the bystanders by speaking

---

[1] *Op. cit.*, p. 97.   [2] Moll, *op. cit.*, pp. 99 and 330.

in a strange language. This unknown tongue proved to be Welsh, which the Englishman had learned, as a child, but had forgotten. The ability to remember, in the normal state, events of the deeper hypnosis varies greatly in individuals. Efforts to recall these events to the subject's mind are often successful, and yet, as a general rule, such events of hypnosis are forgotten.

The most puzzling of hypnotic experiences is closely connected with the facts of memory. It is known as post-hypnotic suggestion, and may be described as the tendency of hypnotic subjects to follow, even in their waking lives, the suggestions of the hypnotist. We must consider this tendency in more detail. The hypnotist, for example, before waking his subject addresses him in some such fashion as the following: "To-morrow, at twelve o'clock, you will move the Lucca della Robia madonna from its present position over the chimney-piece to the empty space between the two windows." At twelve o'clock on the following day, the subject, apparently in his normal condition, actually makes the suggested change, without remembering the suggestion of the hypnotist. The readily hypnotized subject may, in this way, be influenced to perform simple and complicated acts, and also to experience sense-illusions.

It is obvious that the main value, as well as the chief danger, of hypnotism lies in just this susceptibility of the hypnotic subject to post-hypnotic suggestion. Physicians who make use of hypnotism suggest to the patient that he is freed from disturbing symptoms, and that he will remain freed from them after waking. The practice is based on the admitted truth that "a number of diseases can be cured or relieved merely by making the patient believe that he will soon be better, and by firmly implanting this conviction in his mind."[1] To this end, post-hypnotic suggestion has been employed, with distinct success, for more than thirty years by Liebault and Bernheim at Nancy; and

[1] Moll, *op. cit.*, p. 291.

hundreds of doctors, in all parts of the world, have employed like methods. Indeed, the dependent attitude of patient to physician in itself predisposes the patient to fill the conditions of the hypnotized subject. It is not, therefore, surprising to discover that celebrated physicians of antiquity induced what would now be called hypnotic states, for example, the temple sleep which characterized both Greek and Egyptian cures. Not merely nervous diseases, so-called, but all diseases and symptoms which have no anatomical cause have been successfully treated by hypnotism, for example, rheumatic and neuralgic pain, loss of appetite, certain disorders of sight, stammering, chorea and writer's cramp (of central origin). The success of the treatment is dependent on the extent of the hypnosis and on the susceptibility of the subject. It also depends, of course, on the patience, skill and experience of the physician.[1] The objections urged against the therapeutic use of hypnotism are, first, the fact that the patient submits himself to the relatively complete control of another person; and second, the fact that the patient grows in susceptibility, so that he is more readily hypnotized with every treatment.

In unscrupulous hands, the ability to give post-hypnotic suggestions may, of course, be grossly abused. There are reasonably well-attested instances of crimes committed and of large sums of money given away, in accordance with post-hypnotic suggestion. In such cases, the discovery of the guilty hypnotist is made difficult by the fact, already indicated, that the hypnotized subject so seldom remembers the events of the hypnotic state. The best authorities, however, agree in the conclusion that only individuals predisposed to criminal acts can be influenced to actual crime. "It is very difficult," Moll says, "to suggest anything that is opposed to the confirmed habits of the subject. . . . The more an action is repulsive to his disposition the stronger

[1] Cf. Moll, *op. cit.*, Chapter VIII.

is his resistance." On the other hand, a depraved subject may solicit criminal suggestions. The surest means of avoiding the danger of crimes, hypnotically suggested, is the legal restriction of the use of hypnotism to competent physicians and scientists. Some such limitation of the right to hypnotize is warmly recommended by the continental writers, Liegeois, Delacroix and others.[1]

In conclusion, we must briefly outline an entirely different theory of the nature of hypnosis. This is the doctrine, most ably championed by the French physician, Charcot, that hypnosis is a pathological state, in other words, a nerve disease. Charcot distinguishes two main forms, *le petit* and *le grand hypnotisme,* and claims that the latter has three well-marked stages, cataleptic, lethargic, and somnambulic, each capable of excitation through physical stimulation, without suggestion. The suggestibility of the hypnotic subject is, on his view, merely a symptom of the disease. It is fair to say, however, that the theory of Charcot has been completely set aside by the observations of Liebault and Bernheim, in Nancy, and by the conclusions of most modern students of hypnotism.

II. ANALOGY OF ABNORMAL STATES TO THE NORMAL EXPERIENCE

Though we have more than once considered the likeness of abnormal to normal consciousness, it is well now to summarize the resemblances and to emphasize them. It has been shown already that the dream-experience includes all the elements of the waking consciousness, and that the dream illusion, as a whole, closely resembles the absorbed revery in which we do not reflect on the privacy and unreality of our images. These statements apply equally to waking illusions and hallucinations. We have seen already that the percept is usually, though not invariably, more

[1] Cf. Moll, *op. cit.,* Chapter VIII.

intense than the image, and that the only constant distinction is the privacy of imagination, as contrasted with the community of experience in perception. Illusion and hallucination are abnormally vivid sense-experiences, which we incorrectly suppose that we share with other people. From this analysis, it is clear that crystal-gazing induces illusions, simply because it tends to divert attention from one's surroundings, and to concentrate it on an object relatively empty of interest. One is thus absorbed in one's images, and one ceases to compare them with perceptual reality; they therefore gain a fallacious air of being common, instead of individual, experiences. The phenomena, finally, of somnambulism and of automatic writing seem to be instances of ideo-motor or of reflex action.

The essential point of likeness, between the waking consciousness and hypnosis, is the individual's susceptibility, in both the normal and the abnormal state, to the influence of another person. It is idle to deny this relation. The most independent of mortals shapes his actions and judgments, in one particular or another, in accordance with the ideas of somebody else. The picture in which he delighted becomes a crude daub of color, if this influential critic pronounces against it; the theory which he scouted gains dignity and impressiveness, at a word of approval from his mentor. Dull tasks are undertaken, favorite pastimes are given over, action and theory alike are remodelled, at the suggestion of some one whose opinion is valued. Now this everyday truth that an individual does profoundly influence the life of thought and action of other men is the basal principle of hypnosis.

Coördinate with this resemblance of hypnotic state to waking life is the likeness of hypnosis to the dream life, in that it excludes the percepts and images which oppose those of the hypnotist. This analogy of hypnosis to the dream is of real significance. The hypnotic illusion, though differently excited, is, in principle, like the dream illusion — a vivid idea uncompared with perceptual reality. The movements of the hypnotized subject, in response to suggestion, resemble, in like manner, the movements of somnambulism, which is simply the acting out of dream images.

III. DIFFERENCES OF ABNORMAL AND NORMAL STATES

We have no right to obscure the peculiarities of these abnormal states, by insisting only on their likeness to the waking consciousness. The remainder of this chapter is devoted, therefore, to a brief consideration of the two particulars, in which these forms of abnormal consciousness most widely diverge from the waking experience.

(a) *Changes in Personality*

Both dreams and hypnotic states may be characterized by what is known as a change or a doubling of personality; for example, one may dream of being a little child or of attending one's own funeral. In the writer's own experience, such dreams involve no loss of the consciousness of self, but rather a vivid imagination and a failing memory. The dreamer forgets the events of his past experience and even his own appearance, and adopts another environment as his own; yet all the time he is conscious of the old self as the centre of these new experiences. Occasionally, however, a real change of personality appears to occur. For example, a careful observer of dreams, Miss Weed, recalls the following dream.[1] " I seem to be an old minister, lean, tall, with long, thin, white hair. My coat is a long Prince Albert, worn at the elbow; my tie is black. I realize that I am soon to die. I review my whole career as a pastor, call to mind several people and some of the details of the work. I think of some of the sermons I have preached, and feel a strong sense of my shortcom-

[1] " A Study of the Dream Consciousness," *American Journal of Psychology*, Vol. VII., p. 411.

ings." The writer adds: "In this entire dream I do not view the personality which I have assumed as one apart, but as one from within. I do not see the long, gray hair and the black tie, but imagine them as one imagines any bodily characteristic or any article of dress not in direct vision."

The hypnotic state offers many examples of changed personality, so far at least as this can be externally observed. The deeply hypnotized subject, if told that he is Napoleon, is likely to adopt a military stride and to develop pugnacious tendencies. Kraft Ebing's subject, Ilma S——, when it was suggested to her that she was eight years old, played contentedly for hours at a time with a doll, wrote an unformed hand, and made childish errors in spelling words which she normally spelled correctly.

Even more surprising is the discovery or the creation, through hypnotic methods, of regular alternations of personality. One of the best-known of these cases is that of Janet's patient Leonie. We quote a translation, by James, of Janet's account of this subject: "This woman, whose life sounds more like an improbable romance than a genuine history, has had attacks of natural somnambulism since the age of three years. She has been hypnotized constantly by all sorts of persons from the age of sixteen upwards, and she is now forty-five. Whilst her normal life developed in one way in the midst of her poor country surroundings, her second life was passed in drawing-rooms and doctors' offices, and naturally took an entirely different direction. To-day, when in her normal state, this poor peasant woman is a serious and rather sad person, calm and slow, very mild with every one, and extremely timid: to look at her one would never suspect the personage which she contains. But hardly is she put to sleep hypnotically when a metamorphosis occurs. Her face is no longer the same. She keeps her eyes closed, it is true, but the acuteness of her other senses supplies their place. She is gay, noisy, restless, sometimes insupportably so. She remains good-natured, but has acquired a singular tendency to irony and sharp jesting. Nothing is more curious than to hear her after a sitting when she has received a visit from strangers who wished to see her asleep. She gives a word-portrait of them, apes their manners, pretends to know their little ridiculous aspects and passions, and for each invents a romance. To this character must be added the possession of an enormous number of recollections, whose existence she does not even suspect when awake, for her amnesia is then complete. . . . She refuses the name of Leonie and takes that of Leontine (Leonie 2) to which her first magnetizers had accustomed her. 'That good woman is not myself,' she says, 'she is too stupid!' To herself, Leontine or Leonie 2, she attributes all the sensations and all the actions, in a word all the conscious experiences which she has undergone in somnambulism, and knits them together to make the history of her already long life. To Leonie 1 [as M. Janet calls the waking woman] on the other hand, she exclusively ascribes the events lived through in waking hours. But it is the same with her second or deepest state of trance. When after the renewed passes, syncope, etc., she reaches the condition which I have called Leonie 3, she is another person still. Serious and grave, instead of being a restless child, she speaks slowly and moves but little. Again she separates herself from the waking Leonie 1. 'A good but rather stupid woman,' she says, 'and not me.' And she also separates herself from Leonie 2: 'How can you see anything of me in that crazy creature?' she says. 'Fortunately I am nothing for her.'"

Other well-attested instances of changed personality are reported, and several of these occur naturally, or as result of illness, but without hypnotization. The chapter of the James Psychology, which has already been quoted,[1] contains accounts of many of these cases.

[1] *Op. cit.*, Vol. I., Chapter X., "The Consciousness of Self."

2 E

It would be idle to pretend that such experiences have been satisfactorily explained, but an adequate discussion, of the theories which have been advanced, would involve us in a metaphysical consideration of personality. We shall merely, therefore, consider two theoretical tendencies. The first is that of very many writers on abnormal psychology. It supposes that each personality includes, besides the everyday self of the normal consciousness (the supraliminal self, as Mr. Myers calls it),[1] one or more split-off and relatively distinct selves (subliminal selves), the selves of the dream life, the vision and the hypnotic state. The everyday self is, on this theory, usually unconscious of the subliminal experiences, but occasionally takes notice of them, for example, when it remembers visions or dreams. On the other hand, the subliminal self (whether dream-self, hypnotized self, or unexplained second self) ordinarily remembers the experience of the everyday self.

On this theory, it should be noticed, even people who have never observed, in their own experience, any alterations of personality are regarded as none the less made up of supraliminal and subliminal selves. In other words, the normal is explained on the analogy of the abnormal consciousness. The argument, on which the theory is based, may be named an argument from continuity, and runs somewhat as follows: Some dreams and visions and hypnoses involve changes of personality, and must be explained by the hypothesis of a complex personality, made up of supraliminal and subliminal selves; moreover, all abnormal experiences may be accounted for in the same way, and since one hypothesis may serve for all the phenomena, it is reasonable to make use of it.

Opposed to this hypothesis of the subliminal self or selves, is a radically different theoretical tendency, which

[1] "The Subliminal Self," by F. W. H. Myers, *Proceedings of the Society of Psychical Research*, Vol. VII., p. 298, *et al.*

the writer of this book regards as a safer one. This is the effort to account for the abnormal consciousness in terms of the normal. From this point of view, we may take exception to each step of the argument which has just been outlined. We may urge that one has closest knowledge of the everyday, conscious life, and that, therefore, every abnormal phenomenon, which is readily accounted for by analogy with the normal consciousness, should not be explained in any remoter way. In accordance with this general principle, we lay stress on the close resemblance of most phenomena of dreaming, visions, automatic writing and hypnosis, to the different phases of our ordinary waking consciousness. Even so-called changes of personality, as observations of our dreams have shown us, are often merely unusual changes in the imagined environment of the old self. It follows that the subliminal self theory, even if it be required for explanation of genuine changes of personality, should not be invoked to account for simple dreams, for crystal visions, or for light hypnoses.

But we may object also to the initial affirmation of our opponents. In other words, we may deny that changes of personality can be explained only on the subliminal self theory. We readily admit that these phenomena are not explained by analogy with the normal consciousness; Leonie 2's forgetfulness of the first Leonie's husband, the transformation of Mary Reynolds from morose to gay,[1] and the change of Ansel Bourne, the farmer, into Brown, the candy dealer, certainly are not paralleled in ordinary experiences.

We must, therefore, either be content to leave these cases unexplained, or we must advance some additional hypothesis. The theory, already outlined, of distinct selves which are yet one personality, involves, in the opinion of the writer, both a logical and a psychological contradic-

[1] Cf. James, *loc. cit.*

what is meant by ' soul.' The question is not an easy one
to answer, but the outline which follows includes the important features of the soul doctrine. The reflective savage
must have noticed that his thoughts were relatively independent of his body. This must early have impressed him
in connection with his dreams. He would wake from a
dream of hunting in a dusky forest, to find himself lying
at full length in his hut; and a more wakeful companion
would assure him that he had not stirred the whole night
through. Thus he would gain, gradually, a distinction
between the inner life of feelings and the outer life of
things. The savage would discover that the inner life of
his dreams and imaginations was his own, unshared by his
companions, whereas, the external things were acknowledged
by all the people of his family and tribe. He would not,
however, be able to think of the inner life except as a
shadow or image of the outer; and thus he would gain, little
by little, an image of the soul, as a shadowy sort of body,
lighter and more easily moved than his flesh and blood
body, in some way detachable from it, but, on the whole,
inferior to it. The Homeric account of the visit of Odysseus to the souls of the dead Hellenes, in the home of
Hades, well illustrates these aspects of the early conceptions of the soul.

We have not time to dwell on the development of the
soul doctrine, but must simply name the relatively permanent features of the conception, as it appears in philosophical and in psychological systems. In the first place,
the soul is regarded as somewhat which underlies consciousness and has consciousness, but which is not merely
identical with consciousness. That is what is meant by
the common assertion that the soul is a substance. It
is fair to add that most doctrines of soul substance seem
really to retain a trace of the primitive conception that the
soul is a sort of material thing. But in the second place,
the soul is distinguished from the body, primarily because
it has consciousness, but also because it is believed in some

ilar tests should be applied to veridical illusions and hallucinations.

If now we limit our attention to veridical experiences, rigidly scrutinized, we shall doubtless find a number of well-attested instances. We are therefore concerned to suggest the explanation of them. It is evident, in the first place, that veridical phenomena may precede the events to which they refer, quite naturally, without the slightest connection between the vision and the event. For example, a dream of an absent friend may be due to the fact that one has recently re-read his letters, instead of being in any sense related to the fact that he is actually on his way home.

It is, however, believed, by many careful students of veridical dreams and illusions, that there are far too many of them to be explained by mere chance coincidence. The most important alternative theory is that of telepathy. This is the doctrine, that individuals influence each other, by other than the normal means of language and bodily expression. Such a theory is perhaps more common than we realize. Most of us have observed the tendency, of people who know each other well, to make the same remark at the same instant, or to respond, as we say, to unspoken questions. We are apt to account uncritically for such experiences, by supposing a peculiar nearness of the two people and an especial unity of experience. This is essentially what is meant by telepathy. The technical argument for it is based, in part, on the occurrence of veridical phenomena, coinciding in time with the event to which they refer. One may quote, in illustration, the authenticated story[1] of Captain Colt, an officer of the British army, who had a vision on the eighth of September, 1855, of the kneeling image of his brother, a soldier who was then before Sebastopol. The figure had a wound on the right temple. Captain Colt described the

---

[1] "Phantasms of the Living," Vol. I., p. 556.

vision to the members of his household, and both his accounts of it and his statement of the date are substantially corroborated by his sister. A fortnight later, he had news of his brother's death on the eighth of September. His brother's body had been found "in a sort of kneeling posture . . . propped up by other bodies, and the death wound was where it had appeared in the vision."

The argument for the existence of telepathy is strengthened by the records of experimental observations. The original form of these experiments was practically what used to be known as the 'willing-game': the experimenter, by directing his attention to some object in the room, successfully 'willed' the subject to lay hold of it. It is easy to see, however, that in this procedure, the experimenter not only wills the subject's movements, but actually directs them by slight, unintended movements of his own, in the desired direction. The more careful experiments in telepathy consist, therefore, in the reproduction by one person, of pictures drawn or of objects fixedly regarded by another, when the two people are not in contact with each other, and when they have had no opportunity of communication, direct or indirect. Critics of these experiments allege that the subject's imitations are not really similar to the objects drawn or regarded, by the experimenter, but that the observers deceive themselves by fancying resemblances which do not exist. Two of these critics, Lehmann and Hansen, have also proved the existence of 'involuntary whispering,' without movement of the lips, and have shown that, in some telepathic experiments, the subject's imitation of the agent may have been occasioned in this normal way, and not by telepathic influence.

It is therefore necessary to compare the likelihood of telepathic influence with the possibilities of chance coincidence and of unintended communication. Where the experts disagree so widely, the laymen may well withhold their decision. They may, however, avoid consistently two unscientific extremes of thought: on the one hand, the uncritical acceptance of every tale of abnormal experience and, on the other hand, the flat refusal to believe any story, however well authenticated, which contradicts the usual experience of every day.

CONCLUSION

CHAPTER XXVIII

THE HISTORY OF PSYCHOLOGICAL SYSTEMS

THE history of a science is the account of men's systematic observation and thought on a given subject. It is evident that no one can profitably study other men's results except by comparing them with results of his own observation and reflection. For this reason, the study of the history of a science never can replace, or precede, the study of the science itself. When, however, one has made one's own examination of the facts, and one's own reflections and deductions, usually under the guidance and direction of some one teacher and of some particular text-book, it is well to compare the familiar methods and results with the methods and results of other people. Besides serving as basis for the estimation of one's own theories, the study of the history of a science may, furthermore, furnish positive suggestion and may definitely invigorate individual study.

It is very difficult to define the limits of our study, for it is all but impossible to fix the beginnings of psychology. At the outset, it will be remembered, we admitted that scientific study differs in method, not in material, from everyday observation. It is natural, therefore, that the one should melt into the other without any fixed line of demarcation. No one, for example, would reckon Homer among the psychologists, yet the germs of a classification of psychic facts are found, in his nice distinctions between the emotional experiences which he designates by the words μένος, θυμός, καρδία and ἦτορ.

In this chapter, we shall somewhat arbitrarily set out from Plato. This bars out, in the first place, the search for suggestions of psychology in Oriental teachings, but the omission is insignificant, since the Eastern mind is metaphysical, rather than scientific, containing philosophical teachings about the soul, rather than psychological observations of the phenomena of consciousness. A more serious omission is that of the pre-Platonic Greek teaching; for the beginnings of psychology are clearly discernible in the teachings of the Sophists, and Sokrates founded his vigorous ethical doctrine on psychological observation. The teachings both of the Sophists and of Sokrates were, however, in a sense, incorporated in the systems of Plato and of Aristotle.

We are ready now for a preliminary classification of psychological systems, a sort of outline map of the way before us. The first division which suggests itself is that between 'philosophical' and 'scientific' systems. By 'philosophical' psychology is meant simply a combination, and often a confusion, of psychology with philosophy. Such a system includes psychological analysis and classification, else it would not be psychology at all, but it explains and often describes the facts which it observes, by referring them, not to other facts, but to a metaphysical system of reality. This confusion of psychology and philosophy certainly is unjustified, yet all ancient and mediæval systems, and all modern theories, excepting some of the most recent, have shown precisely this confusion. They have treated psychology as a branch of philosophy, and have described its phenomena, not as scientific facts, but as themselves metaphysical realities or else as manifestations of metaphysical reality. There are three main forms of this philosophical psychology: spiritualistic, materialistic and associationist theory.

Spiritualistic psychology, which we shall first consider, is the doctrine that conscious experiences are faculties or activities of a soul. We must first, therefore, ask ourselves

way to control the body. From this condensed account of
the common features of spiritualistic doctrine about the soul,
we shall go on to outline briefly the psychology of Plato.

There is no systematic summary of Plato's psychological
teaching. It is scattered, here and there, through the different dialogues, in close connection with philosophical or
with ethical conclusions. Yet we are justified in admitting
that Plato has a psychology, for not only is his observation
of the life of consciousness keen and discriminating, but he
shows also the clear beginnings of psychological classification. To most students of Plato, this mention of classification is likely to suggest the best known of his divisions of
the soul, an account embodied in the beautiful myth of the
Phaidros. This figures the soul as a charioteer, Reason,
who drives two steeds, a rebellious black horse, symboliz-
ing evil passions, and a gentle white steed, representing
good desires. This enumeration of faculties is certainly,
however, ethical and not psychological, for reason and evil
impulse and good desire are complex states distinguished
for their moral significance. But comparison of the different dialogues will show that Plato elsewhere distin-
guishes sense,[1] memory, passive and active, ($\mu\nu\acute{\eta}\mu\eta$ and
$\dot{\alpha}\nu\acute{\alpha}\mu\nu\eta\sigma\iota\varsigma$),[2] comparison,[3] generalization[4] and impulse.[5]
Sense is sharply distinguished from thought, as a whole,
and is regarded as vastly inferior; and yet, in spite of this low
valuation of sensations, Plato's enumeration of them is far
more accurate than that of many modern writers, for he distinguishes sensations of pleasure, pain, cold and warmth,[6] as
well as sensations of sight, hearing, smell, taste and touch.

An interesting instance of the occasional conflict between philosophy and psychology, in Plato's teaching, is

[1] "Theaitetos," 156 *et al.*
[2] "Philebos," 34; cf. "Theaitetos," 191 *seq.* and 198, and "Phaidon," 73 *seq.*
[3] Cf. "Theaitetos," 184–186.
[4] Cf. "Parmenides," 132; "Phaidon," 74; "Theaitetos," 184–186.
[5] Cf. "Phaidros," 253–254; "Republic," Bk. III., 439 *seq.*
[6] "Theaitetos," 156.

the opposition of his metaphysical doctrine, that the soul is essentially self-moved,[1] to his psychological teaching that bodily changes condition sensations. To tell the truth, this inconsistency is common to spiritualistic systems. Without exception, they are unconsciously dualistic, that is, while they define consciousness as a function of the soul, they also look upon it as in some sense occasioned by bodily changes. Plato definitely formulates this teaching. " Sensation," he says,[2] " is carried through the body to the soul." The cause of sensation, he elsewhere teaches,[3] is the mingling of actual emanations from the organ and from the exciting object, for example, the mingling of sight from the eye and whiteness from the object.

Nearly contemporaneous with the system of Plato was that of a great philosopher, whose view of reality was utterly opposed to Plato's. This is Demokritos, the first of the Greek materialists, a severely consistent and a brilliantly original thinker. He taught that the universe, consciousness included, is in its ultimate reality a complex of moving particles or atoms, differing only in number, in order, in arrangement and in motion. The soul atoms, he held, are fire-atoms, differing from others by being finer, smoother and more mobile. So far, of course, we have only a materialistic philosophy of consciousness. But Demokritos must have attempted a psychological classification, for we are told that he distinguished four colors, and that he regarded black as composed of the others. Such assertions as that sense atoms are finer than thought atoms and that bitterness is made up of angular atoms[4] are a curious mixture of psychology and physics.

This account of Demokritos, meagre as it is, includes almost all which we know of the great thinker's psychology. Greek literature has hardly sustained a greater loss than

---

[1] Cf. " Phaidros," 245.   [2] " Philebos," 33 c.
[3] "Timaios," 66; cf. "Theaitetos."
[4] Cf. Ritter u. Preller, "Historia Philosophiæ Græcæ," 8th ed., 1898, 199 and 200.

that which it met, when the works of Demokritos perished with the great Alexandrian library. Historically, however, the system of Demokritos exerted very little influence, and psychology swung back, with philosophy, to the spiritualistic standpoint of Aristotle. The " Psychology " of Aristotle is the very earliest treatise on psychology, and is well worth reading to-day, not primarily for its great antiquarian interest, but because of its discriminating analysis and classification of the facts of consciousness. The " Psychology " is made up of three Books, of which the first, deeply dyed in metaphysics, is a historical study of soul-theories. Book II. starts out with an exposition of Aristotle's own doctrine of the soul. He defines it now as 'form,' now as 'substance,' and again as 'actuality,' or completeness of the body. From this he goes on to a discussion of sense-perception, setting forth the physical and physiological conditions of sensation, with remarkable detail and system. The opinions of Aristotle on physics and on physiology are not, of course, any longer valuable in themselves. They include, it is true, much which is correct, and much which anticipates the results of later study. The teaching that sound is air vibration,[1] and the doctrine that touch is the 'presupposition of the other senses' and that 'life is constituted by this sense'[2] are examples of Aristotle's successful observation and theory. Yet much which he teaches on these subjects is incomprehensible, for example, his doctrine of light as 'pellucity'; and still more of his teaching is utterly mistaken, for example, his theory that the heart is the bodily centre of consciousness, and that the brain is merely a sort of cooling apparatus to counteract the great heat of the heart. In this last regard, Aristotle is distinctly behind Plato, for Plato taught that the brain is the bodily centre of thought, though not of desire and of sensation. Yet the psychology of Aristotle, as a whole, advances upon that of Plato, precisely in the completeness and consistency with

[1] " Psychology," Bk. II., Chapter VIII.   [2] *Op. cit.*, Bk. III., Chapter XIII.

which he carries out, systematically, the method which Plato had employed incidentally : the classification of psychical experiences by referring them to distinct physical phenomena and to different physiological organs.

To Aristotle, as well as to Plato, consciousness is more than mere sense-perception. His teaching, however, is difficult, because it really includes two distinct conceptions of the unsensuous consciousness. The first of these, one may outline as follows, commenting on it as one proceeds : besides sense and desire,[1] we have thought (τὸ νοεῖν), which has two main forms, imagination (φαντασία), and conception(ὑπόληψις).[2] Imagination is admirably described as the picturing faculty,[3] which does not concern itself with the true or false.[4] Conception, or thought in the narrower sense, is distinguished not from a strictly psychological standpoint, but according as it deals with the true, or with the contingent. Desire is described as ' motive faculty,'[5] is classified as rational or irrational, and is emphatically asserted to depend upon imagination. " No animal," Aristotle says, " can have the faculty of desire unless it have imagination " (ὀρεκτικὸν δὲ οὐκ ἄνευ φαντασίας).[6] This is a long, long step toward the very modern doctrine of volition as essentially anticipatory image.

Aristotle holds, as has been pointed out, a second theory of the unsensational consciousness. In this doctrine, never closely coördinated with the rest of his teaching, he has a curious and comprehensive term by which he designates all the unsensational activities of consciousness : the ' common sense' (κοινὸν αἰσθητήριον). This common, or central, sense has really, according to Aristotle, three functions. In the first place, it is that by which we are conscious of the ' common sensibles ' apprehended by more than one sense : rest, movement, figure and magnitude ;[7] in the second place,

[1] " Psychology," Vol. III., Chapter X.   [2] *Ibid.*, Chapter III., § 5.
[3] *Ibid.*, § 6.   [4] *Ibid.*, § 7.
[5] *Ibid.*, Chapter X.   [6] *Op. cit.*, Bk. III., Chapter X., § 9.
[7] *Op. cit.*, Bk. III., Chapter I., § 5.

it is that by which we compare and discriminate sense-experiences;[1] and finally, it is that by which we recognize sensations as our own, in other words, by which we are self-conscious.[2] We have not space to discuss, in detail, the considerations suggested by this doctrine, as notable for its keen discrimination ... s. It is evi- on-sense are d together. indeed, we nal, yet not nsciousness nination, on mself called erm 'sense,' nmon-sense aching that ' but sensa- t merely of ious. It is, sness 'com- and space-

gy has not philosophi- We cannot, hout a ref- no, and *De* These little nd analysis. 'sychology; ; the third on, in a far itises. systems of , and espe-

, § 1, 425.

cially Aristotle, cut loose from their metaphysical leading strings, and employ the strictly scientific methods, analyzing conscious experiences and classifying them by reference, not to philosophical realities, but to physiological and physical facts. There could hardly be a stronger historical argument for the essentially scientific nature of psychology. Incidentally, also, the study of Greek psychology is of value, in counteracting the modern view that all scientific observation and theory, psychological included, is a purely nineteenth-century product. And there is, finally, a direct advantage in the study of these ancient systems. Nobody, for example, can carefully read the psychological works of Aristotle without being stimulated to keener introspection and to more vigorous thought.

A study of the later Greek psychology would not subserve the aim of this very general survey. We should find very many suggestive expositions, for example, St. Augustine's chapters on memory,[1] but we should discover few new principles; for ancient, mediæval and scholastic psychology alike are dominated by the influence of Plato, and, in greater degree, by that of Aristotle. The only important exception to this statement, the Epikurean doctrine, is modelled on the system of Demokritos.

Our review of Greek psychology has thus disclosed one system, that of Demokritos, whose background of metaphysics is materialism, and two systems based on a spiritualistic, yet dualistic, philosophy. For both Plato and Aristotle taught that conscious phenomena are soul-activities, and in this sense their philosophy is spiritualistic; yet they also taught that consciousness is influenced by bodily phenomena, and by this teaching their systems become dualistic. Modern philosophy contains still another modification of spiritualistic doctrine, namely, parallelism; and an utterly new philosophic conception, that of associationism.

[1] "Confessions," X., 19, and XI., 7.

We shall consider very briefly the psychological systems, whose metaphysical starting-point is parallelism. Descartes[1] introduced into philosophy the conception of psychic and physical events as perfectly parallel but utterly distinct and unlike each other,[2] and as influencing each other at one point only, the pineal gland of the brain.[3] His conception of psychology is therefore practically that of Plato; but his views of bodily phenomena are far more accurate, in spite of the fact that he shares the common belief of his time, that the nerves are mere channels through which the animal spirits, or subtlest particles of the blood, flow from the brain to the muscles.[4] He describes and classifies conscious phenomena as soul-activity, or will (*volonté*), and soul-passivity — perception, imagination and emotion.[5] His detailed account of the emotions derives them from the six basal feelings of wonder, love, hate, desire, joy and sadness. His introspective analysis is both suggestive and discriminating, but unquestionably the chief interest of his work is his vivid description of what he calls the 'causes'[6] of these passions: the variations in pulse, in bodily warmth and in digestive conditions, and his equally accurate description of the 'external signs'[7]: blushing, turning pale, laughing and crying. In all this, Descartes is at his best, and the modern student of the bodily accompaniments of the emotions will find in Descartes's little work not merely an anticipation of the James-Lange theory,[8] but the summarized result of much keen observation.

With the rigid consistency which characterizes all his

---

[1] Réné Descartes, born 1596, died 1650.

[2] Cf. "Meditation," VI : "It is certain that my mind is entirely and truly distinct from my body." Cf. "Principles," Pt. I., VIII.

[3] "Les Passions de l'Ame," Première Partie, Art. 31, 42, *et al.* Cf. "Meditation," VI. Descartes's reason for believing that the pineal gland is 'seat of the soul' is, that the other parts of the brain are double, whereas "there is but one sole and simple thought of the same thing at the same time."

[4] *Ibid.,* Première Partie, Art. 10 *et al.*   [7] *Ibid.,* 2me Partie, Arts. 112 *seq.*
[5] *Ibid.,* Première Partie, Art. 17.   [8] Cf. Chapter XX., p. 294 *seq.*
[6] *Ibid.,* 2me Partie, Arts. 95 *seq.*

thought, Spinoza[1] carries into his psychology the parallelism which he adopts from Descartes. His philosophy may be termed a Monism, that is to say, he teaches that both consciousness (which he calls Thought) and matter (which he calls Extension) are parallel manifestations of a deeper reality, Substance or God. Since, however, on his view, body does not influence mind,[2] any more than mind affects body, the psychology of Spinoza is, in a way, a spiritualistic system. He has also a tendency to regard ideas, without reference to the mind which has them, as determining each other; and in this way his psychology is a forerunner of associationism. He was certainly influenced, in a marked way, by his older English contemporary, Thomas Hobbes, first of British Associationists. Like Descartes, Spinoza centres his psychological interest in the study of the emotions. His doctrine contains important elements of Descartes's teaching, mingled with the theory of Hobbes, that joy and sorrow are, essentially, self-preservation and self-destruction. Both doctrines, however, are modified in accordance with Spinoza's highly individual system. Emotions are defined as "affections of the body, by which its power of motion is increased or diminished, *and the ideas occurring at the same time.*"[3] Emotions are thus regarded no longer, as by Descartes, as effects of bodily change, but merely as close accompaniments of these changes. Though undertaken as a basis for his ethical teaching, Spinoza's analyses and descriptions of the different emotions are discriminating and often brilliant, in spite of the rigid and dogmatic form of the "Ethics," which is made up, like a textbook in geometry, of definitions, axioms, theorems and corollaries.

The psychology of Leibniz, the third of the great continental philosophers of the seventeenth century, is again

---

[1] Baruch de Spinoza, born, Amsterdam, 1632; died, the Hague, 1677.

[2] Cf. "Ethics," Pt. III., Prop. II. "The body cannot determine the mind to thought, neither can the mind determine the body to motion nor rest."

[3] "Ethics," Pt. III., Definition III.

a spiritualistic doctrine. So closely, however, is psychological analysis interwoven with metaphysical doctrine, that it is hardly possible to describe the psychology without a detailed discussion of the metaphysics. Perhaps the most significant contribution of Leibniz to psychology is his sharp distinction between inattentive and attentive consciousness (*petites perceptions* and *apperception*).[1] Later psychology has unjustifiably made this over into a doctrine of unconscious ideas.[2] It should be added that writers of the Leibniz school enlarged the division of conscious functions, current since the days of Aristotle, by expressly recognizing emotions as well as knowledge and volition.[3]

These continental systems may be lightly passed over in this summary, since no one of them has exerted an important influence on psychological theory, whereas each has been immensely significant to the history of philosophy. But though we are justified in this slight treatment of the early continental writers, we must approach the British school in a very different way, for its currents still mingle with the stream of present-day psychological tendencies, and its principles have been formative ones in the growth of modern psychology. The first of English psychologists is Thomas Hobbes,[4] the only Englishman, if we except Herbert Spencer, who has ever produced a complete system of metaphysics. The philosophy of Hobbes is a physical materialism: he reduces all phenomena, facts of consciousness included, to forms of motion, defining sensation as 'some internal motion in the sentient,'[5] and delight as a 'motion proceeding to the heart.'[6]

---

[1] Cf. "New Essays," Preface and Bk. II., Chapter I. (pp. 47 *seq.* and 112 *seq.*, Langley's translation). [2] Cf. this chapter, p. 439.

[3] Cf. Windelband, "History of Philosophy," p. 512.

[4] Hobbes was born in 1588, and died in 1679. His most important psychological work is the "Human Nature," written in 1642, though published later, English Works, Vol. I. See also "De Corpore," 1668, and "Leviathan," Bk. I.

[5] "Concerning Body," English Works, Vol. IV., p. 390.

[6] "Concerning Human Nature," English Works, Vol. I., Chapter VII., p. 31.

Yet, more successfully than any writer who has been named, Hobbes attempts to keep his philosophy out of his psychology, so that his treatises are, to this day, very well worth reading, for their keen analysis and their vigorous expression. They contain also definite anticipations of later theories. For example, the James-Lange emotion theory is clearly suggested by this account of passion: "When the action of an object is continued from the eyes, ears and other organs to the Heart . . . the sense of that motion . . . we either call Delight or Trouble of Mind."[1] And Münsterberg's account of volition as anticipatory idea, is foreshadowed in the definition of will as "the last appetite or aversion immediately adhering to the action."[2]

It should be said also that Hobbes, far more adequately than many who followed him, often treated psychology as a social science of related selves. This view is especially prominent in his analysis of emotions, and two quotations shall conclude this outline, both illustrative of Hobbes's pessimistic belief in the exclusively egoistic and overbearing tendencies of human beings. "Sudden Glory," he says, "is the passion which maketh those Grimaces called Laughter; and is caused either by some sudden art of their own which pleaseth them, or by the apprehension of some deformed thing in another by comparison whereof they suddenly applaud themselves." "Grief for the Calamity of another," he says, a little later, "is Pitty; and ariseth from the imagination that the like calamity may befal himself."[3]

The value of the psychology of Hobbes, is, however, out of all proportion to its influence, which was slight. For the suspicion, right or wrong, of his atheism, and the certainty of his materialism roused among his contemporaries a horror of his doctrines, which greatly reduced the effectiveness of his teaching. It is quite otherwise

---

[1] "Leviathan," Pt. I., Chapter VI. [2] *Ibid.* [3] *Ibid.*

with John Locke,[1] whose great work, the " Essay on Human Understanding," in large measure determined the course of English philosophy. The book, which was very widely read, is like all the treatises which have so far been named, a mixture of psychology and philosophy. It is a curious triple web of idea-theory, mental-faculty doctrine, and philosophy of spirit and matter. Its general merits are the fearlessness and the honesty with which it is written, and the definiteness with which it translates everyday philosophical conceptions into vigorous and unambiguous English. Its main psychological values are two: they can be briefly stated, but their immense importance must not be lost out of sight. First and foremost, the book is a model of honest and independent introspection. It continually drives the student to examine his own experience; and it abounds in assertions of the individuality of introspection. " Can another man," Locke exclaims, " perceive that I am conscious of anything, when I perceive it not myself?"[2] "All that I can say of my book," he later writes of it, "is that it is a copy of my own mind."[3]

In the second place, Locke virtually introduces what a famous opponent called his ' new way by ideas.' That is to say, Locke is first to look at experience not only as a combination of soul-activities or mental faculties, but as a succession of ideas, to be analyzed and classified by the psychologist. This is a conception of the greatest significance, introducing into psychology a method which has never, since Locke's day, been abandoned, and preparing the way for the characteristic system of English psychology.

The next great British philosopher, George Berkeley,[4] perpetuated this psychological method. What is known as the ' empirical ' space theory is, as we have seen,[5] a contribution of Berkeley to psychological theory. Yet Berkeley's theory of ideas and even his space doctrine are strictly

---

[1] 1632–1704. The " Essay " was published in 1690.
[2] " Essay," Bk. II., Chapter I., 19.   [3] Letter to Bishop of Worcester.
[4] 1685–1753.   [5] Cf. Chapter VII., p, 89 *seq*,

subordinated to his metaphysical system, and no one
works approaches Hume's[1] "Treatise on Human N.
in psychological value.

The importance of Hume's psychology is this: it
foundation of British Associationism. This form of
sophical psychology has so dominated the English :
that we must consider its general features before go
to study any expression of it. The underlying conc
of associationism is simply this: each 'idea,' or fact (
sciousness, is viewed as an independent and revivable i
and as endowed with a certain power or force kno
association. A practical addition to most associationis
ries, from Hume's onward, is the conviction that gi
sociation and sensations only, all psychic phenomena
satisfactorily accounted for; in other words, associat
is usually, though not of necessity, a sensationalist do

This definition must now be substantiated by quo
from several writers, including, first, certain stateme
the permanence and revivability of ideas. "Any
tions A, B, and C," says Hartley, one of the earl
associationists, "by being associated with one anotl
such a power over ideas *a, b, c,* that any one of the
tions . . . shall be able to excite in the mind Ideas
rest." Here 'the ideas *a, b,* and *c*' are evidently
on as permanent realities, sometimes in the mind and
times out of it. Priestley's expression, "feelings
ideas have power of recalling," suggests the same
and statements of the same sort could be multiplied.
doctrine of association, as a force, is illustrated by F
definition of association as a 'gentle force,'[2] by Ha
statements about the 'power over ideas' through a
tion,[3] and by Spencer's assertions[4] that feelings 'c
and 'integrate' and compound themselves.

[1] The dates of Hume are 1711-1776. The treatise was published
[2] "Treatise," Bk. I., Pt. I., § 4.
[3] "Observations on Man," Pt. I., Chapter I., Section 2, Prop. X.
[4] "Principles of Psychology," Pt. II. Cf. especially Chapter VII.

We have finally to illustrate the conviction of the associationist, that association is the sufficient explanation of all conscious experience. "Every mental affection and operation," Priestley says, "are but different modes or cases of the Association of Ideas." "All intellectual phenomena," Stuart Mill declares, "are derived from association. . . . The law extends to everything."[1] In accordance with this view, James Mill defines love as association of agreeableness with object, and belief as inseparable association; and Hume makes belief a vivid association.[2]

The list which follows names important British associationists, adding occasionally a word of comment on their books: —

DAVID HUME, 1711–1739.
"Treatise on Human Nature," 1739; "Inquiry," 1749.
DAVID HARTLEY, 1704–1757.
"Observations on Man," 1749. An interesting work, greatly influenced by Newton's theory of vibrations, which Hartley applies awkwardly, though suggestively, to the physiology of the nervous system. The book is a curious combination of physiology and associationist psychology.
ABRAHAM TUCKER, 1705–1774.
"The Light of Nature," 1768–1777. A forgotten book full of good description and lively illustration.
JOSEPH PRIESTLEY, 1733–1804.
Edition of Hartley, 1775. Priestley discards the physiology and morals which 'clog' Hartley's system.
JAMES MILL, 1773–1836, 'the reviver of the Association-theory.'
"Analysis of the Phenomena of Human Mind," 1829.
JOHN STUART MILL, 1806–1873.
Notes on James Mill's "Analysis." Examination of Sir William Hamilton's "Philosophy."
ALEXANDER BAIN, 1818– .
"Senses and Intellect," "Emotions and Will."
HERBERT SPENCER, 1820– .
"Principles of Psychology." (First Ed. 1855.)

Before comment upon the doctrine thus outlined, mention must be made of associationism in Germany, where,

[1] Note to James Mill's "Analysis of the Human Mind."
[2] "Treatise," Bk. I., Pt. III.

indeed, the doctrine is to-day far more important than in
England. Its first great exponent was J. F. Herbart,[1] and
it is represented, in more modern times, by Theodor Lipps,[2]
by Volkmann,[3] and by others. We are best acquainted
with German associationism as a basis of pedagogy, for
Herbart was a pedagogical thinker of great originality and
effectiveness; and his widest influence has been in this
field. The associationism of Herbart is philosophically
peculiar because it is grafted upon a very different type of
theory. Herbart believes in the existence of soul-sub-
stances, and defines ideas as ' self-preservations,' and thus
as activities of the soul. This theory sharply distinguishes
his view from that of the English associationists, who banish ' souls,' and treat ideas as final realities and souls as
entirely *de trop*. Practically, however, the two types of
system closely approach each other, for Herbart makes no
use of his souls to account for psychic phenomena, and
really treats experience as a jostling crowd of ideas which
reënforce or oppose each other. The result, of this constant
activity of the independent and active ideas, he describes as
their alternating disappearance below the threshold of consciousness and their reappearance above it; and the successive sinking and emergence he attributes both to the inherent
force of each idea and to the opposition or assistance of
other ideas. The definition, already given, of associationism is thus in complete accord with Herbart's doctrine.

Associationism is so important, not only as a historical
movement but as a constant tendency, and is yet so mistaken, that the exposition of it cannot be left without comment. It is undeniably an easy form of thought, or at
least of expression. We can readily express many conscious experiences, emotional unrest and deliberation, for

[1] 1776 to 1841. Cf. " Lehrbuch zur Psychologie," 1816 (translation " Text-
book of Psychology," 1891); " Psychologie als Wissenschaft," 1824 (cf. Pt. I.,
L.–III.; Pt. III., L.).
[2] Grundtatsachen d. Seelenlebens, 1883.
[3] Lehrbuch der Psychologie," 1884.

example, as conflicts of ideas; and what is originally metaphor grows to seem like reality. More seriously, in the
second place, the doctrine of permanent and revivable ideas,
possessed of an activity of their own, would offer a satisfactory explanation of certain experiences difficult to account
for. These are, first, the fact that events long forgotten
are recalled. In what state, Herbart asks, is the absent
idea "which is yet in our possession?" And his answer
may be summarized thus: the forgotten idea is below the
threshold of consciousness; it must exist, else we should
never again repossess ourselves of it, that is, remember it;
and yet while it is forgotten we evidently are not conscious
of it. In the same way, the independent but unconscious
existence of ideas would explain the spontaneous occurrence
of ideas, in the midst of our thought of entirely different
things. The name, which flashes upon us when we have
given over trying to remember it, and the unexplained
recollection of a long-forgotten scene are experiences[1]
which argue for the theory of permanent ideas, actively
calling each other up or suppressing each other.

The objections to the theory are, however, perfectly conclusive. In the first place, this doctrine of independent
idea-things is clearly a theory of final reality, that is, a philosophy, and not a psychology; for psychology is primarily
an analysis and classification of conscious experiences.
Furthermore, this doctrine of the idea is flatly self-con-
tradictory and thus invalid. For an idea is a phenomenon, or event of consciousness; it cannot exist when no
one is conscious of it, for it is no more nor less than a fact
of consciousness, a somewhat which is conscious-ed, so to
speak. If we take away its being known, we have taken
away its very being, and nothing is left. So also an idea,
just because it is an event, is temporal, belongs to a given
moment and cannot be revived at another time. Nothing
which I see to-day can actually bring back the idea which I

[1] Cf. Herbart, " Textbook," pp. 148, 174.

had yesterday morning; it is gone as irrevocably as yesterday is gone. My to-day's idea of the Shaw Monument is different from my yesterday's idea of it; this minute's idea of a blue jay is different from the last minute's idea of it. We assume the identity of the two,[1] but it certainly is not an actual identity.

With this exposition and criticism of associationism, our review of philosophical systems of psychology is really concluded. For the sake, however, of fairness to materialistic systems, two reappearances of materialistic psychology must be mentioned. It is characteristic of modern scientific interests that these are physiological in the type of their materialism, and not, like the system of Demokritos, and in less degree like that of Hobbes, a physical materialism. Two groups of writers have espoused this general theory: Condillac,[2] Bonnet[3] and other French writers of the eighteenth century; and Karl Vogt,[4] Louis Büchner[5] and J. Moleschott,[6] German writers of the middle of the nineteenth century. Instead of treating of psychic and physiological facts as coördinate, these men regard the body as a deeper sort of reality than consciousness, and consider consciousness as a function of the brain, teaching that "the brain secretes thought."

From this rapid survey of psychological systems, ancient and modern, we turn to the psychology of the immediate present. It is easy to detect the dominant phase of these present-day systems. 'Psychology as a science' is their war-cry, and however they quarrel among themselves, they are agreed in opposing the traditional conception of psychology as a philosophical discipline. In speaking of

[1] Cf. Chapter XIX., p. 259; and Chapter XII., pp. 161–162.
[2] Cf. especially "Traité des Sensations," 1754.
[3] Cf. "Essai de Psychologie," 1755.
[4] Cf. especially "Köhlerglaube und Wissen," 1854.
[5] Cf. "Kraft und Stoff," 1855.
[6] Cf. "Kreislauf des Lebens," 1852.

scientific psychology, we must, however, guard ourselves against two inadequate conceptions of it. Some writers have held that modern psychology is scientific, simply because it concerns itself so deeply with the physiological conditions of experience. So, Le Conte says that psychology is but another name for nerve-physiology. But though psychology rightly attempts to assign the bodily conditions of consciousness, it does not thereby lose its own identity as a study of conscious phenomena; and, in truth, it considers bodily facts only as these are related to consciousness. Psychology is, therefore, a distinct science, not a branch of physiology.

The modern claim that psychology must be ranked among the sciences is sometimes, furthermore, based solely on the assertion that psychology, giving over the method of introspection, has become experimental. There is certainly no question that modern psychology is through and through experimental. The elementary student begins at once to repeat the well-known experiments on himself; the advanced student investigates experimentally some original problem; the forward movement in psychology is, in a word, by the method of experiment. There are many indications of this progress. The first experiments, carried on by E. H. Weber and elaborated by G. T. Fechner, were psychophysical rather than psychological. They concerned the relation of increase of stimulus to change of sensation, and resulted in the formulation of Weber's Law.[1] The first laboratory, that of Wilhelm Wundt, was founded in 1879. Its early problems concerned reaction-times, applications of Weber's Law and discrimination of intervals, and were largely or wholly attempts to connect psychic phenomena with measurable physical facts. To-day there certainly are more than thirty psychological laboratories, in the United States alone. And, more important than the multi-

[1] Ernst Heinrich Weber, "De Tactu," 1834. Cf. Weber, "Tastsinn u. Gemeingefühl," and Gustav Theodor Fechner, "Elemente der Psychophysik," Leipzig, 1860, especially pp. 134 *seq.*

plication of laboratories and equipments, is the steady increase of scholarly investigators engaged in the experimental study of psychological problems. These problems no longer restricted to the study of purely sensational consciousness, are so widened in their scope that they include the consideration of memory, of thought and even of emotion and volition.

The most obvious distinction of the present-day psychology is certainly, therefore, its experimental methods. The significance of experiment to psychology cannot, indeed, be overestimated. As safeguard against careless introspection, and as stimulus to detailed observation, experiment is of untold value to every psychologist. None the less, we must reject, without qualification, the suggestion of certain writers, that psychology is scientific only in so far as it is experimental. For experiment, as we have seen,[1] is a method of strengthening introspection, not a device for supplanting it. Psychology to-day is as introspective as ever it was, although its introspection is guarded and invigorated by experiment. Not, therefore, because it is experimental, but because, without reference to ultimate reality, it analyzes, classifies and explains conscious experiences, psychology is rightly named a science.

Two conceptions of scientific psychology are recognized by modern writers. The first is the theory of psychology, as study of succeeding ideas conditioned by physiological and physical facts. The most consistent upholders of the system are Münsterberg, Titchener, and a group of recent German writers, of whom we may take G. E. Müller and H. Cornelius as types. The theory is clearly allied to associationism, in that it regards experience as a succession of ideas. But it does not, like associationism, turn a psychological description into a philosophical doctrine by attributing any permanence, or force, or revivability to ideas. Certain upholders of the modern theory make, it

[1] Cf. Chapter L, p. 10.

is true, the old confusion of associationism with sensation-
alism, teaching that the succeeding ideas are reducible to
purely sensational (or to sensational and affective) elements; but others, Meinong [1] and Cornelius,[2] for example,
and, first of them all, William James, teach that the analytic study of ideas discloses other than sensational elements — the feelings of one-ness, of difference, of likeness
and the other relational elements.

The second modern tendency is as closely allied with
the spiritualistic doctrine. It is the conception, expounded
in this book, of psychology as the study of a conscious
self (regarded as fact, not as metaphysical reality) in complex relation with other selves. The affiliation of this
doctrine with spiritualistic psychology, such as Plato's or
Locke's, is obvious. For if one cease thinking of the soul
as possessed of a shadowy reality other than self-consciousness,[3] then at once the 'soul' of the earlier conceptions
turns into the 'self,' the concrete, particular I or you,
realized by every one, without philosophical reflection, as
a fact underlying the ideas. Franz Brentano,[4] G. F. Stout,[5]
J. M. Baldwin [6] and Josiah Royce,[7] may be named as
writers who have treated psychology as a study, not of
ideas but of conscious selves.

The common procedure, it must be confessed, is the
confusion of the two points of view and the vacillation
from one method to another. Wilhelm Wundt, G. T. Ladd,
Harold Höffding and William James are representatives of
this tendency. Wundt, for instance, adds to his analysis
of *Vorstellungen* an uncoördinated doctrine of 'inner activity'; and James oscillates, without explanation, between the

---

[1] "Über Gegenstände höherer Ordnung u. s. w." *Ztsch. f. Psychol.* 1899,
Vol. XXI., pp. 182–272.
  [2] "Psychologie als Erfahrungs wissenschaft." Leipzig, 1897. Cf. "Ueber
Gestaltqualitäten," *Ztsch.*, Vol. XXII., pp. 101 *seq.*
  [3] Cf. p. 426.   [4] "Psychologie," 1874.
  [5] "Analytic Psychology."   [6] "Social and Ethical Interpretations."
  [7] Cf. "Studies in Good and Evil," VI., VIII. and IX.; "Imitation,"
Psychological Review, II., 230.

two methods of regarding consciousness, now as
of thoughts or a succession of 'feelings,' and
set of 'cognitive functions' or 'operations.'

A main purpose of this book has been to
both these conceptions of scientific psychology
and that every conscious experience may be reg
either point of view: as mere idea, adequately
when it is analyzed into its elements, or as th
experience of a self, to be treated not merely as
of structural elements, but as conscious relatic
to other selves.

APPENDIX

SECTION I

STRUCTURE AND FUNCTION OF THE NERVOUS SYSTEM

I

THE bodily changes most closely associated with phenomena of consciousness are certainly those of the nervous system. It is useful, therefore, as introduction to strictly psychological study, to consider, in brief outline, the development, the structure and the function of the nervous system.[1] The embryonic area of the human ovum becomes differentiated at first into two layers, *epiblast* and *hypoblast*, between which a third, the *mesoblast*, is later formed. From these three layers, distinguished by the form and groupings of their cells, are developed all the parts of the animal organism. From the *hypoblast* are derived the epithelial linings of the body; from the *mesoblast* are formed the muscles, the skeleton and the vascular system; and the epiblast is the source of the skin, of important parts of the sense-organs and of the nervous system. Within this epiblast (or ecto-derm) there very early appears a furrow or depression, the medullary groove, whose thickened wall soon closes upon itself, to form a sort of hollow tube which later develops into the cerebro-spinal system. The lower or posterior part of this tube becomes the spinal cord; the forward part is the primitive form of the brain. This forward part very quickly divides itself into three bulbs, called the first, the second and the third cerebral vesicles.

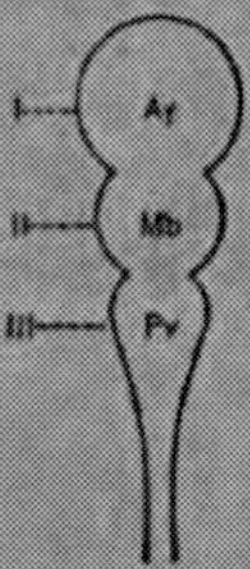

FIG. 9.

These cerebral vesicles, however, undergo such complicated changes, that it is hard to recognize a trace of them in the developed adult brain. The most important of these changes will be briefly enumerated and, in part, illustrated, without the attempt to settle the difficult question of their order: —

First, the number of vesicles increases in two ways: by the

---

[1] See Bibliography.

division of the hind-brain or third vesicle so as to form two parts (4 and 5 in Figure 10) ; and by the outgrowth, from the fore-brain or first vesicle, of two more vesicles, side by side (H), the originals of the cerebral hemispheres. Second, the brain is bent at several points in a ventral or forward direction. The most important of these points are the forward part of the fifth vesicle and the forward part of the mid-brain (x and y in Figure 11). Third, the cerebral hemispheres expand in all directions, so as finally to cover all parts except the hind-brain, folding in upon themselves in such wise as to form what we know as fissures and convolutions. Fourth, all the other vesicle-walls (except the posterior wall of the fifth vesicle) thicken and become differenti-

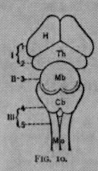

FIG. 10.

ated, first, into the 'basal ganglia,' or 'interior brain' — corpora striata, optic thalami and optic lobes — distinct nerve-centres, around which the hemispheres fold; and second, into the external parts of the 'lower brain': the *crura cerebri*, two bundles of up and down fibres, the *pons*, a band of transverse fibres uniting the two halves of the *cerebellum*, and the *medulla*, mainly a continuation of the *crura*. The cranial nerves, also, take their origin in

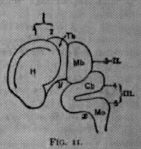

FIG. 11.

the different vesicles. For a description of the parts of the brain, the student is referred to the text-books on physiology. The following is a list of the most important of them, in relation to the primitive vesicles: —

I. FIRST PRIMARY VESICLE	1. Fore-brain	Cerebral hemispheres. Corpora striata. Olfactory bulb.
	2. Inter-brain	Optic thalami. Optic nerve (primary origin).
II. SECOND PRIMARY VESICLE =	3. Mid-brain	Corpora quadrigemina or optic lobes (posterior, *i.e.* dorsal, bodies). Crura cerebri (anterior bodies). Optic nerve (secondary origin).

III. THIRD PRIMARY VESICLE	4. Hind-brain	Cerebellum (dorsal: a double growth like the hemispheres). Pons Varolii (ventral).
	5. After-brain	Medulla oblongata. Auditory nerve.

The development of the cerebral hemispheres is the change especially characteristic of the mammalian brain; and the bending of the brain is the mark of the higher vertebrate. The thickening of the vesicle walls, on the other hand, is quite as noticeable in lower forms of animal life. Birds, for instance, in whom the thin and undeveloped 'pallium' takes the place of the hemispheres, have cerebella and optic lobes far larger, relatively, than those of the human brain.

This will serve as an introductory account, from the standpoint of development, of the cerebro-spinal nerve-centres in their superficial aspect. There are, besides, certain smaller nerve-centres, both the so-called sporadic ganglia and — more important — the sympathetic nerve-system connected with the blood-vessels and viscera of chest and of abdomen. These, however, may be passed by with mere mention, since their activity is seldom or never accompanied by consciousness. Nerve-centres consist of nerve-cells, nerve-fibres, connective tissue and blood-vessels. As they leave the great nerve-centres, the nerve-fibres are massed together into nerve-trunks, but these break up into smaller and smaller branches, terminating finally in the end-organs of eye, ear, nose and so on, and in the muscles of head, trunk, limbs and inner organs. There is thus no part of the human body to which these fibres do not radiate from the nerve-centres.

The nature of these two main forms of nerve-substance must now be more closely studied. A nerve-cell is a mass of protoplasm, grayish in color; it contains a nucleus, branches out into several processes and is embedded in a connective substance, named neuroglia. The nerve-fibres are, as we have seen, the elongated processes of nerve-cells; they are of two sorts, nonmedullated and grayish in color, like the nerve-centres; and medullated, that is, enclosed in an albuminous white covering, the medullary sheath. The gray, non-medullated fibres are most frequent in the centres and in the sympathetic system; the medullated fibres are found on the outer circumference of the spinal cord and, generally speaking, in the interior of the brain. The gray and the white matter, though differing in chemical constitution, are both significant in containing certain highly unstable phosphorized fats. These bring about the chemically sensitive condition of nerve-substance, whose energy is readily yielded when the equilibrium of its molecules is disturbed.

This leads us to a study of the functions of nervous substance. Let us recall that the human body is an organized system of physiological phenomena, in constant and regular succession. This quick succession, or transformation, is perhaps the most noticeable feature of the animal body. Constant chemical changes are involved in respiration and in nutrition, and innumerable muscular changes are facilitated by the anatomical flexibility of the human skeleton, with its more than two hundred bones and its easily moving pivot and ball-and-socket joints. Now the nervous structures of the body form a system, within a system, of extraordinarily shifting and rapidly changing phenomena. Not only the instability of their chemical constitution, but their distribution and arrangement in the body, bring about this result. With nerve-fibres radiating from spinal and from cerebral centres, some organ of the nervous system is, in the first place, affected by every stimulus, external or internal, to any part of the body; and on the other hand, every change within the nervous system communicates itself to the other organs. All this may be summed up in the statement that the nervous system constitutes the most excitable and the most excitory part of the organism. But the functions of nerve-centre and fibre may be distinguished from each other. The latter serves for the conduction of the 'nerve-impulse' or excitation; the nerve-centre, on the other hand, effects the redistribution of impulses. Nerve-fibres are classified as (1) afferent, or ingoing, those which convey to the centre the impulse communicated by some stimulus and (2) efferent, or outgoing, those which convey a nerve-impulse downward or outward from a nerve-centre. So, for example, I touch an icy surface; the end-organs in the skin of my hand are thermally stimulated, and communicate the excitation to an afferent nerve; this conveys the impulse to a spinal centre, where it is redistributed and communicated to an efferent nerve; and this is connected with a muscle whose functioning causes the withdrawal of my hand.

We may now describe, in greater detail, the functions of the different parts of the cerebro-spinal system. Spine and brain, it must be remembered, are made up both of nerve-centres and of nerve-fibres, and therefore serve a double purpose, of conduction and of redistribution. The spinal cord consists of a grayish interior, chiefly composed of nerve-centres, surrounded by an outer, white part made up of medullated nerve-fibres. These nerve-fibres run inward and outward, to and from the muscles and surfaces of trunk and limbs, and also upward and downward to and from the brain. A large number of these fibres cross, in the lower brain, from the right side of the cord to the left side of the brain, and *vice versa ;* and it follows that the stimulation of one side of the body affects the cerebral hemisphere of the opposite side.[1]

When an excitation is transmitted by an afferent nerve to the spinal cord, it may either be immediately redistributed by the spinal nerve-centres to an efferent nerve, or it may be transmitted along one of the upward fibres to a redistributing centre in the brain. This is illustrated by the accompanying diagram, in which the lines *a-b-c* and *a-x-d-y-c* represent respectively a given nervous impulse redistributed in a spinal centre, and the same impulse transmitted to a cerebral centre. It will be observed that the stimulus to the in-going nerve (*ax*) and the bodily movement excited by the outgoing nerve (*yc*) are, in both cases, the same ; but there are two important distinctions between the spinal and the cerebral reaction. Obviously, the spinal reaction follows more swiftly upon the stimulus, and it is, further-more, unaccompanied by consciousness. This last important fact has been estab-lished by the experimental observation

FIG. 12.

that unconscious movements of a limb, in response to stimulation of the skin, occur after such injury to the spinal cord as prevents transmission of excitation to the brain. The spinal cord is thus, first, a centre for unconscious reflex movements from cutaneous stimulation, and second, a transmitter of excitations to the brain.

Within the brain itself, we may also distinguish the functions of its different parts. For our present purpose, we shall regard it as divided into (1) lower brain (medulla, cerebellum, pons and crura), (2) interior-brain (the basal nerve-centres enclosed within the hemispheres), and (3) the hemispheres themselves. Lower brain and interior brain consist of nerve-centres, connected among themselves by transverse fibres, and penetrated also by upward and downward fibres, connecting them, as the diagram

[1] Cf. Fig. 13. p. 454.

suggests, with the spinal centres and with the hemispheres. They therefore transmit to the hemispheres excitations originated in lower portions of the body, and they are also centres for the redistribution both of nervous impulses, transmitted by the spinal cord, and of excitations conducted to them directly by the facial nerves and by the nerves of the special senses. In one

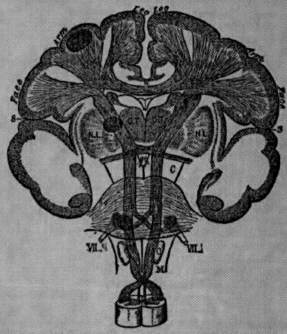

FIG. 13.—Schematic, transverse section of the brain through the Rolandic region. *S*, fissure of Sylvius; *N.C.* and *N.L.*, parts of a corpus striatum; *O.T.*, optic thalamus; *C*, one of the crura; *M*, medulla oblongata; VII., the facial nerves.

centre of the lower brain (the medulla), there are also automatic centres, masses of cells which coördinate excitations from the interior of the body and regulate such automatic movements as the heart-beat, breathing and sneezing. (The two hemispheres, also, are connected with each other by transverse fibres.)

It is a moot question whether sense-consciousness accompanies the functioning of these lower and interior centres. The probability,[1] however, is that in the case of the lower vertebrates, with less developed hemispheres, the excitation of lower and of interior brain is accompanied by consciousness, and that, on the contrary, excitation of the hemispheres is necessary to human consciousness. It is certain that excitation of the hemispheres is the essential cerebral condition of memory and of foresight. The bodily movements characteristic of cerebral activity are, therefore, no longer the unconscious reflexes of the spinal cord nor even acts of which one has a bare sense-perception; they are deliberative acts performed with a memory of past results and an image of future happenings. It follows that the response to a particular stimulation is not, as in the case of a spinal reflex, inevitable and determined. We may illustrate this by a modification of our former example. The unconscious spinal reflex following upon the touch of a hot surface is the withdrawal of the hand. Suppose, however, that the stimulus conducted by the afferent nerve (*a-b*) is transmitted to the hemispheres instead of being at once redistributed in the spinal centres. The centre (*d*), corresponding with the sensation of warmth, is first stimulated, but the impulse is at once transmitted to other brain-centres (*x* and *y*) and the total hemisphere excitation

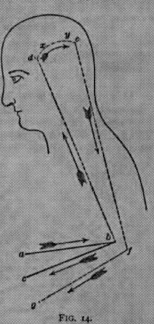

FIG. 14.

is accompanied by the conscious reflection that a hot application will cure neuralgiac pain. The efferent nerve (*e-f*), which is finally stimulated, in turn excites a muscle whose contraction checks the instinctive movement away from the hot surface. Thus the motor response (*e-f-g*), to the excitation transmitted to the hemispheres, is a firmer grasp of the heated object, whereas the instinctive spinal reflex (*a-b-c*) would consist, as we have seen, in the withdrawal of the hand. The following table summarizes these distinctions of bodily activity and consciousness, as associated with different nerve-centres: —

[1] H. Donaldson, *American Journal of Psychology*, Vol. IV.

Organ.	Function.	Activity.	
Spinal cord.	Conduction, Redistribution.	Cutaneous reflex.	No consciousness.
Lower brain.	Conduction, Redistribution.	Automatic.	No consciousness.
Interior brain.	Conduction, Redistribution.	Special-reflex.	Sense-consciousness (?)
Cerebral hemispheres.	Redistribution.	Deliberative.	Perception, Memory, Thought, etc.

It is possible to study, in even greater detail, the relation of the excitation of the hemisphere to different functions of consciousness. For this purpose, it is necessary to gain a clearer notion of the conformation of the hemispheres. It has been shown already that the immense expansion of each hemisphere

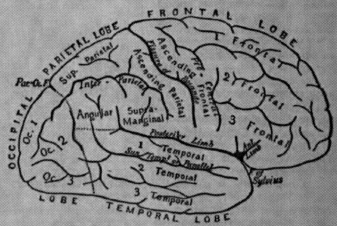

FIG. 15. — Outer Surface of the Right Hemisphere.

results in a folding of its surface in upon itself. Each hemisphere thus consists of an irregular mass of folds, the convolutions, separated by deep gullies, the fissures. The most important of these appear very early in the growth of each embryonic hemisphere, on its outer surface. They are the fissure of Sylvius, which starts from a point below and in front of the middle of each

hemisphere (cf. Figure 15), and runs backward, curving upward
at its termination; and the fissure of Rolando, which runs downward and forward, from the median, upper part of each hemisphere (cf. Figure 15) to a point near to that where the fissure of
Sylvius begins. These fissures and others form the basis of the
ordinary division of the hemisphere into five areas, or lobes.
Roughly speaking, the frontal lobe lies forward of the fissure of
Rolando and above the fissure of Sylvius; the parietal lobe lies
back of the frontal, and also above the fissure of Sylvius; the
occipital lobe lies behind the parietal, and is separated from it
by a fissure which appears most definitely on the median side of
the hemisphere; and the temporal lobe lies below the fissure of

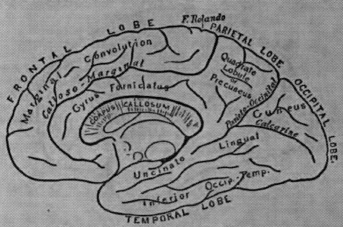

FIG. 16. — Median Surface of the Right Hemisphere.

Sylvius and forward of the occipital lobe. (The fifth lobe, the
'island of Reil,' is folded in within the temporal and the parietal
lobes, and is not represented in the diagram.) On the median
surface of the hemisphere (cf. Figure 16), it is important to distinguish, first, the triangular area of the occipital lobe, called
from its wedge shape the *cuneus;* second, the convolution along
the upper edge, called 'marginal'; and finally, the curving
convolution, called the *uncinate* (or *hippocampus*).

The study of brain areas is important to the psychologist only
for the following reason: investigation has shown that the excitation of certain parts of the brain is accompanied by definite forms
of sense-consciousness and of bodily movement. There is much
dispute, among the anatomists, about special features of cere-

bral localization, but the following results may be accepted as practically assured : —

The excitation of the occipital lobe, especially of that portion of its median surface known as the cuneus (cf. Figure 16), is the cerebral 'centre' of the visual perception of the different colors and shades, and is the centre, also, of movements of the eye-muscles.[1] Nerve-fibres connect the right halves of both retinæ with this visual centre in the right hemisphere, and the left halves of both retinæ with the left visual centre.

The area forward and back of the fissure of Rolando is the so-called 'centre' of cutaneous sensation and of general bodily movements. The excitation of the lower part of it is accom-

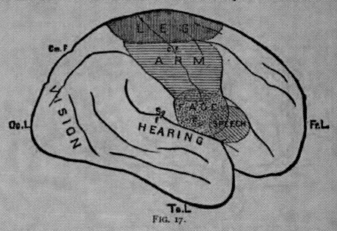

FIG. 17.

panied by the perception of contact with the skin of head and face, and by movements of the head; the excitation of the next higher portion conditions the skin-sensations and the movement of the arms, and so on, so that the very highest part of the Rolandic area is the cerebral 'centre' both of the skin-sensations and of the movements of the feet.

The centre of hearing is the first temporal convolution; the smell-centre and, possibly, the taste-centre are in the uncinate convolution of the median temporal lobe (cf. Figure 16). These are centres also for movements of ear, nostrils and tongue. The following summary of the sensory centres in the hemispheres combines these results : —

[1] Cf. Donaldson, *American Journal of Psychology*, Vol. IV., p. 121; Flechsig, "Gehirn und Seele," 2d edition, 1896, p. 77.

AREAS.	CONSCIOUS PHENOMENA.	BODILY MOVEMENTS.
Occipital lobe.	Of vision.	Of eye-muscles.
Area about fissure of Rolando.	Of cutaneous and 'motor' sensations.	Of { head, trunk, limbs.
Temporal lobe.	Of { hearing, smell, taste?	Of { ear, nostrils, tongue?

It will be observed that this enumeration leaves large areas of the hemispheres without assigned function. The recent researches of a German physiologist, Paul Flechsig, have made it very probable that these areas are the centres of unsensational experiences, the consciousness of pleasantness and unpleasantness, of similarity and difference, of familiarity and of connection. The 'association-centres,' as Flechsig calls them,[1] are included in the unnamed parts of Figure 17. They are distinguished, anatomically, from the sense-centres of the hemispheres, because they are not directly connected, by afferent and efferent nerves, with any end-organs on the surface of the body. On the contrary, they are connected by transverse fibres with the sense-centres, and are only indirectly stimulated by the excitation of these sense-centres. Flechsig has also distinguished 'intermediate' centres between the other two.[2]

II

There are three methods of this study of cerebral localization: the experimental, the pathological and the embryological methods. The first of these proceeds upon two lines. A given area of the brain of an animal is artificially stimulated, — by electricity, for example, — the resulting bodily movements are watched, and the accompanying consciousness is inferred. Or, the particular brain-area is extirpated and the resulting loss of function is carefully studied. For example, a dog's Rolandic region is removed, and the discovery is made that he does not draw back his paw if one pinches it, and that he leaves it unconcernedly in boiling water.

The experimental method, of course, encounters the objection that the functioning of the animal brain may not correspond exactly with that of the human brain. This difficulty is avoided by the pathological method, the careful study, after death, of the brains of patients who have suffered from diseases affecting consciousness. The discovery, for example, of injury to the left

[1] "Gehirn und Seele," pp. 24, 78.   [2] *Neurolog. Centralblatt*, Nov., 1898.

occipital lobe, of persons who have lost the left half of their field of vision, has contributed to the knowledge of the relation of that part of the brain to visual consciousness.

The embryological method, finally, employed with great efficiency by Flechsig, studies the human brain at various stages preceding its complete development, distinguishing the periods at which one sense-centre after another, and, latest of all, the association-centres and the transverse fibres, reach their complete development.

In conclusion, the student should be reminded that any definite explanation of individual psychical characteristics, by discoverable peculiarities of the brain, has, up to this time, eluded every investigator. The weight of the brain, for example, has seemed to some anatomists an indication of intellect, but though the brain of Cuvier weighed 1830 gr., that of Gambetta weighed only 1294 gr., and that of Liebig 1352 gr., as compared with an average of 1340; and the heaviest brain on record belonged to a perfectly commonplace individual. Between circumference of brain and strength of intellect there is also no observable connection. The most recent and most accurate examinations of particular brains confirm this general conclusion; to the surprise of everybody, for example, the accurate microscopic examination of Laura Bridgman's brain disclosed no describable defects in the visual areas; and Dr. Hansemann,[1] who has recently examined the brain of the great scientist Helmholtz, observes that it is not extraordinarily developed.

The basal conclusions which emerge for the psychologist, from all this study of the nervous system, are, therefore, the following: every fact of consciousness, every percept, image, thought, emotion or volition is first necessarily related to a neural phenomenon, that is, to some functioning of the nervous system, and is, therefore, second, accompanied by some other bodily change or changes, mechanical, chemical or thermal; and these changes may be either conscious or unconscious.

SECTION II

APHASIA

The study of aphasia is important to physiologist and to psychologist alike. Defects in the word-consciousness are detected and analyzed with relative ease, and the discovery of the corresponding areas of brain injury has made it possible to suggest the special centres whose excitation conditions visual, auditory or tactile-motor consciousness. On the other hand, the study of

---

[1] Hansemann, *Zeitschrift*, 1899, Vol. XX.

the brain conditions has stimulated and verified the psychological analysis of the word-consciousness.

Aphasia is the general name for diseased conditions of the brain, which affect the patient's consciousness of words. In sensory aphasia, the subject's hearing or reading of words is affected; in motor aphasia, he is unable to speak or to write. In either case, he may or may not know the meaning of words. The patient's speech, for example, may be unaffected, and he may read perfectly, yet spoken words may seem to him like mere inarticulate sounds; or he may hear words and even understand them, he may speak and write, and he may yet be unable to read printed and written words, even those which he himself has written. These forms of sensory aphasia are named word-deafness and alexia respectively. Motor aphasia, also, has two main forms, inability to speak and to write. The latter is called agraphia, and the former is rather ambiguously named pure motor aphasia. In agraphia, the patient reads and speaks understandingly; he can even read what he himself has earlier written, but he cannot write. In pure motor aphasia, a man understands what is said to him, reads printed and written words, and can even write, but his speech is more or less seriously disturbed. He can laugh, cry and sing; but either he misuses words, one in place of another, or he has no words at all, or he speaks incoherently, in what has been called a broth of unintelligible syllables. He may recognize his mistakes and be tormented by them, but he cannot avoid them. Sometimes it happens that the inability to speak affects only objects of a certain sense-class. For example, a man may be able to name the visual and tactile qualities of an object, but unable to name sounds of any kind; or he may be able to name colors and sounds but not tactile qualities: pure motor aphasia is known as acoustic, tactile or optical, according as it affects one class of sensations or another.

All these cases of merely sensory and motor word-disturbance must be contrasted, finally, with the most serious form of aphasia: the inability to understand words, or mental blindness (*Seelenblindheit*), as it is named from one form of it. In this case, the patient hears the word as a word and repeats it, but does not know its meaning; he reads aloud and writes, but does not understand what he reads and writes because his verbal images do not suggest the concrete images which make up what we call the meaning of the word.

It must be remembered that aphasia is due to cerebral disease, not to any injury of end-organs or of muscular apparatus. In word-deafness, or auditory sense aphasia, for instance, the patient is not deaf: he hears as distinctly as ever he did, and he even hears the words that are spoken to him, only he hears them not as words, conventional expressions of some meaning, — understood or not, — but as mere sounds. A spoken sentence seems to him a mere succession of mixed tones and noises. And pure motor aphasia, the inability to speak, occurs without loss of voice or paralysis of lip or of tongue.

We must therefore ask for the cerebral conditions of the different forms of aphasia. These have been discovered, by the study of the brains of aphasic patients, after their death, and certain definite conclusions have been reached by such study. Neurologists agree, in the first place, that disturbances of speech are conditioned by diseased states of the left side of the brain — in left-handed people, of the right side. The conditions of aphasia are, however, known in more detail. Broca found, in 1861, that injury to the third or lowest frontal convolution (the area marked 'speech' on the diagram of page 458) accompanies pure motor aphasia, that is, the inability to speak. Some years later, another neurologist, Wernicke, discovered that injury to the first and second temporal convolution accompanied cases of word-deafness. These discoveries, substantiated by many students of aphasia, have constituted an important argument for the localization of hearing-centres and tactile-motor centres, in the temporal lobe and the lower Rolandic area respectively.

The specific areas for the two diseases concerned with written language, alexia and agraphia, are in the throat and the hand areas of the Rolandic region. It has, furthermore, been abundantly [1] established that word-blindness, or the loss of the meaning of words, is due, not to the derangement of articulatory or word-hearing centre, but rather to the loss of connection between such word-centres and the visual, auditory or tactile centres of concrete images. The man who is unable to tell the meaning of the word 'brush' — though he writes and articulates the word and rightly uses the object — no longer associates the motor or visual image of the act of brushing, with the sight of the word. This absence of the habitual association may be due either to the injury of visual or motor centres, or to injury of the fibres connecting word-centre with other centre. Normally, the articulation-centre is closely connected with the brain-centres for concrete imagery; but sometimes the connection is utterly broken, and again it is curiously altered. Dr. Sommer, for

[1] Cf. Flechsig, "Gehirn und Seele," pp. 44 *seq.*; James, Vol. I., pp. 54 *seq.*

example, tells the story[1] of a patient tested for pure motor aphasia, who seemed to recover from his inability to name objects, in an inexplicably short time. Objects which, a few hours before, he had been unable to name, he now identified with only a slight hesitation. This surprising facility was, however, explained by the discovery that the man was tracing the names of the objects, with his finger tip, on some convenient surface. His hands were then held, but he was detected tracing the names, with the toe of his boot, on the ground; his feet were secured, and a facial contortion betrayed that he was writing the words, with the tip of his tongue, on the roof of his mouth. The sight of an object evidently no longer suggested the appropriate throat-sensation and motions, but did suggest the act of writing, that is to say, the cerebral connection was broken between brain-centre for the concrete visual image of an object and brain-centre for the visual word-image, whereas the connection between concrete image centre and writing centre was unimpaired.

It is evident, from our former study of the diversity in people's imagination-types, that verbal images and percepts differ with different persons. For almost everybody, however, the verbal image includes at least two parts: the sound of the word as heard, and the consciousness of articulating the word. Even when we merely listen and do not actually speak aloud, there is for most of us a slight excitation of the sense-cells in the articulation-centre. This shows the importance of the Broca and Wernicke centres, and it indicates also that the Broca centre in the lower frontal convolution is not merely a motor centre, in other words, that it is not concerned merely in the use of speech, but that it is a sense-centre as well, excited during the word-consciousness of persons of the tactile-motor image-type. But language, by an educated person, is read and written as well as spoken and heard. The word-sound often, therefore, suggests the image of the written or printed word, and it may suggest the movement of writing. The complete percept of a spoken word must, thus, include fused elements of sound and articulation (through actual, peripheral excitation of ear and pharynx) and assimilated elements, both visual and tactual, through the imaged appearance of the word and the imagined act of writing it; and of course this means that, not merely the Wernicke auditory word-centre in the temporal lobe, but visual and tactile areas are excited, in the complete consciousness of a word as word, irrespective of any consciousness of its meaning.[2]

[1] *Zeitschrift für Physiologie und Psychologie*, II., 1891, p. 143.
[2] Cf. Flechsig, *op. cit.*, p. 46.

SECTION III

SENSATIONAL ELEMENTS OF COLOR AND COLORLESS LIGHT

I. Theories

THE outline of color-theories, as given in the second chapter of this book, must be greatly amplified, if it is to be at all commensurate with the sweep of modern discussions and investigations. The earliest of the hypotheses which are at present upheld is that of Thomas Young and Hermann von Helmholtz. This theory teaches, as we know, that there are three elemental colors, red, green and violet, and that colorless light sensations are always occasioned by the mixture of colored lights.[1] The conclusive objections to this theory are, as has been noted, the distinctness of yellow as an elemental experience and the occurrence of colorless light consciousness without mixture of stimuli. The Hering theory of antagonistic color-processes, assimilative and dissimilative, meets these objections, but runs upon other difficulties. These difficulties must be carefully considered, since they form a starting-point for the study of other theories. They are, in the main, the following:[2] (1) It is highly improbable that an assimilative bodily process should condition consciousness. (2) It is inconsistent to suppose that the simultaneous occurrence of opposite color-processes balance each other, and result in an absence of color-consciousness, whereas the opposite processes of the black-white substance, if excited together, occasion the consciousness of gray. (3) As a matter of fact, a mixture of red and green lights does not, as Hering implies, occasion colorless light sensation. On the contrary, the color-stimulus which, mixed with red light, produces a colorless light sensation, is blue-green. This shows that the red and green which are psychically elemental are not physiologically antagonistic.

An answer to certain of these objections is found in Professor G. E. Müller's recent modification of the Hering theory.[3] Müller replaces the conception of assimilation and dissimilation by a hypothesis of reversible chemical action, which meets the first of

---

[1] " Handbuch der Physiologischen Optik," 2te Aufl., 1896, §§ 19, 20, pp. 275 *seq.*, 316 *seq.* This is the most reasonable statement of the theory. But Helmholtz upholds it in a far more indefensible way, teaching that a mixture of color *sensations* gives the sensation of colorless light (*op. cit.*, p. 559). This is introspectively untrue.   [2] Cf. p. 39.
[3] *Ztsch. f. Psych. u. Physiol. d. Sinnesorgane*, 1896 and 1897, X. and XIV., esp. §§ 7, 18, 33, 36. Cf. C. L. Franklin, *Psychological Review*, Vol. VI., p. 70.

the objections to the Hering theory. To avoid the second of these difficulties, the occurrence of colorless light sensation when the black and white retinal processes are in equilibrium, Müller refers these sensations of gray to a black-white excitation constantly going on in the visual brain-centre. This second hypothesis, it will be noted, is logically valid, but it is purely imaginary, and it deprives the color-theory of the supposed advantage of explaining colorless light in the same way in which colors are explained. The third objection to the Hering hypothesis is not met by Müller; and this, in itself, constitutes a reason for abandoning the hypothesis of antagonistic color-processes. It should be added that Müller's introspective analysis of the four color-quality series, red to yellow, yellow to green, green to blue, and blue to red, is a valuable argument for the theory that there are four color-elements.

Another modification of the Hering theory, earlier than that of Müller, must be mentioned. This is the hypothesis of Ebbinghaus,[1] who substitutes, for the Hering conception of assimilative and dissimilative processes, a conception of progressive and antagonistic stages of decomposition of three visual substances. In particular, Ebbinghaus makes the following suppositions: (1) The rod-pigment, called 'visual purple,' by its first stage of decomposition occasions sensations of yellow. In its second phase, this substance is yellow, not purple, and its decomposition conditions sensations of blue. (2) There is a second, an objectively red-green substance, present in the cones, and the first and second processes of its decomposition occasion the colors of green and red; it has never been observed because, in its green phase, it is complementary to the visual purple. (3) A third, invisible substance occasions sensations of white and black, by its progressive decomposition. This theory, however, cannot hold out against the following entirely decisive objections: The different stages of decomposition are, in the first place, successive, and they therefore do not explain any phenomena due to the mixture of lights. Furthermore, there is no support for Ebbinghaus's conjectures about the objective color of visual substances. It is, for example, highly improbable that in every retina so far examined, precisely the antagonistic green and purple phases of the visual substances should have been present.[2]

---

[1] "Theorie des Farbensehens," *Ztsch. f. Psych. u. Physiol. d. Sinnesorgane,* 1893. In his textbook on psychology, 1897, Ebbinghaus does not bring forward this theory.

[2] Cf. C. L. Franklin, *Mind,* N. S., Vol. II., p. 473; Cattell, *Psychological Review,* Vol. I., p. 325.

2 H

From the study of this group of Hering-like theories, we turn, therefore, to the discussion of certain theories of another type. Hering, Müller and Ebbinghaus suppose that the physiological conditions of colorless light sensations must be closely analogous to those of the color-sensations. Wundt, von Kries, König and Christine Ladd Franklin, on the contrary, teach that the two experiences are due to different conditions. The theory of Wundt[1] is simplest and most unelaborated of the four which will be outlined. His doctrine includes the following features: (1) The consciousness of color is due to a photochemical process, called a 'chromatic' retinal process, which varies with the length of the ether-waves falling on the retina. (Wundt's assumption of more than four elementary colors is not an essential feature of his theory.) (2) The sensational elements of white and gray — which, according to Wundt, are identical with brightness — are due to an 'achromatic' retinal process of chemical decomposition, which varies with the amplitude of the ether-waves. (3) The consciousness of black or of 'dark' is due to a third, constant retinal process, and occurs, therefore, without external stimulus, and when opposite ether-wave vibrations cancel each other. This last hypothesis would readily account for the fact, so difficult of explanation on Hering's theory, that a mixture of black and white stimuli do not destroy each other. Wundt also avoids the other difficulties attendant on Hering's theory, but he accomplishes this, in great part at least, by his own indefiniteness. He does not, for example, attempt a description of his achromatic and chromatic processes.

The theories of König, von Kries and Franklin agree in the affirmation that the retinal rods have to do with the conditioning of colorless light sensations. Several of the arguments which conclusively show the correctness of this view have already been enumerated.[2] These arguments may now be restated and amplified. (1) The periphery of the retina, whose excitation gives only colorless light, contains rods, well provided with visual purple, and no cones. (2) The retinæ of night-seeing animals are rich in rods.[3] (3) The visual purple absorbs most readily just that color, green, which is intensest in faint light.[4] (4) Two

---

[1] "Phys. Psych.," I., 536; *Phil. Stud.*, IV., 1887; "Lectures," VI., 103.

[2] Chapter II., p. 40.

[3] This observation was made in 1866 by Max Schultze, who drew the inference that the rods are concerned in faint-light vision.

[4] This discovery was made in 1894 by Professor Arthur König, and Frl. Else Köttgen, through the investigation of an extracted human retina. Cf. Sitzungsberichte d. Akad. d. Wissensch. zu Berlin, Juni, 1894.

mixtures, one of red and blue-green lights and a second of blue and yellow lights, which form grays of precisely similar intensity when looked at by an eye adapted to the light, form grays which differ widely in intensity to an eye adapted to the darkness.[1] This fact is inexplicable on a Hering-Müller hypothesis, for if the colorless light sensation, which follows mixtures of color-stimuli, were due to the activity of a black-white substance, then the sensation would not vary with the composition of the complex color-stimulus: a gray, due to the mixture of red and green, could not change, with the adaptation of the eye, in any other way than the gray due to mixture of blue and yellow, for the retinal condition of the one would be exactly that of the other — activity of white-black substance. The fact accords well, on the other hand, with the theory that rod activity has to do with colorless light sensations, for the visual purple on the rods is renewed in the eye rested by the darkness, but is bleached out in the light. Therefore, the eye adapted to the dark absorbs more green rays than the eye adapted to the light; and grays, due to mixture of 'colors' which seemed alike in a bright light, will have different intensities when the rod-pigment, renewed by the darkness, more readily absorbs the green of the red-green mixture.[2]

From this consideration of the arguments, which support any one of the theories of rod-excitation as condition of colorless light sensation, we must go on to a separate study of each of these different theories, beginning with that of Mrs. C. L. Franklin, already adopted as the most probable of the hypotheses so far advanced.[3] The Franklin theory, in its latest form,[4] lays stress on the following points: (1) Sensational elements of white or gray are due to the complete decomposition of the molecules of a photochemical retinal substance. This substance is found both on the rods and on the cones. On the rods, it exists in an undifferentiated condition, so that it "goes to pieces all at once under the influence of light of any kind";[5] on the cones, it has

[1] This fact was established by C. L. Franklin and by Ebbinghaus. Cf. "Nature," Vol. 48, p. 517; "Theorie des Farbensehens," Separat-Abdruck aus *Ztsch. f. Psych. u. Physiol. d. Sinnesorgane*, 1893, p. 27.
[2] Cf. C. L. Franklin, "The Extended Purkinje Phenomenon," *Psychological Review*, Vol. V., p. 309.
[3] Cf. Chapter II., p. 40.
[4] Müller's "Theory of the Light Sense," *Psychological Review*, Vol. VI., p. 84.
[5] C. L. Franklin, "The Functions of the Rods of the Retina," *Psychological Review*, Vol. III., pp. 71 *seq.* For more detailed, but older, statement of the theory, cf. *Mind*, 1893.

been modified so that its decomposition occurs in two, or in four, stages. But the complete decomposition of the molecules of this substance, whether in the rods or in the cones, excites sensations of white or gray. (2) A sensational element of color is occasioned by one stage in the partial decomposition of the differentiated molecules of the photochemical substance in the cones. These differentiated molecules consist, in this second stage of development, "of two distinct parts, one fitted to be shaken to pieces by light from the warm end of the spectrum [the yellow-producing] and the other by light from the cold end of the spectrum [the blue-producing]; . . . in a third state of development the yellow-producing constituent is in its turn broken up into two parts of such different internal vibration periods that they respond respectively to the red light and the green light of the spectrum."[1] (3) The rod-pigment, or visual purple, is "not the substance whose chemical decomposition affects the optical nerve-ends,"[2] but is a substance which acts "by absorbing (for the purpose of reënforcing faint light vision) a large amount of the light which usually passes entirely through the transparent rods and cones."[3] (4) The sensational element black "is accounted for . . . . as the effect on the nerve-ends of the resting condition of the photochemical substance; it is therefore the antithesis to every color as well as to white."[4]

The proofs in favor of this hypothesis have now to be considered. The features which chiefly distinguish the theory from other rod-excitation theories are the following: (1) The hypothesis of one photochemical substance, both in rods and in cones, composed, on the rods, of undifferentiated molecules (which may be decomposed by ether-waves of any and all lengths) and, on the cones, of molecules so differentiated that distinct parts of them have 'different vibration periods.' (2) The conception of the rod-pigment as a reënforcing agent. (3) The conception of black as qualitatively distinct from white and gray, and as differently occasioned. In favor of the first of these hypotheses, the following considerations may be urged: It is (a) in accordance with physical and chemical conceptions.[5] It is (b) furthermore in close harmony with recent histological investigations. The Spanish neurologist, Ramon y Cajal, and others have shown that

---

[1] C. L. Franklin, *op. cit., Psychological Review*, Vol. VI., p. 84.
[2] *Op. cit., Psychological Review*, Vol. V., p. 332.
[3] *Ibid.*, Vol. VI., p. 80.
[4] "Color-Sensation Theory," *Psychological Review*, Vol. I., p. 171.
[5] Cf. C. L. Franklin, *op. cit., Psychological Review*, Vol. III., p. 72 and *Psychological Review*, Vol. VI., p. 84.

the retinal cones are really rods in a high stage of development.[1] "The fact is very much to the favor of those theories . . . which regard the color function of the cones as a developed form of the rod function." This feature of the Franklin theory has (c) a great advantage over the von Kries and König theories, which are later to be outlined, in that it offers an essentially identical explanation for all colorless light sensations, whether excited peripherally or in some other way. This advantage will be accentuated further on.

For the Franklin theory of the reënforcing function of the rod-pigment, the following arguments are offered: (a) It cannot be supposed that the functioning of the rod-pigment is essential to sensational elements of color or of colorless light, because we see white and grays, as well as all colors, in light so brilliant that it destroys the rod-pigment. (b) The greater intensity, in faint light, of the green rays which are most readily absorbed by the purplish rod-pigment, and the brightening, in faint light, of gray, due to mixture of red and green lights, are facts which are very readily explained by this conception of the rod-pigment as a substance which reënforces faint-light vision. (c) According to this hypothesis, the purplish color of the rod-pigment is highly significant, for "it is adapted to aiding vision in the gloomy depths of the forest, because green light is the light which it absorbs"; and, of course, primitive animal life is mainly passed in the forest.[2]

The Franklin hypothesis concerning black need not here be considered, for it is independent of other parts of the theory, and is mainly based on introspective grounds.[3] It will be well, however, to compare the theory as a whole with other theories of color and colorless light.

Like all theories which explain colorless light sensations by the functioning of a substance in the rods, this hypothesis (1) explains, as the Helmholtz theory cannot, the occurrence of white and gray without mixture of lights; it advances upon the antagonistic color-theories of Hering, Müller and Ebbinghaus, by providing (2) an explanation of the fact that grays, due to different mixtures, which are exactly similar, become dissimilar in changing illumination; and (3) by accounting for the fact that blue-green, not green, is 'complementary' to red; it is furthermore (4) a more definite hypothesis than that of Wundt.

---

[1] Ramon y Cajal's Neuere Beiträge, *Ztsch. f. Psych. u. Physiol. d. Sinnesorgane*, Vol. XVI., 1898, p. 161. Cf. C. L. Franklin, *Psychological Review*, Vol. VI., pp. 212 and 85.

[2] *Op. cit.*, *Psychological Review*, Vol. VI., p. 80.   [3] Cf. Chapter II., p. 30.

We have next, therefore, to compare the Franklin theory with the two remaining rod-excitation theories. Of these, the hypothesis of Professor J. von Kries is the simplest. Von Kries teaches [1] (1) that color-sensations are due to the activity of retinal cones, and (2) that sensational elements of colorless light are due to one of two distinct retinal conditions, either to the functioning of retinal cones or to the combination of three different retinal processes connected with the cones. It is evident that the von Kries theory differs from that of Mrs. Franklin in two main particulars: it is, in the first place, more indefinite, since it does not attempt to describe the activity of either rods or cones. In this respect the Franklin theory, since its hypotheses are reasonable, distinctly advances on that of von Kries. More positively, in the second place, von Kries differs from Mrs. Franklin in insisting that rods and cones are utterly different in function. His chief argument is the fact that colorless light sensations, through peripheral excitation, are differently conditioned from faint-light vision or color-blind vision.[2] This is indeed proved, "since the relative brightness of the spectrum, throughout its length, is not the same in the two cases";[3] but the phenomenon is readily explained in accordance with the Franklin theory, for the periphery in bright light lacks the rod-pigment, whereas this rod-pigment is built up in the retina during faint illumination, and is probably present in great degree in color-blind eyes. The discovery that this phenomenon does not tell in favor of von Kries leaves his theory encumbered with a tremendous burden: the improbability that peripheral gray and faint light gray, which appear to everybody exactly similar, should be due to utterly distinct retinal conditions. This objection von Kries has never satisfactorily answered.

The theory of Professor Arthur König is far more complicated. It agrees with that of von Kries, in that it attributes the colorless light consciousness to two retinal processes, but it involves, as will be shown, an entirely new consideration. König teaches first, that the consciousness of colorless light is due either to the weak decomposition of the rod-pigment in its purplish stage, or to the combined decomposition of the retinal substances; second, that the consciousness of blue is occasioned by the decomposition of the rod-pigment in its second or yellow stage (the visual yellow); and finally, that the other forms of color-sensations are

[1] *Ztsch. f. Psych. u. Physiol. d. Sinnesorgane,* Vol. IX., p. 82, Vol. XV., p. 247; "Abhandlungen," Leipzig, 1897.
[2] *Ztsch.,* Vol. XV.
[3] C. L. Franklin, *Psychological Review,* Vol. V., p. 330.

due to the decomposition of other retinal substances, as yet undiscovered, which are in the pigment layer — not in the rod and cone layer — of the retina. The theory that the consciousness of white and gray, in ordinary foveal vision, in faint light and in color-blindness has another retinal condition than that of peripherally excited sensations of colorless light, is evidently opposed by the grave objection which confronts the von Kries theory: the improbability that sensations subjectively alike should have widely different conditions.[1] The distinctive features of the theory are, however, the following: (1) the statement that the sensational element of blue is occasioned by the strong decomposition of the rod-pigment; (2) the theory that there are color-substances in the pigment layer of the retina. In proof of the first point, König adduces his experimental discovery that the fovea, which contains few rods or none, is blue-blind. His argument for the second hypothesis is an experiment performed by himself and Dr. Zumft:[2] two shadows of a blood-vessel were thrown, by different colored lights, upon the retina; the distance between the shadows was measured, and thus the distance of the blood-vessel from the excited layer of the retina was calculated; this distance was found to vary with the colors of the light, to be greater for red than for blue, and to be greater than the depth of the rod and cone layer. König concludes, as has been said, that the retinal processes which condition red, yellow and probably green, must lie behind the rod and cone layer, in the pigment layer.

In spite of the ingenuity of these arguments, König does not seem, to the writer of this book, to prove his points. The objections urged against both parts of the theory are decisive. The explanation of blue as due to the functioning of the 'visual yellow,' is opposed by the fact that one often sees blue in light strong enough to bleach out the rod-pigment in this yellow stage.[3] König bases this hypothesis on the alleged blue-blindness of the fovea; but this blue-blindness has been disputed,[4] and, in any case, could be otherwise explained. Against the second hypothesis of the theory, the following objections may be urged:[5] (a) "It proves too much," for the depth of the rod and cone

[1] Cf. E. Hering, Pflüger's *Archiv*, Vol. LIX., p. 412.
[2] Über die lichtempfindliche Schicht in der Netzhaut des menschlichen Auges, Sitzungsberichte d. Akad. d. Wissensch. zu Berlin, 1894.
[3] C. L. Franklin, *Psychological Review*, Vol. II., p. 146.
[4] Hering, *op. cit.*, p. 403.
[5] C. L. Franklin, *op. cit.* Cf. Gad, "Der Energium-Satz in der Retina," Separat-Abzug aus Arch. f. Anat. u. Physiol., 1894.

layer and pigment layer together are not equal to the calculated
difference between the retinal shadows.   (*b*) The explanation of
color-sensations as due to the excitation either of rod-pigment or
of substances in the pigment layer, makes it necessary to assign
a new rôle to the retinal cones.   König supposes them to be
lenses for concentrating light on the pigment layer cells.   But
this leaves unexplained the nerve conduction from the fovea,
and it also distinguishes too sharply between the rods and cones,
which, as we know, are anatomically very similar.   It should be
added, however, that the results of König's shadow-experiment
have neither been repeated nor disputed; and that his account
of these results, though justly criticised, has not been replaced
by another explanation.

This discussion of modern color-theories may be concluded
by a rough outline and classification of their most prominent
features.

I. THE THREE-COLOR THEORY OF HELMHOLTZ

(STATEMENT)

Three elemental colors: red, green, violet.

Colorless light sensations only through mixture of color-stimuli.

. Colorless light sensations 'compounds' of color-sensations.

(OBJECTIONS)

Introspection discloses *four* elemental colors.

No explanation for: peripheral, faint light, color-blind, colorless light sensations.

Introspectively untrue.

II. THE THEORIES OF 'ANTAGONISTIC' COLORS OF HERING, MÜLLER, EBBINGHAUS

(STATEMENT)

Four elemental colors: red, green, blue, yellow.

Two pair of antagonistic color-processes: red-green and blue-yellow.

Colorless light sensations through activity of a white-black substance, or through cerebral excitation, when color-processes have neutralized each other.

(MAIN OBJECTIONS)

The mixture of red and green lights does not produce colorless light sensations.

[See text.]

III. THE THEORIES OF COLORLESS LIGHT SENSATION AS DUE TO
ROD-EXCITATION

(*a*) *Theories of von Kries and König*

(STATEMENT)	(OBJECTIONS)
Four color-elements, due to cone-excitation (von Kries) ; or to decomposition of visual-yellow, and pigment layer excitation (König).	[See text.]
Colorless light sensations, due both to rod-excitation and to combination of distinct color-processes.	Improbability of two distinct retinal conditions of subjectively similar sensations.

(*b*) *Theory of C. L. Franklin*

Four color-elements, due to partial decomposition of differentiated molecules (of photochemical substance) in cones.	[For arguments see text.]

Colorless light sensations due to
complete decomposition of :
   (*a*) Undifferentiated molecules in rods.
   (*b*) Differentiated molecules in cones.

II. CERTAIN PHENOMENA OF COLOR-VISION

a. CONTRAST PHENOMENA

There are two forms of contrast, successive and simultaneous. Successive contrast may be illustrated by the following rough experiment: if, with eyes fixed, one looks steadily for twenty or thirty seconds at a square of red paper on a gray surface, and if one then looks off at the gray background, one is conscious, not of the uninterrupted gray field, but of a square of bluish green, which moves, as one's eyes move, across the background.[1] Parallel results follow upon the fixation of small green, blue and yellow surfaces: when the eye is moved to the gray background one sees,

[1] For experiments, cf. Sanford, 124; Titchener, § 11, Exps. (7) and (8).

instead of gray, a second figure, whose color is complementary to that of the stimulus; and if white or black be fixated, the 'negative after-image,' as the contrasting color is called, is black or white.

Here one has an instance of a psychic phenomenon, precisely opposed to that which is the natural consequence of the physical stimulus: yellow light induces the sensational consciousness of blue, blue light induces yellow, and so on. The explanation of these contrast-phenomena must therefore be physiological. According to Fechner, followed by Helmholtz,[1] they are due to retinal fatigue. The retinal process induced by the yellow light, for example, is exhausted by fixation of the yellow paper; when, therefore, the eye is moved to the gray background and the retina is stimulated by colorless light (a combination of ether-waves of all vibration-rates), the retinal processes corresponding to the yellow light are exhausted, and only the unfatigued processes, which condition the consciousness of blue, are excited. This explanation, though most often stated in terms of the Helmholtz theory, is really in accord with any hypothesis of retinal activity as occasioning color-sensations. Hering has shown, however, that the Fechner theory is insufficient to explain all the phenomena involved in successive contrast.[2] In particular, he shows that the background of the negative after-image is always affected in hue or in intensity.

We turn, therefore, to the study of simultaneous contrast. Many everyday phenomena, for example the decided blue of the shadows on a sunlighted field of snow, illustrate what is known as simultaneous contrast. There are also many experimental verifications of the phenomenon.[3] The simplest is the examination of squares or rings of gray, on colored surfaces, through a tissue paper covering, which obscures the outline of the gray figures; these gray figures will then appear in the color complementary to the background, yellow on a blue background, red on bluish green, and so on.

An exact explanation of this curious phenomenon has never been given, but it has been established by Hering, against the teaching of Helmholtz, that the explanation, whatever it is, of simultaneous contrast, must be physiological in its nature. Helmholtz taught that simultaneous contrast is no more nor less than a psychological illusion.[4] According to his theory, we

---

[1] "Physiologische Optik," Ed. 2, pp. 501 *seq.*, 537 *seq.*, §§ 23, 24.
[2] Cf. Hering, "Zur Lehre vom Lichtsinne," especially § 18.
[3] For experiments, cf. Sanford, 152, *b, c, d*; Titchener, § 10, especially Exp. (1), (2), (3).   [4] *Op. cit.*, § 24, p. 559.

'really' see, not a complementary contrast-color but the physically excited, actual gray figure, though we fallaciously suppose that this gray is yellow, if it lies on a blue background, or green, if it is seen against purple. The explanation, for so widespread an illusion, is found in the admitted fact that people are accustomed to look at familiar, colored objects through a complementary colored medium, which makes them seem gray. For example, we see a red brick wall through the green lights of a hall door; the wall seems gray, but we still think of it as red. Or again, the blue gown looks gray in the yellow gaslight, but is known to be blue. The gray figures of the simultaneous contrast experiences are thus, Helmholtz holds, inferred — not actually seen — to be of a color complementary to that of the background. But opposed to this theory of Helmholtz are insurmountable obstacles. In the first place, it directly contradicts our introspection. We not only do not naturally see objects, in simultaneous contrast, as gray, but in most cases we cannot force ourselves to do so; the gray ring on the colored background is immediately, and inevitably, blue or yellow or red. It is highly improbable, in the second place, that our comparatively infrequent and unnoticed experiences of colored objects, in light of complementary color, should have formed in us such a habit of inference as this theory supposes. The Helmholtz theory is disproved, finally, by direct and unambiguous experiments.[1]

It is fair to conclude, with Hering, that simultaneous contrast is physiologically conditioned; in other words, that when one part of the retina is directly excited by a colored light, retinal processes which condition a complementary color are set up in the neighboring retinal regions. This undoubted fact can be stated in terms of any color-theory, but it has never been, in any strict sense explained, or accounted for.[2]

b. COLOR-BLINDNESS

The description and explanation of color-blindness have gone hand in hand with the discussion of color-theories, and fact has not even, always, been clearly distinguished from hypothesis. It was rightly inferred, for example, that if the Helmholtz hypothesis (of three color-processes and no distinct colorless light apparatus) were correct, then color-blindness would consist in the absence of one or other of these color-processes. Accordingly, the ordi-

[1] Cf. Sanford, 155 *a* and *b*; 156 *a* and *b*; Hering, "Beitrag zur Lehre vom Simultankontrast," *Ztsch. f. Psych. u. Physiol. d. Sinnesorgane*, Vol. I., p. 18.
[2] Cf. C. L. Franklin, *Mind*, N. S., Vol. II., 1893.

nary forms of color-blindness were called 'red-blindness' and 'green-blindness.' It has, however, been established by Hering and by others, that the so-called 'red-blind' sees red, not as green-blue — which the Helmholtz theory requires — but as gray, and that he does not see green as green; and conversely, it has been shown that the 'green-blind' sees green as gray and fails to see red as red. This conclusion has been reached both by experiments on the totally red-green blind, which require the matching of different hues and shades, and also by the examination of subjects who are color-blind in one eye only, so that they can compare their color-blind with their normal experiences.[1] Evidently, therefore, the facts of color-blindness definitely contradict the Hemholtz color-theory. Unfortunately, they do not unequivocally pronounce in favor of any one of the other color-theories. A further study of the forms of color-blindness will make this clear.

In his early discussions of color-blindness, Hering supposed the existence of a single form of red-green blindness, in which both red and green were seen as gray. Later investigation has, however, established the fact that there are two distinct types of red-green blindness. In the one, the unmixed red is seen as gray, the yellowish reds and greens are an unsaturated yellow, and even saturated green appears as yellow and not as gray. In the other form of red-green blindness, saturated green seems gray, the yellowish greens and reds are unsaturated yellow, and even red is seen not as gray but as yellow.[2] "It is as if red vision had fallen out and green vision had been turned into yellow vision for the one sort; and for the other sort, it is as if green vision had fallen out and yellow vision had taken the place of red vision."[3] The existence of these different forms of red-green blindness tells against the Hering view that all forms of red-green blindness are due merely to the absence of the red-green substance. Hering's recent explanation of the distinction, as due to individual differences in the yellow spot of the eye, is inadequate; Müller's account of it, as due to an indirect effect of red light on the 'blue-yellow' substance, is extremely complicated, and is, of course, at variance with the Hering theory in its original form; Ebbinghaus's theory, that the distinction is due to individual differences in objectively colored retinal sub-

---

[1] Cf. Hering, "Zur Erklärung der Farbenblindheit, Sonderabdruck," 1880, especially § 5 : "Die Untersuchung einseitiger Störung des Farbensinnes," especially pp. 10 *seq.*

[2] Cf. Wundt, *op. cit.*, 4te Aufl., I., 508, and 510, note 1.

[3] C. L. Franklin, *op. cit., Psychological Review*, Vol. VI., p. 82.

stances, makes use of an unsubstantiated hypothesis. The difference between the red-blind with his gray, yellow and blue spectrum and the green-blind with his yellow, gray and blue spectrum, is thus a crucial difficulty for the Hering hypothesis.

The forms of blue-yellow blindness, and their relation to general color-theory, need not be discussed at length, for so few cases have been described[1] that this form of dichromatic color-blindness is insufficiently established. Either the absence or the rarity of blue-yellow blindness would indicate, we may observe, that blue and yellow were the primitive forms of color-vision, and that red and green, the last to be attained, are the earliest lost. This accords well, it will be noted, with the Franklin theory, that the vibrating portions of the color-molecule, which occasion 'red' and 'green,' are developed out of the portion whose decomposition occasions yellow. The fact, however, may be stated in harmony with still other color-theories.

There are a number of well authenticated cases of achromasia, or total color-blindness, in which the subject sees all the spectral colors as tones of gray. The spectrum of the totally color-blind is probably like that of the normal eye in faint illumination. Two forms of achromasia have been discovered. The first includes cases in which the fovea, which, in the normal eye, contains cones only and no rods, is totally blind, not merely color-blind. Such cases evidently tell in favor of the König, von Kries and Franklin theories, of colorless light sensations as due to retinal processes connected with the rods, since excitation of a retinal area, devoid of rods, produces, in the color-blind, no visual sensations whatever. But at least three cases of another sort have been reported.[2] In these, there was no blindness of the fovea, which must therefore have contained some apparatus for colorless light sensations. These cases have been urged against the theory that cone-processes condition color-vision, whereas rod-processes occasion colorless light sensations. But as Mrs. Franklin points out,[3] this form of color-blindness does not disprove these theories, though it does not support them. For one may either suppose, in general harmony with von Kries or Franklin, (1) that the sensitive foveæ of these three color-blind subjects were unlike the normal, precisely in that they contained not cones but rods — probably without visual purple; or one may suppose (2) that

[1] Cf. Wundt, *op cit.*, Vol. I., p. 509 ; Ebbinghaus, *op cit.*, p. 71.
[2] Cf. Hess and Hering, Pflüger's *Archiv*, 71, 105, reviewed by C. L. Franklin, *Psychological Review*, Vol. V., p. 532.
[3] "The New Cases of Total Color-blindness," *Psychological Review*, Vol. V., p. 503.

these foveæ contained undeveloped cones, provided with the same photochemical substance as the rods; or finally, (3) that these cases of color-blindness, without total blindness of the fovea, are due to no retinal peculiarity whatever, but to some disturbance of the visual centres in the brain. Many facts speak for this last hypothesis. Acquired color-blindness is almost always a symptom of disease of brain or of optic nerve; the effect, which is cerebral, of a dose of santonine, is to induce yellow-blindness; and it certainly is highly probable that color-blindness is due to cerebral rather than to retinal conditions,[1] where there is, otherwise, absolutely undisturbed vision.

These conclusions may now be summarized, with the remark that few of them would remain unchallenged by some students of color-vision: There are two general classes of color-blindness, partial and total. Red-blindness — in which the spectrum order of colors appears as gray, yellow, blue — and green blindness — in which the order is yellow, gray, blue — are the most common form of dichromasia or partial color-blindness; but there are also a few alleged cases of yellow-blue blindness, in which the patient sees grays, reds and greens, but no blues and yellows. There are two forms of achromasia, or total color-blindness: in one, probably retinal in origin, the fovea is totally blind, and there are accompanying defects of vision; in the second form of achromasia, very likely due to cerebral defects, the fovea is not totally blind, and there are no defects of vision, other than the color-blindness. These facts absolutely contradict the Helmholtz theory; are with difficulty harmonized with the Hering theory; support, or at least do not oppose, a theory of the general form of the Franklin hypothesis.

c. THE PURKINJE PHENOMENON

It will be well to summarize here the essential features of a characteristic color-phenomenon, often encountered in our study, under its historic name of 'Purkinje phenomenon.' As first observed, it consists simply in the fact that green and blue,[2] seen in a faint light, have a greater intensity than red and yellow. This is illustrated by the familiar phenomenon that greens and blues keep their color in the twilight far better and far longer than reds and yellows; my bookshelf, for example, as the twilight falls, is a succession of intense greens and blues, broken by dull

[1] Cf. C. L. Franklin, *Psychological Review*, Vol. VII., p. 520.
[2] Cf. C. L. Franklin, *Psychological Review*, Vol. VII., p. 601.

reds and yellows; as the room grows darker, the greens and blues stand out against lighter and darker grays, representing the reds and yellows; and even when these greens and blues have themselves turned to gray, they are distinctly brighter, more nearly white, than the reds and yellows.[1]

A spectrum, therefore, regarded in a very faint light, is a series of grays, darkest at the red end and brightest in the region of green. Up to this point, the Purkinje phenomenon has been described, so far as it affects colors. In recent years it has, however, been shown by Ebbinghaus and by C. L. Franklin, that if two grays, one produced by the mixture of red and blue-green lights, and the other excited by the mixture of blue and yellow lights, be precisely matched in a bright light, the first of the two will grow brighter than the other in a faint light. Mrs. Franklin has suggestively named this observation an extension of the Purkinje phenomenon.

The significance of the Purkinje phenomenon has constantly appeared in our discussion of color-theories. It is the most unambiguous psychological argument for the theory that the visual purple, and consequently the rods with which it is found, are organs of achromatic, or colorless light vision. For the Purkinje phenomenon appears only in faint illumination, and the visual purple is active only in faint light; moreover, the Purkinje phenomenon consists in the intensification of green and secondarily of blue lights, and the visual purple absorbs green rays — and, after green, blue rays — most readily; finally, the Purkinje phenomenon, as has been found,[2] does not occur when the foveæ of normal and partially color-blind eyes are excited, that is to say, it does not occur by excitation of the region of the retina which lacks visual purple and rods.

Mention should be made of Hering's most recent account of the Purkinje phenomenon as due to the 'specific brightening power' of the different colors.[3] This hypothesis has lost its excuse for being, for, at best, it described the Purkinje phenomenon instead of explaining it; and it is logically, as well as physiologically, superseded by the discovery that the visual purple so readily absorbs green and blue rays.

[1] For experiment, cf. Sanford, 142.

[2] Von Kries u. Nagel, *Ztsch. f. Psych. u. Physiol. d. Sinnesorgane*, Vol. XXIII., p. 161, discussed by C.L. Franklin, *Psychological Review*, Vol. VII., p. 600.

[3] This hypothesis, it should be noted, is not identical with Hering's original supposition, which he has now abandoned, that the brightness of a color consists in the brightness of the colorless light mixed with it. Cf. C. L. Franklin, *Psychological Review*, Vol. III., p. 695; Vol. V., p. 332; Vol. VII., p. 604.

SECTION IV

THE PHYSICAL AND THE PHYSIOLOGICAL CONDITIONS OF SENSATIONS OF SMELL

BY ELEANOR A. McC. GAMBLE

JOHANNES MÜLLER is responsible for the hypothesis that odorous particles are in solution when they act upon the end-organs of smell. He supposed them to be dissolved in the liquid which covers the olfactory membrane. The arguments for this hypothesis are as follows: First, amphibia and fishes have central nervous developments and peripheral organs which somewhat resemble the organs of smell in birds and in mammals. Second, if the mucous membrane of the nose becomes dry, as it does in the first stage of rhinitis, smell is impaired. Third, Aronsohn obtained sensations of smell when he poured into the nose, from the height of half a meter, normal saline solutions of odorous matter, of slight concentration, and at 40° C. Against these arguments Zwaardemaker urges the following considerations: First, aquatic mammals have, in a rudimentary state, organs of smell which resemble those of land mammals. This does not look as if these organs could function under water. Second, the drying of the nasal membrane in rhinitis is confined almost entirely to the respiratory membrane, and is conjoined with hyperæmia and with swelling, which constitutes a mechanical hindrance to the passage of odorous particles. Third, it cannot be shown that Aronsohn succeeded in filling the nasal cavities so completely as to exclude all bubbles of air. It is very difficult to drive all the air out of blind pouches.

Against the hypothesis, Zwaardemaker urges further: First, that the hairs of the olfactory cells protrude through the thin layer of liquid which covers the membrane; second, that most odorous substances are insoluble, or soluble to a very slight degree, in water. In a room saturated with perfume or tobacco smoke, although a bit of glass or of cotton-wool will take up the odor, water will not. Gums, æthereal oils and the like are the materials of the perfume industry.[1]

Gaseous particles are given off from the surface of odorous bodies by simple evaporation, by oxidation, by hydrolitic changes,

---

[1] This discussion is found in Zwaardemaker's "Physiologie des Geruchs," Leipzig, 1895, pp. 62–66.

and by more complicated processes of decomposition. Some strongly odorous substances, such as æthereal oils, diffuse themselves in a thin film over the surface of water, and are probably often carried through the air in the form of minute drops. Odorous vapors diffuse slowly; hence their significance in the animal world.

We know much less of the chemistry than of the physics of smell. Certain groups of atoms occur so persistently, in ranges of similar smells, that they would seem to condition these smells. Yet the total composition of these similarly odorous substances differs so much that we can scarcely believe the connection to be direct. Zwaardemaker suggests that the function of these effective groups of atoms may be analogous to the part which chemical composition plays in the absorption of different colored lights. Smells, he supposes, may be conditioned by ether vibrations, which are determined by the intramolecular motions of the tiniest particles of odorous substances. The ether vibrations must be longer or shorter than the light and heat waves. Since very short light waves may be absorbed by a layer of air only a few millimeters thick, and since odors can be detected only near their source, it is probable that odor vibrations are very short rather than comparatively long.[1]

We may hope for a satisfactory classification of odors, only on a physiological basis and by the help of the exhaustion-experiments, initiated by Aronsohn. Zwaardemaker is certainly justified in arguing that if certain zones of the olfactory membrane are especially sensitive to certain smells, these zones must be arranged horizontally from front to back, and not vertically; for the height to which the air is drawn into the nose makes a difference in the intensity but none in the quality of a smell.[2] Other features of Zwaardemaker's theory are the following: The lower cells, taken vertically, may be more sensitive to the heavier odors of an homologous series, and the higher cells to the lighter.[3] Cells are not set apart to some one stimulus exclusively; they are simply more sensitive to one stimulus, and less so to others. Excitations may irradiate from the points especially sensitive to given stimuli, and may overlap. In case they overlap, we have a fusion of odors.[4] The great variety of odors in nature is due to fusion. It is comparable, on the theory of this text-book, to the scales of hues, tints and shades, not to the pure tonal scale. When there is no coincidence of excitations, smells 'compen-

[1] Zwaardemaker, *op. cit.*, pp. 253–254.   [2] *Ibid.*, p. 262.
[3] pp. 272–275.   [4] pp. 278–284.

sate ' or cancel each other.   Since compensation takes place even
when the stimuli are applied to different nostrils, there must be
some central cancellation of excitations.[1]

It should be added that the details of fusion and compensation
are in dispute; and that uniform results are by no means easy to
obtain in exhaustion-experiments.   Such experiments, except for
purposes of illustration, should always be made with an olfac-
tometer, and the subject's breathing should be recorded with
a pneumograph.

SECTION V

END-ORGANS OF PRESSURE AND OF PAIN

I. END-ORGANS OF PRESSURE: VON FREY'S THEORY[2]

At least five sorts of differentiated nerve-endings are found in
or beneath the skin.   There are, in the first place, the hair-bulbs,
from which project the fine hairs which transmit any movement

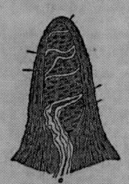

FIG. 18.—A dermic papilla
containing tactile corpuscle
(Meissner's).

with accelerated force: many of the afferent nerves terminate in these bulbs.
There are also four distinct forms of end-
organs:[3] (1) Tactile corpuscles (Meissner's), found in the papillæ of the dermis,
or lower skin, in which several nerves end.
These have a soft core, separated into
several masses by end-plates, in each of
which a nerve-fibre seems to end; they
seldom occur except in the skin of hand
and of foot.   (2) Touch cells, 'of the
same essential structure, but receiving
only one nerve-fibre each, distributed all
over the skin.'   (3) Pacinian corpuscles,
'in the subcutaneous tissue of the hand
and foot, and about the knee-joint.'
(4) End-bulbs, consisting 'of a core with
connective-tissue capsule, found on parts
of the lips, in the conjunctiva, and on mucous membranes of
palate and tongue.'   Besides the nerves ending in the hair-bulbs
and in these special organs, there are nerves with so-called 'free'

[1] *Op. cit.*, pp. 284–287.
[2] Cf. "Untersuchungen, u. s. w."   (See this book, p. 68, footnote.)
[3] Cf. Martin, *op. cit.*, pp. 556 *seq.*

endings, that is to say, nerves terminating in undifferentiated cells.

In the fifth chapter of this book, von Frey's theory that both the hair-bulbs and the tactile corpuscles are end-organs of pressure has been approved; and his theory that the pain-nerves are nerves with free end-organs has been named among the hypotheses regarding the physiological conditions of pain. It will be well, therefore, to outline von Frey's methods and his arguments. His apparatus consists of a large number of light sticks, ten centimeters long, to each of which is fastened, at right angles, a hair from two to three centimeters in length. (For coarse work, a horse-hair is used, otherwise, a human hair — for finest work, the hair of a child.) The diameter of the hair, and thus its pressure area, is measured under the microscope. The force necessary to bend each hair is determined by a delicately poised scale; the number of grams of pressure is calculated from these data. The unit is therefore $\frac{gr}{mm^2}$, "the number of grams pressure necessary to produce a sensation of pressure when the contact surface equals one square millimeter."[1]

Von Frey holds, as has been shown, that there are two sorts of pressure end-organs: first, the hair-bulbs, whose connection with pressure-sensations is proved by the fact that hairy spots are especially sensitive to pressure; and second, the 'tactile corpuscles,' or corpuscles of Meissner. These organs, as has been said, are most frequent on hairless portions of the body, especially on hand and foot, and are entirely absent from some hairy parts of the body. In proof of this second part of the theory, von Frey urges the following facts: (1) The number of these corpuscles of Meissner corresponds with the number of actually discovered pressure-spots. This correspondence has not been observed in the case of any other skin end-organs. For example, there are only 608 Pacinian corpuscles in the palm of the hand — a number far smaller than that of the pressure-spots. (2) The situation of the Meissner corpuscles in the dermis or lower skin accounts for the fact that the pressure-intensity from a very small surface is not proportional to that from a larger surface. For in the case of small stimuli, but not in the case of larger ones, the depth of skin to be stimulated, before the corpuscle of Meissner is affected, actually neutralizes the force of the stimulus. Finally, (3) the connection of the corpuscle through its two or three nerve fibrils with several distinct nerves, differentiates the pressure-

[1] For criticism, cf. W. A. Nagel, Pflüger's *Archiv*, 1895, Vol. LIX., p. 595.

spots in a way which closely corresponds with our keen discrimination of different contacts.

It should be noticed that von Frey's results contradict Goldscheider's, in that Goldscheider finds in hairy areas many
pressure-spots unconnected with the hairs, whereas von Frey
finds but few. Von Frey explains the discrepancy by supposing that Goldscheider used too heavy stimuli, which initiated
excitations radiating from the organ first stimulated.

II. Theories of the Physiological Excitation of Pain

Von Frey's theory of the physiological conditions of pain is
based on his discovery, with the apparatus just described, of certain points on the elbow-joints and on the cornea and conjunctiva
of the eye, which are sensitive to pain and not to pressure; these
argue, he points out, for the existence of special pain-nerves, and
these pain-nerves are, he believes, the nerves which terminate in
free endings, that is to say, in undifferentiated nerve-cells. Von
Frey reaches this conclusion by the following rather complicated
argument: (1) It has been observed that large surfaces excite
sensations of pressure, whose intensity is nearly proportional to
the weight of the stimuli, whereas this proportion is not observed
when the pressure-stimuli have small surfaces. (2) This contrast
can only be explained by the fact that, in the latter case, the thick-
ness of the skin neutralizes the pressure of the stimulating object;
and this indicates that the end-organs of pressure lie deep. Now,
(3) in the case of pain-stimuli this contrast is not observable, and
it follows, according to von Frey, that the pain nerve-endings
must lie nearer the surface. The undifferentiated 'free' nerve-
endings are those which meet this condition.[1]

As has been said, von Frey explains the fact that so few parts
of the body have been found, which are insensitive to pressure
yet sensitive to pain, by supposing that the pain nerve-endings
are far less easily excited than the pressure end-organs. He
also admits the possibility that internal pains are due to direct
excitation of pain nerve-fibres.[2]

It should be added that W. A. Nagel has repeated von Frey's
experiment, and that he finds,[3] in opposition to von Frey, that
conjunctiva and cornea are sensitive to pressure, and, for some
persons, to cold, though not to warmth. He explains von Frey's
results by the supposition that von Frey's hairs pricked the sur-

---

[1] *Op. cit.,* p. 257.   [2] *Op. cit.,* p. 258.
[3] Pflüger's *Archiv,* Vol. LIX., p. 563. Cf. G. W. A. Luckey, *American
Journal of Psychology,* Vol. VII., p. 109.

faces, instead of gently touching them. Nagel concludes that the existence of distinct pain nerves is unproved. The results of his experiments incline him to the Goldscheider theory.

In the diversity of expert opinion the layman may well hesitate, therefore, to decide between the end-organ theory of von Frey and others, and the theories, like that of Goldscheider, which deny a peripheral end-organ of pain while maintaining its sensational character. An ingenious theory, of this second type, that of Professor Z. Oppenheimer,[1] may be briefly mentioned. Dr. Oppenheimer attributes pain to excitation both of cutaneous nerves and of the sympathetic nervous system.

SECTION VI

BODILY MOVEMENTS

SUCH constant reference is made, throughout a treatise on psychology, to the different forms of bodily movement, that it will be convenient to summarize here the distinctions on which various chapters comment in more detail. The forms of bodily movement are grouped together in the following summary:—

BODILY MOVEMENTS

A. IMMEDIATE MOVEMENTS

I. *Automatic Movements.* (Stimulus: within the organism. Always instinctive.)

    a. Without consciousness } 1. Once performed.
    b. With consciousness   } 2. Habitual.

II. *Reflex Movements.* (Stimulus: without the organism.)

    a. Without consciousness.
        1. Instinctive } (*a*) Once performed.
        2. Acquired } (*b*) Habitual.
        (Externally imitative)
    b. With consciousness.
        1. Instinctive } (*a*) Once performed.
        2. Acquired } (*b*) Habitual.

---

[1] "Schmerz u. Temperatur Empfindung," p. 128; cf. Luckey, *op. cit.*

B. Delayed or Ideo-motor Movements
(Following upon anticipatory idea. Always with consciousness.)

I. *Impulsive.* (Unconsciously imitative of anticipatory idea.)
    a. Habitual (self-imitative).
    b. Externally imitative.

II. *Volitional.* (Consciously imitative of anticipatory idea.)
    1. Simple   } (*a*) Habitual.
    2. Deliberative } (*b*) Externally imitative.

SECTION VII

THEORIES OF ATTENTION

There is no subject in psychology concerning which more divergent views are held than this topic of the nature of attention. It is almost correct to say that no one theory has the undivided support even of any one scholar. The following types of theory — including those referred to in the text — are of greatest importance.

I. The Activity Theory

This theory distinguishes attention, as an activity of consciousness, from the passivity of perception and imagination, thus regarding it as a radically different sort of consciousness. In merely perceiving and in imagining, say the upholders of this doctrine, we are clearly inactive and receptive; in attention, on the other hand, we evidently assert ourselves and react upon our environment. This is the view of the books written wholly from the so-called 'spiritualist' standpoint, but it may also be discovered in books written on an utterly different basis. Wundt's theory, for example, of apperception and attention, often presupposes this activity of a self. The objections to the theory may be readily stated. It has been urged [1] (1) that the activity which it presupposes is a metaphysical entity, a mind-activity inferred to account for the facts of attention, not an experience actually observed. This objection certainly holds good against many statements of the activity-theory. When Professor Ladd, for example, says that "primary attention is a form of psychical

[1] Cf. Titchener, "Outline," § 36.

energy,"[1] and again that "attention is . . . a striving and selective, but self-originating activity," it is hard to divorce from his words a metaphysical implication. Yet it is certainly possible, in the opinion of the writer, to discover within one's conscious life the distinct experience of activity — a form of consciousness which is present in will and in belief, and lacking in revery and in perception. But (2) activity, in this sense of will or belief, is something other than attention. This is evident from the fact that even the upholders of the activity-theory admit that attention may be involuntary as well as voluntary ('passive' as well as 'active').

The admission of a passive as well as an active form of attention is, indeed, as Titchener has pointed out, a virtual abandonment of the activity-theory. So long as 'passive' attention is admitted to be attention, and yet to involve no activity, the activity can be no necessary feature of attention. Certain activity-theory psychologists, realizing this dilemma, insist that the activity is present in the earliest stages of consciousness. But once more, (3) activity, in this general sense, is either a metaphysical concept, or else a synonym for self-consciousness, not a designation of any phase of consciousness.

Both Titchener and Münsterberg, in different connections, urge against the activity-theory (4) that the alleged activity is really a consciousness of bodily motions; and this is probably true of many (though not of all) experiences of activity.

The theories of attention which will next be considered are alike, in that they mistake — in the opinion of the writer — the frequent accompaniment or result of attention for attention itself. Historically, most important of these is

II. THE MOTOR THEORY OF ATTENTION

According to this hypothesis, attention consists simply and solely of what we have called its motor results, and of the consciousness of these motor phenomena — adjustment of sense-organs or movements of the scalp, and contraction of inhibitory muscles. The best-known exposition of the view is that of Theodore Ribot.[2] It derives its plausibility from the constant presence in admitted attention, not only of the characteristic

[1] "Psychology, Descriptive and Explanatory," pp. 34 and 37.
[2] "The Psychology of Attention." Cf. Bain, "Emotions and Will," and N. Lange, "Philosophische Studien," Vol. IV. See also summary, James, *op. cit.*, Vol. I., p. 444.

motor accompaniments, but of the little-heeded, readily forgotten, yet persistent feelings of bodily movement. Nevertheless,
introspection shows clearly that by attention we mean something
more than consciousness of bodily motions. It is perfectly certain that the terms are not synonymous in our experience. The
theory of the text, which treats the bodily movements as results
or as accompaniments of the attention-element, clearness, does
justice to their significance, without giving them a false
importance.

III. The Theory of Attention as Affection

This theory is unambiguously stated by Stumpf,[1] who says,
"Aufmerksamkeit ist identisch mit Interesse und Interesse ist
ein Gefühl." Wundt, though he does not expressly relate attention and affection, regards them as alike in two important particulars: both are referred to the self,[2] and both are physiologically
conditioned by excitation of the frontal lobes. Titchener, like
Wundt, does not actually identify attention and affection, but
calls them 'back and front,' obverse and reverse of the same
state, 'two sides of one' experience.' On the other hand, he
does identify interest and affection. "A felt thing," he says, "is
an interesting thing"; "a thing that interests us is a thing, the
idea of which is overlaid with affection." If, therefore, that
view is correct, which is outlined in Chapter XI. of this book,
upheld by Stumpf, and stated by James in the words, "what we
are interested in and what we attend to are synonymous terms,"
then the identification of interest and affection amounts to the
identification of attention and affection. Titchener, however,
would not admit the identity of interest and attention, and really
teaches that attention and affection (which he names interest)
are constant accompaniments. In the opinion of the present
writer,[4] it is untrue to introspection to insist that the attended-to
is invariably pleasant or unpleasant, though it is unquestionably
true that attention is often affectively toned.

IV. Theories which deny Attention as a Positive Form of Consciousness

Two theories which agree in denying that attention adds
anything to consciousness will be briefly named. The first is

[1] "Tonpsychologie," Vol. I., § 4, II., § 22.
[2] "Physiologische Psychologie," Vol. II., Chapter 18, p. 497 ("Zustände
die wir unmittelbar auf ein Leiden oder Thätigkeit unsers Ich beziehen ").
[3] "Primer," § 33.   [4] Cf. Chapter XI., p. 141.

that of F. H. Bradley, who frankly insists[1] that attention is a mere synonym for consciousness, and that inattention is pure unconsciousness.

A more ordinary view, of the same general import, defines attention as inhibition, or exclusion. My attention at a moment of intellectual strain consists, for example, in the fact that I am not conscious of the plainly audible gnawing of a mouse. This theory evidently identifies attention with what we have reckoned as one of its secondary characteristics, its narrowness — or monoideism, as Ribot calls it. Both conceptions of attention are evidently set aside, if we have been right in our discovery of an attention-element, clearness; for such an element would evidently distinguish attention from mere consciousness, and would endow it with a more positive characteristic than its narrowness or exclusiveness.

It should be added that the inhibition theory of attention may be a physiological hypothesis concerning the cerebral condition of attention.

V. THEORIES OF ATTENTION AS ELEMENTAL CONSCIOUSNESS

It is difficult to point to any one writer who holds steadily and consistently to this view; but the activity-theories constantly tend toward expression in these terms. So, Wundt says, that clearness (*Klarheit*) is an element of attention;[2] and this statement implies the existence of a distinct element of consciousness. Titchener's latest account of attention[3] describes it as the (1) clearness of (2) a narrow experience which (3) is constantly accompanied by affections and bodily movements, and (4) is easily reproducible. This accords closely with the conception of this book; and though Titchener does not define clearness, it is easiest to suppose that he virtually conceives it as element of consciousness.

The theory of an attention-element is also clearly suggested by Münsterberg in his doctrine of vividness. He does not, to be sure, define vividness as element of consciousness, since he uses the term 'element' in another sense than that of this book; but he calls vividness a distinct 'variation' or 'dimension' or 'value' of sensation, and explains it, as will be pointed out, by a distinct physiological process.[4]

[1] *Mind*, N. S., Vol., II., 1893, p. 211.
[2] "Physiologische Psychologie," 4te Aufl., Vol. II., p. 271.
[3] "Experimental Psychology," Vol. I., Pt. I., p. 109.
[4] "Psychology and Life," pp. 86, 95–96. Cf. "Grundzuge d. Psychologie," p. 531.

VI. Theories of the Physiological Conditions of Attention

Brief mention must be made, in conclusion, of the theories which have concerned themselves with the physiological conditions of attention. Roughly speaking, these are of three varieties:[1] First, theories which claim an afferent (or sensory) neural excitation for attention. In general, these theories[2] suppose a reënforcement of the brain-excitations which condition inattentive consciousness. The objections to the conception are, first, its vagueness, and second, the fact that on this view there seems to be no conceivable distinction between the physiological condition of sense-intensity (which is surely nothing other than 'reënforced' cerebral excitation) and that of attention. Yet sense-intensity and attention are psychologically perfectly distinct.[3]

In the second place, there are 'motor' theories of attention. The earliest of them attached itself to the Ribot theory of attention, as essentially composed of movements and feelings of movement. It treated this consciousness of movement, after the manner of Wundt and others, as a feeling of 'innervation' or outgoing energy. Ferrier, James, Münsterberg and others, however, proved that this feeling of movement is nothing more than a sensory consciousness of bodily pressure, which must be due to the excitation of cells in the sensory pressure-centre of the brain.[4]

A later 'motor' theory of attention attributes merely inhibitive functions to motor cells and to efferent fibres of the brain.[5] Münsterberg, finally, has still a third 'motor' theory. He explains attention — or vividness — as due to the 'intensity of the discharge' of the nerve-current along the efferent nerves.[6]

The physiological theories of attention, which belong to the third group, explain attention, not as due to the functioning of sensory or of motor cells and fibres, but as due to the activity of cells and fibres in the so-called association-centres. The best known of these hypotheses is that of Wundt,[7] who conceives of

[1] Cf. throughout, A. J. Hamlin, "Attention and Distraction," *American Journal of Psychology*, Vol. VIII., 1896, 1.
[2] Cf. Bastian, *Revue Philosophique*, 1892, p. 353; and Marillier, *ibid.*, Vol. XXVII., p. 566.   [5] Cf. A. J. Hamlin, *op. cit.*, p. 13.
[3] Cf. Chapter XI., pp. 140–141.   [6] "Psychology and Life," pp. 95–96.
[4] Cf. James, *op. cit.*, II. 492 *seq.*   [7] "Physiol. Psychologie," Vol. II., p. 275.

attention as conditioned by the conduction of nervous impulses from sensory centres to the frontal lobes, and thus outward to the motor fibres. The effect of this functioning of the frontal lobe centres is, according to Wundt, in the main inhibitive.

The theory of this book belongs, in a general way, to this third group — that is to say, the conception of a relational attention-element, clearness, implies as corollary the hypothesis that one of the association-centres of the brain is excited in attention. The constancy of the motor accompaniments of attention makes it highly probable, also, that outgoing fibres function in attention. In the opinion of the present writer, our knowledge of brain conditions warrants only some such tentative and general theory of the cerebral conditions of attention.

BIBLIOGRAPHY

This bibliography is incomplete, first, because of the limitations of its compiler's knowledge; second, because of the limitations of this book, which is a general treatise, not a specialist monograph on any subject. On the other hand, this bibliography does not confine itself to English works, and includes references to the monograph and periodical literature of psychology, not only in the hope of inciting some students to psychological research, but in the belief that even elementary students are the better for a wide outlook. With a few exceptions, mainly in the literature of experiment, only books and papers of which the writer has a first-hand knowledge are referred to. Detailed references, in the body of the book, are seldom repeated here; but relatively extended bibliographies are given of certain subjects of which the book does not treat. The lists are arranged in a rough topical order; occasionally, also, the books or essays first named are those which seem, to the writer, of most immediate value to the student. (For complete list of books and essays on psychology published since 1889, cf. the yearly bibliography of the *Zeitschrift für Psychol. u. Physiol. d. Sinnesorgane;* and (since 1894) the Psychological Index now published conjointly by the *Psychological Review, L'Année Psychologique* and the *Zeitschrift.*)

GENERAL PSYCHOLOGY

(This is an incomplete list. In particular it omits all works published, or last issued, before 1890. For references to textbooks of Bain, Spencer, Lipps, Volkmann, Brentano, and Cornelius, see footnotes of Chapter XXVIII.)

William James, Principles of Psychology, I. and II., 1890. Psychology, Briefer Course, 1893.

O. Külpe, Outlines of Psychology, 1895, Eng. Tr. (Macmillan Co.). (This book lays stress on psycho-physical relations and measurements.)

G. F. Stout, Analytic Psychology, I. and II., London and New York, 1896. A Manual of Psychology, 1899.

E. B. Titchener, An Outline of Psychology, 3d ed., 1899.

James Sully, The Human Mind, I. and II., London, 1892.

Harold Höffding, Outlines of Psychology, Eng. Tr., New York, 1891.

G. T. Ladd, Psychology, Descriptive and Explanatory, 1894.

J. M. Baldwin, Handbook of Psychology, I. and II., 1894 and 1890.

John Dewey, Psychology, 1890.

NATURE AND METHODS OF PSYCHOLOGY

Hugo Münsterberg, Psychology and Life, 1899. Grundzüge der Psychologie, Leipzig, 1900.

F. H. Bradley, Phenomenalism in Psychology, *Mind*, N. S., IX., 1900.

M. W. Calkins, Psychology as Science of Selves, *Philos. Rev.*, IX. Elements of Conscious Complexes, *Psych. Rev.*, VII.

G. S. Fullerton, The Psychological Standpoint, *Psych. Rev.*, 1894, I. Psychology and Physiology, *ibid.*, 1896, III., p. 1.

E. W. Scripture, The New Psychology, London and New York, 1897. (Part I.) E. B. Titchener, Structural Psychology, *Philos. Rev.*, VII. James Ward, Modern Psychology, *Mind*, 1893.

PSYCHOLOGY AND NERVE PHYSIOLOGY

Wilhelm Wundt, Grundzüge der Physiologische Psychologie, I. u. II. 4te Aufl., Leipzig, 1893. (Forthcoming translation by Titchener, Macmillan Co.)

George T. Ladd, Elements of Physiological Psychology, 1887.

Th. Ziehen, Introduction to Physiological Psychology, Eng. Tr., 1895.

EXPERIMENTAL PSYCHOLOGY

E. C. Sanford, A Course in Experimental Psychology. Part I., Sensation and Perception, 1898.

E. B. Titchener, Experimental Psychology. Vol. I., Qualitative Experiments. Part I., Students' Manual. Part II., Instructors' Manual. 1901.

Höfler and Witasek, Psychologische Schulversuche, Leipzig, 1900. (See also periodical and monograph literature.)

PERIODICALS AND SERIAL PUBLICATIONS

American Journal of Psychology (Worcester); Psychological Review, (New York); Zeitschrift für Psychologie und Physiologie der

Sinnesorgane (Leipzig); L'Année Psychologique (Paris); Philosophische Studien (Leipzig). Publications of Laboratories. Monograph Supplements of the Psychological Review. (Cf. also the philosophical journals.)

PSYCHOLOGY OF SENSATION

(Cf. throughout E. A. Schäfer, Text-book of Physiology, Vol. II., 1900; M. Foster, Text-book of Physiology, 1895, Bk. III.; Hermann, Handbuch der Physiologie, III., 1879; Ebbinghaus, Grundzüge d. Psychologie, I., Leipzig, 1897; Wundt, Physiolog. Psych., and Külpe, *op. cit.;* Titchener, Exp. Psych., I., Instructor's; Zeitschrift; and Pflüger's Archiv. For bibliographies, cf. Titchener, *op. cit.*, and Sanford.)

Visual Sensations

H. von Helmholtz, Handbuch d. Physiolog. Optik, 2te Aufl., Hamburg and Leipzig, 1896. E. Hering, Zur Lehre vom Lichtsinne, Vienna, 1878. (Cf., for other monographs by Hering, Hermann's Handbuch, *loc. cit.*, Pflüger's Archiv, etc.) H. Aubert, Grundzüge d. Physiol. Optik, 1876. A. Fick, in Hermann's Handbuch, *loc. cit.*

(For further references, cf. above; cf. footnotes of Appendix, Section III.; and cf. reviews, by C. L. Franklin, in the *Psychological Review*, of periodical and monograph literature since 1894.)

Auditory Sensations

C. Stumpf, Tonpsychologie, Leipzig, I., 1883; II., 1890.
H. von Helmholtz, Sensations of Tone, Eng. Tr., London, 1895.
M. Meyer, *Ztschr.*, XI. Cross and Maltby, Proc. Amer. Acad., 1891-92.
(For further references cf. Titchener, *op. cit.*, pp. 51, 72.)

Sensations of Taste and of Smell

(For references, cf. above; cf. footnotes of Chapter IV. and of Appendix, Section IV.; and cf. E. A. McC. Gamble, The Applica-'ility of Weber's Law to Smell, *Amer. Jour. of Psy.*, X., 1898.)

'Cutaneous' Sensations

A. Goldscheider, Gesammelte Abhandlungen, I., II., Leipzig, 1898.
Z. Oppenheimer, Schmerz u. Temperaturempfindung, Berlin, 1893.

(For further references to the important German monographs, cf. footnotes to Chapter V.; and Appendix, Section V.)

F. B. Dresslar, Studies in the Psychology of Touch, *Amer. Jour. of Psy.*, VI. H. Griffing, Sensations from Pressure and Impact, *Monogr. Suppl. of Psych. Rev.*

REACTION-TIMES

J. Jastrow, Time Relations of Mental Phenomena, 1890. L. Lange, Neue Experimente, u. s. w., *Phil. Stud.*, IV., p. 479. E. B. Titchener, Type Theory of the Simple Reaction, *Mind*, 1895, pp. 74, 506; *ibid.*, 1896, p. 236. J. M. Baldwin, Types of Reaction, *Psych. Rev.*, 1895, II., p. 259. Cf. *Mind*, 1896, V., p. 81. N. Alechsieff, *Phil. Stud.*, XVI., 1900.

ALLEGED SENSATIONS FROM INTERNAL EXCITATION

Külpe, *op. cit.*, §§ 22 and 23.

CONSCIOUSNESS OF BODILY POSITION AND MOVEMENT

Titchener, Outline, § 46. James, *op. cit.*, II., pp. 493, 499–500, 503–509, 514, 515. Ferrier, Functions of the Brain, London, 1886. Breuer, Ueber die Funktion der Otolithenapparate, *Pflüger's Archiv*, XLVIII., p. 195. Brown, On Sensations of Motion, *Nature*, XL., 1889, p. 449. E. B. Delabarre, Ueber Bewegungsempfindungen, Freiburg, 1891. E. Mach, Lehre von Bewegungsempfindungen, Leipzig, 1875. Analysis of Sensations, Eng. Tr., Chicago, 1897.

CONSCIOUSNESS OF EXTENSITY OR SPACE

(Cf. H. Münsterberg, Grundzüge, p. 231 *seq.*)

Nativist Theory

Carl Stumpf, Tonpsychologie, II., pp. 51 *seq.* (cf. I., p. 210 and II., p. 550); Ueber den psychologischen Ursprung der Raumvorstellung, Leipzig, 1873. E. Hering, Beiträge zur Physiologie, I. and III., Leipzig, 1861 and 1863. Der Raumsinn u. die Bewegungen des Auges (in Hermann's Handbuch, III.). James, *op. cit.*

Empiricist Theory

H. Spencer, Principles of Psychology, Vol. II., Chapters XIV. and XXII. J. S. Mill, Examination of Sir William Hamilton's Philosophy, Vol. I., Chapter XIII. (Cf. Bain, Senses and Intellect.) Helmholtz, *op. cit.*, § 33, p. 947 *seq.*

The Eye as "Organ" of Consciousness of Extensity

(Cf. Sanford, *op. cit.*, Chapters V. and VII.; Titchener, Exp. Psych., I., Instructor's, §§ 46–48; Aubert, *op. cit.*; Fick and Hering in Hermann's Handbuch, III.)

The Space Consciousness of the Blind

W. Preyer, The Mind of the Child, Vol. II., The Intellect, Appendix C. Raehlmann, *Ztschr.*, II., pp. 73–85. W. Uhtorff, in Beiträge zur Psychologie (Helmholtz Festschrift).

Auditory Localization

M. Matsumoto, Studies from Yale Psycholog. Lab., 1897. W. Preyer, Die Wahrnehmung der Schallrichtung, *Pflüger's Archiv*, XL., 1887. Urbantschitsch, Zur Lehre von der Schallempfindung, *ibid.*, XXIV., 1881. E. Bloch, Das Binaurale Hören, Wiesbaden, 1893. Münsterberg and Pierce, The Localization of Sound, *Psych. Rev.*, I., 1894. C. E. Seashore, Localization of Sound in the Median Plane, *Univ. of Iowa Studies in Psychol.*, 1899. J. R. Angell and W. Fite, Monaural Localisation of Sounds, *Psych. Rev.*, May and Sept., 1901.

Tactual Localization

V. Henri, Ueber die Raumwahrnehmungen d. Tastsinnes, Leipzig, 1898. G. A. Tawney, Ueber die Wahrnehmung zweier Punkte, u. s. w., *Phil. Stud.*, XIII. M. F. Washburn, Ueber den Einfluss d. Gesichtsassociationen, u. s. w., *ibid.*, XI., p. 190.

CONSCIOUSNESS OF TIME AND RHYTHM

General

Höffding, *op. cit.*, pp. 184 *seq.* James, *op. cit.*, I., Chapter XV. Münsterberg, Grundzüge, Chapter 7. Z. Stern, Psychische Präsenzzeit, *Ztschr.*, XIII., p. 332. C. A. Strong, Consciousness and Time, *Psych. Rev.*, III., p. 150. M. W. Calkins, Time, Space and Causality, II. (c), *Mind*, N. S., VIII.

Experimental and Theoretical

E. Meumann, Beiträge zur Psychologie d. Zeitsinns, *Phil. Stud.*, VIII. and IX., 1893. F. Schumann, Über die Schätzung kleiner Zeitgrössen, *Ztschr.*, IV. H. Münsterberg, Zeitausfüllung, Beiträge, IV., p. 89. H. Nicholls, *Amer. Jour. Psy.*, IV., p. 84. L. T.

Stevens, On the Time-Sense, *Mind*, 1885. **T. L. Bolton**, Rhythm, *Amer. Jour. Psy.*, VI., 1893. **E. Meumann**, Unters. zur Psych. u. Aesth. d. Rhythmus, *Phil. Stud.*, X., 1894 (cf. M. K. Smith, *ibid.*, XVI., 1900).

PSYCHOPHYSICAL MEASUREMENTS AND METHODS

Külpe, *op. cit.*, §§ 4–9, *et al.*
(For further references cf. Sanford, p. 362; and add, **L. Martin** and **G. E. Müller**, Zur Analyse der Unterschiedsempfindlichkeit, Leipzig, 1899; **E. A. McC. Gamble**, *op. cit.*)

ATTENTION

(For references, cf. Titchener, Exp. Psych., I., II., p. 187; cf. also footnotes of Chapter XI., and Appendix, Section VII.)

FUSION

Wundt, Physiol. Psych., II., 437 *seq.* Külpe, *op. cit.*, § 42.

ASSOCIATION

Theoretical

M. W. Calkins, Association, *Monogr. Suppl. Psych. Rev.*, 1896. **Arthur Allin**, Über d. Grundprincip d. Association, Berlin, 1895. **F. H. Bradley**, Principles of Logic, 294 *seq.* **Wundt**, *Phil. Stud.*, VII. **A. Bain**, Senses and Intellect, pp. 544–556. (Cf. footnotes of Chapter XXVIII., pp. 438–440.)

Experimental Studies

1. *On Classification of Associations:* Trautscholdt, Philos. Studien, I., pp. 216 ff. Münsterberg, Beiträge, IV. Aschaffenburg, Exp. Studien über Associationen, Leipzig, 1895. Ziehen, Ideenassociation d. Kindes, I. and II. (*Abhandlungen* aus d. Gebiete der Pädagogischen Psych. u. Physiol., Berlin.) Scripture, Über den associativen Verlauf, *Philos. Stud.*, VII., 1892.
2. *On Secondary Laws of Association:* M. W. Calkins, *op. cit.*, Part II.
3. *Mediate Association:* W. Jerusalem, Philosoph. Stud., X. (Cf. Scripture and Münsterberg, *op. cit.*)
4. *On Interference of Associations:* J. A. Bergström, *Amer. Jour. Psy.*, V., p. 356, and VI., p. 433.

2 K

PERCEPTION

(Cf. on Consciousness of Space and of Time.)

IMAGINATION

G. T. Fechner, Elemente d. Psychophysik, 1860, II., XLIV. F. Galton, Inquiries into Human Faculty, 1883, pp. 83 *seq.* Stricker, Studien über die Sprachvorstellungen, 1880. George H. Lewes, Principles of Success in Literature, Chapter III. James, *op. cit.*, II., Chapter XVIII. Sully, The Human Mind, I., Chapter X. W. Lay, Mental Imagery, *Monogr. Suppl. Psych. Rev.*, 1898.

MEMORY

(Cf. references to Burnham and Ebbinghaus in Chapter XVI.)

G. E. Müller and A. Pilzecker, Exp. Beitr. zur Lehre vom Gedächtniss, Leipzig, 1900. (Cf. *Ztschr.* VI., 1893.) E. A. Kirkpatrick, An Experimental Study of Memory, *Psych. Rev.*, I., p. 602 (Verbal *vs.* Concrete Memory). Cf. Wellesley, Psycholog. Lab. Studies, *Psych. Rev.*, V., p. 451 (Modification of Kirkpatrick's Experiment). Harvard Psycholog. Lab. Studies, *Psych. Rev.*, I., pp. 34, 453; III., p. 21. Princeton Psycholog. Lab. Studies, *Psych. Rev.*, II., p. 236 (Memory for Square Size). W. G. Smith, Relation of Attention to Memory; *Mind*, N. S., IV., 1895.

THOUGHT

(Cf. references in Chapters XVII. and XVIII.)

Th. Ribot, Evolution of the General Idea, Eng. Tr., Chicago, 1899. A. Binet, The Psychology of Reasoning, Eng. Tr., 1899.

RECOGNITION

(Cf. references in Chapter XIX.)

THE EMOTIONS

Classification of Emotions

Titchener, Outline, § 56. J. Ward, *Encycl. Brit.*, XX., pp. 67, 70. A. Bain, Feeling and Will, pp. 71–77. and heading of Chapters V.– XV.

Bibliography

Personal Emotion

J. M. Baldwin, Social and Ethical Interpretations in Mental Development, Chapter VI., Section 3. Höffding, *op. cit.*, pp. 242–253.

Æsthetic Emotion

Schopenhauer, The World as Will and Idea, Book III. George Santayana, The Sense of Beauty. Marshall, Pain, Pleasure, and Æsthetics, p. 110 *seq.* Heymans, *Ztschr. f. Psych. u. Phys.*, XL., July, 1896. V. Lee and C. A. Thomas, Beauty and Ugliness, *Contemp. Review*, 1897, Vol. LXXII. Ethel Puffer, Criticism and Æsthetics, *Atlantic Monthly*, 1901. (For further references, cf. Bosanquet, History of Æsthetics, and Marshall, *op. cit.*, Chapter III.)

The Sense of Humor

C. C. Everett, Poetry, Comedy and Duty. Th. Lipps, Psychologie d. Komik (includes criticisms of Kraepelin, Vischer, Lotze, Hecker), *Philosophische Monatshefte*, XXIV. and XXV. E. Kraepelin, Zur Psychologie d. Komischen, *Phil. Stud.*, II. Ziegler, J. Das Komische, Leipzig, 1900.

Bodily Changes
The James-Lange Theory and its Critics

W. James, Principles of Psychology, Chapter XXV. (Briefer Psychology, Chapter XXIV.) The Physical Basis of Emotion, *Psych. Rev.*, I., pp. 516 *seq.* C. Lange, Ueber Gemüthsbewegungen, Tr. by H. Kurella, Leipzig, 1887. J. Dewey, The Theory of Emotion, *Psych. Rev.*, II., 13. W. Wundt, Philos. Stud., VI., p. 349. D. Irons, James's Theory of Emotion, *Mind*, 1894 *et al.* W. L. Worcester, Observations on Some Points in James's Psychology, II., *Monist*, III., p. 285. J. M. Baldwin, The Origin of Emotional Expression, *Psych. Rev.*, I., p. 610.

Biological Considerations

C. Darwin, Expression of the Emotions. J. Dewey, *op. cit.*, *Psych. Rev.*, I., p. 553. (Cf. James, II., pp. 478–479, for references to Spencer, Bell, Manteguzza and others.)

Experimental Studies

J. R. Angell and H. B. Thompson, Organic Processes and Consciousness, *Psych. Rev.*, VI., 1899 (with full references). T. E. Shields, Effect of Odours, etc., upon the Blood-flow, *Journal of Exp. Medicine*, I., 1896. Binet and Courtier, *L'Année Psychologique*, III., 1897. Binet and Henri, *Ibid.* Féré, Sensation et Mouvement, Paris, 1887. A. Lehmann, Hauptgesetze d. Menschl. Gefühlslebens, Ger. Tr., Leipzig, 1892, and Die Körperlichen Aüsserungen, psychischer Zustände, Leipzig, 1899. A. Mosso, Die Temperatur d. Gehirns, Kreislauf d. Blutes, u. s. w., Die Ermüdung. Münsterberg, Beiträge, IV., 216.

VOLITION AND WILL

James, *op. cit.*, II., Chapter XXVI. H. Münsterberg, Die Willenshandlung, Freiburg, 1888, esp. pp. 60–76; The Psychology of the Will, *Psych. Rev.*, 1898; Psychology and Life, pp. 210 *seq.*, Grundzüge, Chapter IX., 7. G. Stout, Analytic Psychology, II., esp. pp. 130–135, 143–148.

BELIEF AND FAITH

Baldwin, Feeling and Will, pp. 148–160. James, *op. cit.*, II., Chapter XXI.

SOCIAL PSYCHOLOGY

To the references of Chapter XXIII. add
G. Tarde, Social Laws, Eng. Tr., 1899. (Cf. La Logique Sociale, L'Opposition Universelle, Paris, Alcan.) H. Spencer, Principles of Sociology. (Cf. references in J. M. Baldwin, Social and Ethical Interpretations.)

COMPARATIVE PSYCHOLOGY

(Cf. Baldwin, Mental Development in the Child and the Race.)

Psychology of Animal Consciousness

C. L. Morgan, Animal Life and Intelligence (esp. Chapters IX. and X.); Comparative Psychology (esp. Chapters XIV., XVI., XX.). Wesley Mills, Animal Intelligence, 1898 (contains 'diaries' of development of young animals). Romanes, Mental Evolution in Animals (esp. Chapters VII.–X., XIX., XX.). J. Lubbock, Ants, Bees and Wasps, 1899. Edward Thorndike, Animal Intelligence, *Monogr. Suppl. to Psych. Rev.*, 1898. James, *op. cit.*, II., pp. 348–355 (on Thought); Chapter XXV., on Instinct. Wundt, Lectures on Human and Animal Psychology, XXIII. and XXIV. R. D. Yerxa, Reaction of Entomastraca to Stimulation by Light. Contributions from Harvard Zool. Lab., No. 108.

Psychology of Child Consciousness

Studies of Individual Children: M. W. Shinn, The Biography of a Baby, 1901 ; Notes on the Development of a Child, University of California. W. Preyer, The Mind of the Child, I. and II., Eng. Tr., Appleton; Mental Development in the Child (a condensation). H. Taine, Sur l'Acquisition du Langage chez les Enfants, *Revue Philos.*, I., 1876 (cf. *Mind*, II., p. 252). Charles Darwin, *Mind*, O. S. II. K. C. Moore, The Mental Development of a Child, *Monogr. Suppl. of Psych. Rev.*

Topical Studies: James Sully, Studies of Childhood, 1896. F. Tracy, The Psychology of Childhood (a summary).

(Cf. G. S. Hall, Earl Barnes, H. W. Brown, S. E. Wiltse, Wellesley College Studies, in the *Pedagogical Seminary* and elsewhere, for studies of children's fears, self-consciousness, religious ideas, imaginations, drawings, etc.)

Nature and Origin of Language: 9. Romanes, Mental Evolution in Man, p. 138; W. D. Whitney, Language and the Study of Language, p. 426 (cf. *Encycl. Brit.* ed. 9, Vol. XVIII.); F. Max Müller, Science of Thought, I., p. 192; James, *op. cit.*, II., p. 356; Morgan, Animal Life and Intelligence, p. 343.

SYNÆSTHESIA

F. Galton, Inquiries into Human Faculty, pp. 114–154. Th. Flournoy, Des Phénomènes de Synopsiè, 1893. Bleuler u. Lehmann, Zwangmässige Lichtempfindungen durch Schall u. s. w., Leipzig, 1881. S. de Mendoza, L. Audition Colarée, Paris, 1890. M. W. Calkins, *Amer. Jour. Psy.*, 1893, V., p. 439, and 1895, VII., p. 20. Beaunis and Binet, *Revue Philosophique*, 1892. G. E. Gruber, *ibid.*, Vol. XXXV., *Ztschr.*, 1893. W. O. Krohn, "Pseudochromesthesia," *Amer. Jour. Psy.*, 1892 (cf. Bibliography). D. S. Jordan, The Colors of Letters, *Pop. Sci. Monthly*, 1891. Binet, *ibid.*, Oct., 1893. G. T. W. Patrick, Number forms, *ibid.*, 1893. D. E. Phillips, *Amer. Jour. of Psych.*, 1897.

ABNORMAL PSYCHOLOGY

(Cf. throughout (except on Dreams), *Proceedings* of Society for Psychical Research. Cf. also J. Jastrow, Fact and Fable in Psychology, 1901.)

Dreams

Summaries: Sante de Sanctis, I Sogni, Turin, 1899. (This is the completest work on the subject, including introspective and experimental investigation.) M. de Manacéine, Sleep, London and New York, 1897, Chapter IV. Radestock, Schlaf u. Traum, 1879. Sully, Illusions, Chapter VII.

Introspective Study: M. W. Calkins, Statistics of Dreams, *Amer. Jour. Psych.*, V., 1893. Wellesley College Studies of Dreams, I. and II., *ibid.*, VII., 1896, and XI., 1900. E. B. Titchener, Taste Dreams, *ibid.*, 1895. (Cf. the classic work of A. Maury, Le Sommeil et les Rêve, 4me ed., Paris, 1878, and Ives Delage, *Revue Scientifique*, 1891.)

Questionnaire Study: F. Heerwagen, Statistische Untersuchungen über Traüme, *Philos. Stud.*, V., 1888. J. Nelson, A Study of Dreams, *Amer. Jour. Psy.*, I.

Hallucinations

(Cf. bibliographies in E. Parish, Hallucinations and Illusions, Eng. Tr., London and New York, 1897.)

Crystal Vision

F. W. H. Myers, The Subliminal Self, *Proc. Soc. Ps. Res.*, VIII., pp. 472 *seq.* (Cf. references in Parish, *op. cit.*, pp. 63–70.)

Automatic Writing

A. Binet, Double Consciousness, Eng. Tr., 1890, pp. 23–33.

Hypnosis

Albert Moll, Hypnotism, Eng. Tr., New York, 1890. James, *op. cit.* II., Chapter XXVII. (cf. brief bibliography, pp. 615, 616). Cf. also *Proc. Soc. Ps. Res.*, and *Revue de l'Hypnotisme*.

Changes in Personality

James, *op. cit.*, I., Chapter X., pp. 373–400. F. W. H. Myers, The Subliminal Self, *Proc. Soc. Ps. Res.*, VII., VIII. and IX. Th. Ribot, Diseases of Personality, Eng. Tr., 1887. Pierre Janet, L'Automatisme Psychologique, 1889.

Telepathy

Frank Podmore, Apparitions and Thought Transference. Gurney, Myers and Podmore, Phantasms of the Living, I., pp. 8–95.

Physical Explanation of Telepathy

Hanssen and Lehmann, Wundt's Philosophische Studien, XI., p. 471; reviewed by W. James, *Psych. Rev.*, III., p. 98; answered by H. Sidgwick, *Proc. Soc. Ps. Res.*, XII., p. 298.

HISTORY OF PSYCHOLOGY

Siebeck, Geschichte der Psychologie, I. and II., 1880, 1884 (through Thomas of Aquino).

STRUCTURE AND FUNCTIONS OF THE NERVOUS SYSTEM

(Cf. Wundt, Physiol. Psychologie; Ebbinghaus, Psychologie; Ladd, Elements; James, Briefer Psychology, Chapters VII., VIII. Foster, *op. cit.*, Book III., Chapters I., II., Sections 1–3.) Flechsig, Gehirn u. Seele, 2te Ausg., Leipzig, 1896; Neurolog. Centralblatt, 1898. H. Donaldson, The Growth of the Brain, London and New York, 1897 (cf. *Amer. Jour. Psy.*, IV.). L. Edinger, Anatomy of Central Nervous System, Eng. Tr., 1899. H. Martin, The Human Body, Chapters XII. and XIII.

INDEX OF SUBJECTS

The Bibliography is not referred to except in the case of subjects mentioned only there.

ABNORMAL CONSCIOUSNESS, 397–423; phenomena, 397 ff., 415 ff.; analogy to normal consciousness, 413 f.; distinction from normal, 415 ff.

Abstraction and abstract notion, 224–226; related to attention, 224; to generalization, 225 f.

Activity (cf. Self-consciousness, Attention).

Æsthetic consciousness (cf. Emotion).

AFFECTIONS, 113–124; two, 113, 122; combined, 122 f.; not always present, 113; not 'attributes,' 114; physical stimuli, 115 f.; physiological conditions, 116 ff.; physiological theories: Marshall's, 120; Titchener's, 121; Münsterberg's, 121. Of animals, 366, 372.

Agraphia, 461, 462.

Air waves, 48 f.

Alexia, 461, 462.

Alimentary 'sensations,' 85.

Altruistic consciousness (cf. Self-consciousness).

Analysis, a method of science, 7; psychological, 17, 149.

ANIMAL CONSCIOUSNESS, 355–381. Inferential study, 355, 380. Sensational: pressure, 357; 'chemical sense,' 357; taste and smell, 358 ff.; temperature, 360; vision, 360 ff., 364; hearing, 363 f. Imagination, 365 f. Reasoning, 368 ff. Attention, 369. Affections, 366, 372. Emotions, 372 ff., 375 ff. Personal and social, 374 ff. Experiments upon, 358, 362, 371.

Anticipation, Feeling of, 300 ff.

APHASIA, 460 ff., 200. Sensory, 461. Motor, 461.

Apperception, 214.

Assimilation, 160.

ASSOCIATION, 159–168; definition, 160; classification, 160, 167; simultaneous, 160; successive, 160 ff.; 'total,' 162; 'partial,' 163 ff.; 'localized,' 163 f.; reference to past experience, 161 f.; illustrations, 161 f.; effect of frequency, recency, and vividness, 167 f.; physiological conditions, 168.

'Association-centres' of brain, 117, 135, 178, 233, 262, 459, 490 f.

ATTENTION, 137–146; identical with interest, 137; elemental attention, or clearness, 137 ff.; narrow, 138; classes: primary and acquired, 139 ff.; not identical with affection, 141; nor with intensity, 142; duration, 142; suggestiveness, 143; in widest sense, 146; relation to abstraction, 224; physiological condition, 490 f.; theories: activity theory, 486 f.; motor theory, 487 f.; affection theory, 141, 488; negative theories, 488 f.; element theory, 137 ff., 489; of animals, 369. In hypnosis, 406 ff.

Attributive elements of consciousness, 113–127.

Auditory (cf. Pitch, Noise, Loudness), of animals, 363 f.; localization, 496.

Automatic writing, 405.

Balance, movements of, 81; consciousness of, 83; physiological conditions, 81 ff.

Basilar membrane, 51 ff.

Beauty, Consciousness of, 278–283.

BELIEF: A belief, 304 f., 313 f.; distinguished from a volition, 304; including feelings of congruence and realness, 304 f. Belief (cf. Faith).

Biological significance, of smell and taste, 63 f., 358; of pain, 73; of emotion, 295 f.; of protective coloring, 362 f.

BRAIN, development, 449 ff.; parts, 450 f.; functions, 452 ff.; weight, 460. (Cf. Cerebral hemispheres, Nervous system, Association centres, Frontal, Occipital, and Temporal lobes, Rolandic area.)

BRIGHTNESS, sensational elements, 42 ff., 478 f.

Cerebellum, function, 82 f., 456; structure, 450 f.

CEREBRAL HEMISPHERES. Development, 449 f.; functions, 453 ff., 27 f.; structure, 456 f.; localization, 457 ff.

Changes in personality, in dreams, 415; in hypnosis, 416 f.; subliminal-self theory, 418 f.

CHILD CONSCIOUSNESS, 382-396. Of the baby: sensational, 384 ff.; affective, 386 ff.; relational, 388 ff.; personal, 389 ff.; of the body, 389 ff. Of the little child: likeness to adult consciousness, 392 f.; difference from adult, 393; emotion, 394 f.; thought, 395; isolation, 396.

Child study, 382 ff.

Circulatory 'sensations,' 85.

Cochlea, 50 ff.

Cold (cf. Temperature).

COLOR, Sensations of, 18-28; sensational elements, 19; color square, 20; color pyramid, 31; complementary, 32; physical conditions, 22 f.; physiological conditions, 23 ff. Theories of color and colorless light consciousness, of: Young, 35 f., 464; Helmholtz, 35 f., 464, 469, 472; Hering, 26 f., 464 f., 469, 472; Franklin, 27, 39 ff., 466 ff., 473; König, 466 f., 470 f., 473; von Kries, 39 ff., 466 f., 470, 473. Contrast, 473 f.; Purkinje phenomenon, 478 f.

Color blindness, 33 f., 475 f.; dichromatic, 33, 476; achromatic, 33, 477.

Colored light, 22 f.; mixture, 32.

COLORLESS LIGHT, Sensations of, 28-42; number of sensational qualities, 29 ff.; physical conditions, 32 ff.; physiological conditions, 34 ff.; theories (cf. Color).

Complexity of consciousness, 149 *et al.*

Conation, 303.

Conception (cf. Generalization).

Concrete, opposed to 'abstract,' 149; opposed to 'verbal,' 190.

Concrete conscious experiences, 149-156.

Consciousness, subject matter of psychology, 3; series of ideas, 149 f., which are causally related, 154 f.; personal, 151, not causally related, 155.

Contact, consciousness of, 66.

Contrast. Visual, 30; successive, 473 f.; simultaneous, 474 f.

Corti, Organs of, 51 ff.

Clang, 159.

Classification, a method of science, 7.

Clearness, elemental attention, 137, 140 f.

Cortex (cf. Cerebral hemispheres).

Crura cerebri, 450.

Crystal vision, 404 f.

Deaf mutes, thought without words, 249.

Depth (cf. Distance).

Difference, Feeling of, 43, 54, 105, 131.

Distance, Consciousness of, 97 ff.

Dizziness, 84.

DREAMS, 397-402; methods of study, 397 f.; nature, 398 f.; sensational elements, 400; affective, 401; relational, 401 f.; will, 402; moral consciousness, 402.

Ear, 49 ff.

Effort, 317 ff.

Element of consciousness, 17, 21, 103 f. (Cf. Sensational element.)

EMOTION, 263-298; complex fact, 263; personal experience, 263 ff.; particularizing, 264 f. Personal emotion: classified, 266; egoistic, 266 ff.; sympathetic, 273 ff.; mixed, 275 f. Impersonal: classified, 277; æsthetic, 277 ff.; 'intellectual,' 283; humor, 284 f. Physiological conditions, 285 ff. 'Expression of emotions,' 294 ff. James-Lange theory, 296 f. Related to instinctive reaction, 295 f. Of animals, 372 ff.

Ennui, 278.

Ether waves, 22, 45.

EXPERIMENT, nature, 10 f.; description of experiments, 30, 32, 33, 34, 55,

68, 70, 81, 212 f., 358, 362, 364, 371; reference, in footnotes, to experiments, 25, 30, 31, 32, 33, 34, 46, 47, 58, 62, 63, 68, 69, 74, 77, 78, 81, 99, 118, 122, 138, 140, 159, 167, 184, 193.

Explanation, a method of science, 8, 150.

EXTENSITY, Consciousness of, 89-102, 106 ff.; sensational theory, 89 ff., 106 f., 110; empirical theory, 90 ff.; visual, 89 ff.; pressure-extensity, 92 f.; sound-extensity, 93 f.; surface, 95 ff.; depth or distance, 97 ff.; innateness, 100 f.; of blind, 496; localization, 496.

Eye, 23 ff.

Facts, definition, 4; internal and external, 6; facts for selves, 6 f.; public and private, 6.

FAITH, 305-307, 311-313, 320; active, 306; personal, 311 f.; distinguished from belief, 311 f.; from consciousness of reality, 311 ff.; duty, 312 f.; conflicting, 319 f.

Familiarity, Feeling of, 131, 254 ff.; experiment, 256; analysis, 259; relational experience, 254; relation to supplementary images, 255 ff.; to bodily attitude, 257; to pleasantness, 258.

Feeling, 150.

Frontal lobes, 117 ff., 286, 288 f.

Fusion, 157-159; nature, 158; degrees, 158; illustration, 159; psychic and physical, 158.

Future, Feeling of, 301.

General notion (cf. below), indistinct, 226; composite, 228; associative of similars, 228 f., 233; verbal, 230; motor, 231 f.

Generality, Feeling of, nature, 222 ff.; physiological condition, 233.

GENERALIZATION, 221-233; generalizing and general notion, 221; generality feeling, 222 ff.; related to perception and imagination, 222 ff.; to abstraction, 224 ff.

Genetic, psychology, 351, 353; theory of space, 100.

Gratitude, 269 f.

Hallucinations, 402-405.

Hardness, Consciousness of, 66.

Hate, 270 ff.

HISTORY OF PSYCHOLOGY, 424-446; classification, 425 f.; Greek psychology, 427 ff.; Continental psychology, 434 f.; British psychology, 435 ff.; associationism, 438 ff.; modern psychology, 442 ff.

Hotness (cf. Temperature).

Humidity (cf. Wetness).

Humor, 'Sense of,' 284 f.

Hypnosis, 406-413; methods, 406; stages, 407; muscular disturbance, 408 f.; illusions, 409 f.; memory, 410 f.; post-hypnotic suggestion, 411 f.; therapeutic use, 412; criminal suggestion, 412 f.; Charcot's theory, 413.

Idea, 149-150.

Illusions, 183-184. (Cf. Dreams, Hallucinations, Hypnosis.)

Image (cf. Imagination). Complex idea, 185 ff., 204 f., 205, 207 ff.

IMAGINATION, 185-209; unshared experience, 188 f.; classification, 190; concrete, 190-197; visual, 191-194; auditory, 195; tactile, 195; of smell and taste, 195 ff.; verbal, 197 ff.; reproductive and creative, 202 f.; development, 209. Of animals, 365 f.

IMITATION, 331-333, 336-337, 339-342, 344-345; distinguished from repetition, 332. Unconscious, 333. Conscious: fashion or tradition, 340; physical or psychic, 340-341. Personal, 341-342. Related to invention, 343-345.

Indifference, through habitual stimuli, 116, 119.

Intellectualist theory, 128, 129.

Intensities, sensational, nature, 106; physiological conditions, 108, 110 f.; physical conditions, 108, 110 f. (Cf. Brightness and Loudness, and cf. also pp. 59, 61, 67, 75, 77.)

Interest (cf. Attention).

Internal excitation, Sensations from, 80-86.

Introspection, The method of psychology, 8 ff.

James–Lange theory, 297, 436.

Joint surfaces, Consciousness from, 69 f.

Judgment, 234-240; a judgment, 234; judging, 234; nature, 234 f.; distinguished from perception and abstraction, 234 f.; analytic and synthetic, 235 ff.; abstract and concrete, 237 f.; distinguished from proposition, 239, from belief, 239 f.; 'negative judgment,' 239; physiological conditions, 234.

Language, related to thought, 248-251.
'Less,' Feeling of (cf. 'More').
Like and dislike, 267 f.
Likeness, Feeling of, 131 f.
Linkage, Feeling of, 301 f.
Localization, auditory, 496; tactual, 496.
Logic, distinguished from psychology, 248.
Loudness, Sensational elements of, 53-54.

'Many,' Feeling of, 131.
Medulla oblongata, 287, 450.
Memory, 210-217; definition, 210; complete or incomplete, 210; methods of improving, 211 ff.: by repetition, 211-212, association, 213, grouping, 213 f., selection, 214 f.; verbal, 215 f.; experiment, 212; physiological conditions, 216.
Moral consciousness, 327-328, 346-347, 402.
'More,' Feeling of, 43, 54, 105, 131.
Motion, Consciousness of, 86-88; of body, 86 f.; on surface of body, 87 f.
Motor organs of brain, 117-118, 127, 286, 288 f.
Movements. Bodily, to preserve balance, 81-83; in affective experience, 118; in emotions, 288 ff.; immediate and ideo-motor, 485 f.
Muscles, Consciousness from, 70.

Nervous system, development, 449 ff.; structure, 451; function, 452 ff.; nerve cells, 451; nerve fibres, 451; nerve centres, 451 (cf. Brain).
Noise, sensational elements, 46-48; physical conditions of, 48 f.; physiological conditions, 49 ff.

Octaves, 47.
Occipital lobes, 27 f., 42, 45, 110.
Odor (cf. Smell).

Oneness, Feeling of, 131.
Opposition, 338-339, 342-346; of reflective social consciousness, 338 f.; 'simple,' 342; related to imitation, 343 ff.
Organic 'sensations,' 84-86.

Pain, Sensations of, 71-76; sensational elements, 71-72; only one quality, 72; differences of, 72; biological value, 73; distinguished from unpleasantness, 71; physical conditions, 73; physiological conditions, 73-75, 484.
Parallelism, 433-434.
Paramnesia, 260.
Particularizing consciousness (cf. Self-consciousness).
Passive consciousness (cf. Self-consciousness, Attention).
Past, Consciousness of, 259.
Percept, complex idea, 169, 179.
PERCEPTION, 169-184; as complex idea, 169; as experience shared with other selves, 169 ff.; passive, 169 f.; tested by community of experience, 171 f.; implies something independent of self, 172 f.; complexity, 173, 176 f.; differentiation, 174, 175; physiological conditions, 178; classification, 179; pure, 179; mixed, 179 ff.; symbolic, 182 f.; illusory, 183 f.
Peripheral organs, 104.
Periphery of retina, 33, 38, 466 f., 470 f.
Phenomenon (cf. Fact).
Philosophy, nature, 4 f.; confused with psychology, 425 f.
PITCH, 46-53; sensational elements, 46 ff.; physical conditions, 48 f.; physiological conditions, 49 ff.
Pleasantness (cf. Affections). Through novel stimuli, 116, 119; relation to feeling of familiarity, 258.
Pons Varolii, 450 f.
Position 'sensations,' 81-84.
PRESSURE, Sensations of, 65-71; alleged qualities, 66; only one quality, 67; pressure intensity, 67; physiological conditions (end-organs), 68, 482 ff.; physical conditions, 71; localization, 496. Of animals, 357.
PSYCHOLOGY, nature, 3 ff.; methods, 7 ff.; divisions, 12 f., 351 ff.; experimental, 10 f.; as science of selves, 6,

12, 151 ff., 352; as science of ideas, 6,
12, 150 f., 352; individual and social, 12,
152 f., 331, 352 f.; introspective and
comparative, 12, 352; normal and
abnormal, 12, 352; distinguished from
logic, 248; from sociology, 333; in
novel and in drama, 322 f.; genetic,
351, 353.
Psycho-physic law, 111, 443.
Purkinje Phenomenon, 478 f.

Qualities, sensational, nature, 18, 105 ff.;
physiological conditions, 106 f., 110 f.;
physical conditions, 107 f., 110 f. (Cf.
Color, Colorless light, Pitch, Noise,
Taste, Smell, Pressure, Pain, Temperature, etc.)

Reaction-times, 495.
Realness, Feeling of, 124-127; not primitive, 126, 329; parallel with unrealness,
126; in volition, 301 f.; in belief, 304 f.;
in faith, 311 ff.; in religious consciousness, 329 f.
REASONING, 240-248; definition, 240;
purely synthetic, 242 f.; analytic, 243 ff.;
relation to intuition, 245; advantages,
246 ff.; of animals, 368 f.
RECOGNITION, 252-262; recognized
percepts and images, 252; personal
experience, 252 ff.; often called
memory, 252, 261; passive, 253; both
private and shared, 253; physiological
condition, 261 f.
RELATIONAL ELEMENTS OF CON-
SCIOUSNESS, 128-136; opposing
theories, 128 ff.; discovered by introspection, 130 f.; enumeration, 130 f.;
nature, 132 ff.; physiological conditions, 135; physical conditions, 135;
in animals, 366 ff.; in dreams, 401.
RELIGIOUS CONSCIOUSNESS, 323-
330; definition, 323; historical forms,
324 f.; rites, 325; personal, 326 ff.;
active, 327; distinguished from moral
consciousness, 327 f.; from æsthetic
consciousness, 328; from conviction
of reality, 329 f.
Respiratory ' sensations,' 85.
Retina, 24, 25.
Rhythm, Consciousness of, 497.
Rolandic area, 70, 75 f., 79, 81, 110 f., 117 f.,
286 ff., 457 ff.

Science, 3 ff. *et al.*
Scorn, 272.
SELF-CONSCIOUSNESS, social, 152 ff.,
331, 352 f. Phases: egoistic and altruistic, 153, 170 f., 188 f., 253 f., 266 ff.,
277 ff., 307 ff., 311 ff., 338, 340 ff., 346 f.;
particularizing and generalizing, 153,
170 f., 219 f., 264, 277; passive and active, 154, 163 f., 253, 264, 306 ff.
Self, distinguished from facts for self, 6 f.
Semicircular canals, 82 ff.
Sensation, 42, 109.
SENSATIONAL ELEMENT, 103-112;
always present, 103; physiological
condition, 104; physical condition,
104; classes, 105 (cf. Qualities, Intensities, Extensities); criteria, 109; table,
110; of animals, 356 ff.; in dreams, 400 f.
Sensationalist theories, 128, 130, 438.
Sensory circle, 69.
Series, Psychological, 43 f., 53 f., 105,
106.
Skin, Functions, 67.
SMELL, Sensations of, 59-64; unnamed,
59 f.; classification, 60; elements, 61;
complexity, 60 f.; fusions, 60, 481;
compensations, 481 f.; physical conditions, 63, 480; physiological conditions,
61 ff., 480; fatigue of end organs, 61 f.;
cerebral centre, 63 f.; of animals, 358 f.
Smoothness, Consciousness of, 66.
SOCIAL CONSCIOUSNESS, 331-347;
forms, 333 ff.; mob consciousness,
333 ff.; reflective, 335 ff. (Cf. Self-
consciousness.)
Sociology, distinguished from Psychology, 333.
Space (cf. Extensity).
Strain sensations, 80-81.
Sympathy, 272-275; phases, 273;
breadth, 273-274; ' organic,' 268.
Synæsthesia, 405, 501.
SYNTHESIS, 157-168; elemental con-
sciousness, 157; objective sense, 157.
(Cf. Fusion and Association.)

TASTE, Sensations of, 55-59; experimental analysis, 55; complexity, 56;
sensational elements, 57; physiological conditions, 57 f.; physical conditions, 58; intensities, 59; of animals,
358 f.
Telepathy, 420-423.

TEMPERATURE, Sensations of, 76–79; sensational qualities, 76 f.; intensities, 77; physical conditions, 77; physiological conditions, 78 f.; animal consciousness of, 360.

Temporal lobes, 53, 59, 63, 110, 457 ff.

Tendons, Organs of strain-consciousness, 81.

Terror, 270–272.

THOUGHT, 218–251; thoughts, 218; thinking, 219 ff.; analysis and classification, 221 ff.; related to language, 248 ff. (Cf. Generalization, Judgment, Reasoning.)

Tickling, Consciousness of, 66.

Time, consciousness of (cf. Past and Future), 496.

Typical personal relations, 321–323.

Unpleasantness (cf. Affections), of pain, 71; through intense and intermittent stimuli, 116, 119.

VISUAL SENSATIONS, 17–45, 464–479 (cf. Color, Colorless light, Brightness). Of animals, 360 f.

VOLITION, 299–303, 313–319; an idea, 299; anticipatory, 300 ff.; distinguished from antecedent idea, 300; independent of result, 302; classification, 313; outer volition, 299, 314 f.; inner volition, 302 f., 313 ff.; with resident end, 314 f.; remote end, 314 f.; simple volition, 303, 315; choice, 303, 315 ff.; without effort, 318; with effort, 318 f.; deliberative, 303, 315 ff.

Wetness, Consciousness of, 66–67.

Wholeness, Feeling of, 131, 234 ff.

WILL, 305–310, 313–320; active, 306; imperious, 307 f.; personal, 306, 309 f.; relatively impersonal, 309 f.; temporal, 310; classes, 313 ff. (cf. Volition); in dreams, 402.

INDEX OF AUTHORS

Names mentioned only in the Bibliography are not repeated in this list.

Allen, G., 196.
Alrutz, S., 78.
Andrews, G. A., 400.
Aristotle, 65, 320, 429.
Aronsohn, E., 480 f.

Bain, A., 89, 439, 487.
Baldwin, J. M., 126, 227, 232, 312, 345, 388, 390, 445.
Bastian, H. C., 490.
Bateson, 361.
Berkeley, G., 98, 223, 437.
Binet, A., 403, 405.
Bonnet, C., 442.
Bradley, F. H., 489.
Brentano, F., 239, 445.
Broca, 462.
Büchner, L., 442.
Burnett, F. H., 394.
Burnham, W., 260.

Charcot, J. M., 413.
Condillac, E. B. de, 442.
Cornelius, H., 444 f.
Cross, C. R., 48.

Darwin, C., 295, 373, 376, 387.
Demokritos, 428, 442.
Descartes, 129, 433.
Dewey, J., 295.
Donaldson, H., 188, 455, 458.

Ebbinghaus, H., 212 f., 465, 469, 472, 476, 479.

Fackenthal, K., 388.
Fechner, G. T., 111, 185, 443.
Ferrier, D., 490.
Flechsig, P., 117 f., 121, 135, 458 f., 462 f.
Foster, M., 52, 70, 75.
Franklin, C. L., 39 f., 464 f., 466 ff., 475 ff.
Frey, M. von, 68, 74, 79, 482 ff.

Galton, F., 193, 198.
Gamble, E. A. McC., 60, 62, 72, 480 f.
Goldscheider, A., 68, 74 f., 484 f.

Hamerton, P. G., 376, 381.
Hamlin, A. J., 490.
Hansen, F. C., 422.
Hartley, D., 438 f.
Hegel, G. W. F., 321.
Helmholtz, H. von, 35, 89, 464, 469, 472, 474 f.
Herbart, J. F., 214, 440 f.
Hering, E., 36 f., 89, 464 f., 466 f., 469, 472, 474 f., 476 f.
Hobbes, T., 434 ff.
Höffding, H., 218, 225, 256, 445.
Hume, D., 202, 253, 438 f.
Huxley, T., 226 f.

James, W., 70, 89, 92, 94 ff., 105, 126, 131 ff., 138, 140, 142, 145, 149 ff., 162 f., 174, 176, 184, 188, 194, 200 f., 211, 213, 216, 222, 225, 244, 253, 295 ff., 304 f., 312, 314, 317 ff., 369 f., 385, 416 f., 445, 487 f.
Janet, Pierre, 416 f.

Kant, I., 129, 238, 282.
Kiesow, F., 57.
Kipling, R., 359, 366, 375.
Kirkpatrick, E. A., 215.
König, A., 466, 469 ff., 473, 477.
Krafft Ebing, R. von, 408, 416.
Kries, J. von, 39, 466, 469 f., 473.
Külpe, O., 58, 67, 115, 188, 194, 227.

Ladd, G. T., 57, 218, 222, 227, 445, 486.
Lange, C., 288, 291 f., 296 f.
Lange, N., 487.
Le Bon, G., 260, 334 f., 338.
Le Conte, J., 443.

510

Lehmann, A., 256, 422.
Leibniz, G. W., 129, 434 f.
Lipps, Th., 440.
Locke, J., 223, 245, 437.
Loti, P., 395.
Lubbock, J., 358, 362.
Luckey, G. W. A., 484 f.

Maltby, M. E., 48.
Marillier, L., 490.
Marshall, H. R., 119 ff.
Martin, H., 482.
Meinong, A., 445.
Meyer, G. H., 188.
Mill, James, 439.
Mill, J. S., 89, 252, 439.
Miller, D., 233.
Mills, W., 358, 360, 364, 377.
Moleschott, J., 442.
Moll, A., 407 f., 410 ff.
Morgan, C. L., 360 ff., 368 ff., 372, 376 f.
Müller, F. M., 249.
Müller, G. E., 20, 464 f., 466 f., 469, 472, 476.
Müller, J., 480.
Münsterberg, H., 121 f., 175, 281, 302, 383, 436, 444, 487, 489 f.
Myers, F. W. H., 418 f.

Nagel, W. A., 483 f.
Nicolay and Hay, 260.

Oppenheimer, Z., 485.

Parish, E., 403 ff.
Paul, 320.
Pfleiderer, E., 324.
Plato, 129, 427 f.
Priestley, J., 438 f.

Ratzel, F., 327.
Ribot, Th., 369, 487, 489.

Royce, J., 171, 232, 341 ff., 391, 445.
Ruskin, J., 203.

Sanford, E. C. (Cf. Index of Subjects, 'Experiments referred to in footnotes.')
Santayana, G., 280, 284.
Schiller, Fr., 282.
Schopenhauer, A., 282 f.
Shinn, M. W., 386, 389.
Sidis, B., 335.
Sommer, R., 462 f.
Spaulding, D. A., 100.
Spencer, H., 89 f., 134, 435, 438 f.
Spinoza, B. de, 129, 434.
Stout, G. F., 239, 445.
Stricker, S., 200.
Stumpf, C., 89, 488.

Tarde, G., 331, 338.
Thompson, E. S., 375, 378 f.
Thorndike, E., 371, 377.
Titchener, E. B., 67, 121, 123, 141 f., 184, 236, 400, 444, 486 ff. (Cf. Index of Subjects, 'Experiments referred to.')
Tracy, F., 385 ff.
Tucker, A., 439.
Tyler, E. B., 324 ff.

Vogt, K., 442.
Volkmann, W. von V., 440.

Ward, J., 89, 188, 280.
Weber, 69, 111, 443.
Weed, S., 400, 402, 415.
Wernicke, 462.
Wiltse, S. E., 383.
Windelband, W., 435.
Wundt, W., 47, 89, 114 f., 121, 214, 218, 222, 227, 443, 445, 466, 469, 486, 488 ff.

Young, Th., 35, 464.

Zwaardemaker, H., 60, 358, 480 f.

Printed in the United States
107458LV00003B/288/A

9 780548 200919